The original edition of this book contained oversized maps. PDF files of these maps can be downloaded from www.elibron.com/maps

ALEXANDER VAN MILLINGEN

BYZANTINE
CONSTANTINOPLE

Elibron Classics
www.elibron.com

BYZANTINE CONSTANTINOPLE

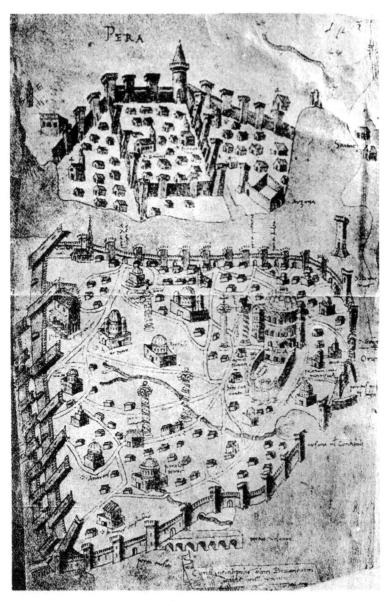

MAP OF CONSTANTINOPLE IN 1422.
(By Bondelmontius.)

BYZANTINE CONSTANTINOPLE

THE WALLS OF THE CITY AND ADJOINING
HISTORICAL SITES

BY

ALEXANDER VAN MILLINGEN, M.A.
PROFESSOR OF HISTORY, ROBERT COLLEGE, CONSTANTINOPLE

WITH MAPS, PLANS, AND ILLUSTRATIONS

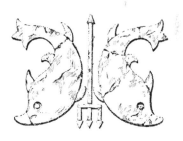

LONDON

JOHN MURRAY, ALBEMARLE STREET

1899

Ἐγὼ δὲ ὡς μητέρα φιλῶ καὶ γὰρ ἐγενόμην πὰρ' αὐτῇ καὶ ἐτράφην ἐκεῖσε, καὶ οὐ δύναμαι περὶ αὐτὴν ἀγνωμονῆσαι.

EMPEROR JULIAN, *Epistle* 58.

LONDON : PRINTED BY WILLIAM CLOWES AND SONS, LIMITED,
STAMFORD STREET AND CHARING CROSS.

PREFACE.

In the following pages I venture to take part in the task of identifying the historical sites of Byzantine or Roman Con-stantinople, with the view of making the events of which that city was the theatre more intelligible and vivid. The new interest now taken in all related to the Byzantine world demands a work of this character.

The attention I have devoted, for many years, to the subject has been sustained by the conviction that the Empire of which New Rome was the capital defended the higher life of mankind against the attacks of formidable antagonists, and rendered eminent service to the cause of human welfare. This is what gives to the archæological study of the city its dignity and importance.

Only a portion of my subject is dealt with in the present volume—the walls of the city, which were the bulwarks of civilization for more than a thousand years, and the adjoining sites and monuments memorable in history.

While availing myself, as the reader will find, of the results obtained by my predecessors in this field of research, I have endeavoured to make my work a fresh and independent investigation of the subject, by constant appeals to the original authorities, and by direct examination of the localities concerned. The difficult questions which must be decided, in order that our knowledge of the old city may be more satisfactory, have been made prominent. Some of them, however, cannot be answered once for all, until excavations are permitted.

By the frequent quotations and references which occur in the course of the following discussions, the student will find himself placed in a position to verify the statements and to weigh the arguments submitted to his consideration. All difference of opinion leading nearer to the truth in the case will be welcomed.

My best thanks are due to the friends and the photographers who have enabled me to provide the book with illustrations, maps, and plans, thus making the study of the subject clearer and more interesting. The plan of the so-called Prisons of Anemas by Hanford W. Edson, Esq., the sketches by Mrs. Walker, the photographs taken by Professor Ormiston, and the maps and plans drawn by Arthur E. Henderson, Esq., are particularly valuable. I wish to express my gratitude also to the many friends who accompanied me on my explorations of the city, thereby facilitating the accomplishment of my work, and associating it with delightful memories.

ALEXANDER VAN MILLINGEN.

ROBERT COLLEGE,
   CONSTANTINOPLE,
      September, 1899.

CONTENTS.

LIST OF ILLUSTRATIONS.

———◆◇◆———

BUST OVER THE GATE OF GYROLIMNÈ.

BYZANTINE CONSTANTINOPLE.

————

CHAPTER I.

THE SITE OF CONSTANTINOPLE—THE LIMITS OF BYZANTIUM.

WITHOUT attempting any elaborate description of the site occupied by Constantinople, such as we have in Gyllius' valuable work on the topography of the city,[1] it is necessary to indicate to the reader, now invited to wander among the ruins of New Rome, the most salient features of the territory he is to explore.

The city is situated at the south-western end of the Bosporus, upon a promontory that shoots out from the European shore of the straits, with its apex up stream, as though to stem the waters that rush from the Black Sea into the Sea of Marmora. To the north, the narrow bay of the Golden Horn runs inland, between steep banks, for some six or seven miles, and forms one of the finest harbours in the world. The Sea of Marmora spreads southwards like a lake, its Asiatic coast bounded by hills and mountains, and fringed with islands. Upon the shore of Asia, facing the eastern side

---

[1] Petrus Gyllius, *De Topographia Constantinopoleos et De illius Antiquitatibus*, liber i. c. 4-18.

B

of the promontory, stand the historic towns of Chrysopolis
(Scutari) and Chalcedon (Kadikeui). The mainland to the
west is an undulating plain that soon meets the horizon. It
offers little to attract the eye in the way of natural beauty,
but in the palmy days of the city it, doubtless, presented a
pleasing landscape of villas and gardens.

The promontory, though strictly speaking a trapezium, is
commonly described as a triangle, on account of the comparative shortness of its eastern side. It is about four miles
long, and from one to four miles wide, with a surface broken
up into hills and plains. The higher ground, which reaches an
elevation of some 250 feet, is massed in two divisions—a large
isolated hill at the south-western corner of the promontory,
and a long ridge, divided, more or less completely, by five
cross valleys into six distinct eminences, overhanging the Golden
Horn. Thus, New Rome boasted of being enthroned upon as
many hills beside the Bosporus, as her elder sister beside the
Tiber.

The two masses of elevated land just described are separated by a broad meadow, through which the stream of the
Lycus flows athwart the promontory into the Sea of Marmora ;
and there is, moreover, a considerable extent of level land along
the shores of the promontory, and in the valleys between the
northern hills.

Few of the hills of Constantinople were known by special
names, and accordingly, as a convenient mode of reference,
they are usually distinguished by numerals.

The First Hill is the one nearest the promontory's apex,
having upon it the Seraglio, St. Irene, St. Sophia, and the
Hippodrome. The Second Hill, divided from the First by the
valley descending from St. Sophia to the Golden Horn, bears
upon its summit the porphyry Column of Constantine the

Great, popularly known as the Burnt Column and Tchemberli
Tash. The Third Hill is separated from the preceding by the
valley of the Grand Bazaar, and is marked by the War Office
and adjacent Fire-Signal Tower, the Mosque of Sultan Bajazet,
and the Mosque of Sultan Suleiman the Magnificent. The
Fourth Hill stands farther back from the water than the
five other hills beside the Golden Horn, and is parted from
the Third Hill by the valley which descends from the aqueduct
of Valens to the harbour. It is surmounted by the Mosque of
Sultan Mehemet the Conqueror. The Fifth Hill is really a
long precipitous spur of the Fourth Hill, protruding almost to
the shore of the Golden Horn in the quarter of the Phanar.
Its summit is crowned by the Mosque of Sultan Selim. Between
it and the Third Hill spreads a broad plain, bounded by the
Fourth Hill on the south, and the Golden Horn on the north.
The Sixth Hill is divided from the Fifth by the valley which
ascends southwards from the Golden Horn at Balat Kapoussi
to the large Byzantine reservoir (Tchoukour Bostan), on the
ridge that runs from the Mosque of Sultan Mehemet to the
Gate of Adrianople. It is distinguished by the ruins of the
Palace of the Porphyrogenitus (Tekfour Serai) and the quarter
of Egri Kapou. Nicetas Choniates styles it the Hill of
Blachernae (βουνὸς τῶν Βλαχερνῶν),[1] and upon it stood the
famous Imperial residence of that name. The Seventh Hill,
occupying the south-western angle of the city, was known, on
account of its arid soil, as the Xerolophos—the Dry Hill.[2]
Upon it are found Avret Bazaar, the pedestal of the Column of
Arcadius, and the quarters of Alti Mermer and Psamathia.

---

[1] Page 722. All references in this work to the Byzantine Authors, unless otherwise stated, are to the Bonn Edition of the *Corpus Scriptorum Historiæ Byzantinæ.*

[2] Anonymus, lib. i. p. 20, in Banduri's *Imperium Orientale;* Constantine Porphyrogenitus, *De Cerimoniis Aulæ Byzantinæ*, p. 501.

Here, then, was a situation where men could build a noble city in the midst of some of the fairest scenery on earth.

But the history of Constantinople cannot be understood unless the extraordinary character of the geographical position of the place is present to the mind.   No city owes so much to its site. The vitality and power of Constantinople are rooted in a unique location.   Nowhere is the influence of geography upon history more strikingly marked.   Here, to a degree that is marvellous, the possibilities of the freest and widest intercourse blend with the possibilities of complete isolation.   No city can be more in the world and out of the world.   It is the meeting-point of some of the most important highways on the globe, whether by sea or land ;   the centre around which diverse, vast, and wealthy countries lie within easy reach, inviting intimate commercial relations, and permitting extended political control.   Here the peninsula of Asia Minor, stretching like a bridge across the seas that sunder Asia and Europe, narrows the waters between the two great continents to a stream only half a mile across. Hither the Mediterranean ascends, through the avenues of the Ægean and the Marmora, from the regions of the south ; while the Euxine and the Azoff spread a pathway to the regions of the north.   Here is a harbour within which the largest and richest fleets can find a perfect shelter.

But no less remarkable is the facility with which the great world, so near at hand, can be excluded.   Access to this point by sea is possible only through the straits of the Hellespont on the one side, and through the straits of the Bosporus on the other —defiles which, when properly guarded, no hostile navy could penetrate.   These channels, with the Sea of Marmora between them, formed, moreover, a natural moat which prevented an Asiatic foe from coming within striking distance of the city ; while the narrow breadth of the promontory on which the city stands allowed the erection of fortifications, along the west, which could be held against immense armies by a comparatively small force.

As Dean Stanley, alluding to the selection of this site for the new capital of the Empire, has observed: "Of all the events of Constantine's life, this choice is the most convincing and enduring proof of his real genius."

Although it does not fall within the scope of this work to discuss the topography of Byzantium before the time of Constantine, it will not be inappropriate to glance at the circuits of the fortifications which successively brought more and more of this historic promontory within their widening compass, until the stronghold of a small band of colonists from Megara became the most splendid city and the mightiest bulwark of the Roman world.

Four such circuits demand notice.

First came the fortifications which constituted the Acropolis of Byzantium.[1] They are represented by the walls, partly Byzantine and partly Turkish, which cling to the steep sides of the Seraglio plateau at the eastern extremity of the First Hill, and support the Imperial Museum, the Kiosk of Sultan Abdul Medjid, and the Imperial Kitchens.

That the Acropolis occupied this point may be inferred from the natural fitness of the rocky eminence at the head of the promontory to form the kind of stronghold around which ancient cities gathered as their nucleus. And this inference is confirmed by the allusions to the Acropolis in Xenophon's graphic account of the visit of the Ten Thousand to Byzantium, on their return from Persia. According to the historian, when those troops, after their expulsion from the city, forced their way back through the western gates, Anaxibius, the Spartan commander of the place, found himself obliged to seek refuge in the Acropolis from the

---

[1] Xenophon, *Anabasis*, vii. c. 1.

fury of the intruders. The soldiers of Xenophon had, however, cut off all access to the fortress from within the city, so that Anaxibius was compelled to reach it by taking a fishing-boat in the harbour, and rowing round the head of the promontory to the side of the city opposite Chalcedon. From that point also he sent to Chalcedon for reinforcements.[1] These movements imply that the Acropolis was near the eastern end of the promontory.

In further support of this conclusion, it may be added that during the excavations made in 1871 for the construction of the Roumelian railroad, an ancient wall was unearthed at a short distance south of Seraglio Point. It ran from east to west, and was built of blocks measuring, in some cases, 7 feet in length, 3 feet 9 inches in width, and over 2 feet in thickness.[2] Judging from its position and character, the wall formed part of the fortifications around the Acropolis.

The second circuit of walls around Byzantium is that described by the Anonymus of the eleventh century and his follower Codinus.[3] Starting from the Tower of the Acropolis at the apex of the promontory, the wall proceeded along the Golden Horn as far west as the Tower of Eugenius, which must have stood beside the gate of that name—the modern Yali Kiosk Kapoussi.[4] There the wall left the shore and made for the Strategion and

---

[1] *Anabasis*, vii. c. 1.

[2] Paspates, Βυζαντιναὶ Μελέται, p. 103. Mordtmann, *Esquisse Topographique de Constantinople*, p. 5. All references to these writers, unless otherwise stated, are to the works here mentioned.

[3] Lib. i. p. 2 ; Codinus, pp. 24, 25. Ἤρχετο δὲ τὸ τεῖχος, καθὰ καὶ νῦν, ἐπὶ τοῦ Βύζαντος ἀπὸ τοῦ πύργου τῆς Ἀκροπόλεως, καὶ διήρχετο εἰς τὸν τοῦ Εὐγενίου πύργον, καὶ ἀνέβαινε μέχρι τοῦ Στρατηγίου, καὶ ἤρχετο εἰς τὸ τοῦ Ἀχιλλέως λουτρόν. Ἡ δὲ ἐκεῖσε ἀψὶς, ἡ λεγομένη τοῦ Οὐρβικίου, πόρτα ἦν χερσαία τῶν Βυζαντίων : καὶ ἀνέβαινεν εἰς τὰ Χαλκοπρατεῖα τὸ τεῖχος ἕως τοῦ λεγομένου Μιλίου· ἦν δὲ κἀκεῖσε πόρτα τῶν Βυζαντίων χερσαία : καὶ διήρχετο εἰς τοὺς πλεκτοὺς κίονας τῶν Τζυκαλαρίων, καὶ κατέβαινεν εἰς Τόπους, καὶ ἀπέκαμπτε πάλιν διὰ τῶν Μαγγάνων καὶ Ἀρκαδιανῶν εἰς τὴν Ἀκρόπολιν.

[4] See below, p. 227.

the Thermæ of Achilles. The former was a level tract of ground
devoted to military exercises—the *Champ de Mars* of Byzantium—and occupied a portion of the plain at the foot of the
Second Hill, between Yali Kiosk Kapoussi and Sirkedji Iskelessi.[1] The Thermæ of Achilles stood near the Strategion ; and
there also was a gate of the city, known in later days as the
Arch of Urbicius. The wall then ascended the slope of the hill to
the Chalcoprateia, or Brass Market, which extended from the
neighbourhood of the site now occupied by the Sublime Porte
to the vicinity of Yeri Batan Serai, the ancient Cisterna Basilica.[2]

The ridge of the promontory was reached at the Milion,
the milestone from which distances from Constantinople were
measured. It stood to the south-west of St. Sophia, and
marked the site of one of the gates of Byzantium. Thence the
line of the fortifications proceeded to the twisted columns of
the Tzycalarii, which, judging from the subsequent course of
the wall, were on the plateau beside St. Irene. Then, the wall
descended to the Sea of Marmora at Topi,[3] somewhere near the
present Seraglio Lighthouse, and, turning northwards, ran along
the shore to the apex of the promontory, past the sites occupied,
subsequently, by the Thermae of Arcadius and the Mangana.

If we are to believe the Anonymus and Codinus, this was
the circuit of Byzantium from the foundation of the city by

---

[1] The site of the Strategion may be determined thus : It was in the Fifth Region
of the city (*Notitia, ad Reg. V.*) ; therefore, either on the northern slope or at the
foot of the Second Hill. Its character as the ground for military exercises required
it to be on the plain at the foot of the hill. In the Strategion were found the
granaries beside the harbour of the Prosphorion (Constant. Porphyr., *De Cerim*,
p. 699), near Sirkidji Iskelessi. At the same time, these granaries were near the
Neorion (*Bagtché Kapoussi*), for they were destroyed by a fire which started in the
Neorion (*Paschal Chron.*, p. 582).

[2] The Chalcoprateia was near the Basilica, or Great Law Courts, the site of which
is marked by the Cistern of Yeri Batan Serai (Cedrenus, vol. i. p. 616 ; cf. Gyllius,
De Top. CP., lib. ii. c. 20, 21). Zonaras, xiv. p. 1212 (Migne Edition), ἐν τῇ
καλουμένῃ βασιλικῇ ἔγγιστα τῶν Χαλκοπρατείων.

[3] See below, p. 256.

Byzas to the time of Constantine the Great. On the latter point, however, these writers were certainly mistaken ; for the circuit of Byzantium was much larger than the one just indicated, not only in the reign of that emperor, but as far back as the year 196 of our era, and even before that date.[1] The statements of the Anonymus and Codinus can therefore be correct only if they refer to the size of the city at a very early period.

One is, indeed, strongly tempted to reject the whole account of this wall as legendary, or as a conjecture based upon the idea that the Arch of Urbicius and the Arch of the Milion represented gates in an old line of bulwarks. But, on the other hand, it is more than probable that Byzantium was not as large, originally, as it became during its most flourishing days, and accordingly the two arches above mentioned may have marked the course of the first walls built beyond the bounds of the Acropolis.

We pass next to the third line of walls which guarded the city, the walls which made Byzantium one of the great fortresses of the ancient world. These fortifications described a circuit of thirty-five stadia,[2] which would bring within the compass of the city most of the territory occupied by the first two hills of the promontory. Along the Golden Horn, the line of the walls extended from the head of the promontory to the western side of the bay that fronts the valley between the Second and Third Hills, the valley of the Grand Bazaar. Three ports, more or less artificial,[3] were found in that bay for the accommodation of the shipping that frequented the busy mart of commerce, one of them being, unquestionably, at the Neorion.[4]

[1] See below, the size of city as given by Dionysius Byzantius.
[2] *Anaplus* of Dionysius Byzantius.   Edition of C. Wescher, Paris, 1874.
[3] Dion Cassius, lxxiv. 14 ; Herodianus, iii. 6.
[4] Beside Bagtchè Kapoussi.   See below, p. 220.

These bulwarks, renowned in antiquity for their strength, were faced with squared blocks of hard stone, bound together with metal clamps, and so closely fitted as to seem a wall of solid rock around the city. One tower was named the Tower of Hercules, on account of its superior size and strength, and seven towers were credited with the ability to echo the slightest sound made by the movements of an enemy, and thus secure the garrison against surprise. From the style of their construction, one would infer that these fortifications were built soon after Pausanias followed up his victory on the field of Platæa by the expulsion of the Persians from Byzantium.

These splendid ramparts were torn down in 196 by Septimius Severus to punish the city for its loyalty to the cause of his rival, Pescennius Niger. In their ruin they presented a scene that made Herodianus[1] hesitate whether to wonder more at the skill of their constructors, or the strength of their destroyers. But the blunder of leaving unguarded the water-way, along which barbarous tribes could descend from the shores of the Euxine to ravage some of the fairest provinces of the Empire, was too glaring not to be speedily recognized and repaired. Even the ruthless destroyer of the city perceived his mistake, and ere long, at the solicitation of his son Caracalla, ordered the reconstruction of the strategic stronghold.

It is with Byzantium as restored by Severus that we are specially concerned, for in that form the city was the immediate predecessor of Constantinople, and affected the character of the new capital to a considerable extent. According to Zosimus, the principal gate in the new walls of Severus stood at the extremity of a line of porticoes erected by that emperor for the embellishment of the city.[2] There Constantine subsequently

[1] I. I.

[2] Page 96: Καὶ τὸ μὲν παλαιὸν εἶχε τὴν πύλην ἐν τῇ συμπληρώσει τῶν στοῶν ἅς Σεβῆρος ὁ βασιλεὺς ᾠκοδομήσατο.

placed the Forum known by his name, so that from the Forum one entered the porticoes in question, and passed beyond the limits of Byzantium.[1]   Now, the site of the Forum of Constantine is one of the points in the topography of the capital of the Eastern Roman Empire concerning which there can be no difference of opinion.   The porphyry column (Burnt Column) which surmounts the Second Hill was the principal ornament of that public place.   Therefore the gate of Byzantium must have stood at a short distance from that column.   According to the clearest statements on the subject, the gate was to the east of the column, the Forum standing immediately beyond the boundary of the old city.[2]

The language of Zosimus, taken alone, suggests, indeed, the idea that the gate of Byzantium had occupied a site to the west of the Forum ; in other words, that the Forum was constructed to the east of the gate, within the line of the wall of Severus.   For, according to the historian, one entered the porticoes of Severus and left the old town, after passing through the arches (δι' ὧν) which stood, respectively, at the eastern and western extremities of the Forum of Constantine.   This was possible, however, only if these various structures, in proceeding from east to west, came in the following order : Forum of Constantine ; porticoes of Severus ; gate of Byzantium.   On this view, the statement that the Forum was " at the place where the gate had stood" would be held to imply that the porticoes between the Forum and the gate were too short to be taken

---

[1] Zosimus, p. 96 : Ἀγορὰν δὲ ἐν τῷ τόπῳ καθ' ὃν ἡ πύλη τὸ ἀρχαῖον ἦν οἰκοδομήσας, . . . ἀψῖδας δύο μαρμάρου προικοννησίου μεγίστας ἀλλήλων ἀντίας ἀπετύπωσε, δι' ὧν ἔνεστιν εἰσιέναι εἰς τὰς Σεβήρου στοὰς, καὶ τῆς πάλαι πόλεως ἐξιέναι.

[2] Theophanes, p. 42, speaking of the column, says it was set up ἀπὸ τοῦ τόπου οὗ ἤρξατο οἰκοδομεῖν τὴν πόλιν, ἐπὶ τὸ δυτικὸν μέρος τῆς ἐπὶ Ῥώμην ἐξιούσης πύλης.

into account in a general indication of the Forum's position. But to interpret Zosimus thus puts him in contradiction, first, with Theophanes, as cited above ; secondly, with Hesychius Milesius,[1] who says that the wall of Byzantium did not go beyond the Forum of Constantine (οὐκ ἔξω τῆς ἐπωνύμου ἀγορᾶς τοῦ βασιλέως) ; thirdly, though that is of less moment, with the Anonymus [2] and Codinus,[3] who explain the circular shape of the Forum as derived from the shape of Constantine's tent when he besieged the city.

Lethaby and Swainson [4] place the Forum between the porticoes of Severus on the east and the gate of Byzantium on the west, putting the western arch of the Forum on the site of the latter. They understand the statement of Zosimus to mean that a person in the Forum could either enter the porticoes *or* leave the old town according as he proceeded eastwards or westwards.

From that gate the wall descended the northern slope of the hill to the Neorion, and thence went eastwards to the head of the promontory.[5] In descending to the Golden Horn the wall kept, probably, to the eastern bank of the valley of the Grand Bazaar, to secure a natural escarpment which would render assault more difficult.

Upon the side towards the Sea of Marmora the wall proceeded from the main gate of the city to the point occupied by the temple of Aphrodite, and to the shore facing Chrysopolis.[6] The temple of the Goddess of Beauty was one of the oldest sanctuaries in Byzantium,[7] and did not entirely disappear until

---

[1] *Fragm. Hist. Græc.*, iv. p. 49.			[2] I. p. 14.			[3] Page 41.

[4] *The Church of Sancta Sophia*, pp. 5, 9.

[5] Zosimus, p. 96, Ἀπὸ δὲ τοῦ βορείου λόφου κατὰ τὸν ἴσον τρόπον, κατιὸν ἄχρι τοῦ λιμένος ὃ καλοῦσι νεώριον, καὶ ἐπέκεινα μέχρι θαλάσσης ἣ κατευθὺ κεῖται τοῦ στόματος δι᾽ οὗ πρὸς τὸν Εὔξεινον ἀνάγονται Πόντον.

[6] *Ibid.*, Τὸ δὲ τεῖχος διὰ τοῦ λόφου καθιέμενον ἦν ἀπὸ τοῦ δυτικοῦ μέρους ἄχρι τοῦ τῆς Ἀφροδίτης ναοῦ, καὶ θαλάσσης τῆς ἀντικρὺ Χρυσοπόλεως.

[7] *Paschal Chron.*, p. 495.

the reign of Theodosius the Great, by whom it was converted
into a carriage-house for the Prætorian Prefect.[1]   It was, consequently, a landmark that would long be remembered.   Malalas [2]
places it within the ancient Acropolis of the city.   Other
authorities likewise put it there, adding that it stood higher up
the hill of the Acropolis than the neighbouring temple of
Poseidon,[3] where it overlooked one of the theatres built
against the Marmora side of the citadel,[4] and faced Chrysopolis.[5]
From these indications it is clear that the temple lay to the
north-east of the site of St. Sophia, and therefore not far from
the site of St. Irene on the Seraglio plateau.

Accordingly, the wall of Severus, upon leaving the western
gate of the city, did not descend to the shore of the Sea of
Marmora, but after proceeding in that direction for some
distance turned south-eastwards, keeping well up the south-
western slopes of the First Hill, until the Seraglio plateau was
reached.[6] As these slopes were for the most part very steep,
the city, when viewed from the Sea of Marmora, presented the
appearance of a great Acropolis upon a hill.

Where precisely the wall reached the Sea of Marmora
opposite Chrysopolis is not stated, but it could not have been
far from the point now occupied by the Seraglio Lighthouse, for
the break in the steep declivity of the First Hill above that point
offered the easiest line of descent from the temple of Aphrodite
to the shore.   Thus it appears that the circuit of the walls
erected by Severus followed, substantially, the course of the
fortifications which he had overthrown.   It is a corroboration

---

[1] Malalas, p. 345.

[2] Page 292.

[3] Hesychius Milesius, *Fragm. Hist. Græc.*, iv. p. 149; Codinus, p. 6.

[4] *Notitia, ad Reg. II.* ; *Paschal Chron.*, p. 495.   [5] Zosimus, p. 96.

[6] As the Sphendonè of the Hippodrome was a construction of Constantine the
Great, the wall of Severus may, near that point, have stood higher up the hill than
is indicated on the Map of Byzantine Constantinople, facing page 19.

of this conclusion to find that the ground outside the wall constructed by Severus—the valley of the Grand Bazaar—answers to the description of the ground outside the wall which he destroyed ; a smooth tract, sloping gently to the water : "Primus post mœnia campus erat peninsulæ cervicis sensim descendentis ad litus, et ne urbs esset insula prohibentis." [1]

To this account of the successive circuits of Byzantium until the time of Constantine, may be added a rapid survey of the internal arrangements and public buildings of the city after its restoration by Severus.[2]

A large portion of the Hippodrome, so famous in the history of Constantinople, was erected by Severus, who left the edifice unfinished owing to his departure for the West. Between the northern end of the Hipprodrome and the subsequent site of St. Sophia was the Tetrastoon, a public square surrounded by porticoes, having the Thermæ of Zeuxippus upon its southern side.

In the Acropolis were placed, as usual, the principal sanctuaries of the city ; the Temples of Artemis, Aphrodite, Apollo, Zeus, Poseidon, and Demeter. Against the steep eastern side of the citadel, Severus constructed a theatre and a Kynegion for the exhibition of wild animals, as the Theatre of Dionysius and the Odeon were built against the Acropolis of Athens.

At a short distance from the apex of the promontory rose the column, still found there, bearing the inscription *Fortunæ Reduci ob devictos Gothos*, in honour of Claudius Gothicus for his victories over the Goths. To the north of the Acropolis was the Stadium ; [3]

---

[1] Dionysius Byzantius. See Gyllius, *De Bosporo Thracio*, ii. c. 2 ; cf. *ibid.*, *De Top. CP.*, i. c. 10.

[2] *Paschal Chron.*, pp. 494, 495 ; cf. Malalas, p. 345 ; *Notitia, ad Reg. II.*

[3] *Notitia, ad Regiones, IV., V., VI.* In the first tower south of Saouk Tchesmè Kapoussi, in the land wall of the Seraglio, is built a stone, inscribed with archaic Greek letters, which probably came from the Stadium. See *Proceedings of the Greek*

then came the ports of the Prosphorion and the Neorion, and in their vicinity the Strategion, the public prison,[1] and the shrine of Achilles and Ajax.[2] The aqueduct which the Emperor Hadrian erected for Byzantium continued to supply the city of Severus.[3]

Nor was the territory without the walls entirely unoccupied. From statements found in Dionysius Byzantius, and from allusions which later writers make to ruined temples in different quarters of Constantinople, it is evident that many hamlets and public edifices existed along the shore of the Golden Horn, and in the valleys and on the hills beyond the city limits. Blachernæ was already established beside the Sixth Hill ; Sycæ, famous for its figs, occupied the site of Galata ; and the Xerolophos was a sacred hill, crowned with a temple of Zeus. [4]

Literary Syllogos of Constantinople, vol. xvi., 1885, *Archæological Supplement,* p. 3. Ἀπομά(χων) αἰχματ(ᾶν), σταδιοδ(ρόμων), ὁ τόπος ἄ(ρχεται).

[1] Codinus, p. 76.

[2] Hesychius Milesius, *Fragm. Hist. Græc.,* iv. p. 149.

[3] *Paschal Chron.,* p. 619.

[4] For buildings, etc., outside the limits of Byzantium, see *Anaplus* of Dionysius Byzantius ; Gyllius, *De Bosporo Thracio,* ii. c. 2, c. 5 ; Codinus, p. 30 ; Anonymus, iii. p 51.

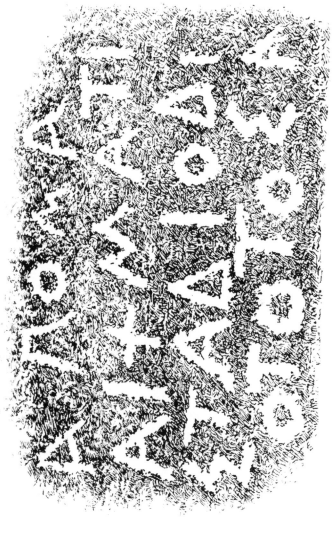

INSCRIPTION FROM THE STADIUM OF BYZANTIUM.
(From *Broken Bits of Byzantium*, by kind permission of Mrs. Walker.)

CHAPTER II.

THE CITY OF CONSTANTINE—ITS LIMITS—FORTIFICATIONS—
INTERIOR ARRANGEMENT.

IN the year 328 of our era, Constantine commenced the transformation of Byzantium into New Rome by widening the
boundaries of the ancient town and erecting new fortifications.
On foot, spear in hand, the emperor traced the limits of the
future capital in person, and when his courtiers, surprised at the
compass of the circuit he set himself to describe, inquired how
far he would proceed, he replied, "Until He stops Who goes
before me."[1] The story expresses a sense of the profound
import of the work begun on that memorable day. It was the
inauguration of an epoch.

We shall endeavour to determine the limits assigned to the
city of Constantine. The data at our command for that purpose
are, it is true, not everything that can be desired ; they are often
vague ; at other times they refer to landmarks which have
disappeared, and the sites of which it is impossible now to
identify ; nevertheless, a careful study of these indications
yields more satisfactory results than might have been antici-
pated under the circumstances.

The new land wall, we shall find, crossed the promontory[2]
along a line a short distance to the east of the Cistern of

[1] Philostorgius, ii. c. 9.   [2] See Map of Byzantine Constantinople.

Mokius on the Seventh Hill, (the Tchoukour Bostan, west of Avret Bazaar), and of the Cistern of Aspar at the head of the valley between the Fourth and Sixth Hills, (the Tchoukour Bostan on the right of the street leading from the Mosque of Sultan Mehemet to the Adrianople Gate). The southern end of the line reached the Sea of Marmora somewhere between the gates known respectively, at present, as Daoud Pasha Kapoussi and Psamathia Kapoussi, while its northern extremity abutted on the Golden Horn, in the neighbourhood of the Stamboul head of the inner bridge. At the same time the seaward walls of Byzantium were repaired, and prolonged to meet the extremities of the new land wall.

That this outline of the city of Constantine is, substantially, correct, will appear from the information which ancient writers have given on the subject.

(a) According to Zosimus,[1] the land wall of the new capital was carried fifteen stadia west of the corresponding wall of Byzantium. The position of the latter, we have already seen, is marked, with sufficient accuracy for our present purpose by the porphyry Column of Constantine which stood close to the main gate of the old Greek town.[2] Proceeding from that column fifteen stadia westwards, we come to a line within a short distance of the reservoirs above mentioned.

(b) In the oldest description of Constantinople—that contained in the *Notitia*[3]—the length of the city is put down as 14,075 Roman feet ; the breadth as 6150 Roman feet. The

---

[1] Pages 96, 97.   [2] See above, p. 10.

[3] *Notitia Dignitatum accedunt Notitia urbis Constantinopolitanæ et Laterculi Provinciarum*, edidit Otto Seeck, p. 243.

The *Notitia*, so far as Constantinople is concerned, will be found in Gyllius' *De Topographia Constantinopoleos*.

" Habet sane longitudo urbis a porta aurea usque ad litus maris directa linea pedum quattuordecim milia septuaginta quinque, latitudo autem pedum sex milia centum quinquaginta."

Notitia belongs to the age of Theodosius II., and might therefore be supposed to give the dimensions of the city after its
enlargement by that emperor. This, however, is not the case.
The size of Constantinople under Theodosius II. is well known,
seeing the ancient walls which still surround Stamboul mark,
with slight modifications, the wider limits of the city in the
fifth century. But the figures of the *Notitia* do not correspond
to the well-ascertained dimensions of the Theodosian city ;
they fall far short of those dimensions, and therefore can
refer only to the length and breadth of the original city of
Constantine. To adhere thus to the original size of the capital
after it had been outgrown is certainly strange, but may be
explained as due to the force of habit. When the *Notitia* was
written, the enlargement of the city by Theodosius was too
recent an event to alter old associations of thought and introduce new points of view. " The City," proper, was still what
Constantine had made it.

The length of the original city was measured from the Porta
Aurea on the west to the sea on the east. Unfortunately, a
serious difference of opinion exists regarding the particular gate
intended by the Porta Aurea. There can be no doubt, however,
that the sea at the eastern end of the line of measurement was
the sea at the head of the promontory ; for only by coming to
that point could the full length of the city be obtained. Consequently, if we take the head of the promontory for our starting-point of measurement, and proceed westwards to a distance
of 14,075 feet, we shall discover the extent of the city of
Constantine in that direction. This course brings us to the
same result as the figures of Zosimus—to the neighbourhood of
the Cisterns of Mokius and Aspar.

Turning next to the breadth of the city, we find that the
only portion of the promontory across which a line of 6150 feet

will stretch from sea to sea lies between the district about the gate Daoud Pasha Kapoussi, beside the Sea of Marmora on the south, and the district about the Stamboul head of the inner bridge on the north; elsewhere the promontory is either narrower or broader. Hence the southern and northern extremities of the land wall of Constantine terminated respectively, as stated above, in these districts.

From these figures we pass to the localities and structures by which Byzantine writers have indicated the course of Constantine's wall.

On the side of the Sea of Marmora the wall extended as far west as the Gate of St. Æmilianus (πόρτα τοῦ ἁγίου Αἰμιλιανοῦ), and the adjoining church of St. Mary Rhabdou (τῆς ἁγίας θεοτόκου τῆς Ῥάβδου).[1] That gate is represented by Daoud Pasha Kapoussi, which stands immediately to the west of Vlanga Bostan.[2]

In crossing from the Sea of Marmora to the Golden Horn, over the Seventh, Fourth, and Fifth Hills, the line of the fortifications was marked by the Exokionion; the Ancient Gate of the Forerunner; the Monastery of St. Dius; the Convent of Icasia; the Cistern of Bonus; the Church of SS. Manuel, Sabel, and Ishmael; the Church, and the Zeugma, or Ferry, of St. Antony in the district of Harmatius, where the fortifications reached the harbour.[3] To this list may be added the Trojan Porticoes and the Cistern of Aspar.

(*a*) The Exokionion (τὸ ἐξωκιόνιον)[4] was a district immediately outside the Constantinian Wall, and obtained its name from a column in the district, bearing the statue of the founder of the city. Owing to a corruption of the name, the quarter was commonly known as the Hexakionion (τὸ ἐξακιόνιον).[5] It is

---

[1] *Paschal Chron.*, p. 494; Anonymus, i. p. 2. [2] See below, p. 264.
[3] Anonymus, i. p. 2; Codinus, p. 25. [4] Anonymus, i. p. 20.
[5] Constant. Porphyr., *De Cer.*, p. 501.

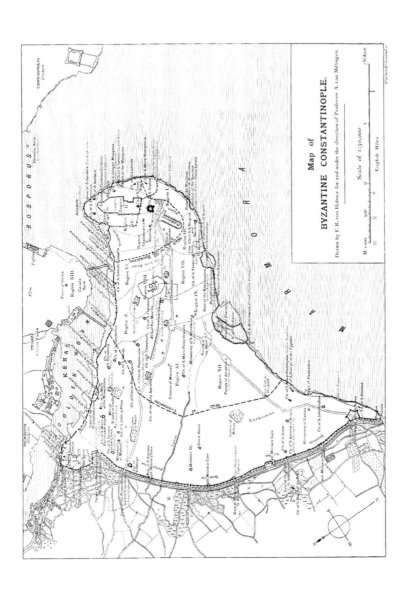

Map of

BYZANTINE CONSTANTINOPLE.

Drawn by F. R. von Hubner for and under the direction of Professor A. van Millingen.

Scale of 1:30,000

celebrated in ecclesiastical history as the extra-mural suburb in which the Arians were allowed to hold their religious services, when Theodosius the Great, the champion of orthodoxy, prohibited heretical worship within the city.[1]   Hence the terms Arians and Exokionitai became synonymous.[2]   In later times the quarter was one of the fashionable parts of the city, containing many fine churches and handsome residences.[3]

Gyllius was disposed to place the Exokionion on the Fifth Hill,[4] basing his opinion on the fact that he found, when he first visited the city, a noble column standing on that hill, about half a mile to the north-west of the Mosque of Sultan Mehemet.[5]

Dr. Mordtmann, on the other hand, maintains that the designation was applied to the extra-mural territory along the whole line of the Constantinian land fortifications.[6]

But the evidence on the subject requires us to place the Exokionion on the Seventh Hill, and to restrict the name to that locality.

For in the account of the triumphal entry of Basil I. through the Golden Gate of the Theodosian Walls, the Exokionion is placed between the Sigma and the Xerolophos.[7]   The Sigma appears in the history of the sedition which overthrew Michael V., (1042), and is described as situated above the Monastery of St. Mary Peribleptos.[8]   Now, regarding the position of that monastery there is no doubt.   The establishment, founded by Romanus Argyrus, was one of the most important monastic

---

[1] *Paschal Chron.*, p. 561 ; Socrates, v. c. 7.   [2] *Ibid., ut supra.*

[3] Theophanes Continuatus, p. 196; Cedrenus, vol. ii. p. 173 ; Nicetas Chon. p. 319.

[4] *De Top. CP.*, iv. c. 1.

[5] On the occasion of his second visit, Gyllius saw the column removed to the Mosque of Sultan Suleiman.

[6] Pages 10, 72.   [7] Constant. Porphyr., *De Cer.*, p. 501.

[8] Cedrenus, vol. ii. p. 540, Ἄνωθεν τῆς περιβλέπτου μονῆς, ἐν τῷ τόπῳ τῷ καλουμένῳ Σίγματι.

houses in Constantinople. Its church survived the Turkish Conquest, and remained in the hands of the Greeks until 1643, when
Sultan Ibrahim granted it to the Armenian community.[1] Since
that time the sacred edifice has twice been destroyed by fire, and
is now rebuilt under the title of St. George. It is popularly known
as Soulou Monastir (the Water Monastery), after its adjoining
ancient cistern, and stands in the quarter of Psamathia, low down
the southern slope of the Seventh Hill.

The Xerolophos was the name of the Seventh Hill in
general,[2] but was sometimes applied, as in the case before us, to
the Forum of Arcadius (Avret Bazaar) upon the hill's summit.[3]

This being so, the Exokionion, which was situated between
the Sigma and the Forum of Arcadius, must have occupied the
upper western slope of the Seventh Hill.

In corroboration of this conclusion two additional facts may
be cited. First, the Church of St. Mokius, the sanctuary accorded
to the Arians for their extra-mural services in the Exokionion,
stood on the Seventh Hill,[4] for it was on the road from the Sigma
to the Forum of Arcadius,[5] and gave name to the large ancient
cistern, the Tchoukour Bostan, to the north-west of the Forum.[6]

In the next place, the district on the Seventh Hill to the
west of Avret Bazaar (Forum of Arcadius) and beside the cistern
of Mokius, still retains the name Exokionion under a Turkish
form, its actual name, Alti Mermer, the district of "the Six
Columns," being, evidently, the Turkish rendering of Hexakionion, the popular Byzantine alias of Exokionion.[7] The Exokionion, therefore, was on the Seventh Hill. Accordingly, the Wall

---

[1] Patriarch Constantius, *Ancient and Modern Constantinople,* p. 86.
[2] *Paschal Chron.,* p. 579.
[3] Socrates, vii. c. 5 ; Constant. Porphyr., *De Cer.,* p. 106.
[4] Banduri, *Imperium Orientale,* v. p. 81 ; *Synaxaria,* May 11.
[5] Constant. Porphyr., *De Cer.,* pp. 55, 56.
[6] Codinus, p. 99 ; Gyllius, *De Top. CP.,* iv. c. 8.
[7] Cf. Paspates, p. 362.

of Constantine crossed that hill along a line to the east of the quarter of Alti Mermer.

(*b*) The next landmark, the Ancient Gate of the Forerunner (Παλαιὰ Πόρτα τοῦ Προδρόμου), elsewhere styled simply the Ancient Gate (Παλαιὰ Πόρτα),[1] furnishes the most precise indication we have of the position of Constantine's wall.   It was a gate which survived the original fortifications of the city, as Temple Bar outlived the wall of London, and became known in later days as the Ancient Gate, on account of its great antiquity.   Its fuller designation, the Ancient Gate of the Forerunner,[2] is explained by the fact that a church dedicated to the Baptist was built against the adjoining wall.   Conversely, the church was distinguished as the Church of the Forerunner at the Ancient Gate (τὴν Παλαιὰν).[3] Manuel Chrysolaras places the entrance to the west of the Forum of Arcadius, and describes it as one of the finest monuments in the city.[4]   It was so wide and lofty that a tower or a full-rigged ship might pass through its portals.   Upon the summit was a marble portico of dazzling whiteness, and before the entrance rose a column, once surmounted by a statue.   When Bondelmontius visited the city, in 1422, the gate was still erect, and is marked on his map of Constantinople as Antiquissima Pulchra Porta.[5]   It survived the Turkish Conquest, when it obtained the name of Isa Kapoussi (the Gate of Jesus), and held its place as late as 1508.   In that year it was overthrown by a great earthquake.   "Isa Kapoussi," says the Turkish historian Solak Zadè, who records the occurrence, "near Avret Bazaar, which had been in existence for 1900 years (*sic*), fell and was levelled to the ground."[6]   But the shadow of the name still

---

[1] Codinus, p. 122.   [2] Codinus, p. 25.

[3] Du Cange, iv. p. 102.   [4] *Patrologia Græca*, vol. clvi. p. 54, Migne.

[5] Another copy of the map of Bondelmontius than that forming the Frontispiece of this work is found at the beginning of Du Cange's *Constantinopolis Christiana.*

[6] For this information I am indebted to Rev. H. O. Dwight, LL.D., of the American Board of Missions.

lingers about the site. A small mosque to the west of Avret Bazaar bears the name Isa Kapoussi Mesdjidi,[1] while the adjoining street is called Isa Kapoussi Sokaki. The mosque is an ancient Christian church, and probably bore in its earlier character a name which accounts for its Turkish appellation.

From these facts it is clear that the Wall of Constantine, in crossing the Seventh Hill, passed very near Isa Kapoussi Mesdjidi, a conclusion in accordance with the position already assigned to the Exokionion. The column outside the Ancient Gate was probably that which gave name to the district. Nowhere could a column bearing the statue of the city's founder stand more appropriately than before this splendid entrance.

(c) Another landmark of the course of the Constantinian ramparts in this part of the city were the Trojan Porticoes (τρῳαδήσιοι ἔμβολοι),[2] which stood so near the wall that it was sometimes named after them, the Trojan wall (τῶν τειχῶν τῶν Τρῳαδησίων).[3]

From their situation in the Twelfth Region,[4] it is probable that they lined the street leading from the Porta Aurea into the city. They were evidently of some architectural importance, and are mentioned on more than one occasion as having been damaged by fire or earthquake.[5] The reason for their name is a matter of conjecture, and no trace of them remains.

(d) Nothing definite regarding the course of the Constantinian Wall can be inferred from the statement that it ran beside the Monastery of St. Dius and the Convent of Icasia, seeing the situation of these establishments cannot be determined more exactly than that they were found near each other, somewhere on the Seventh Hill.

[1] Cf. Paspates, pp. 361–363.
[2] Hesychius Milesius, *Fragm. Hist. Graec.*, vol. iv. p. 154.
[3] *Paschal Chron.*, p. 590.   [4] *Notitia, ad Reg. XII.*
[5] Marcellinus Comes.

The former, ascribed to the time of Theodosius I., is mentioned by Antony of Novgorod in close connection with the Church of St. Mokius and the Church of St. Luke.[1] The Convent of Icasia was founded by the beautiful and accomplished lady of that name,[2] whom the Emperor Theophilus declined to choose for his bride because she disputed the correctness of his ungracious remark that women were the source of evil.

(*e*) The Cistern of Aspar, which, according to the *Paschal Chronicle*,[3] was situated near the ancient city wall, is the old Byzantine reservoir (Tchoukour Bostan), on the right of the street conducting from the Mosque of Sultan Mehemet to the Gate of Adrianople in the Theodosian walls. This is clear from the following evidence. The cistern in question was a very large one, and stood near the Monastery of Manuel,[4] which was founded by the distinguished general of that name in the reign of Theophilus. The church of the monastery is now the Mosque Kefelè Mesdjidi in the quarter of Salmak Tombruk, and a little to the east of it stands the Tchoukour Bostan mentioned above,[5] the only large Byzantine reservoir in the neighbourhood.

This conclusion is again in harmony with the figures of Zosimus and the *Notitia*, which, it will be remembered, brought the line of the Constantinian Wall close to this point.

(*f*) The Cistern of Bonus, the next landmark to be considered, was built by the Patrician Bonus, celebrated in Byzantine history for his brave defence of the capital in 627 against the Avars and the Persians, while the Emperor Heraclius was in Persia carrying war into the enemy's country.[6]

Where this cistern was situated is a matter of dispute which cannot be definitely settled in our present state of knowledge.

---

[1] *Itinéraires Russes en Orient*, p. 103 ; *Traduits pour la Société de l'Orient Latin*, par Madame B. de Khitrovo.

[2] Codinus, p. 123.   [3] Page 593.   [4] Theophanes Continuatus, p. 168.

[5] Paspates, pp. 304–306.   [6] Codinus, p. 99.

Gyllius identified it with a large cistern, three hundred paces in length, which he found robbed of its roof and columns, and turned into a vegetable garden, near the ruins of the Church of St. John in Petra, on the Sixth Hill.[1] The cistern has disappeared since that traveller's day, but as the Wall of Constantine never extended so far west, the identification cannot be correct.

In Dr. Mordtmann's opinion, the Cistern of Bonus was the large open reservoir to the south-west of the Mosque of Sultan Selim, on the Fifth Hill,[2] and there is much to be said in favour of this view.

The Cistern of Bonus was, in the first place, situated in one of the coolest quarters of the city, and beside it, on that account, the Emperor Romanus I. erected a palace,[3] styled the New Palace of Bonus,[4] as a residence during the hot season. Nowhere in Constantinople could a cooler spot be found in summer than the terrace upon which the Mosque of Sultan Selim stands, not to speak of the attractions offered by the superb view of the Golden Horn from that point. Furthermore, the Cistern of Bonus was within a short distance from the Church of the Holy Apostles, seeing that on the eve of the annual service celebrated in that church in commemoration of Constantine the Great, the Imperial Court usually repaired to the Palace of Bonus, in order to be within easy riding distance of the sanctuary on the morning of the festival.[5] A palace near the reservoir beside the Mosque of Sultan Selim would be conveniently near the Church of the Holy Apostles, to suit the emperor on such an occasion. To these considerations can be added, first, the fact that on the way from the Palace of Bonus

---

[1] *De Top. CP.*, iv. c. 4.   [2] Pages 72, 73.
[3] Cedrenus, vol. ii. p. 343.   [4] Constant. Porphyr., *De Cer.*, p. 532.
[5] *Ibid., ut supra.*

to the Church of the Apostles there was an old cistern converted into market gardens,[1] which may have been the reservoir near the Mosque of Sultan Selim ; and, secondly, the fact that the Wall of Constantine, on its way from the Cistern of Aspar to the Golden Horn passed near the site now occupied by the Mosque of Sultan Selim, and, consequently, close to the old cistern adjoining that mosque. But to this identification there is a fatal objection : the Cistern of Bonus was roofed in,[2] whereas the reservoir beside the Mosque of Sultan Selim appears to have always been open.

Dr. Strzygowski has suggested that the Cistern of Bonus stood near Eski Ali Pasha Djamissi,[3] on the northern bank of the valley of the Lycus, and to the south-west of the Mosque of Sultan Mehemet.[4] No traces of a cistern have been found in that locality, but the conjecture satisfies the requirements of the case so far as the proximity of that site to the line of Constantine's wall and to the Church of the Holy Apostles is concerned. Why that position should have been selected for a summer palace is, however, not apparent.

We have said that the Constantinian Wall, upon leaving the Cistern of Aspar, turned sharply to the north-east, and made for the shore of the Golden Horn by running obliquely across the ridge of the Fifth Hill.

This view of the case is required, first, in order to keep the breadth of the city within the limits assigned by the *Notitia ;* and, secondly, by the statement of the same authority that the Eleventh Region—the Region at the north-western angle of the Constantinian city—did not extend to the shore of the Golden Horn : " Nulla parte mari sociata est."[5] For this statement

---

[1] Constant. Porphyr., p. 532.
[2] Anonymus, iii. p. 49, Ἐσκέπασεν αὐτὴν κυλινδρικῷ θόλῳ.
[3] The literary form of the word is Djami'i.
[4] *Die Byzantinischen Wasserbehälter von Konstantinopel*, p. 185.
[5] *Ad Reg. XI.*

implies that the fortifications along the northern front of that Region stood at some distance from the water. But the northern slope of the Fifth Hill is so precipitous, and approaches so close to the Golden Horn that the only available ground for the fortifications on that side of the city would be the plateau of the Fifth Hill, where the large cistern beside the Mosque of Sultan Selim is found.

(*g*) The church dedicated to the three martyr brothers, SS. Manual, Sabel, and Ishmael, must likewise have been on the Fifth Hill ; for it stood where the wall began its descent (κατήρχετο) [1] towards the Golden Horn. This agrees with the statement of the *Synaxaria* that the church was situated beside the land wall of Constantine, upon precipitous ground, and near the Church of St. Elias at the Petrion.[2]

(*h*) As to the district of Harmatius, named after Harmatius, a prominent personage in the reign of Zeno,[3] it must be sought in the plain bounded by the Fifth, Fourth, and Third Hills, and the Golden Horn, the plain known in later days as the Plateia, (Πλατεῖα). To that plain the fortifications of Constantine would necessarily descend from the Fifth Hill, in proceeding on their north-eastern course to the Golden Horn ; and there also the figures of the *Notitia* require the northern end of the walls to terminate. Doubtless in the time of Constantine the bay at this point encroached upon the plain more than at present.

A church dedicated to St. Antony was found in this part of the city by the Archbishop of Novgorod, when he visited Constantinople at the close of the eleventh century. He reached it after paying his devotions in the Church of St. Theodosia, the Church of St. Isaiah, and the Church of St. Laurentius,[4] sanctuaries situated in the plain before us ; the

---

[1] Codinus, p. 25. [2] *Synaxaria*, June 17, 20 ; Anonymus, ii. p. 35.
[3] Anonymus, ii. p. 36. [4] *Itinéraires Russes en Orient*, pp. 104, 105.

first being now the Mosque Gul Djami, near Aya Kapou,[1] while the two last are represented, it is supposed, respectively, by the Mosque of Sheik Mourad and the Mosque of Pour Kouyou, further to the south.[2]   The Archbishop places the Church of St. Antony on higher ground than the Church of St. Laurentius, apparently a short distance up the slope of the Fourth Hill, a position which St. Antony of Harmatius may well have occupied.

(*i*) The locality known as the Zeugma, or Ferry of St. Antony, stood, naturally, beside the shore.   If it cannot be identified with Oun-Kapan Kapoussi, where one of the principal ferries across the Golden Horn has always stood, it must, at all events, have been in that neighbourhood.

(*j*) With the result thus obtained regarding the course of the Constantinian Wall, may now be compared the statement of the *Paschal Chronicle* upon the subject.   According to that authority the old land wall of the city crossed the promontory from the Gate of St. Æmilianus, upon the Sea of Marmora, to the district of the Petrion, upon the Golden Horn.[3]   This statement is of great importance, because made while the wall was still standing ; and it would on that account have been considered sooner, but for certain questions which it raises, and which can be answered more readily now than at a previous stage of our inquiries.   The Chronicler makes the strange mistake of supposing that the wall which he saw stretching from sea to sea was the wall built originally for the defence of Byzantium by Phedalia, the wife of Byzas.   Unfortunately, Byzantine archæologists were not always versed in history.

Setting aside, therefore, the Chronicler's historical opinions,

---

[1] Paspates, pp. 320–322.   [2] *Ibid.*, pp. 381–383.

[3] Page 494, Τὸ παλαιὸν τεῖχος Κωνσταντινουπόλεως, τουτέστιν ἀπὸ τοῦ καλουμένου Πετρίου ἕως τῆς πόρτας τοῦ ἁγίου Αἰμιλιανοῦ, πλησίον τῆς καλουμένης Ῥάβδου.

and attending to the facts under his personal observation, we find him entirely agreed with the Anonymus as regards the point at which the southern extremity of the Wall of Constantine terminated.

For the Gate of St. Æmilianus, by which the former authority marks that extremity, stood close to the Church of St. Mary Rabdou, the indication given by the latter.[1]

The case seems otherwise as regards the northern end of the line, for the Petrion, mentioned in the *Paschal Chronicle*, was, strictly speaking, the district in which the Greek Patriarchate is now situated, the name of the district being still retained by the gate (Petri Kapoussi) at the eastern end of the enclosure around the Patriarchal Church and residence. But this would bring the northern end of the land wall considerably more to the west than the point where we have reason to believe the Church of St. Antony was found. It would also make the city broader than the *Notitia* allows. The discrepancy can, however, be easily removed. For, while the Petrion was pre-eminently the district above indicated, the designation was applied also to territory much further to the east. The Church of St. Laurentius, for example, near which St. Antony's stood, is at one time described as standing in the Plateia,[2] the plain to the east of Petri Kapoussi, while at another time it is spoken of as in the Petrion.[3] Hence the statement of the *Paschal Chronicle* does not conflict with what other authorities affirm respecting the point at which the Constantinian land fortifications reached the Golden Horn.

(*k*) Finally, from the Church of St. Antony the wall proceeded

---

[1] See *Paschal Chron., ut supra.*   [2] Anonymus, ii. pp. 39, 40.

[3] *Bollandists*, May 30, p. 238, Ἐν μαρτυρείῳ τῆς ἁγίας Εὐφημίας τῷ ὄντι πλησίον τοῦ ἁγίου Λαυρεντίου ἐν τῷ Πετρίῳ.

Under August 10, St. Laurentius is described as ἐν Πουλχεριαναῖς and ἐν Πετρίῳ. See below, pp. 206, 207.

along the shore of the Golden Horn to the head of the promontory, thus completing the circuit of the fortifications.

It should, however, be noted that this work of surrounding the city with bulwarks was not executed entirely in the reign of Constantine. A portion of the undertaking—probably the walls defending the shores of the city—was left for his son and successor Constantius to complete.[1]

The following gates, mentioned in Byzantine history, were found, there is reason to believe, in the Constantinian circuit :—

Porta Polyandriou (Πόρτα Πολυανδρίου,[2] the Gate of the Cemetery) stood in the portion of the wall near the Church of the Holy Apostles. It is true that this was one of the names of the Gate of Adrianople in the later Theodosian Walls, but if the name was derived from the Imperial Cemetery beside the Church of the Holy Apostles, there is much probability in Dr. Mordtmann's opinion that the designation belonged originally to the corresponding gate in the Constantinian fortifications, which stood closer to the cemetery.[3]

Another gate was the Porta Atalou (Πόρτα ᾿Ατάλου).[4] It was adorned with the statue of Constantine the Great and the statue of Atalus, after whom the gate was named. Both monuments fell in the earthquake of 740. The presence of the statue of the founder of the city upon the gate, the fact that the damage which the gate sustained in 740 is mentioned in close connection with the injuries done at the same time to the Column of Arcadius on the Xeropholos,[5] and the lack of any proof that the gate stood in the Theodosian Walls, are circumstances which favour the view that it was an entrance in the Wall of Constantine. From its association with the Xerolophos one would infer that the Gate of Atalus was situated on the Seventh Hill, in a

---

[1] Emperor Julian, *Oratio I.*   [2] *Paschal Chron.*, p. 719.
[3] Pages 10, 28. See below, p. 85.   [4] Theophanes, p. 634.   [5] *Ibid., ut supra.*

position corresponding to one of the later Theodosian gates on that eminence.

That the Palaia Porta—Isa Kapoussi, beside the Mosque Isa Kapou Mesdjidi—was a Constantinian gate is beyond dispute. But a difficult, and at the same time important, question occurs in connection with it. Was it the Porta Aurea mentioned in the *Notitia* as the gate from which the length of the city was measured? What renders this a difficult question is the fact that the Porta Aurea of the Theodosian Walls—the celebrated Golden Gate which appears so frequently in the history of the city, and which is now incorporated in the Turkish fortress of the Seven Towers (Yedi Koulè), under the name Yedi Koulè Kapoussi—was already in existence when the *Notitia* was written.[2] That being the case, the presumption is in favour of the opinion that the Golden Gate at Yedi Koulè is the Porta Aurea to which the *Notitia* refers; and this opinion has upon its side the great authority of Dr. Strzygowski.[3] On the other hand, the distance from the Porta Aurea to the sea, as given by the *Notitia*, does not correspond to the distance between Yedi Koulè and the head of the promontory, the latter distance being much greater. To suppose that this discrepancy is due to a mistake which has crept into the figures of the *Notitia* is possible; but the supposition is open to more than one objection. In the first place, such a view obliges us to assume a similar mistake in the figures which that authority gives for the breadth of the city, seeing they do not accord with the breadth of the city along the line of the Theodosian Walls. But even if this objection is waived, and the possibility of a double error admitted in the abstract, the hypothesis of a mistake in the figures before us is attended by another difficulty, which cannot be dismissed so easily. How comes it that figures condemned as inaccurate because they do

---

[1] See above, pp. 21, 22.   [2] See below, p. 62.   [3] See below, p. 61, ref. 5.

not accord with the size of Constantinople under Theodosius II., prove perfectly correct when applied to the dimensions of the city under its founder ?   How come these figures to agree completely with what we learn regarding the length and breadth of the city of Constantine from other data on that subject ?   This cannot be an accident ; the only satisfactory explanation is that the figures in question belonged to the primitive text of the document in which they are found, and never referred to anything else than the original size of the city.   Hence we are compelled to adopt the view that when the *Notitia* was written, two gates bearing the epithet " Golden " existed in Constantinople, one of them in the older circuit of the city, the other in the later fortifications of Theodosius, and that the author of the *Notitia* refers to the earlier entrance.   There is nothing strange in the existence of a Triumphal Gate in the Wall of Constantine, while the duplication of such an entrance for a later line of bulwarks was perfectly natural.

Why the *Notitia* overlooks the second Porta Aurea is explained by the point of view from which that work was written. Its author was concerned with the original city.   A gate in the Wall of Theodosius was only the vestibule of the corresponding Constantinian entrance.

The existence of a Porta Aurea in the Wall of Constantine being thus established, the identification of that gate with the Palaia Porta offers little difficulty.   The Constantinian Porta Aurea, like the Ancient Gate, stood on the Seventh Hill, since the portion of the Via Triumphalis leading from the Exokionion to the Forum of Arcadius was on that eminence.[1]   Like the Ancient Gate, the Porta Aurea was, moreover, distinguished by fine architectural features, as its very epithet implies, and, as the *Notitia* declares, when it states that the city wall bounding the

[1] Constant. Porphyr., *De Cer.*, p. 501.

Twelfth Region, on the Seventh Hill, was remarkable for its monumental character—"Quam (regionem) mœnium sublimior decorat ornatus."[1] Gates so similar in their position and appearance can scarcely have been different entrances.

Of the Constantinian gates along the seaboard of the city, the only one about which anything positive can be affirmed is the Gate of St. Æmilianus, near the Church of St. Mary Rabdou, on the Sea of Marmora. It is now represented by Daoud Pasha Kapoussi.[2]

Dr. Mordtmann[3] suggests the existence of a gate known as the Basilikè Porta beside the Golden Horn, where Ayasma Kapoussi stands; but this conjecture is exceedingly doubtful.

The Wall of Constantine formed the boundary and bulwark of the city for some eighty years, its great service being the protection of the new capital against the Visigoths, who asserted their power in the Balkan Peninsula during the latter part of the fourth century and the earlier portion of the fifth. After the terrible defeat of the Roman arms at Adrianople in 378, the Goths marched upon Constantinople, but soon retired, in view of the hopelessness of an attack upon the fortifications. The bold Alaric never dared to assail these walls; while Gainas, finding he could not carry them by surprise, broke up his camp at the Hebdomon, and withdrew to the interior of Thrace.

It is a mistake, however, to suppose that the original bulwarks of the capital were demolished as soon as the Theodosian Walls were built.[4] On the contrary, the old works continued

[1] *Ad Reg. XII.*   [2] *Paschal Chron.*, p. 494; see below, p. 264.

[3] Pages 7, 8. There is no proof for the existence of a Porta Saturnini in the Constantinian Wall (*Esquisse Top. de CP.*). The author of the "Life of St. Isaacius," in the *Bollandists* (May 31, p. 256, n. 4, p. 259), says that a cell was built for that saint by Saturninus: "Suburbanam, nec procul a civitatis muris (Constantinian) remotam domum." The house of Saturninus himself is described as "extra portam Collarida" (Xerolophos). But nothing is said regarding a gate named after him. Regarding this Basilikè Porta, see below, p. 213.

[4] Nicephorus Callistus, xiv. c. 1.

for a considerable period to form an inner line of defence. We hear of them in the reign of Justinian the Great, when, together with the Wall of Theodosius, they were injured by a violent earthquake.[1] They were in their place also when the *Paschal Chronicle* was written.[2] What their condition precisely was in 740, when the Gate of Atalus was overthrown,[3] cannot be determined, but evidently they had not completely disappeared. Thereafter nothing more is heard of them, and the probability is that they were left to waste away gradually. Remains of ancient walls survived in the neighbourhood of Isa Kapoussi as late as the early part of this century.[4]

INTERIOR ARRANGEMENTS OF THE CITY OF CONSTANTINE.

The work of altering Byzantium to become the seat of government was commenced in 328, and occupied some two years, materials and labourers for the purpose being gathered from all parts of the Empire. Workmen skilled in cutting columns and marble came even from the neighbourhood of Naples,[5] and the forty thousand Gothic troops, known as the Fœderati, lent their strength to push the work forward.[6]

At length, on the 11th of May, A.D. 330,[7] the city of Constantine, destined to rank among the great capitals of the world, and to exert a vast influence over the course of human

---

[1] Malalas, p. 488; Agathias, v. c. 5, 3–8.   [2] Page 494.
[3] Theophanes, p. 634.   [4] Paspates, p. 363.
[5] Lydus, *De Magistratibus*, iii. p. 266.
[6] Jornandes, *De Rebus Get.*, c. 21, "Nam et dum famosissimam et Romæ æmulam in suo nomine conderet civitatem, Gothorum interfuit operatio, qui fœdere inito cum imperatore XL. suorum millia illi in solatio contra gentes varias obtulere, quorum et numerus et millia usque, in Rep. nominantur Fœderati"

In one brief (*Cod. Theod.*, lib. 13, tit. iv. 1) Constantine complains of the dearth of architects; in another (*Cod. Theod.*, lib. 13, tit. iv. 2) he offers to free from taxes thirty-five master artificers if they would bring up their sons in the same professions.

[7] *Paschal Chron.*, p. 529.

affairs, was dedicated with public rejoicings which lasted forty days.[1]

The internal arrangements of the city were determined mainly by the configuration of its site, the position of the buildings taken over from Byzantium, and the desire to reproduce some of the features of Rome.

The principal new works gathered about two nuclei—the chief Gate of Byzantium and the Square of the Tetrastoon.

Immediately without the gate was placed the Forum, named after Constantine.[2] It was elliptical in shape, paved with large stones, and surrounded by a double tier of porticoes ; a lofty marble archway at each extremity of its longer axis led into this area, and in the centre rose a porphyry column, bearing a statue of Apollo crowned with seven rays. The figure represented the founder of the city "shining like the sun" upon the scene of his creation. On the northern side of the Forum a Senate House was erected.[3]

The Tetrastoon was enlarged and embellished, receiving in its new character the name "Augustaion," in honour of Constantine's mother Helena, who bore the title Augusta, and whose statue, set upon a porphyry column, adorned the square.[4]

The Hippodrome was now completed,[5] to become "the axis of the Byzantine world," and there, in addition to other monuments, the Serpent Column from Delphi was placed. The adjoining Thermæ of Zeuxippus were improved.[6] An Imperial Palace,[7] with its main entrance on the southern side of the Augustaion, was built to the east of the Hippodrome, where it stood related to the race-course very much as the Palace of the

---

[1] Banduri, *Imperium Orientale*, lib. v. p. 98.

[2] *Paschal Chron.*, p. 528; Zosimus, p. 96.

[3] Hesychius, *Frag. Hist. Græc.*, iv. p. 154 ; Anonymus, i. p. 13.

[4] *Paschal Chron.*, p. 529, Αὐγουσταῖον.   [5] *Ibid.*, p. 528.

[6] *Ibid.*, p. 529.   [7] *Ibid.*, p. 528.

Cæsars on the Palatine was related to the Circus Maximus. There, at the same time, it commanded the beautiful view presented by the Sea of Marmora, the Prince's Islands, the hilly Asiatic coast, and the snow-capped Bythinian Olympus. Eusebius, who saw the palace in its glory, describes it as "most magnificent;" [1] while Zosimus speaks of it as scarcely inferior to the Imperial Residence in Rome.[2]

On the eastern side of the Augustaion rose the Basilica,[3] where the Senate held its principal meetings. It was entered through a porch supported by six splendid columns of marble, and the building itself was decorated with every possible variety of the same material. There also statues of rare workmanship were placed, such as the Group of the Muses from Helicon, the statue of Zeus from Dodona, and that of Pallas from Lindus.[4]

According to Eusebius, Constantine adorned the city and its suburbs with many churches,[5] the most prominent of them being the Church of Irene [6] and the Church of the Apostles.[7] The former was situated a short distance to the north of the Augustaion, and there, as restored first by Justinian the Great, and later by Leo III., it still stands within the Seraglio enclosure, now an arsenal of Turkish arms.

The Church of the Apostles, with its roof covered with tiles of gilded bronze, crowned the summit of the Fourth Hill, where it has been replaced by the Mosque of the Turkish Conqueror of the city.

There, also, Constantine erected for himself a mausoleum, surrounded by twelve pillars after the number of the Apostles ; [8] and in the porticoes and chapels beside the church most of

---

[1] Eusebius, *Life of Constantine*, iv. 66.   [2] Zosimus, p. 97.

[3] *Paschal Chron.*, pp. 528, 529.   [4] Zosimus, pp. 280, 281.

[5] Eusebius, *Life of Constantine*, iii. 47.   [5] Socrates, i. c. 16.

[7] Eusebius, iv. c. 52-60.   [8] Eusebius, iv. 60.

Constantine's successors and their empresses, as well as the patriarchs of the city, found their last resting-place in sarcophagi of porphyry or marble. Whether Constantine had any part in the erection of St. Sophia is extremely uncertain. Eusebius is silent regarding that church ; Socrates ascribes it to Constantius. Possibly Constantine laid the foundations of the famous sanctuary.

Among other churches ascribed to the founder of the city are those dedicated, respectively, to St. Mokius, St. Acacius, St. Agathonicus, and to Michael the Archangel at Anaplus (Arna-outkeui), on the Bosporus.[1] There is no doubt that in the foundation of New Rome, Constantine emphasized the alliance of the Empire with the Christian Church. "Over the entrance of his palace," says Eusebius, "he caused a rich cross to be erected of gold and precious stones, as a protection and a divine charm against the machinations and evil purposes of his enemies."[2]

Three streets running the length of the city formed the great arteries of communication.[3]

One started from the south-western end of the palace enclosure, and proceeded along the Sea of Marmora to the Church of St. Æmilianus, at the southern extremity of the land wall. At that point was the Harbour of Eleutherius,[4] on the site of Vlanga Bostan, providing the city with what Nature had failed to supply—a harbour of refuge on the southern coast of the promontory.

Another street commenced at the south-eastern end of the palace grounds (Tzycanisterion), and ran first to the point of the Acropolis along the eastern shore of the city, passing on

---

[1] Hesychius Milesius, *Fragm. Hist. Græc.*, p. 154 ; Theophanes, p. 34 ; Sozomon, ii. c. 3.

[2] *Life of Constantine*, iii. c. 48.   [3] Anonymus, i. p. 5 ; Codinus, pp. 22, 23.

[4] Anonymus, iii. p. 46. See below, p. 296.

the way the theatre and amphitheatre of Byzantium. Near the latter Constantine built the Mangana, or Military Arsenal.[1] The street then proceeded westwards along the Golden Horn, past the Temples of Zeus and Poseidon, the Stadium, the Strategion, and the principal harbours of the city, to the Church of St. Antony in the quarter of Harmatius. In the Strategion an equestrian statue of Constantine was placed, and a pillar bearing the edict which bestowed upon the city the name of New Rome, as well as the rights and privileges of the elder capital.[2]

The third street started from the main gate of the palace, and proceeded, first, from the Augustaion to the Forum of Constantine. On reaching the Third Hill it divided into two branches, one leading to the Porta Aurea and the Exokionion, the other to the Church of the Holy Apostles and the Gate of the Polyandrion. This was the main artery of the city, and was named the Mesè (Μεσή) on account of its central position. Porticoes built by Eubulus, one of the senators who accompanied Constantine from Rome, lined both sides of the Mesè, and one side of the two other streets, adding at once to the convenience and beauty of the thoroughfares. The porticoes extending from the Augustaion to the Forum of Constantine were particularly handsome.[3] Upon the summit of all the porticoes walks or terraces were laid out, adorned with countless statues, and commanding views of the city and of the surrounding hills and waters. Thus, the street scenery of Constantinople combined the attractions of Art and Nature.

The water-supply of the new capital was one of the most important undertakings of the day.[4] While the water-works of Byzantium, as improved by Hadrian, continued to be used, they

---

[1] Anonymus, ii. p. 26. See below, p. 250. [2] Socrates, i. c.16.

[3] *Paschal Chron.*, p. 528 ; Lydus, *De Magistratibus*, iii. p. 266.

[4] Anonymus, i. p. 5 ; Codinus, p. 22.

were extended, to render the supply of water more abundant. What exactly was done for that purpose is, however, a matter of conjecture.[1]

To the construction of the aqueducts, porticoes, and fortifications of New Rome sixty centenaria of gold (£2,500,000) were devoted.[2]

The health of the city was consulted by building sewers far underground, and carrying them to the sea.[3]

With the view of drawing population to the new city, Constantine made the wheat hitherto sent from Egypt to Rome the appanage of Constantinople, and ordered the daily free distribution of eighty thousand loaves.[4] The citizens were, moreover, granted the Jus Italicus,[5] while, to attract families of distinction the emperor erected several mansions for presentation to Roman senators.[6] House-building was encouraged by granting estates in Pontus and Asia, on the tenure of maintaining a residence in the new capital.[7]

Furthermore, in virtue of its new dignity, the city was relieved from its subordination to the town of Heraclea,[8] imposed since the time of Septimius Severus, and the members of the public council of New Rome were constituted into a Senate, with the right to bear the title of Clari.[9]

For municipal purposes the city was divided, like Rome, into

---

[1] Cf. Tchihatchef, *Le Bosphore et Constantinople*, chap. ii. ; Andreossy, *Constantinople et le Bosphore de Thrace*, Livre Troisième, " Système des Eaux."

[2] Anonymus, i. p. 5.   [3] *Ibid., ut supra.*

[4] Socrates, ii. c. 13 ; Philostorgius, ii. c. 9.

[5] *Cod. Theod.*, lib. xiv. 13 ; *Cod. Justin.*, xi. 20.

[6] Hesychius Milesius, *Fragm. Hist. Græc.*, iv. p. 154 ; Zosimus, p. 97.

[7] *Cod. Theod.*, Novella 12.

[8] *Paschal Chron.*, p. 530. Because of this subordination of Byzantium to Heraclea, the bishop of the latter city has still the right to preside at the consecration of the patriarch of Constantinople.

[9] Valesian Anonymus, appended to the History of Ammianus Marcellinus. The senators of Rome were styled " Clarissimi."

Fourteen Regions,[1] two of them being outside the circuit of the fortifications, viz. the Thirteenth, which comprised Sycæ (Galata), on the northern side of the Golden Horn, and the Fourteenth, constituting the suburb of Blachernæ, now the quarters of Egri Kapou and Aivan Serai.

[1] *Notitia, ad Regiones.* On the delimitation of the Regions, see Gyllius, *De Topographia Constantinopleos*, l. ii. c. 2, 10, 16 ; l. iii. c. 1, 2, 5, 7, 8, 9 ; l. iv. c. 1, 3, 7, 10, 11 ; and Mordtmann, *Esquisse Topographique de Constantinople*, pp. 2–10. The point on which these authorities differ most widely is regarding the situation of the Seventh Region, Gyllius making it occupy the valley of the Grand Bazaar, on the northern side of the city ; while Mordtmann (pp. 6, 7) places it on the southern slope of the Second Hill, from the Forum of Constantine to the Sea of Marmora. My view (at present) on the subject is indicated in the Map of Byzantine Constantinople.

CHAPTER III.

THE THEODOSIAN WALLS.

THE enduring character of the political reasons which had called the new capital into being, and the commercial advantages which its unique position commanded, favoured such an increase of population, that before eighty-five years had elapsed, the original limits of Constantinople proved too narrow for the crowds gathered within the walls.

So numerous were the inhabitants already in 378, that the Goths, who then appeared before the city after the defeat of the Roman arms at Adrianople, abandoned all hope of capturing a stronghold which could draw upon such multitudes for its defence.[1]

Three years later, Athanaric[2] marvelled at the variety of peoples which poured into the city, as they have ever since, like streams from different points into a common reservoir. Soon the corn fleets of Alexandria, Asia, Syria, and Phœnicia, were unable to provide the city with sufficient bread.[3] The houses were packed so closely that the citizens, whether at home or abroad, felt confined and oppressed, while to walk the streets was dangerous, on account of the number of the beasts of burden that crowded the thoroughfares. Building-ground was in such

---

[1] Ammianus Marcellinus, xxxii. 16.   [2] Jornandes, xxviii.
[3] Eunapius, quoted by Gyllius, *De Top. CP.*, i. c. 5.

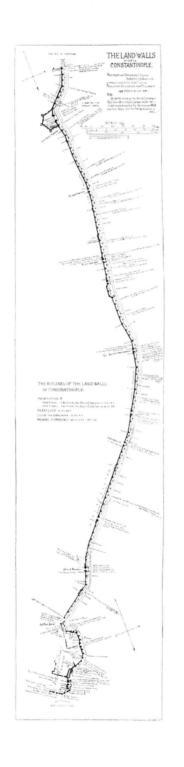

THE LAND WALLS
of the
CONSTANTINOPLE.

THE BUILDERS OF THE LAND WALLS
OF CONSTANTINOPLE

demand that portions of the sea along the shores of the city had
to be filled in, and the erections on that artificial land alone
formed a considerable town.[1]   Sozomon goes so far as to affirm
that Constantinople had grown more populous than Rome.[2]

This increase of the population is explained, in part, by the
attractions which a capital, and especially one founded recently,
offered alike to rich and poor as a place of residence and occupation.   The ecclesiastical dignity of the city, when elevated to
the second rank in the hierarchy of the Church, made it, moreover, the religious centre of the East, and drew a large body of
ecclesiastics and devout persons within its bounds.   The presence
and incursions of the Goths and the Huns south of the Danube
drove many of the original inhabitants of the invaded districts
for shelter behind the fortifications of the city, and led multitudes
of barbarians thither in search of employment or the pleasures
of civilized life.

Then, it must be remembered that no capital is built in
a day.

To make the city worthy of its name involved great labour,
and demanded an army of workmen of every description.   There
were many structures which Constantine had only commenced ;
the completion of the fortifications of the city had been left to
Constantius ; Julian found it necessary to construct a second
harbour on the side of the Sea of Marmora ; Valens was obliged
to improve the water-works of the city by the erection of the fine
aqueduct which spans the valley between the Fourth and Fifth
Hills.   And how large a number of hands such works required
appears from the fact that when the aqueduct was repaired, in
the ninth century, 6000 labourers were brought from the provinces
to Constantinople for the purpose.[3]

Under the rule of the Theodosian dynasty the improvement

---

[1] Zosimus, p. 101.   [2] Sozomon, ii. c. 3.   [3] Theophanes, p. 680.

of the city went forward with leaps and bounds. Most of the public places and buildings enumerated by the *Notitia*, were constructed under the auspices of that House, and transformed the city. A vivid picture of the change is drawn by Themistius,[1] who knew all the phases through which Constantinople had passed, from the reign of Constantius to that of Theodosius the Great. "No longer," exclaims the orator, as he viewed the altered appearance of things around him, "is the vacant ground in the city more extensive than that occupied by buildings ; nor are we cultivating more territory within our walls than we inhabit ; the beauty of the city is not, as heretofore, scattered over it in patches, but covers its whole area like a robe woven to the very fringe. The city gleams with gold and porphyry. It has a (new) Forum, named after the emperor ; it owns Baths, Porticoes, Gymnasia ; and its former extremity is now its centre. Were Constantine to see the capital he founded he would behold a glorious and splendid scene, not a bare and empty void ; he would find it fair, not with apparent, but with real beauty." The mansions of the rich, the orator continues, had become larger and more sumptuous ; the suburbs had expanded ; the place "was full of carpenters, builders, decorators, and artisans of every description, and might fitly be called a work-shop of magnificence." "Should the zeal of the emperor to adorn the city continue," adds Themistius, in prophetic strain, "a wider circuit will be demanded, and the question will arise whether the city added to Constantinople by Theodosius is not more splendid than the city which Constantine added to Byzantium."

The growth of the capital went on under Arcadius, with the result that early in the reign of his son, the younger Theodosius, the enlargement of the city limits, foreseen by Themistius, was carried into effect.

[1] *Oratio*, xviii. p. 222. Edition of Petavius.

But this extension of the boundaries was not made simply to suit the convenience of a large population. It was required also by the need of new bulwarks. Constantinople called for more security, as well as for more room. The barbarians were giving grave reasons for disquiet ; Rome had been captured by the Goths ; the Huns had crossed the Danube, and though repelled, still dreamed of carrying their conquests wherever the sun shone. It was, indeed, time for the Empire to gird on its whole armour.

Fortunately for the eastern portion of the Roman world, Anthemius, the statesman at the head of the Government for six years during the minority of Theodosius II., was eminently qualified for his position by lofty character, distinguished ability, and long experience in the public service. When appointed Prætorian Prefect of the East, in 405, by the Emperor Arcadius, Chrysostom remarked that the appointment conferred more honour on the office than upon Anthemius himself ; and the ecclesiastical historian Socrates extols the prefect as " one of the wisest men of the age." [1] Proceeding, therefore, to do all in his power to promote the security of the State, Anthemius cleared the Balkan Peninsula of the hostile Huns under Uldin, driving them north of the Danube. Then, to prevent the return of the enemy, ·he placed a permanent flotilla of 250 vessels on that river, and strengthened the fortifications of the cities in Illyria ; and to crown the system of defence, he made Constantinople a mighty citadel. The enlargement and refortification of the city was thus part of a comprehensive and far-seeing plan to equip the Roman State in the East for the impending desperate struggle with barbarism ; and of all the services which Anthemius rendered, the most valuable and enduring was the addition he made to the military importance of the capital. The bounds he assigned to

[1] VII. c. I.

the city fixed, substantially, her permanent dimensions, and behind the bulwarks he raised—improved and often repaired, indeed, by his successors—Constantinople acted her great part in the history of the world.

The erection and repair of the fortifications of a city was an undertaking which all citizens were required to assist, in one form or another. On that point the laws were very stringent, and no rank or privilege exempted any one from the obligation to promote the work.[1] One-third of the annual land-tax of the city could be drawn upon to defray the outlay, all expenses above that amount being met by requisitions laid upon the inhabitants. The work of construction was entrusted to the Factions, as several inscriptions on the walls testify. In 447, when the Theodosian fortifications were repaired and extended, the Blues and the Greens furnished, between them, sixteen thousand labourers for the undertaking.[2]

The stone employed upon the fortifications is tertiary limestone, brought from the neighbourhood of Makrikeui, where the hollows and mounds formed in quarrying are still visible. The bricks used are from 1 foot 1 inch to 1 foot 2 inches square, and 2 inches thick. They are sometimes stamped with the name of their manufacturer or donor, and occasionally bear the name of the contemporary emperor, and the indiction in which they were made. Mortar, mixed with powdered brick, was employed in large quantities, lest it should dry without taking hold,[3] and bound the masonry into a solid mass, hard as rock.

The wall of Anthemius was erected in 413,[4] the fifth year of

---

[1] *Cod. Theod.*, lib. viii. tit. xxii.   [2] Anonymus, i. p. 22.

[3] See Choisy, *L'Art de Bâtir chez les Byzantins*, pp. 7-13.

[4] Socrates, vii. c. 1 ; *Cod. Theod.*, "De Operibus Publicis," lex. 51. The law refers to the towers of the new wall, and is addressed to Anthemius as Prætorian Prefect in 413 : " Turres novi muri, qui ad munitionem splendidissimæ urbis extructus

Theodosius II., then about twelve years of age, and is now represented by the inner wall in the fortifications that extend along the west of the city, from the Sea of Marmora to the ruins of the Byzantine Palace, known as Tekfour Serai. The new city limits were thus placed at a distance of one mile to one mile and a half west of the Wall of Constantine.

This change in the position of the landward line of defence involved the extension likewise of the walls along the two shores of the city; but though that portion of the work must have been included in the plan of Anthemius, it was not executed till after his day. As we shall find, the new seaboard of the capital was fortified a quarter of a century later, in 439, under the direction of the Prefect Cyrus, while Theodosius II. was still upon the throne.

The bulwarks of Anthemius saved the city from attack by Attila. They were too formidable for him to venture to assail them.

But they suffered soon at the hands of the power which was to inflict more injury upon the fortifications of Constantinople than any other foe. In 447, only thirty-four years after their construction, the greater portion of the new walls, with fifty-seven towers, was overthrown by a series of violent earthquakes.[1] The disaster was particularly inopportune at the moment it occurred, for already in that year Attila had defeated the armies of Theodosius in three successive engagements, ravaged with fire and sword the provinces of Macedonia and Thrace, and come as near to Constantinople as Athyras (Buyuk Tchekmedjè). He had dictated an ignominious treaty of peace, exacting the cession of territory south of the Danube, the payment of an

est, completo opere, præcipimus eorum usui deputari, per quorum terram idem murus studio ac provisione Tuæ Magnitudinis ex Nostræ Serenitatis arbitrio celebratur."

[1] Marcellinus Comes, "Plurimi urbis Augustæ muri recenti adhuc constructi, cum LVII. turribus, corruerunt."

indemnity of 6000 pounds of gold, and the increase of the annual tribute paid to him by the Eastern Empire from 700 pounds of gold to 2100.

The crisis was, however, met with splendid energy by Constantine, then Prætorian Prefect of the East, and under his direction, as Marcellinus Comes affirms, the walls were restored in less than three months after their overthrow.[1] But besides restoring the shattered bulwarks of his predecessor, Constantine seized the opportunity to render the city a much stronger fortress than even Anthemius had made it. Accordingly, another wall, with a broad and deep moat before it, was erected in front of the Wall of Anthemius, to place the city behind three lines of defence. The walls were flanked by 192 towers, while the ground between the two walls, and that between the Outer Wall and the Moat, provided room for the action of large bodies of troops. These five portions of the fortifications rose tier above tier, and combined to form a barricade 190–207 feet thick, and over 100 feet high.[2]

As an inscription [3] upon the fortifications proclaimed, this was a wall indeed, τὸ καὶ τεῖχος ὄντως—a wall which, so long as ordinary courage survived and the modes of ancient warfare were not superseded, made Constantinople impregnable, and behind which civilization defied the assaults of barbarism for a thousand years.

Three inscriptions commemorating the erection of these noble works of defence have been discovered. Two of them are still found on the Gate Yeni Mevlevi Haneh Kapoussi (Porta Rhousiou), one being in Greek, the other in Latin, as

---

[1] "Intra tres menses, Constantino Præfecto Prætorio opere dante, (muri) reædificati sunt." Cf. Inscription on the Gate Yeni Mevlevi Haneh Kapoussi, p. 47.

[2] Measuring from the bed of the Moat.

[3] It stood on the Outer Wall between the fourth and fifth towers south of the Golden Gate (Paspates, p. 58).

PORTION OF THE THEODOSIAN WALLS (BETWEEN THE GATE OF THE DEUTERON AND YEDI KOULÉ KAPOUSSI).

both languages were then in official use. The former reads to the effect that " In sixty days, by the order of the sceptre-loving Emperor, Constantine the Eparch added wall to wall."

† HMAϹIN EΞHKONTA ΦIΛOϹKHΠTPω BAϹIΛHI †
KωNϹTANTINOϹ YΠAPXOϹ EΔEIMATO TEIXEI TEIXOϹ †

The Latin legend is more boastful : " By the commands of Theodosius, in less than two months, Constantine erected triumphantly these strong walls. Scarcely could Pallas have built so quickly so strong a citadel."

THEODOSII JUSSIS GEMINO NEC MENSE PERACTO †
CONSTANTINUS OVANS HAEC MOENIA FIRMA LOCAVIT
TAM CITO TAM STABILEM PALLAS VIX CONDERET ARCEM †[1]

The third inscription has disappeared from its place on the Porta Xylokerkou, but is preserved in the Greek Anthology.[2] It declared that, " The Emperor Theodosius and Constantine the Eparch of the East built this wall in sixty days."

ΘEYΔOϹIOϹ TOΔE TEIXOϹ ANAΞ KAI YΠAPXOϹ EωAϹ
KωNϹTANTINOϹ ETEYΞAN EN HMAϹIN EΞHKONTA

The shortness of the time assigned to the execution of the work is certainly astonishing. Perhaps the statement of the inscriptions will appear more credible if understood to refer exclusively to the second wall, and if we realize the terror which the Huns then inspired. The dread of Attila, " the Scourge of God," might well prove an incentive to extraordinary performance, and strain every muscle to the utmost tension.

But the question of the time occupied in the reconstruction of the walls is not the only difficulty raised by these inscriptions. They present a question also as regards the official under whose direction that work was executed. For according to them, and Marcellinus Comes, the superintendent of the work was named

---

[1] See illustrations facing pp. 78, 96, 248.
[2] Banduri, *Imperium Orientale*, vii. n. 428.

Constantine.[1] Theophanes and subsequent historians, on the
other hand, ascribe the undertaking to the Prefect Cyrus.[2]
This is a serious discrepancy, and authorities are not agreed in
their mode of dealing with it. Some have proposed to remove
the difficulty by the simple expedient of identifying Constantine
and Cyrus ;[3] while others maintain a distinction of persons, and
reconcile the conflicting statements by understanding them to
refer, respectively, to different occasions on which the walls
were repaired.[4]

Cyrus was one of the most conspicuous figures in the
history of the city during the reign of Theodosius II.[5] On
account of his talents and integrity he held the office of
Prætorian Prefect, and that of Prefect of the City, for four
years, making himself immensely popular by the character of
his administration. During his prefecture, in 439, the new
walls along the shores of the city were constructed. The fires
and earthquakes, moreover, which devastated Constantinople in
the earlier half of the fifth century, afforded him ample opportunity for carrying out civic improvements, and he was to be
seen constantly driving about the city in his chariot to inspect
the public buildings in course of erection, and to push forward
their completion. Among other works, he restored the great
Bath of Achilles, which had been destroyed in the fire of 433,[6]
To him also is ascribed the introduction of the practice of
lighting the shops and streets of the capital at night.[7] He was,
moreover, a man of literary tastes, and a poet, who counted the
Empress Eudoxia, herself a poetess, one of his admirers.[8] In

---

[1] See above, p. 47.
[2] Theophanes, pp. 148, 149 ; Leo Gram., pp. 108, 109.
[3] Patriarch Constantius, Paspates, Mordtmann, Du Cange.
[4] Muralt, *Essai de Chronographie Byzantine, de* 395 *à* 1057, pp. 54, 55.
[5] *Paschal Chron.*, pp. 588, 589.
[6] *Ibid.*, pp. 582, 583.   [7] *Ibid.*, p. 588.   [8] Suidas, *ad vocem* Κύρος.

the competition between Greek and Latin for ascendency as the official language of the Government, he took the side of the former by issuing his decrees in Greek, a practice which made the conservative Lydus style him ironically, "Our Demosthenes." [1]

But in the midst of all his success, Cyrus remained self-possessed and sober-minded. "I do not like Fortune, when she smiles much," [2] he was accustomed to say ; and at length the tide of his prosperity turned. Taking his seat one day in the Hippodrome, he was greeted with a storm of applause. "Constantine," the vast assembly shouted, "founded the city ; Cyrus restored it." For a subject to be so popular was a crime. Theodosius took umbrage at the ovation accorded to the renovator of the city, and Cyrus was dismissed from office, deprived of his property, forced to enter the Church, and sent to Smyrna to succeed four bishops who had perished at the hands of brigands. Upon his arrival in that city on Christmas Day he found his people ill-prepared to receive him, so indignant were they that a man still counted a heathen and a heretic should have been appointed the shepherd of their souls. But a short allocution, which Cyrus delivered in honour of the festival, disarmed the opposition to him, and he spent the last years of his life in the diocese, undisturbed by political turmoils and unmolested by robbers.

Returning to the question of the identity of Cyrus with the Prefect Constantine above mentioned, the strongest argument in favour of that identity is the fact that, commencing with Theophanes, who flourished in the latter part of the eighth century, all historians who refer to the fortification of the city under Theodosius II. ascribe the work to Cyrus. That they

---

[1] Lydus, *De Magistratibus*, iii. p. 235.
[2] Malalas, p. 361, Οὐκ ἀρέσκει μοι τύχη πολλά γελῶσα.

should be mistaken on this point, it may be urged, is extremely improbable. On this view, the occurrence of the name Constantine instead of Cyrus in the inscriptions and in Marcellinus Comes, is explained by the supposition that the former name was the one which Cyrus assumed, as usual under such circumstances, after his conversion to the Christian faith.[1] But surely any name which Cyrus acquired after his dismissal from office could not be employed as his designation in documents anterior to his fall. Perhaps a better explanation is that Cyrus always had both names, one used habitually, the other rarely, and that the latter appears in the inscriptions because more suited than the former to the versification in which they are cast. This, however, does not explain why Marcellinus Comes prefers the name Constantine.

On the other hand, the proposed identification of Cyrus and Constantine is open to serious objections. In the first place, not till the eighth century is the name of Cyrus associated with the land walls of Constantinople. Earlier historians,[2] when speaking of Cyrus and extolling his services, say nothing as to his having been concerned in the fortification of the city in 447.

In the next place, the information of Theophanes and his followers does not seem based upon a thorough investigation of the subject. These writers ignore the fact that under Theodosius II. the land walls were built on two occasions ; they ascribe to Cyrus everything done in the fifth century in the way of enlarging and fortifying the capital, and are silent as regards the connection of the great Anthemius with that work.

The only Byzantine author later than the fifth century who recalls the services of Anthemius is Nicephorus Callistus,[3] and even he represents Cyrus as the associate of that illustrious

---

[1] Paspates, p. 48, quoting Skarlatus Byzantius.
[2] *Paschal Chron.*, Malalas.   [3] Lib. vii. c. 1.

prefect.   If such inaccuracies do not render the testimony of
Theophanes and subsequent historians worthless, they certainly
make one ask whether these writers were not misled by the
great fame of Cyrus on the ground of other achievements, and
especially on account of his share in building the walls along
the shores of the city in 439, to ascribe to him a work which
was really performed by the more obscure Constantine.

THE INNER WALL.

Τὸ κάστρον τὸ μέγα :[1]   Τὸ μέγα τεῖχος.[2]

The Inner Wall was the main bulwark of the capital.   It
stood on a higher level than the Outer Wall, and was, at the
same time, loftier, thicker, and flanked by stronger towers.   In
construction it was a mass of concrete faced on both sides with
blocks of limestone, squared and carefully fitted ; while six
brick courses, each containing five layers of bricks, were laid at
intervals through the thickness of the wall to bind the structure
more firmly.

The wall rises some $30\frac{1}{2}$ feet above the present exterior
ground-level, and about 40 feet above the level within the
city, with a thickness varying from $15\frac{1}{2}$ feet near the base to
$13\frac{1}{2}$ feet at the summit.   The summit had along its outer edge
a battlement, 4 feet 8 inches high, and was reached by flights
of steps, placed generally beside the gates, and set at right angles
to the wall, upon ramps of masonry.

The ninety-six towers, now battered and ruined by weather,
war, and earthquakes, which once guarded this wall, stood from
175 to 181 feet apart, and were from 57 to 60 feet high, with
a projection of 18 to 34 feet.   As many of them are recon-
structions and belong to different periods, they exhibit various

---

[1] Cananus, p. 476.   [2] Nicephorus Gregoras, xiv. p. 711.

forms and different styles of workmanship. Most of them are
square ; others are hexagonal, or heptagonal, or octagonal.

While their structure resembles that of the wall, they are
nevertheless distinct buildings, in compliance with the rule
laid down by military engineers, that a tower should not be
bound in construction with the curtain of the wall behind it.[1]
Thus two buildings differing in weight could settle at different rates without breaking apart along the line of junction.
As an additional precaution a relieving arch was frequently
inserted where the sides of the tower impinged on the wall.[2]

A tower was usually divided by wooden or vaulted floors into
two chambers. Towers with three chambers, like the Tower of
Basil and Constantine at the southern extremity of the wall,
and the Soulou Kaleh beside the Lycus, were rare. The lower
chamber was entered from the city through a large archway.
Occasionally, it communicated also with the terrace between the
two walls by a postern, situated as a rule, for the sake of con-
cealment or easier defence, at the angle formed by the tower
and the curtain-wall. Upon these entrances the chamber
depended for light and air, as its walls had few, if any, loopholes,
lest the tower should be weakened where most exposed to
missiles.

Generally, the lower chamber had no means of communication with the story above it ; at other times a circular aperture,
about $7\frac{1}{2}$ feet in diameter, is found in the crown of the vaulted
floor between the chambers.

The lower portion of a tower had evidently little to do
directly with the defence of the city, but served mainly as a
store-room or guard-house. There, soldiers returning home or

---

[1] Philo of Byzantium. See *Veterum Mathemat. Opera,* s. ix. Edited and Translated by MM. de Rochat et Graux, *Revue de Philologie,* 1879.
[2] Choisy, *L'Art de Bâtir chez les Byzantins,* p. 112.

PORTION OF THE THEODOSIAN WALLS (FROM WITHIN THE CITY).

leaving for the field were allowed to take up their temporary quarters.[1]   The proprietors of the ground upon which the towers stood were also allowed to use them,[2] but this permission referred, doubtless, only to the lower chambers, and that in time of peace.

The upper chamber was entered from the parapet-walk through an arched gateway, and was well lighted on its three other sides by comparatively large windows, commanding wide views, and permitting the occupants to fire freely upon an attacking force.   Flights of steps, similar to the ramps that led to the summit of the wall, conducted to the battlemented roof of the towers.   There, the engines that hurled stones and Greek fire upon the enemy were placed ;[3] and there, sentinels watched the western horizon, day and night, keeping themselves awake at night by shouting to one another along the line.[4]

THE INNER TERRACE.

Ὁ Περίβολος.[5]

The Inner Embankment, or Terrace, between the two walls was 50 to 64 feet broad.   It was named the Peribolos, and accommodated the troops which defended the Outer Wall.

THE OUTER WALL.

Τὸ ἔξω τεῖχος :[6] τὸ ἔξω κάστρον :[7] τὸ μικρόν τεῖχος.[8]

The Outer Wall is from 2 to 6½ feet thick, rising some 10 feet above the present level of the peribolos,[9] and about 27½ feet above the present level of the terrace between the

---

[1] *Cod. Theod.*, "De Metatis," lib. 13.

[2] *Cod. Theod.*, "De Operibus Publicis," lib. 51.

[3] Theophanes, p. 589 ; Phrantzes, p. 281.

[4] Nicephorus Gregoras, ix. p. 408.   [5] Ducas, p. 283.

[6] Constant. Porphyr., *De Cer.*, p. 504.   [7] Cananus, p. 476.

[8] Critobulus, i. c. 34.

[9] Or "Lists, the space between the Inner and the Outer Walls of enceinte or enclosure" (*Violet-le-Duc on Mediæval Fortifications ;* translated by Macdermott).

Outer Wall and the Moat. Its lower portion is a solid wall, which retains the embankment of the peribolos. The upper portion is built, for the most part, in arches, faced on the outer side with hewn blocks of stone, and is frequently supported by a series of arches in concrete, and sometimes, even, by two series of such arches, built against the rear. Besides strengthening the wall, these supporting arches permitted the construction of a battlement and parapet-walk on the summit, and, moreover, formed chambers, 8½ feet deep, where troops could be quartered, or remain under cover, while engaging the enemy through the loophole in the western wall of each chamber.

The towers which flanked this wall[1] were much smaller than those of the inner line. They are some 30 to 35 feet high, with a projection of about 16 feet beyond the curtain-wall. They alternate with the great towers to the rear, thus putting both walls more completely under cover. It would seem as if the towers of this line were intended to be alternately square and crescent in shape, so frequently do these forms succeed one another. That this arrangement was not always maintained is due, probably, to changes made in the course of repairs.

Each tower had a chamber on the level of the peribolos, provided with small windows. The lower portion of most of the towers was generally a solid substructure ; but in the case of square towers it was often a small chamber reached from the Outer Terrace through a small postern, and leading to a subterranean passage running towards the city. These passages may either have permitted secret communication with different parts of the fortifications, or formed channels in which water-pipes were laid.

---

[1] Only seventy out of the ninety-six towers in this wall can now be identified.

Notwithstanding the comparative inferiority of the Outer Wall, it was an important line of defence, for it sheltered the troops which engaged the enemy at close quarters. Both in the siege of 1422,[1] and in that of 1453,[2] the most desperate fighting occurred here.

THE OUTER TERRACE.

Τὸ ἔξω παρατείχιον.[3]

The embankment or terrace between the Outer Wall and the Moat is some 61 feet broad. While affording room for the action of troops under cover of the battlement upon the scarp of the Moat,[4] its chief function was to widen the distance between the besiegers and the besieged.

THE MOAT.

Τάφρος : σοῦδα.[5]

The Moat is over 61 feet wide. Its original depth, which doubtless varied with the character of the ground it traversed, cannot be determined until excavations are allowed, for the market-gardens and *débris* which now occupy it have raised the level of the bed. In front of the Golden Gate, where it was probably always deepest, on account of the importance of that entrance, its depth is still 22 feet. The masonry of the scarp and counterscarp is 5 feet thick, and was supported by buttresses to withstand the pressure of the elevated ground on either side of

---

[1] Cananus, p. 475.

[2] Ducas, pp. 266, 283, 286; Critobulus, i. c. 34; Leonard of Scio, p. 936, thinks this was poor strategy, rendered necessary by the bad condition of the Inner Wall. "Operosa autem protegendi vallum et antemurale nostris fuit; quod contra animum meum semper fuit, qui suadebam in refugium muros altos non deserendos, qui si ob imbres negligentiamque vel scissi, vel inermes propugnaculis essent, qui non deserti, praesidium urbi salutis contulisset."

[3] Constant. Porphyr., *De Cer.*, p. 438.

[4] Ducas, p. 266, Ἐν τῇ τάφρῳ.   [5] Cananus, pp. 461, 462.

the Moat.   The battlement upon the scarp formed a breastwork
about 6½ feet high.

At several points along its course the Moat is crossed by
low walls, dividing it into so many sections or compartments.
They are generally opposite a tower of the Outer or Inner Wall,
and taper from the base to a sharp edge along the summit, to
prevent their being used as bridges by an enemy.   On their
southern side, where the ground falls away, they are supported
by buttresses.

Dr. Paspates [1] was the first to call attention to these structures, and to him, also, belongs the credit of having thrown
some light upon their use.   They were, in his opinion, aqueducts, and dams or batardeaux, by means of which water was
conveyed to the Moat, and kept in position there.   But this
service, Dr. Paspates believed, was performed by them only in
case of a siege, when they were broken open, and allowed to run
into the Moat.   At other times, when no hostile attack was
apprehended, they carried water across the Moat into the city,
for the supply of the ordinary needs of the population.

That many of these structures, if not all, were aqueducts
admits of no doubt, for some have been found to contain
earthenware water-pipes, while others of them still carry into
the city water brought by underground conduits from the hills
on the west of the fortifications ; and that they were dams seems
the only explanation of the buttresses built against their lower
side, as though to resist the pressure of water descending from
a higher level.

Certainly Dr. Paspates' view has very much in its favour.   It
is, however, not altogether free from difficulties.   To begin with,
the idea that the Moat was flooded only during a siege does
not agree with the representations of Manuel Chrysolaras and

---

[1] Pages 7–13.

AQUEDUCT ACROSS THE MOAT OF THE THEODOSIAN WALLS.

COIN OF THE EMPEROR THEODOSIUS II.
(From Du Cange.)

Bondelmontius on that point. The former writer, in his famous description of Constantinople, speaks as if the Moat was always full of water. According to him, it contained so much water that the city seemed to stand upon the sea-shore, even when viewed from the side of the land.[1] The Italian traveller describes the Moat as a " vallum aquarum surgentium." [2]

Are these statements mere rhetorical flourishes? If not, then water must have been introduced into the Moat by some other means than by the aqueducts which traverse it, for these, as Dr. Paspates himself admits, ordinarily took water into the city. Unfortunately, it is impossible, under present circumstances, to examine the Moat thoroughly, or to explore the territory without the city to discover underground conduits, and thus settle the question at issue. One can only ask, as a matter for future investigation, whether, on the view that the Moat was always flooded, the water required for the purpose was not brought by underground conduits that emptied themselves a little above the bed of the Moat. The mouth of what appears to be such a conduit is seen in the counterscarp of the Moat immediately below the fifth aqueduct to the south of Top Kapoussi. If water was brought thus to the elevation of Top Kapoussi and Edirnè Kapoussi, sufficient pressure to flood the rest of the Moat would be obtained.

But, in the next place, it must be added that objections can be urged against the opinion that the Moat was flooded even in time of war. The necessary quantity of water could ill be spared by a city which required all available water for the wants of its inhabitants, especially at the season of the year when sieges were conducted. Then, there is the fact that in

---

[1] Page 40, Τὸ δὲ πλῆθος τῶν ἐν αὐταῖς (τάφροις) ὑδάτων, ὥστε ᾧ μέρει μόνον ἐλείπετο, καὶ ταύτῃ δοκεῖν πελαγίαν τὴν πόλιν εἶναι διὰ τούτων.

[2] *Librum Insularum Archipelagi*, p. 121. Leipsic, 1824.

the accounts we have of the sieges of the city, all contemporary
historians are silent as to the presence of water in the Moat,
notwithstanding frequent allusions to that part of the fortifications.

Furthermore, there are statements which imply the absence
of water in the Moat during a siege. Pusculus, for instance,
giving a minute account of the measures adopted in 1453 to
place the city in a state of defence, refers to the deepening of
the Moat, but says nothing about water in it. "Fossaque
cavant, atque aggere terræ educto, muros forti munimine
cingunt."[1] If water had been introduced into the Moat on
this occasion, Pusculus could hardly have ignored the fact.

Again, in the Slavic account of the last siege of the city we
are informed that the Greeks opened mines through the counterscarp of the Moat, to blow up the Turks who approached the
fortifications : "Les assiégés pendant le jour combattaient les
Turcs, et pendant la nuit descendaient dans les fossés, perçaient
les murailles du fossé du côté des champs, minaient la terre sous
le mur à beaucoup d'endroits, et remplissaient les mines de
poudre et de vases remplis de poudre."[2]   If such action was
possible, there could be no water in the Moat.

[1] IV. 138, 139.

[2] Dethier, *Siéges de Constantinople*, ii. p. 1085 ; cf. Mijatovich, *Constantine, Last
Emperor of the Greeks*, pp. 185, 186.   Some 24 of these aqueducts or dams can still
be identified : 2 between the Sea of Marmora and the Golden Gate ; 1 between that
gate and the Gate of the Deuteron ; 6 or 7 between the Gate of the Deuteron and the
Gate of Selivria ; 5 between the Gate of Selivria and the Gate Yeni Mevlevi Haneh
Kapoussi ; 5 between Yeni Mevlevi Haneh Kapoussi and Top Kapoussi ; 2 between
Top Kapoussi and the Gate of the Pempton ; 3 between the Gate of the Pempton and
Edirnè Kapoussi ; 2 between Edirnè Kapoussi and the northern end of the Moat.

CHAPTER IV.

THE GATES IN THE THEODOSIAN WALLS.

THE GOLDEN GATE.

THE Theodosian Walls were pierced by ten gates, and by several small posterns.

Of the former, some led only to the different parts of the fortifications, serving exclusively the convenience of the garrison. These may be styled Military Gates. Others connected the capital, moreover, with the outside world by means of bridges thrown across the Moat,[1] and constituted the Public Gates of the city. The two series followed one another in alternate order, the military entrances being known by numbers, the public entrances by proper names. Both were double gateways, as they pierced the two walls. The inner gateway, being the principal one, was guarded by two large towers, which projected far beyond the curtain-wall to obtain a good flank fire, and to command at the same time the outer gateway. Thus also the passage from the area between the gateways to the peribolos, on either side, was rendered exceedingly narrow and capable of easy defence. In view of its great importance, the outer gateway of the Golden Gate also was defended by two towers, projecting from the rear of the wall towards the city.

[1] Pusculus, iv. 137, 138, " Pontes qui ad mœnia ducunt dirumpunt."

For the sake of security against surprise the posterns were few in number, and occurred chiefly in the great wall and its towers, leading to the peribolos. It is rare to find a postern in a tower of the Outer Wall opening on the parateichion.

Proceeding northwards from the Sea of Marmora, there is a postern immediately to the north of the first tower of the Inner Wall. It is an arched entrance, with the laureated monogram "XP." inscribed above it.

The handsome gateway between the seventh and eighth towers north of the Sea of Marmora, Yedi Koulè Kapoussi, is the triumphal gate known, from the gilding upon it, as the Porta Aurea. Its identity cannot be questioned, for the site and aspect of the entrance correspond exactly to the description given of the Golden Gate by Byzantine historians and other authorities.

It is, what the Porta Aurea was, the gateway nearest the Sea of Marmora,[1] and at the southern extremity of the Theodosian Walls,[2] constructed of marble, and flanked by two great marble towers.[3] Beside its outer portal, moreover, were found the bas-reliefs which adorned the Golden Gate, and upon it traces of an inscription which expressly named it the Porta Aurea are still visible. The inscription read as follows:

HAEC LOCA THEVDOSIVS DECORAT POST FATA TYRANNI.
AVREA SAECLA GERIT QVI PORTAM CONSTRVIT AVRO.

The history of our knowledge of this inscription is curious. There is no mention made of the legend by any writer before 1453, unless Radulphus de Diceto alludes to it when he states that in 1189 an old resident of the city pointed a Templar to certain words upon the Golden Gate, foretelling the capture

---

[1] Pusculus, iv. 151, "Aurea Porta datur ponto vicina sonanti."
[2] Cananus, p. 460.
[3] Cantacuzene, iv. pp. 292, 293; Manuel Chrysolaras, p. 48.

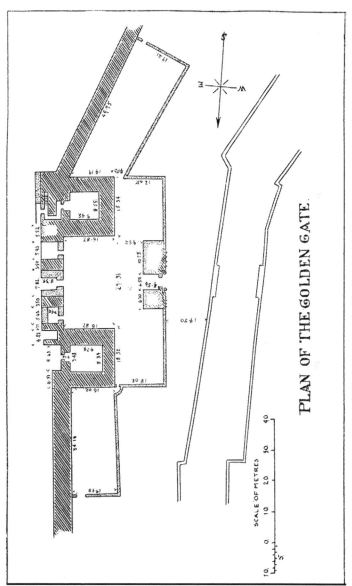

PLAN OF THE GOLDEN GATE.

SCALE OF METRES

(This plan was taken by Monsieur Adolphe Burdet.)

of Constantinople by the Crusaders.[1]   And of all the visitors to the city since the Turkish Conquest, Dallaway is the only one who speaks of having seen the inscription in its place.[2]

The inscription is cited first by Sirmondi[3] and Du Cange,[4] the former of whom quotes it in his annotations upon Sidonius Apollonius, as furnishing a parallel to that poet's mode of spelling the name Theodosius with a *v* instead of an *o* for the sake of the metre.   How Sirmondi and Du Cange, neither of whom ever visited Constantinople, became acquainted with the inscription does not appear.

Matters remained in this position until 1891, when the attention of Professor J. Strzygowski[5] was arrested by certain holes in the voussoirs of the central archway, both on its western and eastern faces.   The holes are such as are found on stones to which metal letters are riveted with bolts.

Here, then, was conclusive evidence that the Porta Aurea had once borne an inscription, and here, Professor Strzygowski divined, was also the means by which the genuineness of the legend given by Sirmondi and Du Cange could be verified. Accordingly, a comparison between the arrangement of the holes on the arch and the forms of the letters in the legend was instituted.   As several of the original voussoirs of the arch had been removed and replaced by others without holes in them, the comparison could not be complete ; but so far as it was possible to proceed the correspondence was all that could be desired.   Where H, for example, occurred in the inscription, the

---

[1] *Historiæ Anglicanæ Scriptores Antiqui*, p. 642.   London, 1652.
[2] See French translation of his work, *Constantinople Ancienne et Moderne*, 1798, vol. i. p. 28, where, quoting the legend, he says, "On y lit encore ces vers."
[3] *Opera Varia*, vol. i., Paris, 1696 ; Paneg. Maioriani, *Carmen V.*, 354.
[4] *Constantinopolis Christiana*, lib. i. p. 52.
[5] The brilliant monograph of Dr. Strzygowski on the Golden Gate is found in the *Jahrbuch des Kaiserlich Deutschen Archæologischen Instituts*, Band viii., 1893, Erstes Heft.

holes on the archway are arranged thus, : : ; where an A stood,
the holes are placed thus, ∴ ; where V came, their position is ∵ ;
and so on, to an extent which verifies the inscription beyond
dispute.   Thus, also, it has been ascertained that the letters were
of metal, probably gilt bronze, and that the words "Haec loca
Thevdosivs decorat post fata Tyranni" stood on the western face
of the arch, while the words "Avrea saecla gerit qvi portam
constrvit avro" were found on the opposite side.

The preservation of the inscription is a matter of very great
importance, for it furnishes valuable and interesting information
as to the circumstances under which the Porta Aurea was
erected.   From the fact that the entrance is found in the
Theodosian Walls it is natural to infer that the Porta Aurea
was a contemporaneous building, and that the emperor extolled
in the inscription is Theodosius II.   But that inference is pre-
cluded by the statement that the arch was set up after the sup-
pression of a usurper, *post fata tyranni.*   For Theodosius II.
was not called to suppress the usurpation of his imperial
authority at any time during his reign, much less in 413, when
the Wall of Anthemius, in which the Porta Aurea stands, was
built.   On the other hand, Theodosius the Great crushed two
serious attempts to dispute his rule, first in 388, when he
defeated Maximus, and again in 395, when he put down the
rebellion of Eugenius.   Hence, as Du Cange first pointed out,
the Porta Aurea is a monument erected in the reign of Theodosius the Great, in honour of his victory over one of the
rebels above mentioned.   It could not, however, have been de-
signed to commemorate the defeat of Eugenius, seeing that
Theodosius never returned to Constantinople after that event,
and died four months later in the city of Milan.   It must,
therefore, have been reared in honour of the victory over
Maximus, a success which the conqueror regarded with feelings

of peculiar satisfaction and pride, celebrating it by one triumphal entry into Rome, in the spring of 389, and by another into Constantinople, when he returned to the eastern capital in 391.[1] Accordingly, the Porta Aurea was originally an Arch of Triumph, erected some time between 388 and 391, to welcome Theodosius the Great upon his return from his successful expedition against the formidable rebellion of Maximus in the West. It united with the Column of Theodosius in the Forum of Taurus, and the Column of Arcadius in the Forum on the Xerolophus, and the Obelisk in the Hippodrome,[2] in perpetuating the memory of the great emperor's warlike achievements.

In corroboration of the date thus assigned to the monument, it may be added that the only Imperial statue placed over the Porta Aurea was that of Theodosius the Great, while the group of elephants which formed one of the ornaments of the gate was supposed to represent the elephants attached to the car of that emperor on the occasion of his triumphal entry into the city.[3]

There is, however, an objection to this view concerning the age of the Porta Aurea, which, whatever its force, should not be overlooked in a full discussion of the subject. The inscription describes the monument as a gateway, " Qui portam construit auro."[4] But such a designation does not seem consistent with the fact that we have here a building which belongs to the age of Theodosius the Great, when the city walls in which the arch stands did not exist, as they are the work of his grandson. How could an isolated arch be, then, styled a gateway? Can

---

[1] Zosimus, p. 234.

[2] Cf. the inscription on the pedestal of the obelisk—

> " Difficilis quondam dominis parere serenis
> Jussus, et extinctis palmam portare tyrannis
> Omnia Theodosio cedunt," etc.

[3] See below, pp. 64, 65.

[4] Malalas, p. 360, ascribes the decoration of the gate with gold to Theodosius II.

the difficulty be removed by any other instance of a similar use of the term "Porta"? Or is the employment of the term in the case before us explained by the supposition that in the reign of Theodosius the Great the city had spread beyond the Constantinian Wall, and reached the line marked by the Porta Aurea, so that an arch at that point was practically an entrance into the city? May not that suburban district have been protected by some slight fortified works? Or was the Porta Aurea so named in anticipation of the fulfilment of the prediction of Themistius, that the growth of the city under Theodosius the Great would ere long necessitate the erection of new walls?[1] Was it built in that emperor's reign to indicate to a succeeding generation the line along which the new bulwarks of the capital should be built?

The Porta Aurea was the State Entrance into the capital,[2] and was remarkable both for its architectural splendour and its military strength. It was built of large squared blocks of polished marble, fitted together without cement, and was flanked by two great towers constructed of the same material. Like the Triumphal Arch of Severus and that of Constantine at Rome, it had three archways, the central one being wider and loftier than those on either side.

The gates glittered with gold,[3] and numerous statues and other sculptured ornaments were placed at suitable points.[4]

Of these embellishments the following are mentioned: a cross, which was blown down by a hurricane in the reign of Justinian;[5] a Victory, which fell in an earthquake in the reign of Michael III.;[6] a crowned female figure, representing the Fortune of the city;[7] a statue of Theodosius the Great,

---

[1] See above, p. 42.
[2] Nicephorus, *Patriarcha CP.*, p. 59 ; Constant. Porphyr., *De Cer.*, pp. 500, 506.
[3] Malalas, p. 360.   [4] Codinus, p. 48.   [5] Cedrenus, vol. i. p. 675.
[6] *Ibid.*, ii. p. 173.   [7] Codinus, *ut supra.*

THE GOLDEN GATE (INNER).

overthrown by the earthquake at the close of the reign of Leo the Isaurian ;[1] a bronze group of four elephants ;[2] the gates of Mompseuesta, gilded and placed here by Nicephorus Phocas, as a trophy of his campaign in Cilicia.[3]   At the south-western angle of the northern tower the Roman eagle still spreads its wings ; the laureated monogram " XP " appears above the central archway on the city side of the gateway ; and several crosses are scattered over the building.

In later days, when taste had altered, the scene of the Crucifixion was painted within one of the lateral archways, while the Scene of the Final Judgment was represented in the other.[4] Traces of frescoes are visible on the inner walls of the southern archway, and suggest the possibility of its having been used as a chapel.

The whole aspect of the gateway must have been more imposing when the parapet on the towers and on the wall over the arches was intact, and gave the building its full elevation.

Two columns crowned with graceful capitals adorned the outer gateway, while the wall north and south was decorated with twelve bas-reliefs, executed with considerable skill, and representing classical subjects.   Remains of the marble cornices and of the pilasters which framed the bas-reliefs are still found in the wall, and from the descriptions of the slabs given by Manuel Chrysolaras, Gyllius, Sir Thomas Roe, and others, a fair idea of the nature of the subjects treated can be formed.[5]   Six bas-reliefs were placed on either side of the entrance, grouped in triplets, one above another, each panel being supported by pilasters, round or rectangular.

---

[1] Theophanes, p. 634.
[2] Cedrenus, vol. i. p. 567.
[3] *Ibid.*, ii. p. 363.
[4] *Itinéraires Russes en Orient*, p. 239.
[5] Manuel Chrys., p. 48 ; Gyllius, *De Top. CP.*, iv. c. 9 ; Adolf Michaelis, *Ancient Marbles in Great Britain*, pp. 10–14, translated by C. A. M. Fennell.   See Wheler, Grelot, Gerlach, Bulliardus, Spon, and Monograph of Dr. Strzygowski.

F

On the northern slabs the subjects pourtrayed were : Prometheus tortured ; a youth pursuing a horse, and trying to pull off its rider ; a satyr, between a woman with a vessel of water behind her, and a savage man, or Hercules, holding a whip ; Labours of Hercules (on three slabs).

The bas-reliefs to the south were of superior workmanship, and represented : Endymion asleep, a shepherd's lute in his hand, with Selene and Cupid descending towards him ; Hercules leading dogs ; two peasants carrying grapes ; Pegasus and three female figures, one of them attempting to hold him back ; the fall of Phaëthon ; Hercules and a stag.[1]

---

[1] The first two bas-reliefs to the north of the gate, and the first and fourth to the south, as superior in workmanship, came very near being removed to England, through the efforts of Sir Thomas Roe, ambassador to the Porte from 1621 to 1628, and of a certain Mr. Petty, who was sent to the East by the Earl of Arundel to procure works of Ancient Art. The finds were to be divided between that nobleman and the Duke of Buckingham. The correspondence on the subject will be found in *The Negotiations of Sir Thomas Roe in his Embassy to the Ottoman Porte,* published in London, 1740 (see pp. 386, 387, 444, 445, 495, 512, 534, 535) ; in Michaelis' *Ancient Marbles in Great Britain ;* and, partially, in Dr. Strzygowski's *Monograph on the Golden Gate.*

" Promise to obteyne them," wrote Sir Thomas Roe, in May, 1625, " I cannot, because they stand upon the ancient gate, the most conspicuous of the cytte, though now mured up, beeing the entrance by the castell called the Seauen Towers, and neuer opened since the Greek emperors lost yt : to offer to steale them, no man dares to deface the cheefe seate of the grand signor : to procure them by fauour, is more impossible, such enuy they bear vnto us. There is only then one way left ; by corruption of some churchman, to dislike them, as against their law ; and vnder that pretence to take them downe to be brought into some priuat place : from whence, after the matter is cold and unsuspected, they may be conveyed. I haue practised for the four, and am offered to haue it done for 600 crownes."

A year later he had to write, " Those on the Porta Aurea are like to stand, till they fall by tyme : I haue vsed all meanes, and once bought them, and deposed, 3 moneths, 500 dollers. Without authority, the danger and impossibility were alike ; therefore I dealt with the great treasurer, who in these tymes is greedy of any mony, and hee had consented to deliuer them into a boat without any hazard of my part. The last weeke hee rode himself to see them, and carried the surueigher of the citty walls with him ; but the Castellano and the people beganne to mutine, and fell vpon a strange conceite ; insomuch that hee was forced to retyre, and presently sent for my enterpreter, demanding if I had any old booke of prophesy : inferring, that those statues were enchanted, and that wee knew, when they should bee taken downe, some great alteration should befall this cytty. . . . In conclusion, hee sent to mee, to think, nor mention no more that place, which might cost his life, and bring mee into

As the Porta Triumphalis of Constantinople, the Golden Gate was the scene of many historical events and imposing ceremonies.

So long as the inauguration of an emperor upon his accession to the throne was celebrated at the Hebdomon (Makrikeui), it was through the Golden Gate that a new sovereign entered his capital on the way to the Imperial Palace beside St. Sophia. Marcian (450),[1] Leo I. (457),[2] Basiliscus (476),[3] Phocas (602),[4] Leo the Armenian (813),[5] and Nicephorus Phocas (963),[6] were welcomed as emperors by the city authorities at this portal.

Distinguished visitors to the Byzantine Court, also, were sometimes allowed to enter the city by this gate, as a mark of special honour. The Legates of Pope Hormisdas were met here upon their arrival on a mission to Justin I.:[7] here, in 708, Pope Constantine was received with great ceremony, when he came to confer with Justinian II.:[8] and here, in the reign of Basil II., the Legates of Pope Hadrian II. were admitted.[9] Under Romanus Lecapenus, the procession which bore through the city to St. Sophia the Icon of Christ, brought from Edessa, entered at the Porta Aurea.[10]

It was, however, on the return of an emperor to the city after a victorious campaign that the Porta Aurea fulfilled its highest purpose, and presented a brilliant spectacle of life and splendour.

Through this triumphal arch came Theodosius the Great, after his defeat of Maximus ;[11] by it Heraclius entered the capital

trouble ; so that I despair to effect therein your graces seruice : and it is true, though I could not gett the stones, yet I allmost raised an insurrection in that part of the cytty."

[1] *Paschal Chron.*, p. 590.
[2] Constant. Porphyr., *De Cer.*, p. 414.
[3] Theophanes, p. 186.
[4] *Paschal Chron.*, p. 693.
[5] Theophanes, p. 784.
[6] Constant. Porphyr., *De Cer.*, p. 438.
[7] Anastasius Bibliothecarius.
[8] *Ibid.*
[9] Guillelmus Bibliothecarius, *in Hadriano II.*
[10] Theophanes Cont., p. 432.
[11] Zosimus, p. 234.

to celebrate the success of his Persian expeditions;[1] through it passed Constantine Copronymus, after the defeat of the Bulgarians;[2] Theophilus, on two occasions, after the repulse of the Saracens;[3] Basil I., after his successes at Tephrice and Germanicia;[4] Zimisces, after his victories over the Russians under Swiatoslaf;[5] Basil II., after the slaughter of the Bulgarians;[6] and, for the last time, Michael Palæologus, upon the restoration of the Greek Empire in 1261.[7]

It would seem that, in accordance with old Roman custom, victorious generals, below Imperial rank, were not allowed to enter the city in triumph through this gate. Belisarius,[8] Maurice,[9] Nicephorus Phocas, before he became emperor,[10] and Leo his brother,[11] celebrated their respective triumphs over the Vandals, Persians and Saracens, in the Hippodrome and the great street of the city.[12]

An Imperial triumphal procession[13] was marshalled on the plain in front of the Golden Gate,[14] and awaited there the arrival of the emperor, either from the Hebdomon or from the Palace of Blachernæ. The principal captives, divided into several companies, and guarded by bands of soldiers, led the march. Next followed the standards and weapons and other spoils of war. Then, seated on a magnificent white charger, came the emperor himself, arrayed in robes embroidered with gold and pearls, his crown on his head, his sceptre in his right hand, his

---

[1] See illustration facing p. 334.   [2] Theophanes, p. 668.

[3] Constant. Porphyr., *De Cer.*, pp. 503, 504.   [4] *Ibid.*, p. 498.

[5] Leo Diaconus, p. 158.   [6] Cedrenus, vol. ii. p. 475.

[7] Pachymeres, vol. i. p. 160.

[8] Procopius, *De Bello Vand.*, ii. c. 9 ; Theophanes, p. 309.

[9] Theophanes, p. 388.   [10] Leo Diaconus, p. 28.

[11] *Ibid.*, p. 23.   [12] Theophanes, p. 309.

[13] For the descriptions of the triumphs accorded to Basil I. and Theophilus, see Constant. Porphyr., *De Cer.*, pp. 498–508.

[14] Constant. Porphyr., *De Cer.*, p. 499, Ἐν δὲ τῷ λιβαδίῳ τῷ ἔξω τῆς χρυσῆς πόρτας.

THE GOLDEN GATE (OUTER).

victorious sword by his side. Close to him rode his son, or the
Cæsar of the·day, another resplendent figure of light, also on a
white horse. Upon reaching the gate the victor might, like
Theophilus, dismount for a few moments, and falling thrice upon
his face, humbly acknowledge the Divine aid to which he owed
the triumph of his arms. At length the Imperial *cortége* passed
through the great archway. The civic authorities came forward
and did homage, offering the conqueror a crown of gold and a
laurel wreath, and accepting from him a rich largess in return ;
the Factions rent the air with shouts—" Glory to God, who restores
our sovereigns to us, crowned with victory ! Glory to God, who
has magnified you, Emperors of the Romans ! Glory to Thee,
All-Holy Trinity, for we behold our Emperors victorious ! Welcome, Victors, most valiant sovereigns !"[1] And then the glitter-
ing procession wended its way to the Great Palace, through the
dense crowds that packed the Mesè and the principal Fora of
the city, all gay with banners, flowers, and evergreens.

Sometimes the emperor, as in the case of Heraclius,[2] rode in a
chariot instead of on horseback ; or the occupant of the triumphal
car might be, as on the occasion of the triumph of Zimisces, the
Icon of the Virgin.[3] Michael Palæologus entered the city on
foot, walking as far as the Church of St. John Studius before he
mounted his horse.[4] On the occasion of the second triumph of
Theophilus, the beautiful custom was introduced of making
children take part in the ceremonial with wreaths of flowers.[5]

But besides serving as a State entrance into the city,
the Porta Aurea was one of the strongest positions in the

---

[1] On the pier to the left of the central archway are painted in red the words,
ΠΟΛΛΑ ΤΑ ΕΤΗ ΤѠΝ ΒΑϹΙΛΕѠΝ ; while on the pier to the right are the
words, Ο Θ͠Ϲ ΚΑΛѠϹ ΗΝΕΝΓΕΝ ϹΕ ; lingering echoes of the shouts that
shook the gate on a day of triumph.

[2] See illustration facing p. 334.   [3] Leo Diaconus, p. 158.
[4] Pachymeres, vol. i. p. 160.   [5] Constant. Porphyr., p. 508.

fortifications.[1] The four towers at its gateways, the deep moat
in front, and the transverse walls across the peribolos on either
hand, guarding approach from that direction, constituted a
veritable citadel. Cantacuzene repaired it, and speaks of it as an
almost impregnable acropolis, capable of being provisioned for
three years, and strong enough to defy the whole city in time
of civil strife.[2] Hence the great difficulty he found in persuading
the Latin garrison which held it on his behalf, in 1354, to
surrender the place to his rival John VI. Palæologus.

The Golden Gate, therefore, figures also in the military annals
of Constantinople. In the reign of Anastasius I. it was the
object of special attack by Vitalianus at the head of his Huns
and Bulgarians.[3] Repeated attempts were made upon it by the
Saracens in the siege of 673–675.[4] Crum stood before it in the
reign of Leo the Armenian, and there he invoked the aid of his
gods against the city, by offering human sacrifices and by the
lustration of his army with sea-water in which he had bathed
his feet.[5] His demand to plant his spear in the gate put an
end to the negotiations for peace. In 913 the Bulgarians, under
their king Simeon, were again arrayed before the entrance.[6]
Here, also, in 1347, John Cantacuzene was admitted by his
partisans.[7]

John Palæologus, upon receiving the surrender of the gate
foolishly dismantled the towers, lest they should be turned

---

[1] Τὸ κατὰ τὴν χρυσῆν καλουμένην φρούριον, Cantacuzene, iv. p. 292. It was
not, however, the fortress known as the Strongylon, Cyclobion, Castrum Rotundum
(Procopius, *De Aed.*, iv. c. 8 ; Theophanes, p. 541 ; Anastasius, *in Hormisda PP.* ;
Guillelmus Biblioth. *in Hadriano II.*). That fortress stood outside the city, near
the Hebdomon (Makrikeui), three miles to the west of the Golden Gate (Theophanes,
pp. 541, 608). See below, p. 326.

[2] Cantacuzene, iv. pp. 293, 301, 302. The southern tower projects 55 feet 7 inches
from the wall, and is 60 feet 5 inches broad ; the corresponding dimensions of the
northern tower are 55½ feet, and 60 feet 4 inches.

[3] Marcellinus Comes.   [4] Theophanes, p. 541.   [5] *Ibid.*, p. 785.
[6] Theophanes Cont., p. 385.   [7] Cantacuzene, iii. pp. 606, 607.

against him, in the fickle political fortunes of the day.[1] He did not, however, carry the work of destruction so far as to be unable to use the position as an "acropolis" when besieged, in 1376, by his rebellious son, Andronicus.[2] Later, when Sultan Bajazet threatened the city, an attempt was made to restore the towers, and even to increase the strength of this point in the fortifications.[3] With materials taken from the churches of All Saints, the Forty Martyrs, and St. Mokius, the towers were rebuilt, and a fortress extending to the sea was erected within the city walls, similar to the Castle of the Seven Towers constructed afterwards by Mehemet the Conqueror, in 1457. Upon hearing of this action, Bajazet sent peremptory orders to John Palæologus to pull down the new fortifications, and compelled obedience by threatening to put out the eyes of Manuel, the heir to the throne, at that time a hostage at Brousa. The humiliation affected the emperor, then seriously ill, so keenly as to hasten his death. Subsequently, however, probably after the defeat of Bajazet by Tamerlane at Angora, the defences at the Golden Gate were restored; for the Russian pilgrim who was in Constantinople between 1435 and 1453 speaks of visiting the Castle of the Emperor Kalo Jean.[4]

In 1390, Manuel II., with a small body of troops, entered the city by this gate and drove away his nephew John, who had usurped the throne.[5] During the siege of 1453 the gate was defended by Manuel of Liguria with 200 men, and before it the Sultan planted a cannon and other engines of assault.[6]

Between the second and third towers to the north of the Golden Gate is an entrance known at present, like the Porta

---

[1] Cantacuzene, iv. p. 304.   [2] Chalcocondylas, p. 62.   [3] Ducas, pp. 47, 48.

[4] *Itinéraires Russes en Orient*, p. 239, "Chateau de l'Empereur Kalojean. Il a trois entrées."

[5] See Muralt, ad annum, *Essai de Chronographie Byzantine*, vol. ii.

[6] Phrantzes, p. 253.

Aurea, also by the name Yedi Koulè Kapoussi.   Dr. Paspates
thinks it is of Turkish origin.[1]   It has certainly undergone repair
in Turkish times, as an inscription upon it in honour of Sultan
Achmet III. testifies; but traces of Byzantine workmanship about
the gate prove that it belongs to the period of the Empire;[2] and
this conclusion is supported by the consideration that, since the
Porta Aurea was a State entrance, another gate was required in
its immediate neighbourhood for the use of the public in this
quarter of the capital.   Hence the proximity of the two gateways.

Regarding the name of the entrance opinions differ.   Some
authorities regard the gate as the Porta Rhegiou ('Ρηγίου), the
Gate of Rhegium,[3] mentioned in the Greek Anthology.[4]   But
this identification cannot be maintained, for the Porta Rhegiou
was one of two entrances which bore an inscription in honour
of Theodosius II. and the Prefect Constantine, and both those
entrances, as will appear in the sequel, stood elsewhere in the line
of the fortifications.[5]

The gate went, probably, by the designation of the Golden
Gate,[6] near which it stands, just as it now bears the name given
to the latter entrance since the Turkish Conquest.   A common
name for gates so near each other was perfectly natural; and on
this view certain incidents in the history of the Golden Gate
become more intelligible.   For instance : when Basil, the founder
of the Macedonian dynasty, reached Constantinople in his early
youth, a homeless adventurer in search of fortune, it is related that
he entered the city about sunset through the Golden Gate, and

---

[1] Paspates, p. 78.

[2] Mordtmann, p. 13.   Above the gate, on the side facing the city, is a slab with
the figure of the Roman eagle.

[3] Patriarch Constantius, *Ancient and Modern Constantinople*, p. 19.

[4] Banduri, *Imp. Orient.*, vii. p. 150.

[5] See below, pp. 78, 91.   [6] Mordtmann, p. 13.

YEDI KOULÉ KAPOUSSI.

(By kind permission of Phené Spiers, Esq., F.S.A.)

laid himself down to sleep on the steps of the adjoining Monastery of St. Diomed.[1]   If the only Golden Gate were the Porta Aurea strictly so called, it is difficult to understand how the poor way-farer was admitted by an entrance reserved for the emperor's use ; whereas the matter becomes clear if that name designated also an adjoining public gate.   Again, when the historian Nicetas Choniates,[2] accompanied by his family and some friends, left the city five days after its capture by the Crusaders in 1204, he made his way out, according to his own statement, by the Golden Gate.   In this case also, it does not seem probable that the captors of the city would have allowed a gate of such military importance as the Porta Aurea to be freely used by a company of fugitives.   The escape appears more feasible if the Golden Gate to which Nicetas refers was the humbler entrance in the neighbourhood of the Porta Aurea.

[1] Theophanes Cont., p. 223.   [2] Page 779.

CHAPTER V.

THE GATES IN THE THEODOSIAN WALLS—*continued.*

THE entrance between the thirteenth and fourteenth towers to
the north of the Golden Gate was the Second Military Gate,
τοῦ Δευτέρου.[1] Its identity is established by its position in the
order of the gates ; for between it and the Fifth Military Gate,
regarding the situation of which there can be no doubt,[2] two
military gates intervene. It must therefore be itself the second
of that series of entrances.

Hence, it follows that the quarter of the city known as the
Deuteron (τὸ Δεύτερον) was the district to the rear of this gate.
This fact can be proved also independently by the following
indications. The district in question was without the Walls of
Constantine ;[3] it lay to the west of the Exokionion, the Palaia
Porta, and the Cistern of Mokius ;[4] it was, on the one hand,
near the last street of the city,[5] the street leading to the Golden
Gate, and, on the other, contained the Gate Melantiados,[6] now
Selivri Kapoussi.[7] Consequently, it was the district behind the
portion of the walls in which the gate before us is situated. This
in turn supports the identification of the gate as that of the
Deuteron. It is the finest and largest of the military gates, and

---

[1] Codinus, p. 97.   [2] See below, p. 81.   [3] Sozomon, iv. c. 2.
[4] Anonymus, i. p. 38.   [5] Procopius, *De Aed.*, i. c. 3.
[6] *Synaxaria*, Octob. 25.   [7] See below, pp. 76, 77.

may sometimes have served as a public gate in the period of the Empire, as it has since.

Of the churches in the Deuteron quarter, the most noted were the Church of the SS. Notarii, attributed to Chrysostom,[1] and the Church of St. Anna, a foundation of Justinian the Great.[2] Others of less importance were dedicated respectively to St. Timothy,[3] St. George,[4] St. Theodore,[5] and St. Paul the Patriarch.[6]

The next public entrance (Selivri Kapoussi) is situated between the thirteenth and fourteenth towers north of the Gate of the Deuteron. Its present name appears shortly before the Turkish Conquest ($\pi\acute{\nu}\lambda\eta$ $\tau\hat{\eta}\varsigma$ $\Sigma\eta\lambda\nu\beta\rho\acute{\iota}a\varsigma$),[7] and alludes to the fact that the entrance is at the head of the road to Selivria ; but its earlier and more usual designation was the Gate of the Pegè, *i.e.* the Spring ($\Pi\acute{\nu}\lambda\eta$ $\tau\hat{\eta}\varsigma$ $\Pi\eta\gamma\hat{\eta}\varsigma$),[8] because it led to the celebrated Holy Spring (now Baloukli), about half a mile to the west. This name for the entrance is found in the inscription placed on the back of the southern gateway tower, in commemoration of repairs made in the year 1433 or 1438.[9]

The gate possessed considerable importance owing to its proximity to the Holy Spring,[10] which, with its healing waters and shrines, its cypress groves, meadows, and delightful air, formed one of the most popular resorts in the neighbourhood of the city.[11] There the emperors had a palace and hunting park, to which they often retired for recreation, especially in the spring of the year. On the Festival of the Ascension the emperor visited the " Life-giving Pegè " in state, sometimes

---

[1] *Synaxaria*, Oct. 25.   [2] Procopius, *De Æd.*, i. c. 3.

[3] *Synaxaria*, June 10.   [4] *Ibid.*, April 23.   [5] *Ibid.*, April 22.

[6] Nicephorus Callistus, xii. c. 14.   [7] Phrantzes, p. 253.

[8] Constant. Porphyr., *De Cer.*, p. 109.   [9] See below, pp. 106, 107.

[10] It is still held in great repute, and on the Friday of Greek Easter week is visited by immense crowds of devotees, as in the olden time.

[11] Procopius, *De Æd.*, i. c. 3.

riding thither through the city, at other times proceeding in his barge as far as the Marmora extremity of the walls, and then mounting horse for the rest of the way.[1] But in either case, the Imperial *cortége* came up to this gate, and was received there by the body of household troops called the Numeri. It was on returning from such a visit to the Pegè that the Emperor Nicephorus Phocas was mobbed and stoned, as he rode from the Forum of Constantine to the Great Palace beside the Hippodrome.[2]

The gate is memorable in history as the entrance through which, in 1261, Alexius Strategopoulos, the general of Michael Palæologus, penetrated into the city,[3] and brought the ill-starred Latin Empire of Constantinople to an end. For greater security the Latins had built up the entrance ; but a band of the assailants, aided by friends within the fortifications, climbed over the walls, killed the drowsy guards, broke down the barricade, and flung the gates open for the restoration of the Greek power. By this gate, in 1376, Andronicus entered, after besieging the city for thirty-two days, and usurped the throne of his father, John VI. Palæologus.[4] In the siege of 1422 Sultan Murad pitched his tent within the grounds of the Church of the Pegè ;[5] while during the siege of 1453 a battery of three guns played against the walls in the vicinity of this entrance.[6]

There is reason to think that the gate styled Porta Melantiados (Μελαντιάδος)[7] and Pylè Melandesia (Μελανδησία),[8] should be identified with the Gate of the Pegè. Hitherto, indeed, the Porta Melantiados has been identified with the next public gate, Yeni Mevlevi Haneh Kapoussi ;[9] but that view runs counter

---

[1] Constant. Porphyr., *De Cer.*, p. 109.   [2] Leo Diaconus, iv. p. 64.
[3] Pachymeres, vol. i. p. 142; Niceph. Greg., iv. p. 85.
[4] See Muralt, *Essai de Chronographie Byzantine*, vol. ii.
[5] Ducas, p. 184.   [6] Nicolo Barbaro, p. 733.
[7] *Paschal Chron.*, p. 590.   [8] *Synaxaria*, Oct. 25.
[9] Paspates, p. 47 ; Mordtmann, p. 15.

THE GATE OF THE PEGÈ.

to the fact that the Porta Melantiados stood in the Deuteron,[1] whereas the next public gate was, we shall find, in the quarter of the city called, after the Third Military Gate, the Triton (τὸ Τρίτον).[2]   Unless, therefore, the Porta Melantiados is identified with the Gate of the Pegè, it cannot be identified with any other entrance in the Theodosian Walls.

That the Gate of the Pegè had originally another name is certain, since the Holy Spring did not come into repute until the reign of Leo I.,[3] nearly half a century after the erection of the Wall of Anthemius.   And no other name could have been so appropriate as the Porta Melantiados, for the road issuing from the gate led to Melantiada, a town near the Athyras[4] (Buyuk Tchekmedjè) on the road to Selivria.   The town is mentioned in the Itinerary of the Emperor Antoninus as Melantrada and Melanciada, at the distance of nineteen miles from Byzantium ; and there on different occasions the Huns, the Goths,[5] and the Avars[6] halted on their march towards Constantinople.

At the gate Porta Melantiados, Chrysaphius, the minister and evil genius of Theodosius II., was killed in 450 by the son of John the Vandal, in revenge for the execution of the latter.[7] It has been suggested that the Mosque of Khadin Ibrahim Pasha within the gate stands on the site of the Church of St. Anna in the Deuteron.[8]   It may, however, mark the site of the Church of the SS. Notarii, which stood near the Porta Melantiados.

The Third Military Gate is but a short distance from the Gate of the Pegè, being situated between the fourth and fifth

---

[1] *Synaxaria*, Oct. 25.   Ἐν τῇ Μελανδησία πόρτῃ, ἐν αὐτῇ τῇ Κωνσταντινούπολει, τοποθεσίᾳ τοῦ Δευτέρου.

[2] See below, p. 78.   [3] Nicephorus Callistus, xv. c. 25, c. 28.

[4] Agathias, v. c. 14, c. 20.   [5] Marcellinus Comes, *ad Zenonem.*

[6] *Paschal Chron.*, p. 717.   [7] *Ibid.*, p. 590.   [8] Mordtmann, p. 78.

towers to the north. To the rear of the entrance was the quarter called the Triton (τὸ Τρίτον),[1] and, more commonly, the Sigma (Σίγμα) ;[2] the latter designation being derived, probably, from the curve in the line of the walls immediately beyond the gate. What precisely was the object of the curve is not apparent. One authority explains it as intended for the accommodation of the courtiers and troops that assembled here on the occasion of an Imperial visit to the Pegè.[3] But the Theodosian Walls were built before the Pegè came into repute ;[4] and the visits of the emperors to the Holy Spring were not so frequent or so important as to affect the construction of the walls in such a manner.

In the quarter of the Sigma stood a column, bearing the statue of Theodosius II., erected by Chrysaphius.[5] And there, in the riot of 1042, the Emperor Michael Calaphates and his uncle Constantine were blinded, having been dragged thither from the Monastery of Studius, where they had sought sanctuary.[6]

The most noted churches in the quarter were dedicated respectively to the Theotokos,[7] St. Stephen, and St. Isaacius.[8] The site of the first is, in the opinion of Dr. Paspates, marked by the remains of an old Byzantine cistern off the street leading from the Guard-house of Alti Mermer to the Mosque of Yol Getchen.[9]

The next public gate, Yeni Mevlevi Haneh Kapoussi, situated between the tenth and eleventh towers north of the Third Military Gate, was known by two names, Porta Rhegiou ('Ρηγίου),[10] the Gate of Rhegium, and Porta Rhousiou (τοῦ 'Ρουσίου),[11] the

---

[1] *Menæa*, May 30, as quoted by Du Cange, *Constantinopolis Christiana*, ii. p. 178.
[2] Constant. Porphyr., *De Cer.*, p. 501 ; Cedrenus, vol. ii. p. 540.
[3] Mordtmann, pp. 14, 15.   [4] See above, p. 77.   [5] Codinus, p. 47.
[6] Cedrenus, vol. ii. p. 540.   [7] Theophanes Cont., p. 323.   [8] Codinus, p. 126.
[9] Pages 378–389.   [10] Banduri, *Imp. Orient.*, vii. p. 150.
[11] Theophanes, pp. 355, 358.

THE GATE OF RHEGIUM.

Gate of the Red Faction. That it bore the former name is established by the fact that the inscription in honour of Theodosius II. and the Prefect Constantine, which was placed, according to the Anthology, on the Gate of Rhegium, is actually found on the lintel of this entrance.[1] The name alluded to Rhegium (Kutchuk Tchekmedjè), a town twelve miles distant, upon the Sea of Marmora, whither the road leading westward conducted.

The title of the gate to the second name rests partly upon the consideration that the name cannot be claimed for any other entrance in the walls, and partly upon the fact that two circumstances connected with the gate can thus be satisfactorily explained. In the first place, the seven shafts employed to form the lintel, posts, and sill of the gateway are covered with red wash, as though to mark the entrance with the colour of the Red Faction. Secondly, on the northern face of the southern gateway-tower is an inscription, unfortunately mutilated, such as the Factions placed upon a structure in the erection of which they were concerned. The legend as preserved reads thus: "The Fortune of Constantine, our God-protected Emperor triumphs * * *."

† ΝΙΚΑ Η ΤΥΧΗ
ΚωΝϹΤΑΝΤΙΝΟΥ ΤΟΥ ΘΕΟ
ΦΥΛΑΚΤΟΥ ΗΜωΝ ΔΕϹΠΟΤΟΥ
†   †

The missing words with which the inscription closed were at some date intentionally effaced, but analogy makes it exceedingly probable that they were ΚΑΙ ΡΟΥϹΙωΝ, "and of the Reds."[2]

The number of inscriptions about this entrance is remarkable,

---

[1] See above, pp. 46, 47.

[2] The inscription is found in the C. I. G., No. 8789. Dr. Paspates compares it with No. 8788 in that collection. ΝΙΚΑ Η ΤΥΧΗ ΚωΝϹΤΑΝΤΙΝΟΥ ΜΕΓΑΛΟΥ ΒΑϹΙΛΕωϹ ΤΟΥ ϹΥϹΤΑΤΙΚΟΥ ΝΙΚΗΤΟΥ ΚΑΙ ΒΕΝΕΤωΝ (of the Blues) ΕΥΝωΟΥΝΤωΝ. See below, p. 102.

five being on the gateway itself, and two on its southern tower.
Of the former those commemorating the erection of the Theodosian fortifications in 447 are of special importance and
interest ;[1] another records the repair of the Outer Wall under
Justin II. and his Empress Sophia.[2] Indistinct traces of the
fourth are visible on the southern side of the gateway ;
while the fifth, too fragmentary to yield a meaning, is on the
tympanum, arranged on either side of a niche for Icons,[3]
for the gates of the city were, as a rule, placed under the ward of
some heavenly guardian. This gate was closed with a portcullis.

The Fourth Military Gate stood between the ninth and tenth
towers to the north of the Porta Rhousiou. The northern
corbel of the outer gateway is an inscribed stone brought from
some other building erected by a certain Georgius.[4]

Top Kapoussi, between the sixth and seventh towers north of
the Fourth Military Gate, is the Gate of St. Romanus (πόρτα τοῦ
Ἁγίου Ρωμάνου)[5] so named after an adjoining church of that
dedication. Its identity may be established in the following
manner: According to Cananus,[6] the Gate of St. Romanus and
the Gate of Charisius stood on opposite sides of the Lycus. The
Gate of St. Romanus, therefore, must have been either Top
Kapoussi, on the southern side of that stream, or one of the two
gates on the stream's northern bank, viz. the walled-up entrance
at the foot of that bank, or Edirnè Kapoussi upon the summit.
That it was the gate on the southern side of the Lycus is clear,
from the statements of Critobulus and Phrantzes,[7] that in the

---

[1] See above, p. 47.   [2] See below, p. 97.

[3] Choiseul-Gouffier, *Voyage pittoresque dans l'Empire Ottoman, etc.*, vol. iv. p. 17,
speaking of this gate, says, "Sur le cintre de cette porte sont les représentations de
quelques saints, donc les Turcs ont effacé le visage." Cf. Paspates, p. 51.

[4] Mordtmann, p. 15.   [5] *Paschal Chron.*, p. 720.

[6] *De Constantinopoli Expugnata*, p. 462.

[7] Critobulus, i. c. 23, c. 27 (*Fragmenta Historicorum Græcorum*, vol. v.);
Phrantzes, p. 237.

THE GATE OF ST. ROMANUS.

THE GATE OF CHARISIUS.

siege of 1453 the Turkish troops which invested the walls extending from the Gate of Charisius (Edirnè Kapoussi) to the Golden Horn were on the Sultan's *left, i.e.* to the north of the position he occupied.   But the tent of the Sultan was opposite the Gate of St. Romanus.[1]   Hence, the Gate of Charisius was one of the gates to the north of the Lycus, and, consequently, the Gate of St. Romanus stood at Top Kapoussi, to the south. In harmony with this conclusion is the order in which the two gates are mentioned by Pusculus and Dolfin when describing the positions occupied by the defenders of the walls from the Sea of Marmora to the Golden Horn.   Proceeding from south to north in their account of the defence, these writers place the Gate of St. Romanus before, *i.e.* to the south of, the Gate of Charisius.[2]

The Church of St. Romanus must have been a very old foundation, for it is ascribed to the Empress Helena.   It claimed to possess the relics of the prophet Daniel and of St. Nicetas.[3]

The entrance between the second and third towers north of the Lycus, or between the thirteenth and fourteenth towers north of the Gate of St. Romanus, is the Fifth Military Gate, the Gate of the Pempton (τοῦ Πέμπτου).[4]   It is identified by the fact that it occupies the position which the *Paschal Chronicle* assigns to the Gate of the Pempton ; namely, between the Gate of St. Romanus and the Gate of the Polyandrion—one of the names, as we shall find,[5] of Edirnè Kapoussi.

Some authorities[6] have maintained, indeed, that this entrance was the Gate of Charisius.   But this opinion is refuted by the fact that the Gate of Charisius, as its whole history proves, was not a military gate, but one of the public gates of the city.[7]

---

[1] Critobulus ; Phrantzes, *ut supra.*

[2] Pusculus, iv.   Compare lines 165 and 169.   Cf. Dolfin, s. 54.

[3] Anonymus, iii. p. 55; *Itinéraires Russes en Orient,* p. 103.

[4] *Paschal Chron.,* p. 719.   [5] See below, p. 84.

[6] *E.g.* Dethier, *Le Bosphore et Consple.,* p. 50.   [7] See below, p. 83.

G

Furthermore, the author of the *Metrical Chronicle* and Cananus expressly distinguish the Gate of Charisius from the gate situated beside the Lycus.[1]

To the rear of the entrance was the district of the Pempton, containing the Church of St. Kyriakè and the meadow through which the Lycus flows to the Sea of Marmora. The meadow appears to have been a popular resort before the Theodosian Walls were built, if not also subsequently. Here, about the time of Easter, 404, the Emperor Arcadius came to take exercise on horseback, and here he found three thousand white-robed cate-chumens assembled. They proved to be persons who had recently been baptized by Chrysostom, in the Thermæ Con-stantianæ, near the Church of the Holy Apostles, notwithstand-ing his deposition on account of his quarrel with the Empress Eudoxia. Arcadius was extremely annoyed by the encounter, and ordered his guards to drive the crowd off the ground.[2]

While riding down one of the slopes of the Lycus valley, in 450, Theodosius II. fell from his horse and sustained a spinal injury, which caused his death a few days later. The Gate of the Pempton was probably the entrance through which the dying emperor was carried on a litter from the scene of the accident into the city.[3]

---

[1] *Metrical Chronicle,* lines 371–429 ; cf. statement ἐγέρθη Γεωργίου δόμος . . . πρὸς πύλην τὴν Χαρσίαν with statement πύλην ἐάσας ἀνοικτὴν τὴν ποταμοῦ πλησίον εἰς ἥν τῆς μάρτυρος ναὸς Κυριακῆς ὁρᾶται. See *Byzantinshe Analecten,* von Hernn Joseph Müller, "Situngs Berechte der K. Akademie der Wissenshaften Philisoph. Hist.," Classe B. 9, 1852. Cf. Cananus, p. 462, ἦν γὰρ ὁ τόπος καὶ σοῦδα καὶ πύργος πλησίον Κυριακῆς τῆς ἁγίας, μέσον Ῥωμανοῦ τοῦ ἁγίου καὶ τῆς Χαρσῆς τε τὴν πύλην, καὶ πλησιέστηρον τούτων εἰς τὸν ποταμόν τὸν ἐπονομαζόμενον Λύκον.

[2] Palladius, *Dialogus de Vita J. Chrysostomi,* Migne, xlvii. p. 34. In front of St. Irene in the Seraglio grounds, is preserved the pedestal on which stood the porphyry column bearing the silver statue of the Empress Eudoxia, the occasion of Chrysostom's banishment.

[3] *Paschal Chron.,* p. 589, Εἰσῆλθεν λεκτικίῳ ἀπὸ Λευκοῦ ποταμοῦ.

The next public gate, Edirnè Kapoussi, between the eighth
and ninth towers to the north of the Fifth Military Gate, was
named the Gate of Charisius (τοῦ Χαρισίου).   The name, which
appears in a great variety of forms, occurs first in Peter
Magister,[1] a writer of Justinian's reign, and was derived, according to the Anonymus, from Charisius, the head of the Blue
Faction, when the Theodosian Walls were built.[2]   While some
authorities, as already intimated, have attached this name to the
Gate of the Pempton, others have supposed that it belonged to
the entrance now known as Egri Kapou.[3]   This, as will be
shown in the proper place, is likewise a mistake.[4]

The grounds on which the Gate of Charisius must be identified with the Edirnè Kapoussi are these:[5] From the statements
of Cananus and Critobulus, already considered in determining
the position of the Gate of St. Romanus,[6] it is clear that the
Gate of Charisius was one of the two gates on the northern
bank of the Lycus; either the gate at the foot of that bank
or Edirnè Kapoussi upon the summit.   That it was not the
former is clearly proved by the fact that Cananus and the
Metrical Chronicle, as already cited, distinguished the Gate of
Charisius from the entrance beside the Lycus.   The Gate of
Charisius was, therefore, Edirnè Kapoussi, the gate on the
summit of the bank.

Again, the Gate of Charisius was, like Edirnè Kapoussi,
at the head of the street leading to the Church of the Holy
Apostles.   This is evident from the circumstance that when
Justinian the Great, returning to the city from the West, visited

---

[1] Constant. Porphyr., *De Cer.*, p. 497.

[2] Anonymus, iii. p. 50.

[3] Paspates, p. 68.

[4] See below, p. 124.

[5] Dr. Mordtmann was the first to establish the fact.   For a full statement of his
view, see *Esquisse Topographique de Consple.*, pp. 16-29.

[6] See above, pp. 80, 81.

on his way to the palace the tomb of the Empress Theodora at the Holy Apostles', he entered the capital by the Gate of Charisius instead of by the Golden Gate,[1] because the former entrance led directly to the Imperial Cemetery near that church.

To these arguments may be added the fact that near the Gate of Charisius was a Church of St. George,[2] the guardian of the entrance, and that a Byzantine church dedicated to that saint stood immediately to the south-east of Edirnè Kapoussi as late as the year 1556, when it was appropriated by Sultan Suleiman for the construction of the Mosque of Mihrimah. At the same time the Greek community received by way of compensation a site for another church to the north-west of the gate, and there the present Church of St. George was built to preserve the traditions of other days.[3] Lastly, like Edirnè Kapoussi, the Gate of Charisius stood at a point from which one could readily proceed to the Church of the Chora (Kahriyeh Djamissi), the Church of St. John in Petra (Bogdan Serai), and the Palace of Blachernæ.[4]

Another name for the Gate of Charisius was the Gate of the Polyandrion, or the Myriandron (Πόρτα τοῦ Πολυανδρίου, τοῦ Μυριάνδρου), the Gate of the Cemetery. This follows from the fact that whereas the respective names of the three gates

[1] Constant. Porphyr., *De Cer.*, p. 497. In 1299, Andronicus II. also entered the city by this entrance in great state, after an absence of two years (Pachymeres, vol. ii. p. 290).

[2] Anna Comn., ii. pp. 124, 129; *Metrical Chronicle*, 371-429.

[3] Patriarch Constantius, *Ancient and Modern Constantinople*, p. 105. The church possesses two ancient *Lectionaries*, one containing the Epistles, the other the Gospels. The history of the latter is interesting. The MS. was presented to the Church of St. Sophia, in 1438, by a monk named Arsenius, of Crete. It was taken, the same year, by the Patriarch Joseph to Ferrara, when he proceeded to that city to attend the council called to negotiate the union of the Western and Eastern Churches. Upon his death in Florence the year following it was returned to St. Sophia. Some time after the fall of Constantinople it came into the hands of a certain Manuel, son of Constantine, by whom it was given, in 1568, to the church in which it is now treasured.

[4] Ducas, p. 288.

in the walls crossing the valley of the Lycus are usually given as the Gate of Charisius, Gate of the Pempton, the Gate of St. Romanus, we find the first name omitted in a passage of the *Paschal Chronicle* referring to those entrances, and the Gate of the Polyandrion mentioned instead.[1] Evidently, the Gate of Charisius and the Gate of the Polyandrion were different names for the same gate.

The latter designation was peculiarly appropriate to an entrance on the direct road to the Imperial Cemetery. Probably a public cemetery stood also outside the gate, where a large Turkish cemetery is now situated, and that may have been another reason for the name of the gate.[2]

With the portion of the walls between the Gate of St. Romanus and the Gate of Charisius, memorable historical events are associated which cannot be passed over without some notice, however brief.

On account of its central position in the line of the land fortifications, this part of the walls was named the Mesoteichion (Μεσοτείχιον).[3] It was also known as the Myriandrion,[4] on

---

[1] *Paschal Chron.*, pp. 719, 720 ; cf. Anonymus, i. p. 22, with iii. p. 50.

[2] In the foundations of one of the towers to the north of the Gate of the Pempton, pulled down in 1868 for the sake of building material, a large number of marble tombstones were found, some being plain slabs, others bearing inscriptions. Among the latter, several were to the memory of persons connected with the body of auxiliary troops, styled the Fœderati. Such Gothic names as Walderic, Saphnas, Bertilas, Epoktoric, occurred in the epitaphs, *e.g.*—

    † ΕΝΘΔΕ   ΚΤΑ . . . Ι Ο
    ΤΗϹ ΜΑΚΑΡΙΑϹ ΜΝΗΜΗϹ ϹΕΦΝΑϹ
    ΔΕϹΠΟΤΙΚΟϹ ΠΙϹΤΟϹ ΦΟΙΔΕΡΑΤΟϹ ΕΤΕΛΕΥ
    ΤΗϹΕΝ ΔΕ ΜΗ ΝΟΕΜΒΡΙѠ ΚΔ ΗΜΕΡΑ Β
    ΙΝΔ Β.

See Paspates, pp. 33, 34 ; *Proceedings of the Greek Literary Syllogos of Consple.*, vol. xvi., 1885 ; *Archæological Supplement*, pp. 17-23. Some of the stones are in the Imperial Museum.

[3] Critobulus, i. c. 26, c. 31.

[4] Phrantzes, p. 253 ; Critobulus, i. c. 26 ; Leonard of Scio, "In loco arduo Miliandri, quo urbs titubabat."

account of its proximity to the Gate of Polyandrion; the portion to the south of the Lycus being further distinguished as the Murus Bacchatareus,[1] after the Tower Baccaturea near the Gate of St. Romanus.[2]

Owing to the configuration of the ground traversed by the Mesoteichion, it was at this point that a besieging army generally delivered the chief attack. Here stood the gates opening upon the streets which commanded the hills of the city; here was the weakest part of the fortifications, the channel of the Lycus rendering a deep moat impossible, while the dip in the line of walls, as they descended and ascended the slopes of the valley, put the defenders below the level occupied by the besiegers. Here, then, for Constantinople was the "Valley of Decision"— here, in the armour of the city, the "heel of Achilles."

In the siege of 626 by the Avars, the first siege which the Theodosian Walls sustained, the principal attack was made from twelve towers which the enemy built before the fortifications extending from the Gate of Charisius to the Gate of the Pempton, and thence to the Gate of St. Romanus.[3]

Upon the Gate of Charisius attempts were made: by Justinian II. and his allies for the recovery of his throne in 705;[4] by Alexius Branas against Isaac Angelus in 1185;[5] by John Cantacuzene in 1345;[6] and through it the Comneni entered in 1081, by bribing the German guards (Nemitzi) at the gate, and wrested the sceptre from the hand of Nicephorus Botoniates.[7]

In 1206, during the struggle in which the Latins, soon after their capture of the city, involved themselves with Joannicus, King of Bulgaria, a raid was made upon the Gate of St. Romanus

[1] *Leonard of Scio.*, Migne, vol. clix. pp. 929, 940.   [2] Dolfin, s. 31.
[3] *Paschal Chron.*, pp. 719, 720.   [4] Theophanes, p. 573.   [5] Nicetas Chon., p. 493.
[6] Cantacuzene, iii. p. 525.   [7] Anna Comn., ii. p. 124.

VIEW ACROSS THE VALLEY OF THE LYCUS (LOOKING NORTH).

and the adjacent quarter by Bulgarian troops encamped near the capital.[1] In 1328 the gate was opened to admit Andronicus III. by two partisans, who stupefied the guards with drink, and then assisted a company of his soldiers to scale the walls with rope ladders.[2] In 1379 John VI. Palæologus and his son Manuel, after effecting their escape from the prison of Anemas, and making terms with Sultan Bajazet, entered the city by this gate, and obliged Andronicus IV. to retire from the throne he had usurped.[3]

But it was in the sieges of the city by the Turks that this portion of the walls was attacked most fiercely, as well as defended with the greatest heroism.   Here in 1422 Sultan Murad brought cannon to bear, for the first time, upon the fortifications of Constantinople.   His fire was directed mainly at an old half-ruined tower beside the Lycus ; but the new weapon of warfare was still too weak to break Byzantine masonry, and seventy balls struck the tower without producing the slightest effect.[4]

In the siege of 1453 this portion of the walls was assailed by Sultan Mehemet himself with the bravest of his troops and his heaviest artillery, his tent being pitched, as already stated, about half a mile to the west of the Gate of St. Romanus.[5]   At the Murus Bacchatareus fought the Emperor Constantine, with his 400 Genoese allies, under the command of the brave Guistiniani, who had come to perform prodigies of valour " per benefitio de la Christiantade et per honor del mundo."   The three brothers, Paul, Antony, and Troilus, defended the Myriandrion, "with the courage of Horatius Cocles."

---

[1] Nicetas Chon., p. 824.

[2] Cantacuzene, i. p. 291 ; Nicephorus Greg., ix. pp. 419, 420.

[3] See Muralt, *Essai de Chronographie Byzantine*, vol. ii.   See below, pp. 162, 163.

[4] Cananus, pp. 461, 462.

[5] Compare the narratives of Phrantzes, pp. 246, 253 ; Critobulus, i. c. 23, 27, 31, 34, 60 ; Ducas, p. 275 ; Leonard of Scio (*Migne*, vol. clix.).

As the struggle proceeded two towers of the Inner Wall and a large portion of the Outer Wall were battered to pieces by the Turkish cannon. The enemy also succeeded in filling the moat at this point with earth and stones, to secure an unobstructed roadway into the city whenever a breach was effected.

On the other hand, Giustiniani repaired the breach in the Outer Wall by the erection of a palisade, covered in front with hides and strengthened on the rear by a rampart of stones, earth, branches, and herbage of every description, all welded together with mortar, and supported by an embankment of earth. Between this barricade and the Inner Wall he furthermore excavated a trench, to replace to some extent the moat which had been rendered useless ; and to maintain his communications with the interior of the city he opened a postern in the great wall.

Against these extemporized defences assault after assault dashed in all its strength and fury, only to be hurled back and broken. Meanwhile, more and more of the Inner and Outer Walls fell under the Turkish fire, and the Sultan decided to make a general attack at daybreak on the 29th of May. The onset upon the Mesoteichion, directed by the Sultan in person, was, however, repeatedly repelled, and the day threatened to go against the assailants, when a Turkish missile struck Giustiniani and forced him to leave the field. His soldiers refused to continue the struggle, abandoned their post, and disheartened their Greek comrades. The Sultan, perceiving the change in the situation, roused his janissaries to make a supreme effort. They swept forward, carried the barricade, filled the trench behind it with corpses of the defenders, and passing over, poured into the doomed city through every available opening. Some made their way through the breach in the great wall, others entered by the postern which Giustiniani had opened,[1] while others cut a path through the heap of dead bodies which blocked the Gate of Charisius. The heroic emperor refused to survive his empire, and found death near the Gate of St. Romanus.[2] And through that gate, about midday, the Sultan entered, the master of the city of Constantine. It was the close of an epoch.

The next Theodosian gate stands between the last tower in the Outer Wall to the north of the Gate of Charisius and the old Byzantine Palace now called Tekfour Serai. In its present condition the entrance pierces only the Outer Wall; for the Inner Wall terminates abruptly a little to the south of the palace, having been broken away, probably when that edifice was erected. By way of compensation the Outer Wall was then raised higher and built thicker, and flanked by a large tower.

According to its place in the order of the gates, this entrance should be the Sixth Military Gate; and the smallness of its dimensions is in keeping with this view. But as it led to a Circus built of timber beside the Church of St. Mamas without the walls, it was styled Porta Xylokerkou (Ξυλοκέρκου),[3] Gate of the Wooden Circus, or more briefly, Kerko Porta (Κερκόπορτα),[4] the Gate of the Circus.

---

[1] Critobulus, i. c. 60.   [2] Phrantzes, p. 287.
[3] Cantacuzene, iii. p. 558 ; Theophanes, p. 667.
[4] Ducas, p. 282. The Circus was known as the Circus of St. Mamas, because of its proximity to that church, and appears frequently in Byzantine history.

The district associated with the Church of St. Mamas (Zonaras, xvi. c. 5, ἐν τῇ κατὰ τὸ Στενὸν τοποθεσίᾳ τῇ τοῦ ἁγίου Μάμαντος καλουμένῃ) must have occupied the valley which extends from the Golden Horn southwards to the village of Ortakdjilar, the territory between Eyoub (Cosmidion) and Aivan Serai at the north-western angle of the city. The church itself, with its monastery (Cantacuzene, iv. pp. 107, 259), stood, probably, on the high ground near Ortakdjilar. Owing to its charming situation, the suburb was a favourite resort, and boasted of an Imperial palace, a hippodrome, a portico, a harbour, and, possibly, the

In support of this identification there is first the fact that the Gate of the Xylokerkus, like the gate before us, was an entrance

bridge across the Golden Horn. The indications for the determination of the site of the suburb are: (1) it stood nearer the Golden Horn than the Gate of Charisius did; for in the military demonstration which Constantine Copronymus made before the land walls, against the rebel Artavasdes, by marching up and down between the Gate of Charisius and the Golden Gate, the emperor reached St. Mamas and encamped there, after passing the former entrance on his march northwards (Theophanes, pp. 645, 646). (2) The Hippodrome of St. Mamas was in Blachernæ (ἐν Βλαχέρναις . . . ἐν τῷ ἱππικῷ τοῦ ἁγίου Μάμαντος— Theophanes, p. 667), a term which could be used to designate even the district of the Cosmidion (*Paschal Chron.*, p. 725, τὴν ἐκκλησίαν τῶν ἁγίων Κοσμᾶ καὶ Δαμιανοῦ, ἐν Βλαχέρναις). (3) The suburb stood near the Cosmidion; hence the facility with which the Bulgarians under Crum were able to ravage St. Mamas from their camp near the Church SS. Cosmas and Damianus (Theophanes, pp. 613, 614). (4) The suburb was near the water; for it had a harbour (Theophanes, p. 591). It is also described as situated on the Propontis (Genesius, p. 102), on the Euxine (Theophanes Cont., p. 197), on the Stenon, the Bosporus (Zonaras, *ut supra*), these names being applied in a wide sense. (5) At the same time the Church of St. Mamas stood near the walls (Zonaras, xiv. p. 1272, πλησίον τοῦ τείχους), and near the gate named Porta Xylokerkou (Cedrenus, i. p. 707). This does not necessarily imply that the church was immediately outside the gate, but it intimates that the church was at no very great distance from the gate, and could be easily reached from it; as, for example, the Church of the Pegè stands related to the Gate of Selivria (see above, p. 73). Such language would be appropriate if a branch road leading to St. Mamas and the Golden Horn left the great road, parallel to the walls, at the point opposite the Porta Xylokerkou.

The suburb owed much to Leo the Great, who took up his residence there for six months, after the terrible conflagration which devastated the city in the twelfth year of his reign (*Paschal Chron.*, p. 598). To him are ascribed all the constructions for which the suburb was celebrated; the harbour and portico (*Paschal Chron., ut supra*), the church, the palace, and the hippodrome (Anonymus, iii. pp. 57, 58; Codinus, p. 115). The Church of St. Mamas is, however, ascribed also to an officer in the reign of Justinian the Great, and to the sister of the Emperor Maurice (see Du Cange, *Constantinopolis Christiana*, iv. p. 185). There Maurice and his family were buried, after their execution by Phocas (Codinus, p. 121). The palace was frequented by Michael III., and there he was murdered by Basil I. (Theophanes Cont., p. 210). To it the Empress Irene and her son Constantine VI. retired from the city on the occasion of the severe earthquake of 790 (Theophanes, pp. 719, 720), and in it the marriage of Constantine VI. with Theodota was celebrated (*Ibid.* p. 728). It was burnt down by Crum of Bulgaria (*Ibid.* pp. 785, 786), but must have been rebuilt soon, for Theophilus took up his quarters there on the eve of his first triumphal entrance into the city (Constant. Porphyr., *De Cer.*, p. 504). The hippodrome may have been, originally, the one which Constantine the Great constructed of wood, outside the city, and in which the adherents of Chrysostom assembled after the bishop's deposition (Sozomon, viii. c. 21, συνῆλθον πρὸ τοῦ ἄστεος εἰς τινα χῶρον in the Walls of Theodosius, for it bore an inscription, which has unfortunately disappeared, in honour of that emperor and the Prefect Constantine, similar to the legend on the Porta Rhegiou.[1] In the next place, the Gate of the Xylokerkus, like the entrance before us, was in the vicinity of the Gate of Charisius, and below a palace[2] (Tekfour Serai).

The history of the gate has an interest of its own. When the Emperor Frederick Barbarossa was at Philippopolis, on his way to the Holy Land at the head of the Third Crusade, the prevalent suspicion that he had designs upon the Byzantine Empire found expression in the prophecy of a certain Dositheos, a monk of the Monastery of St. John Studius, that the German emperor would capture Constantinople, and penetrate into the city through this entrance.   Thereupon, with the view of averting the calamity and preventing the fulfilment of the prophecy, Isaac Angelus ordered the gate to be securely built up.[3]   In 1346 the partisans of John Cantacuzene proposed to admit him into the city by breaking the gate open, after its long close.[4]

But what gives to the Kerko Porta its chief renown is the part which, according to Ducas, it played in the catastrophe of

---

ὅν Κωνσταντίνος ὁ βασιλεὺς, μήπω τὴν πόλιν συνοικήσας, εἰς ἱπποδρόμου θέαν ἐκάθηρε, ξύλοις περιτειχίσας).   There Michael III. took part in chariot races (Theophanes Cont., p. 197; cf. Theophanes, p. 731).   Crum carried away some of the works of Art which adorned it (Theophanes, pp. 785, 786).   The harbour of St. Mamas appears as the station of a fleet in the struggle between Anastasius II. and Theodosius III. (Theophanes, pp. 591, 592), and in the struggle between Artavasdes and Constantine Copronymus (*Ibid.*, pp. 645, 646).

[1] Banduri, *Imp. Orient.*, vii. p. 150, n. 428, ΘΕΥΔΟCΙΟC ΤΟΔΕ ΤΕΙΧΟC ΑΝΑΞ ΚΑΙ ΥΠΑΡΧΟC ΕωΑC ΚωΝCΤΑΝΤΙΝΟC ΕΤΕΥΞΑΝ ΕΝ ΗΜΑCΙΝ ΕΞΗΚΟΝΤΑ.   The gate appears in the reign of Anastasius I. (491-518), when a nun residing near it was mobbed and killed for sharing the emperor's heretical opinions (Zonaras, xiv. c. 3, p. 1220, Migne).   This is another evidence of its Theodosian origin.   It must have stood in the portion of the Theodosian Walls that still remain, for it is mentioned in the reign of John Cantacuzene.

[2] Ducas, pp. 282-286.   Cf. Anonymus, iii. p. 50.

[3] Nicetas Chon., pp. 528, 529.   [4] Cantacuzene, iii. p. 558.

1453, under the following circumstances. A large portion of the Outer Wall, at the Mesoteichion, having been overthrown by the Turkish cannon, the besieged were unable to issue from the city to the peribolos without being exposed to the enemy's fire. In this extremity some old men, who knew the fortifications well, informed the emperor of a secret postern long closed up and buried underground, at the lower part of the palace, by which communication with the peribolos might be established.[1] This was done, to the great advantage of the Greeks. But on the last day of the siege, while the enemy was attempting to scale the walls with ladders at several points, a band of fifty Turkish nobles detected the newly opened entrance, rushed in, and mounting the walls from the interior of the city, killed or drove off the defenders on the summit. Thus a portion of the fortifications was secured against which scaling-ladders could be applied without any difficulty, and soon a considerable Turkish force stood on the Inner Wall, planted their standards on the towers, and opened a rear fire upon the Greeks, who were fighting in the peribolos to prevent the Turks from entering at the great breach. The cry rose that the city was taken, whereupon an indescribable panic seized the Greeks, already disheartened by the loss of Giustiniani, and, abandoning all further resistance, they fled into the city through the Gate of Charisius, many being trampled to death in the rout. The emperor fell at his post ; and the Turks poured into the city without opposition.[2] The fate of Constantinople was thus sealed by the opening of the Kerko Porta.

But here a difficulty occurs. In one very important particular the Kerko Porta, as described by Ducas, does not

---

[1] Ducas, p. 282, Παραπόρτιον ἕν πρὸ πολλῶν χρόνων ἀσφαλῶς πεφραγμένον, ὑπόγαιον, πρὸς τὸ κάτωθεν μέρος τοῦ παλατίου.

[2] Ducas, pp. 282–286.

correspond to the character of the entrance with which it has
been identified. The gate which the historian had in mind led
to the peribolos, the terrace between the two Theodosian walls,
whereas the gate below Tekfour Serai opens on the parateichion, the terrace between the Outer Wall and the Moat. This
discrepancy may, however, be removed to some extent by supposing that under the name of the Kerko Porta, Ducas referred

THE (SO-CALLED) KERKO PORTA.[1]

to the postern which Dr. Paspates[2] found in the transverse wall
built across the northern end of the peribolos, where the Inner
Wall of Theodosius terminates abruptly a little to the south
of Tekfour Serai. The postern was discovered in 1864, after
some houses which concealed it from view had been destroyed

---

[1] From *Broken Bits of Byzantium.*   (By kind permission of Mrs. Walker.)
[2] Pages 63–67. Dr. Paspates regarded the Kerko Porta and the Porta Xylokerkou
as different gates. The latter, he held, has disappeared.

by fire. It was 10½ feet high by 6 feet wide, and although the old wall in which it stood has been, for the most part, pulled down and replaced by a new construction, the outline of the ancient postern can still be traced. Such an entrance might be buried out of sight, and be generally forgotten ; and to open it, when recalled to mind in 1453, was to provide the defenders of the city with a secret passage, as they hoped, to the peribolos and the rear of the Outer Wall, where the contest was to be maintained to the bitter end.

The suggestion of Dr. Paspates that this was the entrance at which the incidents recorded by Ducas occurred may, therefore, be accepted. But, from the nature of the case, an entrance in such a position could not have been, strictly speaking, the Gate of the Circus, and to call it the Kerko Porta was therefore not perfectly accurate. That was, properly, the name of the gate below Tekfour Serai. Still, the mistake was not very serious, and, under the circumstances, was not strange. Two entrances so near each other could easily be confounded in the report of the events in the neighbourhood, especially when the postern in the transverse wall had no special name, of its own.

Dr. Mordtmann[1] thinks that the postern near the Kerko Porta was the one which Giustiniani, according to Critobulus,[2] opened in the Inner Wall to facilitate communication with the peribolos. The latter postern, however, is represented as near the position occupied by Giustiniani and the emperor, while the former is described as far from that point.[8]

---

[1] Page 27.   [2] I. c. 60.   [3] Ducas, p. 286.

CHAPTER VI.

REPAIRS ON THE THEODOSIAN WALLS.

THE maintenance of the bulwarks of the city in proper order was naturally a matter of supreme importance, and although the task was sometimes neglected when no enemy threatened, it was, on the whole, attended to with the promptitude and fidelity which so vital a concern demanded. There was little occasion for repairs, it is true, on account of injuries sustained in the shock of war, for until the invention of gunpowder the engines employed in battering the walls were either not powerful enough, or could not be planted sufficiently near the fortifications, to produce much effect. Most of the damage done to the walls was due to the action of the weather, and, above all, to the violent and frequent earthquakes which shook Constantinople in the course of the Middle Ages.

The charge of keeping the fortifications in repair was given to special officers, known under the titles, Domestic of the Walls (ὁ Δομέστικος τῶν Τειχέων),[1] Governor of the Wall (Ἄρχων τοῦ Τείχους),[2] Count of the Walls (Κόμης τῶν Τειχέων).[3]

(1) The earliest record of repairs is, probably, the Latin

---

[1] Codinus, *De Officiis*, p. 41; Constant. Porphyr., *De Cer.*, p. 589.

[2] Theophanes, p. 616.

[3] Constant. Porphyr., *De Cer.*, p. 6. *Ibid.*, p. 295, speaks of the τοῦ τειχεώτου.

inscription on the lintel of the inner gateway of the Porta of
the Pempton.   It reads:

PORTARUM VALID † DO FIRMAVIT LIMINE MUROS
PUSAEUS MAGNO NON MINOR ANTHEMIO.

The age of the inscription cannot be precisely determined,
but the employment of Latin, the Gothic form of the D in the
word *valido*, the allusion to Anthemius, and the situation of the
legend upon the Inner Wall, taken together, point to an early
date.

From the statement of the inscription it would seem that
soon after the erection of the wall by Anthemius, either this
gate or all the gates in the line of the new fortifications had to
be strengthened.   The only Pusæus known in history who could
have presumed to compare himself with Anthemius was consul
in 467, in the reign of Leo I.[1]   There may, however, have
been an earlier personage of that name.

(2) A considerable portion of the Inner Wall (τὰ ἔσω τείχη)
was injured by an earthquake in 578, the fourth year of the reign
of Zeno ;[2] but no record of the repairs executed in consequence
of the disaster has been preserved.

(3) The frequent shocks of earthquake felt in Constantinople
during the reign of Justinian the Great damaged the walls on,
at least, three occasions ; in 542 and 554, when the injury done
was most serious in the neighbourhood of the Golden Gate ;[3] and
again in 558, when both the Constantinian and the Theodosian
Walls were rudely shaken, the latter suffering chiefly in the
portion between the Golden Gate and the Porta Rhousiou.[4]   So
great was the damage sustained by the city and vicinity on the
last occasion that for thirty days the emperor refused to wear
his crown.

---

[1] *Paschal Chron.*, p. 595.   [2] Theophanes, p. 195.
[3] *Ibid.*, pp. 345, 355.   [4] *Ibid.*, pp. 357, 358.

INSCRIPTIONS ON THE GATE OF RHEGIUM.

(4) An inscription on the Gate Rhousiou commemorates the restoration of the Outer Wall in the reign of Justin II. Whether the work was rendered necessary by some particular accident does not appear ; but a wall so slight in its structure would naturally need extensive repair when a century old. With Justin the inscription associates the Empress Sophia, noted for her interest in the public works of the day, and also names Narses and Stephen, as the officials who had charge of the repairs. The latter officer is otherwise unknown. Narses, who held the offices of Spatharius and Sacellarius, superintended also the restoration of the Harbour of Julian in the same reign.[1] Subsequently he was sent, with large funds, on a mission to the Avars to persuade them to raise the siege of Sirmium. But the ship which carried the money was totally wrecked on the way, and Narses took the misfortune so much to heart that he fell ill and died.[2]

The inscription in honour of Justin was to the following effect : [3]

† ΑΝΕΝΕѠΘΗ ΤΟ ΠΡΟΤΕΙΧΙϹΜΑ ΤΟΥ ΘΕΟΔΟϹΙΑΚΟΥ
ΤΕΙΧΟΥϹ ΕΠΙ ΙΟΥϹΤΙΝΟΥ ΚΑΙ ϹΟΦΙΑϹ ΤѠΝ ΕΥϹΕ-
ΒΕϹΤΑΤѠΝ ΗΜѠΝ ΔΕϹΠΟΤѠΝ ΔΙΑ ΝΑΡϹΟΥ ΤΟΥ
ΕΝΔΟΞΟΤΑΤΟΥ ϹΠΑΘΑΡΙΟΥ ΚΑΙ ϹΑΚΕΛΛΑΡΙΟΥ ΚΑΙ
ϹΤΕΦΑΝΟΥ ΑΝΗΚΟΝΤΟϹ ΕΙϹ ΥΠΟΥΡΓΙΑΝ ΔΟΥΛΟϹ
ΤѠΝ ΕΥϹΕΒΑϹΤΑΤѠΝ ΔΕϹΠΟΤѠΝ †

"The Outwork of the Theodosian Wall was restored under Justin and Sophia, our most pious Sovereigns, by Narses, the most glorious Spatharius and Sacellarius, and Stephen, who belonged to the service, a servant of the most pious Sovereigns."

(5) The next repairs on record were executed early in the eighth century, in view of the formidable preparations made by

---

[1] Codinus, p. 86.

[2] *John of Ephesus :* translation by R. Payne Smith.

[3] See illustration facing p. 96, for copy of the inscription with its errors in orthography.

H

the Saracens for a second attack upon Constantinople.   Anastasius II. then strengthened the land walls, as well as the other fortifications of the city ;[1] and thus contributed to the signal repulse of the enemy in 718 by Leo the Isaurian, at that great crisis in the history of Christendom.

(6) Repairs were again demanded in 740, in the reign of Leo the Isaurian, owing to the injuries caused by a long series of earthquakes during eleven months.   So extensive was the work of restoration required, that to provide the necessary funds Leo was obliged to increase the taxes.[2]

Several inscriptions commemorating the repairs executed by that emperor, in conjunction with his son and colleague Constantine Copronymus, have been found upon towers of the Inner Wall.

(*a*) One stood on the seventh tower north of the Sea of Marmora :

† ΛΕωΝ ΟΥΝ ΚωΝΟΤΑΝΤΙΝω ΟΚΗΠΤΟΥΧΟΙ ΤΟΝΔΕ ΗΓΕΙΡΑΝ ΠΥΡΓΟΝ ΤωΝ ΒΑΘΡωΝ ΟΥΜΠΤωΘΕΝΤΑ †

"Leo with Constantine, wielders of the sceptre, erected from the foundations this tower which had fallen."

(*b*) Another was placed on the ninth tower north of the Golden Gate, in letters formed of brick :

IC	XC
NI	KA

ΛΕωΝΤΟΟ ΚΑΙ ΚωΝΟΤΑΝΤΗΝΟΥ ΜΕΓΑΛΟΝ
ΒΑΟΙΛΕωΝ ΚΑΙ ΑΥΤΟΚΡΑΤωΡΟΝ ΠΟΛΛΑ ΤΑ ΕΤΗ

"Many be the years of Leo and Constantine, Great Kings and Emperors."

---

[1] Theophanes, p. 589.
[2] *Ibid.*, pp. 634, 635.   The tax was called "dikeraton," because it was equal to two keratia (1*s*. ½*d*.), or one-twelfth of a nomisma (12*s*. 6*d*.).   Cf. Finlay, *History of the Byzantine Empire*, i. pp. 37, 38.

TOWER OF THE THEODOSIAN WALLS (WITH INSCRIPTION IN HONOUR OF THE
EMPERORS LEO III. AND CONSTANTINE V.).

(*c*) A similar inscription was found on the third tower north of the Second Military Gate:

ΛΕΟΝΤΟϹ ΚΑΙ ΚωΝϹΤΑΝΤΙΝΟΥ

ΜΕΓΑΛωΝ ΒΑϹΙΛΕωΝ ΚΑΙ ΑΥΤΟΚΡΑΤωΡωΝ ΠΟΛΑ ΤΑ ΕΤΗ

(*d*) On the second tower north of the Gate of the Pegè was an inscription similar to that on the seventh tower north of the Sea of Marmora. The raised letters are beautifully cut on a band of marble:

(*e*) The ninth tower north of the same gate bore two inscriptions. The higher was in honour, apparently, of an Emperor Constantine; the lower reads:

† ΝΙΚΑ Η ΤΥΧΗ ΛΕΟΝΤΟϹ ΚΑΙ ΚωΝΤΑΝΤΙΝΟΥ ΤωΝ
ΘΕωΦΥΛΑΚΤωΝ ΔΕϹΠΟΤωΝ ΚΑΙ ΗΡΙΝΗϹ ΤΗϹ ΕΥϹΕ-
ΒΕϹΤΑΤΗϹ ΗΜωΝ ΑΥΓΟΥϹΤΗϹ

"The Fortune of Leo and Constantine, the God-protected Sovereigns, and of Irene, our most pious Augusta, triumphs."

If this inscription belongs to the reign of Leo the Isaurian, the Empress Irene here mentioned must be Irene, the first wife of Constantine Copronymus. In that case Maria, the wife of Leo himself, must have been dead[1] when the repairs which the

---

[1] The date of her death is not known. Muralt is mistaken in saying that she died in 750. The Maria who died in that year was the second wife of Constantine Copronymus; not the widow, as Muralt has it, of Leo III. Cf. Nicephorus, Patriarch of Consple., p. 73.

inscription commemorates were executed. Irene was married to Constantine in 732, and died in 749 or 750.

It is possible, however, that the inscription should be assigned to the reign of Leo IV. and Constantine VI., so different is it from the inscriptions which belong undoubtedly to the time of Leo the Isaurian. If so, the empress named is the famous Irene who blinded her son, usurped his throne, restored the use of Icons, and gave occasion for the revival of the Roman Empire in the West by Charlemagne.

Below the inscription several monograms are found.

(*f*) There is an interesting inscription, in letters of brick, constituting a prayer for the safety of the city, on the fourth tower north of the Gate Rhousiou :

ΧΡΙϹΤΕ ω ΘΕΟϹ ΑΤΑΡΑΧΟΝ ΚΑΙ ΑΠΟΛΕΜΟΝ ΦΥΛΑΤΤΕ ΤΗΝ ΠΟΛΙΝ ϹΟΥ ΝΙΚΑ ΤΟ ΜΕΝΟϹ ΤωΝ ΠΟΛΕΜΙωΝ

"O Christ, God, preserve Thy city undisturbed, and free from war. Conquer the wrath of the enemies."

It is the utterance of the purpose embodied in the erection of the splendid bulwarks of the city, and might have been inscribed upon them at any period of their history. It has been assigned to Constantine IX., when sole ruler after the death of Basil II. (1025–1028) ;[1] but the employment of brick in the construction of the letters favours the view that the legend belongs to the reign of Leo the Isaurian.

(7) Fragments of inscriptions recording repairs by Michael

---

[1] *Proceedings of the Greek Literary Syllogos of Consple.*, vol. xvi., 1885 : *Archæological Supplement*, pp. 34, 35.

II. and his son Theophilus have been found in the neighbourhood of the Gate of Charisius (Edirnè Kapoussi).[1] These
emperors were specially distinguished for their attention to the
state of the fortifications along the shores of the city, but
it would have been strange if sovereigns so concerned for the
security of the capital had entirely neglected the condition of
the land walls.

(8) The earthquake of 975, towards the close of the reign of
Zimisces,[2] left its mark upon the walls of the city, and two
inscriptions commemorate the repairs executed in consequence
by his successors, Basil II. and Constantine IX.

One of the inscriptions is on the huge, pentagonal, three-
storied tower at the junction of the land walls with the defences
along the Sea of Marmora.   The legend reads:

"Tower of Basil and Constantine, faithful Emperors in Christ, pious
Kings of the Romans."

The device

IC	XP
NI	KA

is found over two windows in the northern side of the tower.

The other inscription is on the northern gateway-tower of
the Gate of the Pegè:

† ΠΥΡΓΟϹ ΒΑϹΙΛΕΙΟΥ ΚΑΙ ΚωΝϹΤΑΝΤΙΝΟΥ ΕΝ
ΧΡΙϹΤω ΑΥΤΟΚΡΑΤΟΡωΝ †

"Tower of Basil and Constantine, Emperors in Christ."

---

[1] *Proceedings of the Greek Literary Syllogos of Consple.*, vol. xvi., 1885: *Archæological Supplement*, p. 30.

[2] Leo Diaconus, pp. 175, 176.

Possibly the two following inscriptions on the northern side of the southern tower of the Gate Rhousiou refer to the same emperors:[1]

"The Fortune of Constantine, our God-protected Sovereign, triumphs."

The second inscription is mutilated, but manifestly refers to repairs in the reign of Basil:

> † ΑΝΕΝΕѠΘΗ ΕΠΙ ΑΥ . . .
> ΤΑΤΟΥ Α . . .
> ΤΟΡΟΟ ΤΟΥ ΒΑϹΙΛΕ
> ΕΝ ΙΝ ΙΑ †

(9) An inscription on the fourth tower from the Sea of Marmora records repairs by the Emperor Romanus:

"Romanus, the Great Emperor of all the Romans, the Most Great, erected this tower new from the foundations."

As four emperors bore the name Romanus, it is not certain to which of them reference is here made. The fact that earthquakes occurred in the reign of Romanus III. Argyrus, first in 1032, and again in 1033,[2] is in favour of the view that the inscription was in his honour.

(10) During the period of the Comneni, particular attention

---

[1] Paspates, pp. 46, 47.   [2] Cedrenus, vol. ii. pp. 500, 503, 504.

DIAGRAM SHOWING THE INTERIOR OF A TOWER IN THE THEODOSIAN WALLS.

was given to the state of the fortifications by Manuel Comnenus,[1] and by Andronicus I. Comnenus.[2]   As will appear in the sequel, the former was concerned mainly with the defences in the neighbourhood of the Palace of Blachernæ, beyond the Theodosian Walls.   The interest of Andronicus in the matter was roused by fear lest the Normans, who had captured and sacked Thessalonica in 1185, would advance upon the capital.   After making a minute inspection of the walls in person, Andronicus ordered the immediate repair of the portions fallen into decay, as well as the removal of all houses whose proximity to the fortifications might facilitate escalade.

(11) Under the Palæologi, the Walls of Theodosius, after their long service of eight centuries, demanded frequent and extensive restoration, in view of the dangers which menaced them.

Hence, on the recovery of Constantinople from the Latins in 1261, Michael Palæologus, fearing the Western Powers would attempt to regain the place, took measures to put the fortifications in a proper state of defence.   His chief attention was devoted to the improvement of the bulwarks guarding the shores of the city, as those most exposed to attack by the maritime states of Europe, but he did not overlook the land walls.[3]

(12) In 1317, general repairs were again undertaken by Andronicus II. Palæologus, with money bequeathed by his wife, the Empress Irene, who died in that year.[4]   The only indication, however, of the fact is now found beyond the Theodosian lines.[5]

(13) The Theodosian Walls were injured once more by the great earthquake of October, 1344, during the minority of John VI. Palæologus.[6]   The disaster occurred when the struggle between Apocaucus and Cantacuzene for the control of affairs

[1] Cinnamus, p. 274.
[2] Nicetas Chon., pp. 414, 415.
[3] Pachymeres, vol. i. pp. 186, 187.
[4] Nicephorus Greg., vii. p. 275.
[5] See below, p. 126.
[6] Nicephorus Greg., xiv. pp. 694–696.

was at its height, and the ruin of the fortifications made the position of the former, who then held the city, extremely critical, seeing his rival was preparing to besiege him. Apocaucus proceeded, therefore, to reconstruct the fallen bulwarks with the utmost despatch and thoroughness. The Inner Wall and the Outer Wall were repaired from one end of the line to the other, and the parapet along the Moat was raised to the height of a man ;[1] proceedings which made this the most extensive restoration of the Theodosian Walls since 447. It was completed in January 1345, before Cantacuzene appeared to attack the capital.

(14) Mention has already been made of the repair of the Golden Gate by Cantacuzene, and the erection of a fortress behind that entrance by John VI. Palæologus, the prototype of the Turkish Castle of the Seven Towers.[2]

(15) The last restoration of the Theodosian bulwarks, on an extensive scale, was undertaken by John VII. Palæologus, (1425–1448), the Outer Wall being the portion principally concerned in the matter.

Evidently the task proved difficult, for the numerous inscriptions which celebrate the achievement bear dates extending from 1433–1444, and show that the work proceeded slowly, and with frequent interruptions, due, doubtless, to the low state of the Imperial exchequer. The letters of the legends are incised on small marble slabs, and are filled with lead, exhibiting poor workmanship both in form and arrangement.

One of the inscriptions was placed on the outer tower nearest the Sea of Marmora :[3]

IωAN
Xω AYTO
KPATOPOC TOY
ΠΑΛΑΙΟΛΟΓΟΥ.

"(Tower) of John Palæologus, Emperor in Christ."

---

[1] Nicephorus Greg., xiv. p. 711.   [2] See above, pp. 70, 71.   [3] Paspates, p. 59.

A similar inscription is on the second outer tower north of the Golden Gate:

"(Tower) of John Palæologus, Emperor in Christ; in the year 1444."

Another is on the fifth outer tower north of the Second Military Gate:

> ΙѠΑΝΝΟΥ ΕΝ ΧѠ
> ΑΥΤΟΚΡΑΤΟ
> ΡΟΟ ΤΟΥ ΠΑΛΑΙΟΛΟΓΟΥ
> ΚΑΤΑ ΜΗΝΑ
> ΙΟΥΝΙΟΥ ΤΟΥ Ϛ
> ϖΜΗ ΕΤΟΥΟ (6948).

"(Tower) of John Palæologus, Emperor in Christ; in the month of June of the year 1440."

On the twelfth tower north of the same gate is a fractured slab which bore the legend:

† ΙѠ ΕΝ ΧѠ ΑΥΤΟΚΡΑΤΟΡΟΟ ΤΟΥ ΠΑΛΑΙΟΛΟΓΟΥ
ΚΑΤΑ ΜΗΝΑ ΑΠΡΙΛΙΟΥ ΤΟΥ ϚϖΜΒ ΕΤΟΥΟ (6942).

"(Tower) of John Palæologus, Emperor in Christ; in the month of April of the year 1434."

Traces of similar inscriptions appear on the first and second towers north of the Gate of the Pegè ; while on the third tower in that direction are the words:

IωOY EN Xω AYTO
KPOTOPOC TOY ΠΑΛΑΙΟΛΟΓΟΥ KATA MHNA IANOY
APION TOY
SπMZ ETOYC (6947).

"(Tower) of John Palæologus, Emperor in Christ; in the month of January of the year 1839."

An inscription to the same effect stood on the first and the second towers north of the Third Military Gate. On the third tower beyond the entrance was the legend :

Iω EN Xω
AYTOKPA
TOPOC TOY ΠΑΛΑΙ
ΛΟΓΟΥ KATA MHNA OKTOB
TOY SπMς ETOYC (6946).

"(Tower) of John Palæologus, Emperor in Christ ; in the month of October of the year 1438."

On the outer tower, now demolished, opposite the Porta of the Pempton, was an inscription from which we learn the great extent of the repairs undertaken in this reign.[1] That work comprised the whole of the Outer Wall :

† ANEKAINICE TO KACTPON OΛON Iω Xω AY
TOKPATωP O ΠΑΛΑΙΟΛΟΓΟC ETEI SπMA (6941).

"John Palæolous, Emperor in Christ, restored the whole fortification ; in the year 1433."

In the course of the repairs made at this time, the Gate of the Pegè was restored at the expense of Manuel Bryennius Leontari, as an inscription high up on the back of the southern tower of the gate proclaims:[2]

† ANEKAINICΘH H
ΘEOCOCTOC ΠΥΛΗ AYTH
THC ZωOΔOXOY ΠHΓHC ΔIA

[1] Paspates, p. 45.   [2] Compare Paspates, pp. 54, 55, with Mordtmann, p. 14.

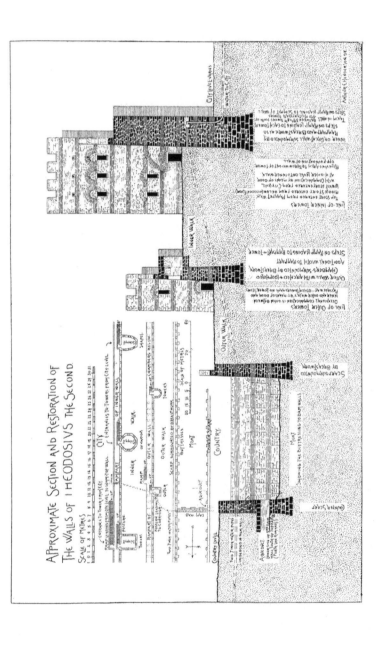

APPROXIMATE SECTION AND RESTORATION OF
THE WALLS OF THEODOSIVS THE SECOND

SCALE OF METRES

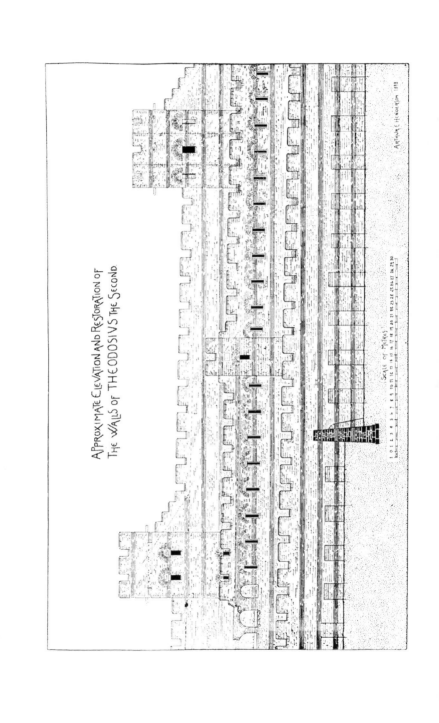

Approximate Elevation and Restoration of
The Walls of THEODOSIVS The Second

Scale of Metres

Arthur Henderson 1938

CYNΔPOMHC KAI EΞOΔOY MA
NOYHΛ BPYENNIOY TOY ΛE
ONTAPI EΠI BACIΛEIAC
TωN EYCEBECTATωN (or EYCEBωN) BACIΛEωN
IωANNOY KAI MAPIAC
TωN ΠAΛAIOΛOΓωN
EN MHNI MAI
EN ETEI ϛ𝟳Mϛ (or A) (6946 or 6941).

"This God-protected gate of the Life-giving Spring was restored with the co-operation and at the expense of Manuel Bryennius Leontari, in the reign of the most pious sovereigns John and Maria Palæologi; in the month of May, in the year 1438 (or 1433)."

The Empress Maria who is mentioned in the inscription was the daughter of Alexius, Emperor of Trebizond, and the third wife of John VII. Palæologus, from 1427–1440.[1]   Manuel Bryennius Leontari was probably the Bryennius Leontari who defended the Gate of Charisius in the siege of 1453.[2]

To the same reign, probably, belonged the work recorded on a tower between the Gate of Charisius and Tekfour Serai.   The inscription was fragmentary, consisting of the letters ENICΘH H KO, evidently ANEKENICΘH H KOPTINA[3] ("The curtain-wall was restored").   The lettering and the form of expression resembled the style of an unmutilated inscription on the walls near the Sea of Marmora, commemorating repairs on that side of the city, in 1448, by George, Despot of Servia;[4] and in view of this resemblance, it is safe to conclude that a part of the money sent by the Servian king to fortify Constantinople against the common enemy was spent upon the land wall.

To the period of John VII. Palæologus, probably, must be

---

[1] Du Cange, *Familiæ Augustæ Byzantinæ*, p. 246.

[2] Zorzo Dolfin, s. 54.

[3] *Proceedings of the Greek Literary Syllogos of Consple.*, vol. xvi., 1885: *Archæological Supplement*, p. 38.

[4] Du Cange, *Familiæ Augustæ Byzantinæ; Familiæ Sclavonicæ*, ix. p. 336.

assigned the inscription which stands on the fifth tower north of
the Gate of Charisius:[1]

ΝΙΚΟΛΑΟΥ
ΚΑΒΑΛΛΑΡΙΟΥ
ΤΟΥ ΑΓΑΛΟΝΟϹ

"(Tower) of Nicholas Agalon, Cabalarius."

(16) On the first outer tower north of the Golden Gate, and
on the outer tower opposite the Gate of the Pempton, the name
Manuel Igari was found, placed a little below the inscriptions
on those towers in honour of John VII. Palæologus.[2]

At first it might be supposed that we have here the name of
the officer who superintended the repair of the fortifications in
the reign of that emperor. But, according to Leonard of Scio,[3]
Manuel Iagari, along with a certain monk, Neophytus of Rhodes,
had charge of such work immediately before the final siege,
while Constantine Dragoses, the last of the Byzantine emperors,
was making pathetic efforts to avert inevitable doom. Leonard
accuses Manuel and Neophytus of having, even at that crisis,
when the fate of the city hung in the balance, embezzled a large
part of the funds devoted to the restoration of the walls, thereby
leaving the fortifications in a state which made a successful
defence impossible: " Idcirco urbs prædonum incuria, in tanta
tempesta periit." It is said that after the capture of the city
the Turks discovered a considerable portion of the stolen money
concealed in a jar.

---

[1] Paspates, p. 42.   [2] *Ibid.*, p. 45.
[3] *Historia Cpolitanæ Urbis a Mahumete II. Captæ, per modum Epistolæ, die
Augusti, anno* 1453, *ad Nicolaum V.*, *Rom. Pont.*, Migne, vol. clix. p. 936.

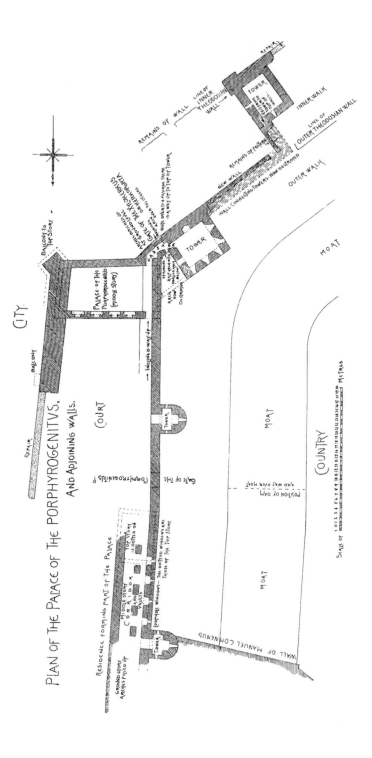

PLAN OF THE PALACE OF THE PORPHYROGENITVS,
AND ADJOINING WALLS.

CITY

REPAIR

BALCONY

BALCONY TO TOP STORY

Palace of the Porphyrogenitvs (MIDDLE STORY)

COURT

Gate of the Porphyrogenitus?

INCLINED WAY UP

Gate of the Porphyrogenitvs?

NOTE OVERLY EXPANSE THERE IS A WAY TO TOP OF TOWER

communication between tower and the room over the gate

ARCH
STAIRWAY

ARCH
NICHE HALF BURIED
MODERN BUILDINGS BELOW

NEW WALL

WALL CONNECTING TOWERS, NOW DESTROYED

REMAINS OF POSTERN

TOWER

TOWER

REMAINS OF WALL

LINE OF INNER THEODOSIAN WALL

OUTER THEODOSIAN WALL

LINE OF THEODOSIAN WALL

INNER WALK

OUTER WALK

REPAIR

RESIDENCE FORMING PART OF THE PALACE

TOP STORY LOOKING ON

MIDDLE STORY CORRIDOR AND VAULTS

TOP STORY WINDOWS — THE DOTTED WINDOWS ARE THOSE OF THE TOP STORY

GROUND STORY ARCHES FILLED UP

TOWER

TOWER

WALL OF MANUEL COMNENUS

MOAT

MOAT

MOAT

POSITION OF DAM AND WAY OVER MOAT

COUNTRY

Scale of   Metres

CHAPTER VII.

THE PALACE OF THE PORPHYROGENITUS.

THE ruined Byzantine palace, commonly styled Tekfour Serai, beside the Porta Xylokerkou was the Imperial residence, known as the Palace of the Porphyrogenitus (τὰ βασίλεια τοῦ Πορφυρο-γεννήτου : οἱ τοῦ Πορφυρογεννήτου οἶκοι),[1] and formed an annex to the great Palace of Blachernæ, which stood lower down the hill.

It is true, Gyllius supposed it to be the Palace of the Heb-domon, and his opinion, though contrary to all the evidence on the subject, has been generally accepted as correct. But the proof that the suburb of the Hebdomon was situated at Makri-keui, upon the Sea of Marmora, is overwhelming, and conse-quently the Palace of the Hebdomon must be sought in that neighbourhood.[2]

The evidence for the proper Byzantine name of Tekfour Serai [3] occurs in the passage in which Critobolus describes the positions occupied by the various divisions of the Turkish army, during the siege of 1453. According to that authority, the Turkish left

[1] Critobolus, i. c. 27 ; Cantacuzene, i. p. 305.
[2] See below, Chap. XIX.
[3] Tekfour Serai means Palace of the Sovereign, from a Persian word signifying Wearer of the Crown, Crowned Head. Leunclavius (*Pandectes Historiæ Turcicæ*, s. 56, Migne, vol. clix.) says that the Turks, in his day, styled the emperor, Tegguires. The derivation of Tekfour from the Greek τοῦ κυρίου is untenable.

wing extended from the Xylo Porta (beside the Golden Horn) [1]
to the Palace of the Porphyrogenitus, which was situated upon a
slope, and thence to the Gate of Charisius (Edirnè Kapoussi).[2]
The site thus assigned to the Palace of the Porphyrogenitus
corresponds exactly to that of Tekfour Serai, which stands on
the steep ascent leading from Egri Kapou to the Gate of
Adrianople.

All other references to the Palace of the Porphyrogenitus are
in accord with this conclusion, so far, at least, as they imply
the proximity of that residence to the Palace of Blachernæ.
When, for instance, Andronicus III., in 1328, entered Constantinople by the Gate of St. Romanus to wrest the government from the feeble hands of his grandfather Andronicus II.,
he took up his quarters, we are told, in the Palace of the
Porphyrogenitus, to be near the palace occupied by the
elder sovereign.[3]   That Andronicus II. was at the Palace of
Blachernæ is manifest from the fact that the peasants who witnessed the entrance of the rebel grandson into the city ran and
reported the event to the guards stationed at the Gate Gyrolimnè,[4] a gate leading directly to the Palace of Blachernæ.[5]

Again, the Palace of the Porphyrogenitus was occupied by
John Cantacuzene, in 1347, while negotiating with the Dowager-
Empress Anna of Savoy to be acknowledged the colleague of her
son, John Palæologus.[6]   Upon taking possession of that residence
he issued strict injunctions that no attack should be made upon
the palace in which the empress and her son were then living.
But the followers of Cantacuzene, hearing that Anna hesitated
to come to terms, disobeyed his orders and seized the fort at

---

[1] See below, p. 173.

[2] I. c. 27. Ἀπὸ τῆς Ξυλίνης πύλης ἀνιόντι μέχρι τῶν βασιλείων τοῦ
Πορφυρογεννήτου, καὶ φθάνοντι μέχρι τῆς λεγομένης πύλης τοῦ Χαρισοῦ.

[3] Cantacuzene, i. p. 305.   [4] Nicephorus Greg., ix. p. 420.

[5] See below, p. 127.   [6] Cantacuzene, iii. p. 607.

THE PALACE OF THE PORPHYROGENITUS (SOUTHERN FAÇADE).

THE PALACE OF THE PORPHYROGENITUS (NORTHERN FAÇADE).

Blachernæ, named the Castelion, which guarded that palace.[1]
Evidently the Palace of Blachernæ and the Palace of the Por-
phyrogenitus stood near each other.   Seven years later, John
Palæologus himself, upon his capture of the city, made the
Palace of the Porphyrogenitus his headquarters while arranging
for the abdication of Cantacuzene.[2]   And from the narrative
of the events on that occasion it is, again, manifest that the
Palace of the Porphyrogenitus was in the neighbourhood of the
Castelion and the Palace of Blachernæ.

By this identification, a flood of light is shed upon the
incidents of Byzantine history to which allusion has just been
made.

The palace, an oblong building in three stories, stands
between the two parallel walls which descend from the Porta
Xylokerkou for a short distance, towards the Golden Horn.
Its long sides, facing respectively north and south, are transverse
to the walls, while its short western and eastern sides rest, at the
level of the second story, upon the summit of the walls.

Its roof and two upper floors have disappeared, and nothing
remains but an empty shell.   The northern façade was supported
by pillars and piers, and its whole surface was decorated with
beautiful and varied patterns in mosaic, formed of small pieces of
brick and stone.   The numerous windows of the building were
framed in marble, and, with the graceful balconies on the
east and south, looked out upon the superb views which the
lofty position of the palace commanded.   The western façade,
being the most exposed to hostile missiles, was screened by a large
tower built on the west side of the Porta Xylokerkou, to the
injury, however, of the gate, which was thus partially blocked up.

A transverse wall erected at some distance to the north made

[1] Cantacuzene, iii. pp. 611, 612 ; Nicephorus Greg., xv. pp. 774-779.
[2] Cantacuzene, iv. pp. 290, 291.

the area between the two walls, upon which the palace rests, a spacious court, communicating by a gate at its north-eastern corner with the city, while a gate in the western wall led to the parateichion.[1]   The latter entrance is, probably, the one known as the Postern of the Porphyrogenitus, by which forty-two partisans of John Cantacuzene made good their escape from the city in 1341.[2]

According to Salzenberg, the palace belongs to the earlier half

MONOGRAM OF THE PALÆOLOGI.[3]

of the ninth century, and was the work of the Emperor Theophilus.[4]   But the name of the building is in favour of the view that we have here an erection of the Emperor Constantine Porphyrogenitus, and consequently a monument of the Art of the tenth century.   Constantine Porphyrogenitus was noted for the number of palaces he erected.[5]

[1] Tafferner (see below, p. 113, reference 5) speaks of a propylæum supported by ten fine columns as the entrance to the court of the palace from the city.

[2] Cantacuzene, iii. p. 138, Τὴν τοῦ Πορφυρογεννήτου προςαγορευομένην πυλίδα.

[3] From *Broken Bits of Byzantium.*   (By kind permission of Mrs. Walker.)

[4] Salzenberg, *Altchristliche Baudenkmæler von Constantinopel*, p. 125.

[5] Theophanes Cont., p. 450.   The date of the building is by no means settled. Dr. Paspates (p. 65) thinks it older than the time of Theodosius II. ; Dr. Mordtmann (p. 33) assigns it to the reign of that emperor.   It is a question for experts in Art to determine.

THE PALACE OF THE PORPHYROGENITUS (VIEW OF INTERIOR).

At the north-western end of the court stood another residence, the western façade of which, pierced by spacious windows, still surmounts the outer wall of the court. Over the second window (from the south) was inscribed the monogram of the legend on the arms of the Palæologi ;[1] Βασιλεὺς Βασιλέων Βασιλεύων Βασιλεύουσι.

Dr. Paspates[2] regarded this building as the Monastery of the Seven Orders of the Angels, mentioned by Cantacuzene ;[3] but that monastery, and the gate named after it, were at Thessalonica, and not at Constantinople. The building formed part of the Palace of the Porphyrogenitus.

Bullialdus, the annotator of Ducas,[4] speaking of the palace, says that the double-headed eagle of the Palæologi was to be seen on the lintel of one of the doors ; that the capitals of the pillars in the building bore the lilies of France ; and that several armorial shields were found there with the monogram—

These ornaments may be indications of repairs made by different occupants of the palace.[5]

---

[1] Paspates, p. 42.
[3] Lib. i. p. 268.
[2] Pages 62, 63.
[4] Page 612.

[5] Tafferner, chaplain to the Embassy sent by the Emperor Leopold I. to the Ottoman Court (*Cæsarea Legatio quam, mandante Augustissimo Rom. Imperatore Leopoldi I. ad Portam Ottomanicam, suscepit, perficitque Excellentissimus Dominus Walterus Comes de Leslie*, 1688), gives in his account of the mission (pp. 92, 93) the following description of the palace in his day :—" Præteriri non potuit quin inviseretur aula magni Constantini : Regia hæc ad Occidentem mœnibus adhæret ; nobilia sublimibus operibus instructissimo olim colle locata : tribus substructionibus moles assurrexerat ; altius nullum in tota urbe domicilium. Palatij coronis superstes marmore inciso elaborata tectum fulcit, ventis et imbribus pervium. Vastæ et eminentes præter sacræ antiquitatis ædilitatem è pario lapide fenestræ liquidò demonstrant, cujus palatij ornamenta fuerint, cujus aulæ etiamnum ruinæ sint. Propylæum decem columnæ magnitudinis et artificij dignitate conspicuæ sustinent : ejus in angulo desolatus, et ruderibus scatens puteus mœret. Pergula è centro prominens universæ

I

urbis conspectum explicat. Columnis constat auro passim illitis, cujus radios color viridis extiamnum animat. Grandiora lapidum fragmenta, cum primis fabricæ orna-mentis, ac fulcris cæteris in Moschèas translata sunt : sola tantæ molis vestigia, atque ex ungue cadaver nunc restat. Muro extimo meridiem versùs insertum parieti visitur Oratoriolum hominibus recipiendis sex opportunum : Angustia loci persuadet privatæ illud pietati Constantini sacrum fuisse. Squallet turpiter hæc Imperatorij operis majestas nunc inter arbusta, atque hederas et sive cœli injurias, sive immanitatem barbarorum, sive Christianorum incuriam accuses, non absimilem cum tempore rebus cæteris, utcunque floreant, internecionem minatur."

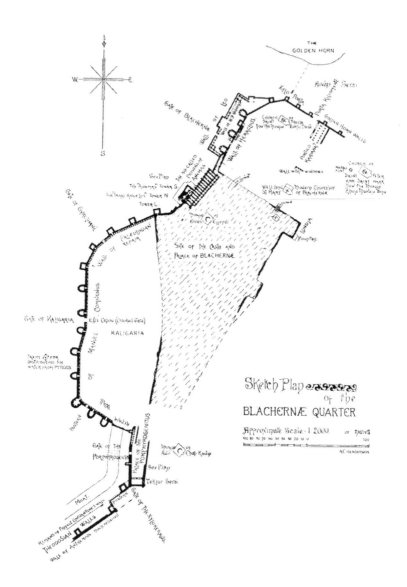

THE
GOLDEN HORN

W ⟶ E

S

Aïvân Seraï

Gate of BLACHERNÆ

WALL OF Iço

Kylo Porta

Porta Kiliomene
Golden Horn Walls

WALL OF HERACLIUS

Phanâr Kapou

Church of Saint Mary
Pou Tchoque Kork Sou

WALL with windows

CHURCH OF
SAINT MARY
AND SAINT MARK
Pou Tche Tchoque
Khoga Mustafa Pasha

See Plan

The "Anemas" Tower S.

The Isaac Angelus Tower N.

TOWER L.

WALL (and) Modern Church of
ST MARY of BLACHERNÆ

WALL OF
PALÆOLOGIAN
REPAIR

Tomb of
Hiros Celepdi

Tomb of
Egri Capou (Crooked Gate)

Site of the Castle and
Palace of BLACHERNÆ

Londa

Pompeg:

Gate of GYRROLINE

WALL OF MANUEL Comnenus

Gate of KALIGARIA

Egri Capou (Crooked Gate)

KALIGARIA

WALL OF MANUEL

Taxim Cistern for
distributing the
water from Pyrgos

Postern

Postern

Gate of THE
PORPHYROGENITUS

See Plan

PALACE OR HOUSE OF THE
PORPHYROGENITUS

Tower D.
Chah Kapou

Tekfur Seraï

MOAT

Postern

Remains of Repair (Constantine's) Wall

Gate of THK Xylokerkus

THEODOSIAN WALLS

WALL OF ANTHEMIUS (Doubly restored)

Sketch Plan
of the
BLACHERNÆ QUARTER

Approximate Scale · 1 2000   or metres

100 90 80 70 60 50 40 30 20 10 0   120

A.C. Henderson

CHAPTER VIII.

THE FORTIFICATIONS ON THE NORTH-WESTERN SIDE OF THE CITY, BEFORE THE SEVENTH CENTURY.

AT the Gate of the Xylokerkus, or the Kerko Porta, the Theodosian Walls come to an abrupt termination, and the line of defence from that point to the Golden Horn is continued by fortifications which, for the most part, did not exist before the seventh century. Along the greater portion of their course these bulwarks consisted of a single wall, without a moat ; but at a short distance from the water, where they stand on level ground, they formed a double wall, which was at one time protected by a moat and constituted a citadel at the north-western angle of the city.

With the exception of that citadel's outer wall, erected by Leo the Armenian, the defences from the Kerko Porta to the Golden Horn have usually been ascribed to the Emperor Heraclius.[1] But this opinion is at variance both with history, and with the striking diversity in construction exhibited by the various portions of the works. As a matter of fact, the fortifications extending from the Kerko Porta to the Golden Horn comprise walls that belong to, at least, three periods : the Wall of Heraclius, the Wall of Leo, and the Wall of Manuel

[1] Paspates, p. 19.

Comnenus.[1] Curiously enough, the Wall of Manuel Comnenus, though latest in time, stands first in order of position, for it intervenes between the Theodosian Walls, on the one hand, and the Heraclian and Leonine Walls, on the other.

Here, therefore, a question presents itself which must be answered before proceeding to the study of the walls just mentioned. If the various portions of the fortifications between the Kerko Porta and the Golden Horn did not come, respectively, into existence until the seventh, ninth, and eleventh centuries, how was the north-western side of the city defended previous to the erection of those walls?

Two answers have been given to this important and very difficult question. Both agree in maintaining that the city was defended on the north-west by the prolongation of the Theodosian Walls; but they differ as regards the precise direction in which the walls were carried down to the Golden Horn.

One view is that the Theodosian Walls upon leaving the Kerko Porta turned north-eastwards, to follow the *eastern* spur of the Sixth Hill,[2] along a line terminating somewhere in the vicinity of Balat Kapoussi.[3] According to this view, the quarter of Blachernæ, which until 627 lay outside the city limits,[4] was the territory situated between the spur just mentioned and the line occupied eventually by the Walls of Comnenus and Heraclius.

The second view on the subject is that the two Theodosian Walls were carried northwards along the *western* spur of the Sixth Hill, and enclosed it on every side. On this supposition, the suburb of Blachernæ, with its celebrated Church of the

---

[1] Dr. Mordtmann was the first to prove this. See below, p. 122.

[2] The Sixth Hill sends three spurs towards the Golden Horn, which may be distinguished as the eastern, middle, and western.

[3] This is the view of Dr. Paspates, pp. 2, 3, 92.

[4] Procopius (*De Æd.*, i. c. 3), speaking of the Church of Blachernæ, describes it as situated πρὸ τοῦ περιβόλου, ἐν χώρῳ καλουμένῳ Βλαχέρναις. Cf. *Paschal Chron.*, p. 726.

Theotokos, without the fortifications, was the plain extending from the foot of the western spur of the Sixth Hill to the Golden Horn, the plain occupied now by the quarter of Aivan Serai.[1]

In support of the first opinion, there is the undoubted fact that the Theodosian Walls, as they approach the Kerko Porta, bend north-eastwards, so that if continued in that direction they would reach the Golden Horn near the Greek Church of St. Demetrius, to the west of Balat Kapoussi.

The opinion that the Theodosian Walls were carried to the foot of the western spur of the Sixth Hill rests upon the fact that traces of old fortifications enclosing that spur are still distinctly visible; while the Theodosian Moat is, moreover, continued towards Aivan Serai, until it is stopped by the Wall of Manuel, which runs transversely to it.[2]

The fortifications referred to are found mostly to the rear of the Comnenian Wall, but portions of them are seen also to the north of it.

One line of the fortifications proceeded from the Kerko Porta along the western flank of the spur, and joined the city walls a little to the south of the "Tower of Isaac Angelus;" another line ran from that gate along the eastern side of the spur to the fountain Tsinar Tchesmè in the quarter of Londja, a short distance to the south-east of the Holy Well which marks the site of the Church of Blachernæ; while a third wall, facing the Golden Horn, defended the northern side of the spur, and abutted against the city walls, very near the southern end of the Wall of Heraclius.[3]   Within the acropolis formed by these

---

[1] This is the view of Dr. Mordtmann, p. 11.

[2] Previous to the erection of Manuel's Wall, the Moat may have continued further north, protecting the wall along the western side of the spur.

[3] Cf. Paspates, pp. 92–99, regarding the remains of the walls around the spur, the area they enclose, and their character. According to him, the wall on the eastern side of the spur measures m. 157.81 in length, and is in some parts m. 13–14 high;

works of defence, the Palace of Blachernæ and the Palace of the Porphyrogenitus were in due time erected.

Both answers to the question before us have much in their favour, and possibly the truth on the subject is to be found in their combination. Their respective values as rival theories will, perhaps, be more easily estimated, if we begin with the consideration of the second answer.

That the western spur of the Sixth Hill was a fortified position early in the history of the city can scarcely be disputed. It must have been so, to commence at the lowest date, before the erection of the Wall of the Emperor Manuel in the twelfth century ; for it was to get clear of the fortifications on that spur that the Comnenian Wall describes the remarkable detour it makes in proceeding from the court of the Palace of the Porphyrogenitus towards the Golden Horn, running out westwards for a considerable distance before taking a northerly course in the direction of the harbour. Then, there is reason to believe that the spur was fortified as early as the seventh century. This is implied in the accounts we have of the siege of Constantinople by the Avars in 627, when we hear of fortifications, named the Wall of Blachernæ,[1] the Pteron[2] or Proteichisma,[3] outside of which stood the Church of Blachernæ and the Church of St. Nicholas.[4]

For these sanctuaries were situated precisely at the foot of the western spur of the Sixth Hill, the site of the former being marked by the Holy Well of Blachernæ at Aivan Serai, that of

the wall along the northern side of the spur is m. 180.90 long, and m. 13-14 high ; the wall on the western side of the spur is m. 35 long, and as high as the adjoining walls of the city.

[1] *Paschal Chron.*, p. 724, τὸ τεῖχος Βλαχερνῶν. This was before the erection of the Wall of Heraclius.

[2] *Ibid.*, p. 726, ἔξωθεν τοῦ καλουμένου Πτεροῦ.

[3] Nicephorus, Patriarcha CP., p. 20, τὸ Βλαχερνῶν προτείχισμα τὸ καλούμενον Πτερόν.

[4] *Paschal Chron., ut supra ;* cf. Procopius, *De Æd.*, i. c. 3, c. 6.

Archway leading to the Gate of the Xylokerkus (Screen Tower).

THE PALACE OF THE PORPHYROGENITUS (FROM THE WEST).

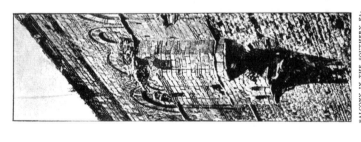

BALCONY IN THE SOUTHERN FA-
ÇADE OF THE PALACE OF THE
PORPHYROGENITUS.

the latter by the Holy Well in the ground between the Wall of
Heraclius and the Wall of Leo.

It is also in favour of the presence of fortifications on the
spur in the seventh century to find that the historians of the
Avar siege are silent as to any danger incurred by the Palace
of Blachernæ, which stood on the spur, when the Church of
St. Nicholas was burnt down, and when the Church of Blachernæ
narrowly escaped the same fate.   A similar silence is observed
as to any advantage derived by the palace from the erection
of the Wall of Heraclius, at the close of the war.

But the age of these fortifications may be carried back to a
still earlier date than the seventh century; for, according to the
Notitia, the Fourteenth Region of the city, which stood on the
Sixth Hill, was defended by a wall of its own, *proprio muro
vallata,* so as to appear a distinct town.[1]   The fortifications
on the Sixth Hill may therefore claim to have originally constituted the defences of that Region, and therefore to be as
old, at least, as the reign of Theodosius II.

But although the origin of the fortifications around the
western spur of the Sixth Hill may thus be carried so far back,
it is a mistake to regard them as a structural prolongation of the
Theodosian Walls.   On the contrary, they are distinct and
independent constructions.   They proceed northwards, while the
latter make for the north-east; so that the Wall of Anthemius,
if produced, would stand to the east of the former, while the
Wall of the Prefect Constantine under similar circumstances
would cut them transversely.   Furthermore, the outer wall,
north of the Kerko Porta, is built almost at right angles
against the wall of the Prefect Constantine, with a distinct line
of junction, and stands so close to the Kerko Porta that the gate,
what with the wall on one side and the tower screening the

---

[1] *Notitia, ad Reg. XIV.*

western façade of the Palace of Porphyrogenitus [1] upon the other, is almost crushed between them. Such a situation could never have been assigned to the gate, if the walls on either hand belonged to the same construction. It should also be added that the masonry of the walls around the spur is different from that in the Walls of Theodosius.

How the non-Theodosian character of the walls to the north of the Kerko Porta is to be accounted for admits of more than one explanation. It may be due to changes in works of Theodosian origin, or to the fact that they are works of an earlier period,[2] or to the fact that they are works of a later age. On the supposition that these fortifications defended originally the Fourteenth Region, the second explanation is the most probable, for the division of the city into Regions was anterior to Theodosius II., and there is every reason to believe that the isolated Fourteenth Region was a fortified suburb from the earliest period of its history.[3]

Accordingly, the second answer to the question how the north-western side of the city was defended before the erection of the Walls of Heraclius, Leo, and Manuel Comnenus, would have more in its favour if it maintained that the defence was effected by the junction of the Theodosian Walls with pre-existing fortifications around the western spur of the Sixth Hill.[4]

The chief difficulty attending this view is that the *Notitia*

---

[1] See above, p. 111. See also illustration facing p. 118.

[2] With alterations made in the course of time by repairs.

[3] *Notitia, ad Reg. XIV.* "Regio sane licet in urbis quartadecima numeretur, tamen quia spatio interjecto divisa est, muro proprio vallata alterius quomodo speciem civitatis ostendit."

Dionysius Byzantius derives the name Blachernæ from a barbarian chieftain who was settled there. If so, it is extremely probable that the Sixth Hill was fortified, to some extent, even before the foundation of Constantinople. See Gyllius, *De Top. CP.*, iv. c. 5.

[4] On this view, a wall must, also, be supposed to have proceeded from Londja to the Golden Horn, completing the circuit of the fortifications around the city.

speaks of the Fourteenth Region as still an isolated suburb in the reign of Theodosius II.[1]

As regards the opinion that the Theodosian Walls proceeded from the Kerko Porta to the Golden Horn in a north-eastern course and reached the water between the Church of St. Demetrius and Balat Kapoussi, it has upon its side the patent fact that those walls, if produced according to their trend at the Kerko Porta, would certainly follow the line indicated. On this view, the walls around the western spur of the Sixth Hill were either the fortifications of the Fourteenth Region (modified), or walls built expressly to defend the Palace of Blachernæ, after the fifth century.

The trend of the walls at the Kerko Porta affords, unquestionably, a very strong argument for this view of the case. But the view is open to objections. The absence of all traces of the walls along the line indicated should, perhaps, not be pressed, as such works are apt to disappear when superseded. A more serious objection is that the Theodosian Moat does not follow the north-eastern course of the walls, but proceeds northwards, for a short distance, in the direction of Aivan Serai.

Furthermore, if the western spur of the Sixth Hill was already fortified when the Theodosian Walls were built, it is reasonable to suppose that the land defences of the city were completed by the simple expedient of uniting the new works with the old. Any other proceeding appears cumbrous and superfluous.

Still, after all is said, the information we have is so meagre, the changes made in the walls beside the Kerko Porta have manifestly been so numerous, that a decided judgment upon the point at issue does not seem warranted by the evidence at our command.

[1] *Notitia, ad Reg. XIV.*

CHAPTER IX.

THE WALL OF THE EMPEROR MANUEL COMNENUS.

ACCORDING to Nicetas Choniates,[1] a portion of the city fortifications was erected by the Emperor Manuel Comnenus.

The historian alludes to that work when describing the site upon which the Crusaders established their camp in 1203, and from his account of the matter there can be no doubt regarding the portion intended. The Latin camp, says Nicetas,[2] was pitched on the hill which faced the western front of the Palace of Blachernæ, and which was separated from the city walls by a strip of level ground, extending from the Golden Horn, on the north, to the wall built by the Emperor Manuel, on the south. This is an unmistakable description of the hill which stands to the west of the fortifications between the Golden Horn and Egri Kapou, and which is separated from those fortifications by a narrow plain, as by a trench or gorge. Consequently, the wall erected by the Emperor Manuel must be sought at the plain's southern extremity ; and there, precisely, commences a line of wall which displays, as far as the north-western corner of the

[1] Page 719 ; cf. *Ibid.*, p. 500 ; Cinnamus, p. 274.

[2] *Ut supra*, Περὶ τὸ γεώλοφον ἀφ' οὗπερ ὁρατὰ μὲν τὰ ἐν Βλαχέρναις ἀνάκτορα, ὁπόσα νένευκε πρὸς ἑσπέραν. Περὶ δὲ γε τὴν τούτου ὑπόβασιν ὑπτιάζει τις αὔλειος, πρὸς μεσημβρίαν μὲν ἐς τὸ τεῖχος λήγουσα ὅπερ ἔρυμα τῶν ἀρχείων ὁ βασιλεὺς ἀνήγειρε Μανουὴλ, κατὰ δὲ βορρᾶν ἄνεμον τῇ θαλάσσῃ ἐγγίζουσα.

TOWER OF THE WALL OF THE EMPEROR MANUEL COMNENUS.

court of the Palace of the Porphyrogenitus, a style of workmanship perfectly distinct from any found elsewhere in the bulwarks
of the city.

The object of building this wall was to add to the security of
the Palace of Blachernæ, which became the favourite residence
of the Imperial Court in the reign of Alexius Comnenus,[1]
and which Manuel himself enlarged and beautified.[2] The
new wall was not only stronger than the earlier defences of
the palace, but had also the advantage of removing the point
of attack against this part of the city to a greater distance from
the Imperial residence. At the same time, the older fortifications
were allowed to remain as a second line of defence.

In construction the wall is a series of lofty arches closed on
the outer face, and built of larger blocks of stone[3] than those
generally employed in the Walls of Theodosius. On account of
the steepness of the slope on which it, for the most part, stands,
it was unprotected by a moat, but to compensate for this lack
the wall was more massive, and flanked by stronger towers
than other portions of the fortifications. At the summit the
wall measured fifteen feet in thickness. Of its nine towers, the
first six, commencing from the court of the Palace of the Porphyrogenitus, are alternately round and octagonal; the seventh and
eighth are octagonal; the last is square.

The wall was provided with a public gate and, apparently,
two posterns.

One postern, opening on the Theodosian parateicheion, was
in the curtain[4] extending from the outer wall of the court of
the Palace of the Porphyrogenitus to the first tower of Manuel's
Wall. The other postern stood between the second and third

---

[1] Anna Comn., vi. p. 275, *et passim.*
[2] Nicetas Chon., p. 269; Benjamin of Toledo, p. 12.
[3] As a rule, two to four courses of stone, alternating with six to nine courses of brick.
[4] This is a piece of Turkish repair, in which the lintel of a postern is found.

towers, and is remarkable for being the only entrance in the city walls furnished with a drip-stone. Dr. Paspates[1] identified it with the Paraportion of St. Kallinikus; but the postern of that name is mentioned in history before the erection of Manuel's Wall.

Between the sixth and seventh towers was the Public Gate, now styled Egri Kapou. By some authorities, as already stated,[2] it has been identified with the Porta Charisiou, but it is, beyond question, the Porta Kaligaria, so conspicuous in the last siege of the city.[3] This is clear from the following circumstances: The Porta Kaligaria pierced the wall which protected the quarter known, owing to the manufacture of military shoes (caliga) there, as the Kaligaria (ἐν τοῖς Καλιγαρίοις). That wall stood near the palace of the emperor; it was a single line of fortifications, distinguished for its strength, but without a moat.[4] It occupied, moreover, such a position that from one of its towers the Emperor Constantine Dragoses and his friend the historian Phrantzes were able to reconnoître, early in the morning of the fatal 29th of May, the operations of the Turkish army before the Theodosian Walls, and hear the ominous sounds of the preparations for the last assault.[5] All these particulars hold true only of the wall in which Egri Kapou is situated; and hence that gate must be the Porta Kaligaria.

The only inscription found on the Wall of Manuel consists of the two words, ΥΠΕΡ ΕΥΧΗC, on a stone built into the left side of the entrance which leads from within the city into the square tower above mentioned.

In the siege of 1453, this wall, on account of its proximity to

[1] Page 62.   [2] See above, p. 83.   [3] Pusculus, iv. 177.
[4] Nicolo Barbaro, p. 794, "Questa Calegaria si xe apresso del palazzo de, l'imperador;" p. 784, "Li no ve iera barbacani." Leonard of Scio, "Ad partem illam murorum simplicium, qua nec fossatis, nec antemurali tutebatur, Calegariam dictam." Again he says, "Murus ad Caligariam erat perlatus, fortisque."
[5] Phrantzes, p. 280.

the Palace of Blachernæ, was the object of special attack ; but all the attempts of the Turkish gunners and miners failed to open a breach in it.[1]   A battery of three cannon, one of them the huge piece cast by Orban, played against these bulwarks with such little effect that the Sultan ordered the guns to be transferred to the battery before the Gate of St. Romanus.[2] The skilled miners who were brought from the district around Novobrodo, in Servia, to undermine the wall succeeded in shaking down only part of an old tower, and all the mines they opened were countermined by John Grant, a German engineer in the service of the Greeks.[3]

The tower from which the emperor and Phrantzes reconnoitred the Turkish movements was, Dr. Paspates thinks, the noble tower which stands at the point where the wall bends to descend the slope towards the Golden Horn.[4]

The portion of the fortifications, some 453 feet in length, extending from the square tower in the wall just described to the fourth tower to the north (the tower bearing an inscription in honour of Isaac Angelus),[5] is considered by one authority to be also a part of the Wall of Manuel Comnenus.[6]   If so, it must have undergone great alterations since that emperor's time, for in its construction and general appearance it is very different from the Comnenian ramparts.   It is built of smaller blocks of stone ; its bricks are much slighter in make ; its arches less filled with masonry ; its four towers are all square, and glaringly inferior to the splendid towers in Manuel's undoubted work ; while, immediately to the south of the square tower above

---

[1] Leonard of Scio, " Horribilem perinde bombardam (quamquam major alai quam vix bovum quinquagenta centum juga vehebant) ob partem illam . . . lapide qui palmis meis undecim ex meis ambibat in gyro, ex ea murum conterebant."

[2] *Ibid.*   [3] *Ibid.;* N. Barbaro, May 16, 21–25 ; Phrantzes, p. 244.

[4] Paspates, p. 22 ; Phrantzes, p. 280.

[5] See below, p. 132.   The tower is marked L on Map facing p. 115.

[6] Mordtmann, p. 35.

mentioned one can see, from within the city, a line of junction
between the wall to the south and the wall to the north of that
tower, indicating in the plainest possible manner the juxtaposi-
tion of two perfectly distinct structures. And in point of fact,
three inscriptions recording repairs are found on the latter wall.
One inscription, on the fourth tower, belongs to the reign of Isaac
Angelus[1] and bears the date 1188. Another is seen among the
Turkish repairs executed on the city side of the second tower
of the wall, and records the date, "In the year 6824 (1317),
November 4;" the year, as we have seen, in which Irene, the
empress of Andronicus II., died, leaving large sums of money,
which that emperor devoted, mainly, to the restoration of the
bulwarks of the capital.[2] The third inscription stands on the
curtain between the third and fourth towers of the wall, immediately below the parapet, and commemorates repairs executed
in 1441 by John VII. Palæologus, who was concerned in the
reconstruction of the Outer Theodosian Wall. It reads :

ΙѠΑΝΝΗC ΕΝ ΧѠ ΤѠ
ѲѠ ΠΙCΤΟC ΒΑCΙΛΕΥC
ΚΑΙ ΑΥΤΟΚΡΑΤѠΡ ΡѠΜΑΙѠΝ
Ο ΠΑΛΑΙΟΛΟΓΟC ΚΑΤΑ ΜΗΝΑ
ΑΥΓΟΥCΤΟΥ ΤΗ Δ
ΤΟΥ ϚⲯΜѲ ΕΤΟΥC (6949).

"John Palæologus, faithful King and Emperor of the Romans, in Christ,
God ; on the second of the month of August of the year 1441."

To the north of the second tower in the wall before us is a
gateway which answers to the description of the Gate of Gyrolimnè (πύλη τῆς Γυρολίμνης) ; for the Gate of Gyrolimnè, like
this entrance, stood in the immediate vicinity of the Palace of
Blachernæ, and was so near the hill on which the Crusaders

---

[1] See below, p. 132.
[2] See above, p. 103. The inscription is now reversed, and stands a little above
the base of the tower.

Tower with inscription of Isaac Angelus.

THE PALÆOLOGIAN WALL, NORTH OF THE WALL OF THE EMPEROR MANUEL COMNENUS.

THE GATE OF GYROLIMNÈ.

encamped in 1203 that the Greeks stationed at the gate and the enemy on the hill were almost within speaking distance.[1]

The gate derived its name from a sheet of water called the Silver Lake (Ἀργυρὰ Λίμνη), at the head of the Golden Horn, and beside which was an Imperial palace.[2] The gate was at the service of the Palace of Blachernæ, a fact which, doubtless, explains the decoration of the arch of the entrance with three Imperial busts.[3]

Several historical reminiscences are attached to the gate. Through it, probably, the leaders of the Fourth Crusade went to and fro in carrying on their negotiations with Isaac Angelus.[4] By it Andronicus the Younger went forth in hunter's garb, with his dogs and falcons, as if to follow the chase, but in reality to join his adherents and raise the standard of revolt against his grandfather.[5] Hither that prince came thrice in the course of his rebellion, and held parley with the officials of the palace, as they stood upon the walls, regarding terms of peace ;[6] and here the intelligence that he had entered the city was brought by the peasants who had seen him admitted early in the morning through the Gate of St. Romanus.[7]

To this gate Cantacuzene also came at the head of his troops in 1343, to sound the disposition of the capital during his contest with Apocaucus and the Empress Anna.[8]

---

[1] Nicetas Chon., pp. 719, 720.

[2] Anna Comnena, x. p. 48 ; Albert Aquensis, lib. ii. c. 10, speaks of certain gates, versus Sanctum Argenteum ; while Tudebodus Imitatus et Continuatus (*Auteurs Occidentaux sur les Croisades*, vol. iii. p. 178) states that Bohemond, who, according to Anna Comnena (x. p. 61) and Ville-Hardouin (c. 33), lodged at the Monastery of SS. Cosmas and Damianus, in the Cosmidion (Eyoub), was assigned quarters—extra civitatem in Sancto Argenteo. The Sanctus Argenteus of these writers was doubtless the church dedicated to the saints above mentioned, who were styled the Anargyri (Without Money). The name of the bay and the epithet of the saints were probably connected.

[3] See foot of List of Illustrations.

[4] Ville-Hardouin, c. 39, 40, 46, 47.

[5] Cantacuzene, i. pp. 89, 90.

[6] *Ibid.*, i. pp. 255, 289, 290.

[7] Nicephorus Greg., ix. pp. 420, 421.

[8] Cantacuzene, iii. p. 501.

THE PALACE OF BLACHERNÆ.

Τὸ ἐν Βλαχέρναις Βασίλειον, Παλάτιον.

Until the site of the Palace of Blachernæ is excavated, little can be added to the information which Du Cange [1] and Paspates [2] have collected respecting that Imperial residence, from the statements made on the subject by writers during the Byzantine period.   If the quarter of Egri Kapou, on the western spur of the Sixth Hill, was included in the Fourteenth Region of the city, the Palace of Blachernæ appears first as the palace which, according to the *Notitia,* adorned that Region.[3]   In the reign of Anastasius I. the residence was enlarged by the addition of the Triclinus Anastasiacus (Τρίκλινος 'Αναστασιακὸς),[4] and in the tenth century [5] it boasted, moreover, of the Triclinus of the Holy Shrine (Τρίκλινος τῆς ἀγίας σοροῦ), named so in honour of the shrine in which the robe and mantle of the Theotokos were kept in the Church of Blachernæ ; the Triclinus Danubius (Τρίκλινος Δανουβιὸς) ; and the Portico Josephiacus (τὸν Πόρτικα 'Ιωσηφιακὸν). Under Alexius I. Comnenus it was frequently occupied by the Court, and there the emperor received the leaders of the First Crusade, Peter the Hermit, Godfrey of Bouillon, Bohemond, and others.[6]   By Manuel Comnenus it was repaired and embellished [7] to an extent which obtained for it the name of the New Palace,[8] and it was one of the sights of the capital with which he entertained Amaury, King of Jerusalem.[9]   The lofty building named after the Empress Irene,[10] and, probably, the Domus Polytimos,[11]

---

[1] *Constantinopolis Christiana,* ii. pp. 130–132.

[2] Chap. iv.

[3] *Notitia, ad Reg. XIV.*

[4] Suidas, *Ad vocem, Anastasius.*

[5] Constant. Porphyr., *De Cer.*, pp. 542, 543.

[6] Anna Comn., x. pp. 36, 54, 63.

[7] Nicetas Chon., p. 269.

[8] William of Tyre, xx. c. 24.

[9] William of Tyre, *ut supra.*

[10] Nicetas Chon., p. 720.

[11] *Ibid.*, p. 351.

Palaeologian Repairs.

GENERAL VIEW OF THE WALL OF THE EMPEROR MANUEL COMNENUS.

were the work of Manuel Comnenus. He also increased, as we have seen, the security of the palace by the erection of new bulwarks; to which Isaac Angelus added a tower.[1] In 1203 the palace was the scene of the negotiations between the latter emperor and the envoys of Baldwin of Flanders and Henrico Dandolo, the leaders of the Fourth Crusade.[2] In 1204, upon the capture of the city by the Crusaders, it surrendered to Henry, the brother of Baldwin,[3] but the Latin emperors seem to have preferred the Palace of the Bucoleon for their residence.

Baldwin II., however, resided in the Palace of Blachernæ, and left it in such a filthy condition that when taken possession of by the Greeks in 1261, Michael Palæologus could not occupy it until it had been thoroughly cleaned and renovated.[4] It was the usual residence of the Byzantine Court during the period of the Palæologi,[5] and from this palace the last emperor who sat upon the throne of Constantinople went forth to die "in the winding-sheet of his empire."[6] All descriptions of the palace agree in representing it as of extraordinary splendour.[7] Foreign visitors could not find words in which to give an idea of its magnificence and wealth. According to them, its exterior appearance was incomparable in beauty, while within it was decorated with gold, and mosaics, and colours, and marbles, and columns, and jewels, at a cost hard to estimate, and with a skill that could be found nowhere else in the world.[8]

The hill on which the palace stood was partly artificial, to furnish a suitable platform or terrace for the group of buildings which composed the residence, and to afford wide

---

[1] See below, p. 143.
[2] Ville-Hardouin, c. 39.
[3] *Ibid.*, c. 55.
[4] Pachymeres, vol. i. pp. 144, 161.
[5] Cantacuzene, i. p. 305; iv. pp. 290, 291; Nicephorus Greg., ix. p. 420, etc.
[6] Phrantzes, p. 280.
[7] Nicetas Chon., p. 269.
[8] See Benjamin of Toledo, and Odo de Dogilo, iv. p. 37, both of whom visited the palace in the reign of Manuel Comnenus.

K

views over the harbour, the city, and the country beyond the
walls—"triplicem habitantibus jucunditatem offerens," as Odo
de Dogilo aptly remarks, "mare, campus, urbemque, alterius
despicit." The palace derived much of its importance from its
proximity to the venerated shrine of the Theotokos of Blachernæ.
And the ease with which the country could be reached from it,
to enjoy the pleasures of the chase, must not be overlooked in
explaining the favour with which the palace was regarded.[1] It
should be added that the palace stood within the fortified enclosure[2] around the western spur of the Sixth Hill, the Castelion
of Blachernæ (Τὸ ἐν Βλαχέρναις φρούριον, μέρος καὶ αὐτὸ τοῦ περὶ
τὰ βασίλεια φρουρίου ὃν Καστέλιον προσαγορευόμενον).[3]

---

[1] Cantacuzene, i. pp. 89, 90.   [2] See Map facing p. 115.
[3] Cantacuzene, iii. pp. 611, 612; Nicephorus Greg., xv. pp. 774–779.

PLAN OF THE SO-CALLED PRISON OF ANEMAS.

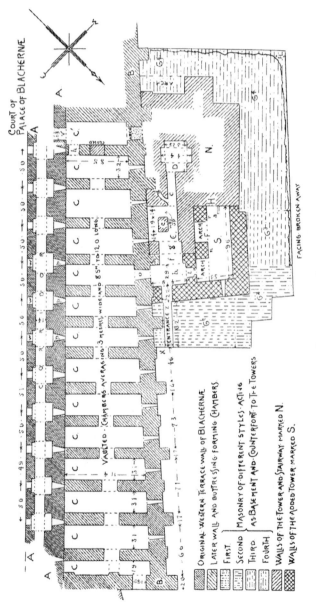

Court of Palace of Blacherne

Vaulted Chambers averaging 3 metres wide and 8⋅5″ to 12⋅0 long.

FACING BROKEN AWAY

SCALE OF METRES

Original Western Terrace Wall of Blacherne
Later Wall and Buttressing forming Chambers
First
Second ⎱ Masonry of different styles, acting
Third ⎰ as Basement and Counterfort to the Towers
Fourth
Walls of the Tower and Stairway marked N.
Walls of the added Tower marked S.

CHAPTER X.

THE TOWER OF ANEMAS—THE TOWER OF ISAAC ANGELUS.

THE next portion of the walls to be considered, beginning at the tower marked with an inscription in honour of Isaac Angelus,[1] and terminating at the junction of the Wall of Heraclius with the Wall of Leo, has undergone many changes in the course of its history, and, consequently, presents problems which cannot be solved in the actual state of our knowledge. After all is said on the subject, there will be room for wide difference of opinion.

Originally, it would seem, this portion of the walls formed part of the defences around the outlying Fourteenth Region of the city ; later, it constituted the north-western front of the enclosure around the Palace of Blachernæ.

It is remarkable for its dimensions, rising in some places 68 feet above the exterior ground-level, with a thickness varying from $33\frac{1}{4}$ to $61\frac{1}{2}$ feet. Inside the city the ground reaches the level of the parapet-walk.

The wall is flanked by three towers, the second and third being built side by side, with one of their walls in common. In the body of the wall behind the twin towers, and for some distance to the north of them, were three stories of twelve

---

[1] See below, p. 132.

chambers, presenting in their ruin the most impressive spectacle to be found in the circuit of the fortifications.

The first[1] of the three towers stands at the south-western angle of the enclosure around the Palace of Blachernæ, where the fortifications around the western spur of the Sixth Hill, to the rear of the Wall of Manuel, join the wall now under consideration ; the tower's upper chamber being on the level of the palace area. Upon the tower is the following inscription, in honour of the Emperor Isaac Angelus :

ΠΡΟϹΤΑΞΙ ΑΥΤΟΚΡΑΤΟΡΟϹ ΑΓΓΕΛΟΥ ΙΑϹΑΑΚΙΟΥ
ΠΥΡΓΟϹ ΕΚ ΠΑΡΑϹΤΑϹΕωϹ ΔΙΜΕΗΙ ΒΑϹΙΛΕΙΟΥ ΕΤ
ϚΠΧΙ (6696).[2]

"Tower, by command of the Emperor Isaac Angelus, under the superintendence of Basil . . . (?) in the year 1188."

The twin towers rise to a great height, and are supported along their base by a massive buttress or counter-fort,[1] $G^1 G^2 G^3 G^4$, that stands 23 feet above the present ground-level, and projects from $19\frac{1}{2}$ to 26 feet beyond the towers.

The tower N, an irregular quadrilateral building in two stories, measures 48 feet by 43 feet ; the tower S, also quadrilateral, is 36 feet by 47 feet. But although closely associated, the two buildings differ greatly in style of construction. The masonry of N is irregular, having a large number of pillars inserted into it ; often partially, so that many of them project like mock artillery. On the other hand, the tower S is carefully put together with the usual alternate courses of stone and brickwork, and is, moreover, ornamented with a string-course. A similar diversity of style is observable in the counter-fort. The portion about the tower N is built of small stones roughly joined, whereas the portion about the tower S consists of

---

[1] See tower L, in Map facing p. 115.
[2] See illustration facing p. 248.

splendid large blocks, regularly hewn, and carefully fitted. Manifestly the towers are not the work of the same period.

The tower N is commonly regarded as the tower of Isaac Angelus; while the tower S has been considered, since Dr. Paspates propounded the opinion, to be the Tower of Anemas,[1] which stood in the vicinity of the Palace of Blachernæ, and is famous in the annals of Constantinople as a prison for political offenders of high rank. The chambers in the body of the wall, behind and to the north of the towers, Dr. Paspates thinks, were the cells of that celebrated prison.

How far these views are correct can be determined only after the towers and the chambers in the adjoining wall have been carefully surveyed. The plan attached to this chapter will render the survey easier and clearer.[2]

At x was a small arched postern, by which one entered the vaulted tunnel Z, that led through the counter-fort G' to the gateway l in the north-eastern side of the tower S. The sill of the postern x is now nearly 10 feet above the exterior ground-level, but originally it was higher, so that persons could pass in and out only by means of a ladder that could be withdrawn at pleasure. The postern x, the tunnel Z, and the gateway l are now built up with solid masonry to the spring of the vault, obliging the explorer to make his way on his hands and knees in a most uncomfortable manner.[3] Judging from the carefulness of the work, the passage was blocked before the Turkish Conquest.

---

[1] Pages 22–32, where Dr. Paspates gives an interesting account of his discovery and exploration of the chambers.

[2] The plan was taken by Mr. Hanford W. Edson, formerly Instructor in Mathematics at Robert College. It was drawn by Professor Alfred Hamlin, of Columbia College, and revised by Mr. Arthur E. Henderson, Architect.

[3] Since the above was written this way of entering the tower and chambers has been closed. One gains admittance now at the opening v, from the courtyard of the Mosque of Aivas Effendi.

By the gateway l one enters the lofty vestibule b, now in total darkness, so that all further exploration requires the aid of artificial light. The original floor of the vestibule is buried below a mass of earth which stands at the present level of Z and l.

In the wall to the right is a low arched niche, i; in the wall g, directly in front of the explorer, a wide breach opens into E; while in the wall to the left is a loophole O, now on the level of the present floor of b.

Crawling first through O, one finds one's self in a spacious vaulted hall, some 200 feet long, and from 29 to 40 feet wide. The lower portion of the hall is filled with *débris* and earth, piled unevenly upon the floor, in great mounds and deep hollows, which add indeed to the weirdness of the scene, but, unfortunately, render a complete exploration of the interior impossible.

Thirteen buttress-walls, pierced by three arches superposed, run transversely across the hall, from the wall AA to the wall BB, and divide the interior into fourteen compartments, which average nearly 10 feet in breadth, and vary in length from about 27 to 40 feet; the walls AA and BB standing further apart, as they proceed from south-west to north-east.

These compartments, excepting the first and last, were divided, as the cavities for fixing joists in the buttresses prove, into three stories of twelve chambers, the superposed arches affording continuous communication between the chambers on the different floors. The chambers on the ground floor, so far as appears, were totally dark, but those on the two upper stories received light and air through the large loophole in the wall BB, with which each of them was provided. The compartment C′ led to the chamber in the second story of the tower N, and at

the same time communicated at v with the terrace on which
the Palace of Blachernæ stood, and where the Mosque of Aivas
Effendi is now erected.

The face of the wall AA is pierced by two tiers of loopholes, which are openings in two superposed corridors or
galleries constructed in the body of the wall AA. These
loopholes occur at irregular distances from the buttress-walls,
and some of them are partially closed by the latter, while others
are completely so.

As the galleries in AA are blocked with earth at various
points, they cannot be explored thoroughly. At the north-
eastern end, the upper gallery opens on the garden of a Turkish
house near the Heraclian Wall. Whether the south-western
end communicated with the court of the Palace of Blachernæ
cannot be determined.

Returning to the vestibule *b*, and crawling next through the
opening at *i*, the explorer finds himself in F, a vaulted
chamber over 29 feet long, and about 17 feet wide. What
the original height of the apartment was cannot be ascertained,
the floor being covered with a deep bed of fine dark loam,
but the ceiling is still some 23 feet high. Below a line
nearly 14 feet from the ceiling, as a sloping ledge at that
elevation makes evident, the north-eastern and north-western
walls of the apartment are much thicker than above that
point. Over the ledge in the north-eastern wall is a loophole.
The south-eastern wall is strengthened with two arches ;
while the ceiling is pierced by a circular hole, which com-
municates with the room on the higher story of the tower.
When first explored by Dr. Paspates, a well nearly 18 feet
deep was found sunk in the floor.[1]

---

[1] In the opinion of some authorities, *e.g.* Professor Strzygowski, this apartment
was a cistern.

Before leaving the chamber the explorer should notice the shaft of a pillar which protrudes from the south-western wall, like the shafts of the pillars built into the open sides of the tower N.

Returning once more to the vestibule *b*, we proceed to the breach in the wall *g*, and enter E. That the breach was made on a systematic plan is clear from the half-arch *f*, which was constructed to support the building after the wall *g* had been weakened by the opening made in it.

E was a stairway-turret, in which an inclined plane, without steps, winded about the newel, *e*, upwards and downwards. The turret is filled with earth to the present level of the vestibule *b*, so that one cannot descend the stairway below that point ; but there can be no doubt whatever that the stairway conducted to the original floor of the vestibule *b*, and to the gateway *l*, and thence to the tunnel and postern in the counterfort. Whether it led also to an entrance to the chambers C C C cannot be discovered under existing circumstances. The object of the breach in *g* was to establish communication between the stairway, the vestibule *b*, and the tunnel Z, after the original means of communication between them had been blocked by raising the floors of the tunnel and the vestibule to their present level, in the manner already described.

The stairway winds thirteen times about its newel, and ascends to within a short distance of the summit of the turret. The summit was open, and stood on the level of the court of the Palace of Blachernæ ; but the opening could be reached from the stairway only by means of a ladder removable at the pleasure of the guardians of the palace, and was, doubtless, closed with an iron door for the sake of greater security.

The walls of the turret were pierced by four loop-holes ; two, placed one above the other, looking towards the north-west,

and two, similarly arranged, facing the north-east. Those on
the lower level are closed, but the two higher ones have
been enlarged, and admit to the fine L-shaped chamber in
the upper story of the tower, the chamber above F and the
vestibule *b*.

The chamber measures some 39 feet by 33 feet, and was
lighted by a large square window in the north-western wall.
A circular aperture in the floor communicated with F ; and a

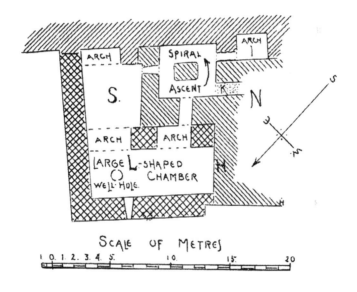

THE L-SHAPED CHAMBER IN UPPER STORY OF TOWER S.

corresponding aperture in the vaulted ceiling opened on the roof
of the tower. The walls are furnished with numerous air-
passages, to prevent dampness, and are covered with a thin
coating of plaster. The vault of the ceiling, if we may judge
from the small cavities for joists below the spring of the arch,
was concealed by woodwork. Indeed, a portion of one of the
cross-beams is still in its place.

The stairway communicated, moreover, with the tower N, through narrow vaulted passages that pierce the north-eastern wall of the tower at three points ; first, at the original level of the vestibule *b*, and then at the level of the two tiers of loopholes. These passages are choked with earth, but by the partial excavation of the lowest one of them access was obtained to the small chamber D. It had no windows, but a round aperture in the ceiling connected it with some unexplored part of the tower.

From this survey of the buildings before us some satisfactory inferences may certainly be drawn regarding their history and character ; although several points must remain obscure until the removal of the earth accumulated within the ruins renders a complete exploration possible.

In the first place, the character of these walls and towers can be understood only in the light of the fact that whatever other function belonged to them, they were intended to support the terraced hill on which the Palace of Blachernæ, to their rear, was constructed. The unusual height and thickness of the walls, the extent to which buttresses are here employed, were not demanded by purely military considerations. Such features are explicable only upon the view that the fortifications of the city at this point served also as a retaining wall, whereby the Imperial residence could be built upon an elevation beyond the reach of escalade, and where it would command a wide prospect of the city and surrounding country. In fact, the buildings before us resemble the immense substructures raised on the Palatine hill by Septimius Severus and Caracalla to support the platform on which the Ædes Severianæ were erected.[1]

In the next place, there are at several points in these

[1] Cf. Lanciani, *The Ruins and Excavations of Ancient Rome*, pp. 178, 179, 182.

"THE TOWER OF ANEMAS" AND "THE TOWER OF ISAAC ANGELUS" (FROM THE SOUTH-WEST).

buildings so many alterations; there is so much undoing of
work done, either rendering it useless or diverting it from its
original purpose, that these various constructions cannot be
treated as parts of an edifice built on a single systematic
plan, but as an agglomeration of different erections, put up at
various periods to serve new requirements arising from time
to time. For instance, the loopholes in the wall AA have no
symmetrical relation to the buttress-walls that divide the compartments C; some of them, as already stated, are partially
closed by the buttresses; others are entirely so, their
existence being discoverable only from the interior of the
galleries in the body of that wall. It is hard to believe that
such inconsistent arrangements can be the work of one mind
and hand.

Again: the tower S and the tower N block the windows in
four of the compartments C. Surely the same builder would
not thus go back upon his work. Once more; the loopholes
in the stairway-turret afford no light in their present position,
the lower pair being closed, the upper pair forming entrances
to the L-shaped chamber. This is not an original arrangement.

In view of such peculiarities, the following conclusions
regarding these buildings seem the most reasonable, in the
present state of our knowledge:

(1) The wall AA was at one time the only erection here;
and the two galleries, constructed in the thickness of the wall
formed with their loopholes two tiers of batteries, so to speak,
for the discharge of missiles upon an enemy attacking this
quarter of the city. A similar system of defence was employed for the protection of the smaller residence forming part
of the Palace of the Porphyrogenitus,[1] and for the protection

---

[1] See the loophole windows in plan of that residence, facing p. 109.

of the Palace of the Bucoleon, situated on the city walls near Tchatlady Kapou.[1]

When precisely the wall AA was erected cannot be determined; but, judging from its height, and the manner in which it was equipped for defence, the probable opinion is that this was done after the Palace of Blachernæ had assumed considerable importance. Possibly, the work belongs to the reign of Anastasius I.[2]

(2) At some later period the wall BB, equipped with buttresses within and without, was erected to support the wall AA. The demand for such support was doubtless occasioned by additions to the Palace of Blachernæ, which already in the tenth century comprised several edifices on the hill behind the wall AA.[3]

As BB superseded the original function of the galleries in AA, it was a matter of little moment how many of the loopholes in the latter were more or less masked by the buttresses built transversely between the two walls. It would be enough to retain a few loopholes to light the galleries. At the same time, advantage was taken of the buttresses to construct, in the space between AA and BB, three stories of chambers, for such purpose as the authorities of the palace might decide.

(3) The manner in which the towers S and N block the windows in four of the compartments C is evidence that these towers were additions made later than the age of BB. This view is corroborated by the marked difference between the masonry of the towers and the masonry of the wall BB, against which they are built.

(4) The towers S and N are so different in their respective styles of construction that they cannot be contemporaneous buildings.

---

[1] See below, p. 273.   [2] See above, p. 128.   [3] *Ut supra.*

(5) The tower S is later than the tower N, for their common wall, H, is strictly the north-eastern side of the tower N, as the similarity of the masonry of H to that of the other sides of N makes perfectly plain.   This similarity is manifest not only in the general features of the work, but also in the insertion of marble shafts into the wall H ; in one instance partially, after the odd fashion adopted so extensively in the open sides of the tower N.   Furthermore, the manner in which the walls of the chamber F and the L-shaped chamber in the tower S impinge upon the wall H shows that the former were built against the latter, and that they are posterior in age.

(6) The stairway-turret E, as the loopholes in its sides prove, stood, at one time, in the open light and air.   If so, it must be older than the apartments b, F, L, in the tower S, which enclose it.

(7) The passages communicating between the stairway and the chambers in the tower N render it almost certain that the stairway-turret was constructed at the same time as that tower. Thus, also, a short and private way from the Palace of Blachernæ to the country beyond the city bounds was provided ; for it may be confidently assumed that at the foot of the stairway there was a small gate, corresponding to the gate l, and the postern x at the mouth of the tunnel Z.

(8) When the stairway-turret was enclosed by the vestibule b, the chamber F, and the L-shaped chamber, the lower loopholes of the turret were built up as superfluous, while the upper ones were widened to form entrances to the L-shaped chamber. Accordingly, the tower S is an old stairway-turret enclosed within later constructions.

(9) In view of some great danger, access to the tower S from without the city was blocked by building up the postern x, the tunnel Z, the gate l, and the vestibule b, to their actual level. The portion of the passage still left open was too narrow to be

forced by an enemy, and yet was convenient to be retained for the sake of ventilation, or as a way in and out in some emergency. At the same time, a breach was made in the wall *g* to place the elevated floor of the vestibule into communication with the stairway-turret E.

(10) What precise object the chambers C in the body of the city wall were intended to serve is open to discussion. In the opinion of Dr. Paspates, who was the first to explore them, they were prison-cells. Possibly the lowest series of these chambers may have been employed for that purpose ; but, taken as a whole, the suite of apartments between AA and BB do not convey the impression of being places of confinement. Their spaciousness, their number, the free communication between them, the size of the windows in the two upper stories, the proximity of the windows to the floor, are not the characteristics of dungeons.

It is not impossible that these chambers were store-rooms or barracks,[1] and that through the loopholes in the wall BB the palace was defended as, previously, through the openings in AA.

Communication between the three stories must have been maintained by means of wooden stairs or ladders. In the north-eastern wall of C'—the chamber which gave access from the court of the Palace of Blachernæ at *v* to the second story of the tower N—there was an archway, now filled up, opening upon the level of the highest series of chambers C. When the archway was closed, communication was held through a breach at *h*. Possibly the same series of chambers was entered from the north-eastern end of the upper gallery in AA. Contrary to what might be supposed, there was no access to the two upper series

---

[1] Speaking of similar substructures below the Domus Gaiana in the Palace of the Cæsars at Rome, Lanciani remarks : " We gain by them the true idea of the human fourmillière of slaves, servants, freedmen, and guards, which lived and moved and worked in the substrata of the Palatine, serving the court in silence and almost in darkness " (*The Ruins and Excavations of Ancient Rome*, p. 150).

of chambers from the stairway-turret. Whether the lowest series could be reached by a door at the foot of the stairway cannot be ascertained, on account of the earth in which the lower portion of the stairway lies buried. But it is extremely improbable that such was the case, for the stairway-turret belongs, we have seen, to a later age than the chambers in the body of the adjoining wall.

With these points made clear, we are in a position to consider how far the identification of the towers N and S, respectively, with the historical towers of Isaac Angelus and Anemas can be established.

According to Nicetas Choniates, the Tower of Isaac Angelus stood at the Palace of Blachernæ, and was built by that emperor to buttress and to defend the palace, and to form, at the same time, a residence for his personal use.[1] It was constructed with materials taken from ruined churches on the neighbouring sea-shore, and from various public buildings in the city, ruthlessly torn down for the purpose.[2]

This account makes it certain, in the first place, that the Tower of Isaac Angelus was one of the three towers which flank the portion of the city walls now under consideration, the portion which forms the north-western side of the enclosure around the Palace of Blachernæ ; for these towers, and they only, at once defended and supported the terrace upon which that palace stood.

This being the case, it is natural to suppose that the Tower of Isaac Angelus is the tower which bears the inscription in his honour.[3] But this opinion is attended with difficulties. For

---

[1] Nicetas Chon., pp. 580, 581, Προθέμενος δὲ καὶ πύργον τεκτήνασθαι κατὰ τὸ ἐν Βλαχέρναις παλάτιον, ἅμα μὲν εἰς ἔρυμα τῶν ἀνακτόρων, ὡς ἔφασκε, καὶ ὑπέρεισμα, ἅμα δὲ καὶ εἰς ἐνοίκησιν ἑαυτῷ.

[2] *Ibid. ut supra.*

[3] See above, p. 132. The tower is marked L on the Map which faces p. 115.

the tower in question does not differ in any marked manner from an ordinary tower in the fortifications of the city. It is not specially fitted for a residence, nor does it possess features which render it worthy to have a place in history among the notable buildings erected by a sovereign. Furthermore, it is not constructed, to any striking degree, with materials drawn from other edifices.

To all this it is possible to reply that we do not see the tower in its original condition ; that its upper story, which stood on the level of the palace area to the rear, is gone ; that the tower, as it stands, consists largely of Turkish repairs ; that the extent to which, in its original state, it resembled, or failed to resemble, the description of the Tower of Isaac Angelus as given by Nicetas, cannot be accurately known, and that, consequently, the question regarding the identity of the tower must be decided by the inscription found upon the building. There is force in this rejoinder ; and it is the conclusion we must adopt, if there are not stronger reasons for identifying the Tower of Isaac Angelus with one or other of the two adjoining towers, N and S.

The claims of the tower N to be the Tower of Isaac Angelus rest upon its strong resemblance to the description which Nicetas has given of the latter building. His description seems a photograph of that tower. Like the Tower of Isaac Angelus, the tower N, besides defending and supporting the Palace of Blachernæ, was pre-eminently a residential tower ; and the numerous pillars employed in its construction betray clearly the fact that it was built with materials taken from other edifices, some of which may well have been churches. The upper story, which was reached from the court of the palace behind it, formed a spacious apartment $22\frac{1}{4}$ by $27\frac{1}{2}$ feet, and about 18 feet high. Its north-western wall was pierced by three large round-headed windows, opening, as pillars placed below them for supports indicate, upon a balcony

Wall containing chambers.

"THE TOWER OF ANEMAS" AND "THE TOWER OF ISAAC ANGELUS" (FROM THE NORTH-WEST).

which commanded a beautiful view of the country about the head of the Golden Horn.   Another window led to a small balcony on the south-western side of the tower, while a fifth looked towards the Golden Horn and the hills beyond.   The apartment might well be styled the Belvedere of the Palace of Blachernæ. The lower story of the tower, which was reached by a short flight of steps descending from the palace court to the vestibule C^1, cannot be explored, being filled with earth; but, judging from its arched entrance and the large square window in the north-western wall, it was a commodious room, with the advantage of affording more privacy than the apartment above it.   What was the object of the dark rooms situated below these two stories, at different levels of the tower, and reached from the stairway-turret outside it, is open to discussion.   The stairway, as already intimated, led also to the surrounding country.   Taking all these features of the tower N into consideration, a very strong case can be made in favour of the opinion that it is the Tower of Isaac Angelus.

How this conclusion should affect our views regarding the inscription in honour of that emperor found on the tower L is a point about which minds may differ.   The inscription may be in its proper place, and thereby prove that the tower it marks was also an erection of Isaac Angelus, although not the one to which Nicetas refers.   And some countenance is lent to this view by a certain similarity in the Byzantine masonry of the towers L and N.   But, on the hypothesis that L and N were both erected by Isaac Angelus, it is extremely strange that the inscription in his honour should have been placed upon the inferior tower, and not upon the one which formed his residence and had some architectural pretension s.

This objection can be met, indeed, either by assuming that another inscription in honour of Isaac Angelus stood on

L

the tower N, but has disappeared; or, with Dr. Paspates,[1] it may be maintained that the inscription is not in its proper place, but belonged originally to the counter-fort supporting the tower N, and was transferred thence to the tower L when the latter was repaired.

In favour of this alternative it may be urged that the tower L has, manifestly, undergone repair; that some of the materials used for that purpose may have been taken from the counter-fort G[4], which has been to a great extent stripped of its facing; and that the inscription on the tower L is not in a symmetrical position, being too much to the left, and somewhat too high for the size of its lettering. But to all this there is the serious objection that the inscribed slab is found in the Byzantine portion of the tower; while the idea that the counter-fort G[4] was defaced in Byzantine days for the sake of repairing the tower L is against all probability.

We pass next to the identification of the Tower of Anemas with the tower S. The Tower of Anemas is first mentioned by Anna Comnena in the twelfth century, as the prison in which a certain Anemas was confined for having taken a leading part in a conspiracy to assassinate her father, the Emperor Alexius Comnenus. According to the Imperial authoress, it was a tower in the city walls in the neighbourhood of the Palace of Blachernæ, and owed its name to the circumstance that Anemas was the first prisoner who occupied it.[2]

Another indication of the situation of the tower is given by Leonard of Scio,[3] when he states that the towers " Avenides "

---

[1] Page 39.

[2] Anna Comn., xii. 161, 162, where the prison of Anemas, ἡ τοῦ Ἀνεμᾶ εἱρκτή, is described as πύργος δ᾽ ἦν εἰς τις τῶν ἀγχοῦ τῶν ἐν Βλαχέρναις ἀνακτόρων διακειμένων τειχῶν τῆς πόλεως: also p. 161, τὸν ἀγχοῦ τῶν ἀνακτόρων ᾠκοδομημένον πύργον.

[3] See his Epistle to Pope Nicholas V.

stood near the Xylo Porta, the gate at the extremity of the land-walls beside the Golden Horn.   To this should be added the indication that the tower was one of a group, for Phrantzes[1] and Leonard of Scio employ the plural form, "the Anemas Towers."

Whether the tower was an erection of Alexius Comnenus or an earlier building is not recorded ; but in either case it was in existence in the reign of that emperor, and, consequently, was older than any work belonging to the time of Isaac Angelus.

With these indications as the basis for a decision, can the claim that the tower S is the Tower of Anemas be maintained ? The tower answers to the description of Anna Comnena in being a tower in the city walls close to the Palace of Blachernæ. Nor is its situation at variance with the statement of Leonard of Scio that it stood in the neighbourhood of the Xylo Porta, although there are three towers between it and that gate.   Furthermore, it is one of a pair of towers that might be designated the Towers of Anemas.

The main reason, however, which induced Dr. Paspates to identify the tower S with the prison of Anemas was the proximity of the tower to the chambers C in the adjoining wall, which he regarded as prison-cells.   This view of the character of those chambers is, for reasons already intimated, extremely doubtful.   But even if prison-cells, that fact alone would not be conclusive proof that they were the prison of Anemas. For the prison of Anemas is always described as a tower ; and by no stretch of language can that designation be applied to the chambers in the body of the wall.[2]

---

[1] Page 51, Ἐν τοῖς πύργοις τοῖς λεγομένοις Ἀδεμανίδες πλησίον Βλαχέρνων. The name Anemas appears first in Theophanes, p. 749, as the surname of a certain Bardanius, τὸ ἐπίκλην Ἀνεμᾶν, in the reign of Nicephorus I., 802–811.

[2] The Byzantine authors who refer to the Prison of Anemas in express terms are: Anna Comnena, xii. pp, 161, 162 ; Nicetas Choniates, p. 455 (ἡ τοῦ Ἀνεμᾶ

The force of this objection would, indeed, be met if proof were forthcoming that the tower S gave access to the chambers C, and formed an integral part of a common system. But the evidence is all on the other side. From the manner in which the tower S blocks the windows of some of the chambers, it is clear, as already observed, that the tower S and the adjoining chambers belong to different periods, and were built without regard to each other. There is no trace of any means of communication between the tower and the two upper series of chambers, and we have no reason to think, but the reverse, that the lowest series of chambers could be reached from it. So far as the chambers are concerned, the tower S is an independent building, upon whose identity they throw no light Whether it was the prison of Anemas must be determined by its own character. Was it suitable for a prison? Above all, is its age compatible with the view that it was the prison of Anemas?

In answer to the former question, it cannot be denied that the tower S could be used as a place of confinement. The chamber F, which is supposed to have been a cistern, may have been a dungeon. The L-shaped chamber in the second story may have served for the detention of great personages placed under arrest. Still, on the whole, the tower S seems rather an extension of the residential tower N than a dungeon.

But the point of most importance in the whole discussion is the comparative ages of the towers N and S. As a building in existence when Alexius Comnenus occupied the throne of Constantinople, the Tower of Anemas was, at least, seventy years

φρουρὰ); Pachymeres, vol. i. p. 378; Cantacuzene, lib. ii. p. 329; Phrantzes, p. 51; Ducas, p. 45. Once, Pachymeres (vol. ii. p. 409) speaks of ταῖς κατὰ τὰς Βλαχέρνας εἱρκταῖς, in which the Despot Michael and his family were confined.

older than the Tower of Isaac Angelus. Hence, if the tower S is the former, it must be older than the tower N, which Dr. Paspates identifies with the Tower of Isaac Angelus. But the evidence which has been submitted goes to prove that the tower S is more recent than the tower N. These towers, therefore, cannot be, respectively, the Tower of Anemas and the Tower of Isaac Angelus. Nothing can prove that the tower S is the Tower of Anemas, until S is shown to be earlier than N, or the identification of the tower N with the Tower of Isaac Angelus is abandoned as erroneous.

Dr. Paspates,[1] indeed, assigned the tower S to the reign of Theophilus in the ninth century, on the ground that a block of stone upon which some letters of that emperor's name are inscribed is built into the tower's north-western face. But a little attention to the way in which that stone is fitted into the masonry will make it perfectly evident that the stone has not been placed there to bear part of an inscription, but as ordinary material of construction, obtained from some other edifice. Consequently, it throws no light upon the age of the tower.

Where, then, was the Tower of Anemas ? Perhaps, in our present state of knowledge, no answer which will commend itself as perfectly satisfactory can be given to the question.

The simplest solution of the difficult problem is that the tower L, which bears the inscription in honour of Isaac Angelus, is, after all, the tower erected by that emperor, though greatly altered by injuries and repairs ; and that the towers N and S together constituted the prison-tower of Anemas, S being a later addition.

Others may prefer to hold the view that the tower N is the Tower of Anemas, and the tower S that of Isaac Angelus, pointing in support of this opinion to the cells in the tower N,

[1] Page 31.

reached from the stairway by narrow vaulted passages. This would mean, practically, that the Tower of Isaac Angelus was the Tower of Anemas renovated and enlarged.

Possibly, others may be disposed, notwithstanding the inscription of Isaac Angelus upon it, to regard the tower L as the Tower of Anemas, and the tower N, with the later addition of S, as that of Isaac Angelus.

If none of these views is acceptable, we must fall back upon the opinion which prevailed before Dr. Paspates discovered the chambers adjoining the tower N and S, viz. that the towers N and S together formed the Tower of Isaac Angelus, and that the Tower of Anemas was one of the three towers in the Heraclian Wall.

This was the view of the Patriarch Constantius,[1] who writes : " The Tower of Anemas still exists. On its side facing the Holy Well of Blachernæ it has a large window, with a smaller one above."

This opinion prevailed in Constantinople also in the sixteenth century, for Leunclavius was informed by Zygomales that the Towers of Anemas were the Towers of the Pentapyrgion,[2] the name given to the citadel formed by the Walls of Heraclius and Leo.

There is nothing in this view opposed to the fact that the Tower of Anemas stood in the city walls near the Palace of

---

[1] *Ancient and Modern Consple.*, pp. 11, 45. The patriarch supposed that the Palace of Blachernæ stood within the enclosure formed by the Wall of Heraclius and the Wall of Leo. *Ibid.*, p. 44.

[2] *Pand. Hist. Turc.*, s. 206.

NOTE.—For the illustrations facing respectively pp. 150, 156, and for the lower illustration facing p. 162, I am indebted to the kindness of my colleague, Professor W. Ormiston. The photographs were taken on the 10th of July, 1894, shortly before the occurrence of the severe earthquake which has made that day memorable in Constantinople. Our situation in the chambers at such a time was not enviable. But we learned that day what an earthquake meant in the old history of the walls of the city.

VIEW OF THE INTERIOR OF "THE PRISON OF ANEMAS" LOOKING NORTH-WEST (BEING THE SUBSTRUCTURES SUPPORTING THE PALACE OF BLACHERNÆ).

Blachernæ ; and a strong argument in its favour may be based upon the association of the tower with the Xylo Porta by Leonard of Scio, when he relates to Pope Nicholas how Jerome from Italy, and Leonardo de Langasco from Genoa, at the head of their companions-in-arms, guarded the Xylo Porta and the towers named Avenides (clearly Anemades) : "Hieronymus Italianus, Leonardus de Langasco, Genovensis, cum multis sociis, Xylo Portam et turres quos Avenides vocant, impensis cardinalis reparatas, spectabant." [1]   This statement is repeated by Zorzo Dolfin. [2]

The Xylo Porta, without question, was at Aivan Serai Kapoussi, to the north of the Wall of Heraclius, and immediately beside the Golden Horn ; [3] and the towers which would most appropriately be entrusted to soldiers defending that entrance are the towers nearest to it, *viz.* the three towers of the Heraclian Wall.   At all events, the designation, "turres Avenides," as used by Leonard of Scio, must include them, even if it comprised others also.

One thing is certain ; the commonly accepted view that the towers N and S represent, respectively, the historical Towers of Isaac Angelus and of Anemas must, in one way or another, be corrected.

NOTE.

Two or three additional passages which bear upon the question under discussion may be noticed, notwithstanding their vagueness.

The statement of Phrantzes (p. 252), among others, that in the siege of 1453 the charge of the palace and all about it was entrusted to Minotto, the Baillus of the

---

[1] See his Epistle to Pope Nicholas V.

[2] Dolfin, s. 64, "Hieronymo Italiano, Leonardo da Languasto Genoexe, cum molti compagni, la porta Chsilo et le Torre Anemande, le qual el cardinal a sue spese hauea reparato, diffensaua."

[3] See below, p. 173.

+—

Venetian colony, might be employed in favour of the view that the "turres Avenides" which Leonard of Scio associates with the Xylo Porta, and assigns to Jerome and Leonardus de Langasco, could not be the towers S and N, but the towers of the Heraclian Wall. For the towers S and N, being attached to the Palace of Blachernæ, would fall under the care of Minotto. There is force in the argument. But it is weakened by statements of Pusculus (iv. 173) and Zorzo Dolfin (s. 55), which imply that the palace defended by Minotto was the Palace of the Porphyrogenitus. For both of these writers place the Gate of the Palace (see above, p. 47) between the Gate of Charisius (Edirnè Kapoussi) and the Gate of the Kaligaria (Egri Kapou), and Pusculus describes the palace concerned as "Regia celsa," an apt description of a building seated, like Tekfour Serai, upon the walls.

The references made to the Tower of Anemas, though not under its name, by the Spanish ambassador Clavijo, who visited the Byzantine Court in 1403, should not be overlooked (see *Constantinople, ses Sanctuaires et ses Reliques*, translated into French by Ph. Bruun, Odessa). Speaking of the Church of Blachernæ (p. 15), he describes it as "située dans la ville près d'un châteaufort, servant de demeure aux empereurs ; ce fort a été démoli par un empereur, parce qu'il y avait été enfermé par son fils." The fact that Clavijo identifies the Church of Blachernæ by its vicinity to the Tower of Anemas may be pressed into the service of the opinion that the tower in question stood in the Wall of Heraclius. For there is no more appropriate way of indicating the situation of that church than by saying that it stands a little to the rear of the Heraclian Wall. So appropriate is that mode of identification, that the Patriarch Constantius has recourse to it when, conversely, he indicates the situation of the Tower of Anemas (which he considered to be the southernmost Heraclian tower) : "The Tower of Anemas still exists," he says. "On its side facing the Holy Well of Blachernæ it has a large window, with a smaller one above" (see above, p. 150). But, unfortunately, to describe one building as "near" another is often the most tantalizing aid to its discovery that can be offered. The towers S and N cannot be said to be far from the Church of Blachernæ. Perhaps some injury to one of the Heraclian towers might explain the statement of Clavijo, that the Tower of Anemas had been destroyed ; but could he have mistaken the citadel formed by the Walls of Heraclius and Leo for an Imperial residence? Such language suggests rather the towers S and N.

Again, the declaration of the Spanish envoy that the tower ("une prison très profonde et obscure ") had been demolished by the Emperor John VI. Palæologus ("*L'empereur s'empressa de démolir la tour où il avait été enferme,*" pp. 19, 20) might seem to imply that the tower has disappeared, and thus to relieve us from all the labour involved in the effort to identify it. But the statement of Leonard of Scio that the "turres Avenides" were repaired by Cardinal Isidore ("impensis cardinalis reparatas "), while it confirms the declaration of Clavijo to some extent, is opposed to the idea of the total destruction and disappearance of the famous prison-tower.

Or, the statement that the Tower of Anemas was demolished, when combined with the statement that it was repaired, might seem to open a way out of the difficulties involved in regarding the tower S as the Tower of Anemas, although more recent than the tower N. May not the tower S be, in its present form, a reconstruction, after the reign of Isaac Angelus, of a tower originally older than that emperor's day, and be thus at once more ancient and more modern than the tower N? But this solution of the puzzle cannot be allowed ; there is the fatal objection that the common wall H belonged first to the tower N.

Finally, in the Venetian account of the attempt made by Carlo Zen to liberate

John VI. Palæologus from the Tower of Anemas, Zen is represented as reaching the foot of the tower in a boat, and clambering up to the window of the prison by means of a rope. This would exclude the claim of a Heraclian tower to be the Tower of Anemas, for that wall could not be reached by boat. One might approach the towers S and N in that way, if the moat before Leo's Wall extended from the Golden Horn to the Wall of Manuel Comnenus, and was full of water. But this is an extremely improbable supposition, when we hear nothing of the sort in the history of the attack upon this side of the city by the Crusaders in 1203, notwithstanding the minute description of the territory from the pen of Nicetas Choniates and other historians of that time. Nor is such a thing mentioned in the history of the last siege, when the moat before the Wall of Leo was reconstructed. The whole story of Carlo Zen's efforts to deliver John Palæologus savours too much of romance to have any topographical value. The story may be read in Le Beau's *Histoire du Bas-Empire*, vol. xii. pp. 174-179.

CHAPTER XI.

INMATES OF THE PRISON OF ANEMAS.

MICHAEL ANEMAS, the first to occupy the prison, and from whom it obtained its name,[1] was a descendant of Emir Abd-el-Aziz ben Omar ben Choaib, known in Byzantine history as Courapas, and famous as the defender of Crete, when Nicephoras Phocas wrested that island from the Saracens, in the reign of Romanus II.[2]

Upon the return of the victorious troops to the capital, the Emir and his family were carried to Constantinople to grace the triumph with which the success of Nicephorus was celebrated. And as the vanquished chief, his wives, his eldest son Anemas, and other members of his family, all clothed in long white robes, passed along the triumphal way in chains, the dignity of their demeanour attracted universal attention, and produced a most favourable impression. To the credit of the conquerors, be it said, the Emir was, thereafter, treated with all due regard and generosity. He received a large estate in the neighbourhood of the capital, and was allowed to end his days in peace, surrounded by his friends, and unmolested on account of his

---

[1] Anna Comn., xii. pp. 161, 162.

[2] See Schlumberger, *Un Empereur Byzantin au Dixième Siècle*, chap. ii., for a brilliant account of the conquest of Crete by Nicephoras Phocas in 962 ; cf. Leo Diaconus, *Historia*, lib. i. et ii.

faith.   Had he seen his way to renounce the creed of his fathers he would have been created a senator.

His son Anemas embraced Christianity, entered the army of the Empire, and took part in the war against the Russians during the reign of Zimisces, when he distinguished himself by his bravery, and fell in battle in personal encounter with Swiatoslaf, the Russian king.

A martial spirit continued to characterize the family in subsequent generations, and was not least conspicuous in Michael Anemas and his three brothers, the representatives of the race under Alexius Comnenus.   But they allowed themselves to become involved in a conspiracy against that emperor, and upon the discovery of the plot were condemned to imprisonment and the loss of their eyes.

To accompany the infliction of punishment with every circumstance that could humiliate the criminal, and excite popular contempt and derision was after the heart of those times. Accordingly, Michael Anemas and his companions, attired in sacking, with their beards plucked out, their heads shorn and crowned with the horns and the intestines of oxen and sheep, were led forth, mounted sideways on oxen, and in this guise, conducted first around the court of the Great Palace, and then along the Mesè of the city, crowded with excited spectators. But the appearance of the guilty men excited commiseration rather than ridicule.   The agony of Michael, as he implored to be put to death rather than to suffer blindness, touched all hearts.   Even Anna Comnena, who witnessed the scene, and whose filial sentiments might have hardened her heart against the conspirators, was so deeply affected that she determined to do all in her power to save Michael from the cruel loss of his eyes.   Finding her mother, Anna brought her to the harrowing spectacle, certain it would have the desired effect.   The empress was overwhelmed to tears, and hastening back to the palace, prevailed upon Alexius to spare the prisoners' sight. By this time the unhappy men were approaching the Amastrianon, a public place where stood an arch on which was a bas-relief representing two hands pierced by a spear. Once a criminal on his way to execution passed that point he was beyond the reach of the Imperial clemency. A few moments more, and the messenger of mercy sent by Alexius would have been too late. But just before the doomed men reached the fatal point, the order for the mitigation of their sentence was delivered, and Anemas was simply imprisoned in the tower which was to perpetuate his name. There he remained for a considerable period; but at length was pardoned and set free.[1]

Before Anemas was released, another notable personage was committed to the tower, Georgius, Duke of Trebizond, who attempted, in 1107, to establish the independence of his province; as though to anticipate the creation of the Empire of Trebizond in the thirteenth century.

He proved a refractory prisoner, venting his rage in unceasing imprecations upon the head of his Imperial master. With the hope of conciliating the rebel, he was repeatedly visited by his old friend, the Cæsar Nicephorus Bryennius, the husband of Anna Comnena. For a long time, however, all friendly overtures proved unavailing. But at last the tedium of protracted confinement broke the prisoner's spirit, and induced him to submit; upon which he was liberated, and loaded with wealth and honours.[2]

The next inmate of the tower was the Emperor Andronicus Comnenus, of infamous memory, upon his capture after his flight from the insurrection which his vices and tyranny had provoked in the capital, in 1185. To Andronicus imprisonment was no

[1] Anna Comn., xii. pp. 153-161. [2] *Ibid.*, pp. 161-164.

CHAMBER IN "THE PRISON OF ANEMAS."

new experience, for already, during the reign of Manuel Comnenus, he had been imprisoned twice elsewhere. On both these
occasions, however, he had succeeded in effecting his escape.
But the prison of Anemas was to prove his last, and he quitted
it, only to die at the hands of his infuriated subjects. On the
eve of his execution he was bound with chains about the neck
and feet, like some wild animal, and dragged into the presence
of his successor, Isaac Angelus, to be subjected to every indignity.
He was reviled, beaten, struck on the mouth; he had his
hair and beard plucked, his teeth knocked out, his right hand
struck off with an axe, and then was sent back to his cell, and
left there without food or water or attention of any kind for
several days. When brought forth for execution, he was
dressed like a slave, blinded of one eye, mounted upon a
mangy camel, and led in mock triumph through the streets of
the city to the Hippodrome, amidst a storm of hatred and insult,
seldom, if ever, witnessed under similar circumstances in a
civilized community. At the Hippodrome he was hung by the
feet on the architrave of two short columns which stood beside
the figures of a wolf and a hyena, his natural associates. But
neither his pitiable condition, nor his quiet endurance of pain,
nor his pathetic cry, "Kyrie Eleison, Why dost Thou break the
bruised reed?" excited the slightest commiseration. Additional
and indescribable insults were heaped upon the fallen tyrant, until
his agony was brought to an end by three men who plunged their
swords into his body, to exhibit their dexterity in the use of arms.[1]

In the course of the following century a different personage
figured in the history of the prison. This was Veccus, Chartophylax of St. Sophia at the time of his confinement, and subsequently Patriarch of Constantinople.[2] He incurred the
displeasure of Michael Palæologus by opposing the union of

[1] Nicetas Chon., pp. 452-458.   [2] Pachymeres, vol. i. pp. 374-403.

the Eastern and Western Churches, through which the emperor
hoped to secure the goodwill and assistance of the Pope in
maintaining the newly recovered throne of Constantinople.
Before an assembly convened to discuss the question in the
presence of Michael, Veccus, who had been appointed the
spokesman of the opponents of the Imperial policy on account
of his abilities, denounced the Latins as heretics with whom
ecclesiastical communion was simply impossible. The emperor
resented the affront, but, unwilling to make it the official
ground of proceedings against the popular champion of orthodoxy, sought other reasons for punishing him. Accordingly,
he accused Veccus of having thwarted the marriage which had
been arranged between the Princess Anna and the second
son of the Kral of Servia; another of Michael's measures
to make his position secure.

The charge had some foundation. For upon the completion
of the negotiations for the marriage, the bride-elect had started
for her destined home under the care of Veccus and of the
Patriarch of Constantinople. But when the party reached
Berœa, Veccus, acting on the private instructions of the empress,
left Anna and the patriarch, and pushed forward to investigate
the character and manners of the people among whom the
princess was to cast her lot. The primitive and boorish
ways of the Servian Court did not commend themselves
to Veccus, as a suitable environment for a lady brought up in
the palaces of Constantinople. The splendour of the tent which
Veccus occupied was lost upon the Kral; while the eunuchs in
the household of the Byzantine princess shocked the sovereign's
unsophisticated mind. Pointing to the wife of his elder son,
simply attired, and busy spinning wool, the rough monarch
exclaimed, " That is how we treat our brides ! " Nor was Veccus
more favourably impressed by other experiences. The embassy

which the Kral sent to welcome the bride-elect was robbed on the journey by brigands ; and the Byzantine envoys awoke one morning to find that all their fine horses had been stolen during the night. Under these circumstances, Veccus thought the wisest course was to conduct Anna back to Constantinople ; [1] and for this action Michael now saw fit to prosecute him.

But the court which was appointed to try Veccus declined to judge a priest in the service of the patriarch without that prelate's orders ; and as such orders were not forthcoming, the trial could not proceed. At this juncture, Veccus had an interview with the emperor and proposed, for the sake of peace, to resign office and emoluments, and to go into exile. Michael did not condescend a reply. Whereupon the Chartophylax, fearing the worst, sought asylum in the Church of St. Sophia, and there awaited the Imperial decision. He was soon summoned to appear again before the emperor, the order being written in vermilion ink, as a mark of esteem and a pledge of personal safety. But on the road to the palace he was treacherously arrested, and carried off to the prison of Anemas under charge of the Varangian guards.

With Veccus out of the way, Michael pushed the matter of the union of the churches more hopefully, and in furtherance of the Imperial policy caused a list of passages favourable to the orthodox character of the Latin Church to be compiled from the writings of theologians of repute, and submitted to the patriarch and his clergy for consideration. The patriarch replied by presenting a list of counter passages, and the situation remained what it had been before Veccus was imprisoned. Thereupon the suggestion was made that the first list should be forwarded to the cell of the Chartophylax. Such a man, it was urged, would never alter his views unless convinced by

[1] For the account of the mission to Servia, see Pachymeres, vol. i. pp. 350–355.

reason. The suggestion was adopted, and after reading the extracts, Veccus acknowledged that the argument for the union of the Churches was stronger than he had hitherto believed. His mind, however, he added, could not be satisfied on the point at issue by the perusal of isolated passages, torn from their connection, and he therefore begged permission to study the works from which the extracts submitted to him had been taken, pleading as an excuse that he was more versed in the writings of classic authors than in patristic learning. Upon this he was released, and provided with the books necessary for the full prosecution of his inquiries.

The result was that, ere long, he found himself in agreement with the emperor, and the scheme for the union of the Churches was pursued with renewed ardour. Delegates proceeded from Constantinople to the Council assembled at Lyons, and there on June 29, 1274, the two great divisions of Christendom were formally united. On the second day of June in the following year Veccus was elevated to the patriarchal throne.[1]

It is natural to suspect that the prison of Anemas had a share in the conversion of Veccus. But the historian Pachymeres ascribes the change to candour of judgment and sincere love of the truth. Certain it is that Veccus suffered for the views he adopted, and died twenty-five years later in the prison of the Castle of St. Gregorius, near Helenopolis (Yalova), a martyr to his convictions.[2]

The Tower of Anemas was probably also the prison to which the Despot Michael was committed by Andronicus II. on the charge of treason. He had been created Despot by Michael Palæologus, and was married to the Princess Anna, above

---

[1] For the circumstances attending the imprisonment of Veccus, see Pachymeres vol. i. pp. 374–403.

[2] Pachymeres, vol. ii. p. 270.

mentioned, after the failure of the Servian marriage to which reference has been made. Upon her death, he fell into disgrace at the Court for marrying a daughter of the Bulgarian king Terter, the repudiated wife of the King of Servia. To this he added treasonable offences, and was, therefore, confined with his wife and children in the prison attached to the Great Palace. On attempting to escape, he was removed to the prison at Blachernæ [1] for greater security.

Another inmate of the prison of Anemas was Syrghiannes, a political adventurer conspicuous for his intrigues during the struggle between Andronicus II. and Andronicus III., taking sometimes the one side and sometimes the other.

He had been immured elsewhere for five years on the charge of conspiracy to assassinate the elder emperor, but in 1322, at the instance of John Cantacuzene, then Grand Domestic, he was transferred to the Tower of Anemas as a more tolerable place of confinement, in the hope of conciliating him ; and there he was permitted to receive visits from his mother, and even to have his wife and children with him.[2] Ultimately he was released, but the old spirit was too strong to be vanquished by suffering or by kindness. He returned to a life of intrigue and rebellion, and his career was closed by the hands of assassins.

Later in the century, members of the Imperial family were once more imprisoned in the Tower of Anemas, under circumstances which afford a vivid picture of an empire weakened by domestic feuds, and distracted by the rival ambitions of foreign powers that were awaiting its dissolution, and ready to appropriate its territories.

---

[1] Pachymeres, vol. ii. pp. 304, 396, 408, 409, where the prison is styled ταῖς κατὰ τὰς Βλαχέρνας εἱρκταις.

[2] Cantacuzene, i. pp. 171, 172 ; ii. pp. 329-332, 457.

There John VI. Palæologus imprisoned his eldest son
Andronicus, and there, upon the escape of the latter, he was
himself imprisoned with his two younger sons, Manuel and
Theodore.

Andronicus had been excluded from the succession to the
throne, on account, it is said, of his indifference to the financial
straits of his father, when the latter was detained at Venice for
inability to meet the demands of creditors. The disinherited
prince, seeking an opportunity for revenge, found a kindred
spirit in a son of Amurath I., Saoudji, who was jealous of his
younger brother Bajazet, because the Sultan's favourite child.
The two princes, bound by a common grievance, joined forces to
supplant their respective parents on the throne, and raised the
standard of revolt. Amurath crushed the rebellion with remorse-
less severity, and after putting out the eyes of his own son, called
upon the emperor to punish Andronicus in the same manner.
Andronicus was consequently committed to the Tower of Anemas,
along with his wife and his son John, a child only five years old,
and there he and his little boy underwent the operation of being
blinded. The cruel deed was, however, performed so imperfectly
that Andronicus recovered the use of one eye, while his son
suffered only from a squint. Two years were thus passed in the
tower, after which the prisoners were released, either through the
intervention of the Genoese, at the price of the concession to
them of the island of Tenedos, or in compliance with the
demand of Bajazet.

Free to act, Andronicus made terms both with the Sultan
and the Genoese, and relying upon their favour, suddenly
appeared before the capital. As the emperor and his son Manuel
happened to be staying at the Palace of the Pegè, outside the
walls, they were easily captured, and upon the surrender of the
city they were, in their turn, sent, along with Theodore, to the

ENTRANCE OF PASSAGE FROM THE STAIRWAY IN
"THE TOWER OF ANEMAS" TO CHAMBER D
IN "THE TOWER OF ISAAC ANGELUS."
(For this view I am indebted to the late Dr. Ledyard)

CORRIDOR IN THE ORIGINAL WESTERN TERRACE WALL OF THE PALACE OF
BLACHERNÆ (LOOKING SOUTH-WEST).
(*See Plan facing page* 131.)

Tower of Anemas, "as Zeus cast his father Chronos and his brothers Pluto and Poseidon into the nether world."

Bajazet advised Andronicus to establish his position by putting the prisoners to death, but to that depth of inhumanity the rebellious son would not descend. Matters remained in this condition for two years, and then the captives managed to escape. Precisely how they found their way out of the tower is a question upon which authorities differ. According to Phrantzes, it was by some deception practised on their Bulgarian guards. Ducas ascribes the escape to the skill of a certain Angelus, surnamed Diabolus, and known by the soubriquet of Diabol-angelus; but whether the deliverance was effected through the angelic power or the satanic cunning of the man, the historian is unable to decide. Chalcocondylas says that the Imperial captives broke through the walls of their dungeon with an iron tool, furnished by the servant who brought their food. According to Venetian authorities, two ineffectual attempts to save the emperor were made by Carlo Zen, on the condition that the island of Tenedos would be granted to the Republic of Venice, thus rescinding the concession of the island to the Genoese by Andronicus. The first attempt, it is said, failed because the emperor refused to escape without his sons; the second, owing to the detection of the plot to deliver him.[1] Once out of prison, John Palæologus and his son Manuel repaired to the Court of Bajazet, prevailed upon him to espouse their cause, and so compelled Andronicus to surrender the throne.[2]

Thus the history of the Tower of Anemas reflects the civil broils, the tyranny, the ecclesiastical dissensions, the political feebleness, and the inability to withstand foreign aggression, which marked the decline and fall of the Byzantine Empire.

[1] Langier, *Histoire de la Republique de Venise*, vol. iv. pp. 251, 253.
[2] The history of the imprisonment of these Imperial personages is found in Phrantzes, pp. 49–57; Ducas, pp. 43–46; Chalcocondylas, pp. 40–46, 51, 60–64.

CHAPTER XII.

THE WALL OF THE EMPEROR HERACLIUS : THE WALL OF THE EMPEROR LEO THE ARMENIAN.

THE fortifications extending from the north-western angle of the enclosure around the Palace of Blachernæ to the Golden Horn consist of two parallel lines, connected by transverse walls, so as to form a citadel beside the Golden Horn. The inner wall belongs to the reign of Heraclius ; the outer is an erection of Leo. V., the Armenian.

The Heraclian Wall was constructed in 627, under the following circumstances :— [1]

Until that year the quarter of Blachernæ, at the foot of the Sixth Hill, was a suburb immediately outside the fortifications.[2] The fact that the suburb and its celebrated Church of the Theotokos, containing, it was believed, the girdle of the Blessed Virgin, were thus exposed to the attacks of an enemy did not occasion serious concern. In the opinion of the devout citizens of Constantinople, the shrine, so far from needing protection, formed one of the strongest bulwarks of the capital. At the worst, when danger threatened, the treasures of the

---

[1] *Paschal Chron.*, p. 726, Τούτῳ τῷ ἔτει ἐκτίσθη τὸ τεῖχος πέριξ τοῦ οἴκου τῆς δεσποίνης ἡμῶν τῆς θεοτόκου, ἔξωθεν τοῦ καλουμένου Πτεροῦ.

[2] *Ibid.*, Procopius, *De Æd.*, lib. i. c. 3 ; *Paschal Chron.*, p. 702.

sanctuary could be readily transported into the city, as was done in the reign of Justinian the Great.[1]

But in 627, Constantinople learned what a siege really meant. Persia and the Empire were then at war with each other; and while Heraclius was carrying the campaign into the enemy's country, a Persian army had encamped at Chalcedon for the purpose of joining the Avars in laying siege to the capital.[2]

As the Byzantine fleet, however, commanded the Bosporus, the allies could not unite their forces, and the Avars were left to act alone. The undertaking proved too difficult for the barbarians, notwithstanding the vigour with which it was conducted, and the siege was raised. But before retiring, a troop of Avaric horse set itself to devastate the suburbs, and having fired the Church of SS. Cosmas and Damianus, and the Church of St. Nicholas, dashed into the open ground beside the Church of Blachernæ, intent upon devoting also that sacred edifice to the flames. For some reason, that purpose was not carried into effect, and the church escaped all injury. This marvellous deliverance enhanced, indeed, the reputation of the Theotokos, but it likewise aroused a sense of the danger to which her shrine was liable, and so the Government of the day ordered the immediate erection of a wall along the western side of the Blachernæ quarter, to place the church beyond the reach of hostile attack in future. The wall was known, until the erection of the Wall of Leo, as the Single Wall of Blachernæ (Μονοτείχος Βλαχερνῶν:[3] τεῖχος τῶν Βλαχερνῶν).[4]

The wall is flanked by three fine hexagonal towers, built towards their summit in brick, perhaps, as Dr. Paspates[5] suggests, in order to lighten the weight of constructions erected on marshy

---

[1] Theophanes, p. 361.

[2] For account of the siege, see *Paschal Chronicle*, pp. 715–726; Nicephorus Patriarcha CP., pp. 20, 21.   [3] Theophanes, pp. 568, 592.

[4] Theophanes Cont., p. 618.   [5] Pages 37, 38.

ground.   They are among the finest towers in the circuit of
the fortifications.   The interior of the southernmost tower, the
only one which can be safely examined, measures $32\frac{1}{2}$ by about
19 feet, and was in three stories.   Upon the face of the tower
is an inscription, in letters formed with pieces of marble, in
honour of the Emperor Michael, probably Michael II.

Between the first and second towers is a gate, named the
Gate of Blachernæ (πόρτα τοῦ Μονοτείχους τῶν Βλαχερνῶν),[1]
after the quarter before which it stood.

It has been generally supposed that the Wall of Heraclius
comprised not only the portion of the city walls just indicated,
but the whole line of fortifications extending from the Kerko
Porta to the Golden Horn.[2]   The evidence on the subject is,
however, in favour of the opinion that the Wall of Heraclius was
only the portion of the fortifications before us.   It is the extent
implied in the description of the Heraclian Wall, as a wall erected
to bring the Church of Blachernæ within the line of the city
bulwarks.[3]   That is an apt description of a wall extending from the
foot of the Sixth Hill to the Golden Horn ; it is a very inadequate
description of a line of bulwarks from the Kerko Porta to the
harbour.   In the next place, more extensive fortifications were not
required to protect the church, seeing it was well defended on
the south by the acropolis on the western spur of the Sixth
Hill.   All that was necessary for the further security of the
church was a wall on the west side of the plain on which it
stood.   Furthermore, the fortifications extending from the
Kerko Porta to the foot of the Sixth Hill, commonly ascribed to
Heraclius, have been proved to be the work of other hands, the
greater part being the Wall of Manuel Comnenus,[4] while the

[1] Theophanes, p. 592 ; Cedrenus, vol. i. p. 787.
[2] Paspates, p. 19.
[3] *Paschal Chron.*, p. 726 ; Nicephorus, *Patriarcha CP.*, p. 21.
[4] See above, Chapter IX.

Wall of Heraclius.   Wall containing chambers.   "Tower of Anemas."   "Tower of Isaac Angelus."   Mosque of Aivas Effendi
Wall of Leo I.   on site of the Palace of Blachernæ

GENERAL VIEW OF THE WALLS OF THE CITY FROM THE HILL ON WHICH THE CRUSADERS ENCAMPED IN 1203.

remainder formed, originally, the defences of the Fourteenth Region.

The Wall of Leo the Armenian was erected in 813 to strengthen the defence of this part of the capital, in view of the preparations which the Bulgarians under Crum were making for a second attack upon Constantinople.[1] Crum had retired from his first assault upon the city, resolved not only to retrieve the defeat he had sustained, but also to punish the treacherous attempt upon his life, when he was proceeding to negotiate terms of peace with the emperor.

Arrangements had been made for holding a conference between the two sovereigns at a short distance to the west of the Heraclian Wall, on the explicit understanding that all persons present were to attend unarmed ; so little confidence had the two parties in each other. But in flagrant breach of this agreement, Leo placed three bowmen in ambush near the place of meeting, with orders to shoot at the Bulgarian king, upon a preconcerted signal. In due time Crum arrived ; but he had scarcely dismounted from his horse when his suspicions of a plot were aroused, and, springing into his saddle, he galloped back towards his camp. The arrows of the soldiers in ambush flew after him, wounding him although he escaped with his life.

The Byzantine historian who records the incident explains the failure of the plot as a Divine punishment upon the sins of his countrymen.[2] Crum saw the dastardly act in a different light, and, vowing vengeance, withdrew to Bulgaria to prepare for another war. He died before he could carry out his intention, but meanwhile Leo had put himself in readiness for the expected

[1] Theophanes Cont., pp. 612-618; Συναθροίσας λαὸν πολὺν καὶ τεχνίτας ἤρξατο κτίζειν ἕτερον τεῖχος ἔξωθεν τοῦ τείχους τῶν Βλαχερνῶν, κόψας καὶ τὴν σούδαν πλατεῖαν.

[2] Theophanes, p. 785; Theophanes Cont., pp. 612-618.

attack by constructing a new wall and a broad moat in front of the Wall of Heraclius.

The Wall of Leo stands 77 feet to the west of the Wall of Heraclius, running parallel to it for some 260 feet, after which it turns to join the walls along the Golden Horn. Its parapet-walk was supported upon arches, which served at the same time to buttress the wall itself, a comparatively slight structure about 8 feet thick. With the view of increasing the wall's capacity for defence, it was flanked by four small towers, while its lower portion was pierced by numerous loopholes. Two of the towers were on the side facing the Golden Horn, and the other two guarded the extremities of the side looking towards the country on the west. The latter towers projected inwards from the rear of the wall, and between them was a gateway corresponding to the Heraclian Gate of Blachernæ.

The citadel formed by the Walls of Heraclius and Leo was designated the Brachionion of Blachernæ (τὸ βραχιόνιον τῶν Βλαχερνῶν).[1] Subsequent to the Turkish Conquest it was named after the five more conspicuous towers which guarded the enclosure, the Pentapyrgion,[2] on the analogy of the Hepta-pyrgion, or Castle of Severn Towers (Yedi Koulè) at the southern end of the land walls.

Near the southern end of the wall, where it has evidently undergone repair, two inscriptions are found. One is in honour of Michael II. and Theophilus, the great Emperors:

ΜΙΧΑΗΛ ΚΑΙ ΘΕΟΦΙΛΟΥ ΜΕΓΑ . . Ν ΒΑCΙ. . . .

The other gives the date †ϛΤΛ† (822), which belonged to the sole reign of the former emperor. These repairs were probably

[1] Anna Comn., ii. p. 104.

[2] Leunclavius, *Pand. Hist. Turc.*, s. 200. The Pentapyrgion mentioned by Constantine Porphyrogenitus was a piece of furniture in the form of a castle with five towers, kept in the Great Palace.

made when Thomas, the rival of Michael for the throne, attacked
the fortifications in this quarter. It was precisely in the year
822 that the rebel general encamped beside the Monastery of
SS. Cosmas and Damianus (above Eyoub), and then, armed with
battering-rams and scaling-ladders, advanced to the assault of the
towers of Blachernæ, behind which the standard of Michael
floated over the Church of the Theotokos.[1]

The tower at the north-western corner of the enclosure was
reconstructed by the Emperor Romanus, as an inscription upon
it proclaims :

圖 FROM A PHOTO

"The Tower of St. Nicholas was restored from the foundations, under
Romanus, the Christ-loving Sovereign."

To which of the four emperors named Romanus the work
should be assigned is not easy to decide. The tower must have
derived its name from the Church of S. Nicholas in this vicinity,
for the site of that church is marked by the Holy Well which
still flows amid the graves and trees of the Turkish cemetery
within the Brachionion of Blachernæ, an object of veneration
alike to Moslems and orthodox Greeks. The grounds on which
the opinion rests are that, previous to the erection of the
Heraclian Wall, the church is described as without the city
bounds, in the district of Blachernæ ;[2] while after the erection
of Leo's Wall it is spoken of as within the city limits, and close
to the gate by which persons proceeded from the Blachernæ
quarter to the Cosmidion.[3] This is exactly how a building

[1] Theophanes Cont., pp. 60, 61 ; Cedrenus, vol. ii. pp. 81–83.
[2] Procopius, *De Æd.*, i. c. 6 ; *Paschal Chron.*, pp. 724, 725.
[3] Anna Comn., x. p. 48; *Itinéraires Russes en Orient.*, p. 124. The church
was dedicated to SS. Priscus and Nicholas (Procopius, *ut supra*). The Holy Well

beside the Holy Well between the two walls, and near the Gate of Blachernæ which pierces them, would be described under such circumstances.

The proximity of these walls to the Palace of Blachernæ, as well as their comparative weakness, combined to make them the scene of many historical events.

While the Wall of Heraclius stood alone, it was through the Gate of Blachernæ that Apsimarus was admitted by his adherents, in 698, to supplant Leontius ; [1] by the same entrance Justinian II., in 705, attempted to force his way into the city to dethrone Apsimarus ; [2] and through it, again, Theodosius III., in 716, entered and deposed Anastasius II.[3] It was before the Heraclian Wall that Crum and Leo the Armenian met to confer, under the circumstances already narrated.

This portion of the fortifications continued to be a favourite point of attack also after the erection of Leo's Wall. Here, as above stated, the rebel Thomas sought to break into the city in 822 ; [4] here, in 924, Simeon of Bulgaria and Romanus Lecapenus

is now regarded as that of St. Basil (Patriarch Constantius, *Ancient and Modern Consple.*, p. 44). Whether the church should be identified with the Church of St. Nicholas, τὰ Βασιλίδου (Codinus, p. 125, Paspates, p. 34), is doubtful.

The Cosmidion, now Eyoub, obtained its name from the celebrated Church and Monastery of SS. Cosmas and Damianus in the district. The church was founded by Paulinus, the friend of Theodosius II., and the victim of his jealousy, and is therefore sometimes described as ἐν τοῖς Παυλίνου. It stood on the hill at the head of the Golden Horn, commanding the most beautiful view of the harbour, and constituted, with the walls around it, an acropolis (Procopius, *De Æd*. i. c. 6). It was restored by Justinian the Great, and was famed for miraculous cures. The two saints had been what would now be termed "medical missionaries," and exercised their art gratuitously ; hence, their epithet Ἀνάργυροι (without money). Owing to the strategical position of the monastery, it was frequently seized by assailants of the city, as, for example, by the Avars (*Paschal Chron.*, p. 725), and by the rebel Thomas (Theophanes Cont., p. 59). It was granted to Bohemond by Alexius Comnenus, and was consequently known as the Castle of Bohemond (William of Tyre, ii. pp. 84, 85). Andronicus II. Palæologus dismantled the fortress, lest it should be used by the Catalans (Pachymeres, vol. ii. p. 592).

[1] Theophanes, p. 568.   [2] *Ibid.*, p. 573.   [3] *Ibid.*, p. 592.
[4] Theophanes Cont., pp. 60, 61 ; Cedrenus, vol. ii. pp. 81–83.

met to conclude peace,[1] taking the greatest precautions against the repetition of the treachery which disgraced the former meeting of a Bulgarian king with a Byzantine emperor. In 1047, in the reign of Constantine Monomachus, the rebel general Tornikius took up his position before these walls, and having routed a company of raw recruits who had sallied forth against him by the Gate of Blachernæ, would have rushed into the city with the fugitives, had not the difficulty of crossing the moat given the defenders of the walls time to close the entrance.[2]

Through the Gate of Blachernæ the friends of Alexius Comnenus sallied from the city, in 1081, to join the standard of revolt against Nicephorus Botoniates ; and it was at the Imperial stables outside the gate that they obtained horses to reach as fast as possible the Monastery of SS. Cosmas and Damianus, baffling pursuit by having taken the precaution to ham-string the animals they did not require.[3] In 1097, Godfrey de Bouillon encamped on the hills and plains without these walls. While the negotiations with the crafty Alexius Comnenus were proceeding, the envoys of the Crusaders were on one occasion detained so long by the emperor as to arouse suspicions of treachery on his part ; whereupon a band of Crusaders rushed from the camp at the Cosmidion, and in their attempt to enter the city and rescue their comrades set fire to the Gate of Blachernæ.[4]

In 1203 these fortifications were attacked by the land forces of the Fourth Crusade.[5] The Venetian fleet, bearing the banner of St. Mark, occupied the Golden Horn, under the command of Dandolo ; the army of the expedition under Baldwin held the hill immediately to the west of the Palace of Blachernæ. Upon

---

[1] Cedrenus, vol. ii. p. 304 ; Theophanes Cont., pp. 406-409.

[2] Cedrenus, vol. ii. p. 563.

[3] Anna Comn., ii. p. 104.   [4] *Ibid.*, x. p. 48.

[5] For the account of the assault, see Ville-Hardouin, *Conquête de Consple.*, c. 35 ; Nicetas Chon., pp. 719-723 ; Count Hugo, in *Tafel et Thomas*, p. 309.

the walls and towers of the citadel stood the Varangian guards, composed mainly of Englishmen and Danes, loyal to their trust, and the peers of the invaders in courage and strength. Alexius III. and his courtiers watched the scene from the palace windows. At length, on the 17th of July, the Crusaders delivered a grand assault by sea and land ; the army attacking the fortress formed by the Walls of Heraclius and Leo ; the fleet attempting the adjoining fortifications along the harbour. With the help of ladders, fifteen knights and sergeants scaled the outer Wall, and engaged the defenders on the summit in a desperate struggle. It was a bold attempt, but the odds were too great, and the assailants, leaving two of their number prisoners, were driven off by the swords and battle-axes of the Varangians. Many other Crusaders, also, who had advanced to support the attack, were wounded, and the day went so hard against the Latins at this point that Dandolo, who had captured twenty-five towers of the harbour fortifications, was obliged to abandon the advantage he had gained, and hastened with his ships to protect his worsted allies.

Finally, in 1453, the moat before these walls, which had been filled with earth in the course of time, was excavated by the crews of the Venetian galleys present at the siege under the command of Aluxio Diedo. It was made 200 paces long and 8 feet wide, the emperor and his courtiers being present at the work, while two sentries, stationed on the neighbouring hill, watched the Turkish outposts.[1]

From the northern extremity of the Heraclian Wall, a short wall was carried to the water's edge, across the western end of the street that runs along the shore of the Golden Horn, outside the Harbour Walls ; thus protecting the latter line of fortifications from attack by the land forces of an enemy.

[1] Barbaro, pp. 719–722.

At the same time, for the convenience of traffic, the wall was pierced by a gate, named, from its material, the Xylo Porta (Ξυλόπορτα, Ξυλίνη), the Wooden Gate.[1]   It was in its place as late as 1868, and bore an inscription in honour of Theophilus.[2] Very probably, the wall was erected by that emperor when he reconstructed the defences along the harbour.   In accordance with its situation, the Xylo Porta is described sometimes as the gate at the northern extremity of the land fortifications;[3] and sometimes as the gate at the western end of the walls along the Golden Horn.[4]

Du Cange[5] identified the Porta Xylo Kerkou with this gate. But the former was an entrance in the Theodosian lines;[6] it led directly into the city, and was built up in the reign of Isaac Angelus[7]—facts which did not hold true of the Xylo Porta. Furthermore, Ducas expressly distinguishes the two entrances.[8] Or the facts in the case may be stated thus: The Gate of the Xylokerkus was in existence before the erection of the wall in which the Xylo Porta stood; the former entrance being not later than the reign of Anastasius I., in the fifth century, the latter not earlier than the reign of Heraclius, in the seventh century, when the wall on the west of Blachernæ was erected.   Therefore the two entrances cannot be the same gate under different names.

In Dr. Mordtmann's opinion,[9] the Postern of Kallinicus (τὸ τῆς Καλλινίκου παραπόρτιον), mentioned by Byzantine writers,[10] was the Xylo Porta under an earlier name.   And what is

---

[1] Cananus, p. 460; Phrantzes, p. 237; cf. Ducas, p. 263.

[2] Paspates, p. 61.

[3] Cananus, pp. 460, 470, 472; Critobulus, i. c. 27; Phrantzes, p. 237.

[4] Cantacuzene, iv. p. 214; Pusculus, iv. 179.

[5] *Constantinopolis Christiana*, lib. i. c. 15, p. 49.

[6] Banduri, *Imperium Orientale*, lib. vii. p. 150.

[7] Nicetas Chon., p. 529.   [8] Ducas, p. 282.

[9] Page 37.   [10] Cedrenus, vol. i. p. 784; Theophanes, p. 583.

known regarding that postern lends support to this view.   Like
the Xylo Porta, the Postern of Kallinicus stood near the Church
of Blachernæ,[1] and led to the Church of SS. Cosmas and
Damianus in the Cosmidion,[2] as well as to the bridge across the
head of the Golden Horn.[3]   The identity is confirmed by the
fact that the bridge to which the road issuing from the Xylo
Porta conducted was sometimes called the Bridge of St. Kallinicus, after a church of that dedication in its neighbourhood.[4]

THE BRIDGE ACROSS THE GOLDEN HORN.

The earliest mention of a bridge across the Golden Horn is
found in the *Notitia*.[5]   It was situated in the Fourteenth Region,
and, like the bridge across the Tiber, was a wooden structure,
"pontem sublicium."   This was superseded by a bridge of stone,[6]
which Justinian the Great constructed in 528, "so that one might
pass," as the *Paschal Chronicle*[7] expresses it, "from the opposite
side (ἀπὸ τῆς ἀντι πέραν) to the all-happy city."   The new building went by various names in the course of its long history.   It
was known as the Bridge of Justinian (ἡ Ἰουστινιανοῦ γέφυρα),[8] in
honour of its constructor ; as the Bridge of St. Kallinicus (ἡ γέφυρα
τοῦ ἁγίου Καλλινίκου),[9] after a church dedicated to that saint near
its southern end ; as the Bridge of St. Panteleemon (ἡ τοῦ ἁγίου
Παντελεήμονος γέφυρα),[10] after a church of that name at its northern
end ; as the Bridge of Camels (ἡ τῆς Καμήλου γέφυρα),[11] on account,
probably, of its frequent use by caravans of camels, bringing

---

[1] Theophanes, pp. 582, 583.   [2] *Ibid., ut supra.*
[3] *Paschal Chron.*, p. 720.   [4] Theophanes Cont., p. 340.
[5] *Ad Reg. XIV.*   [6] Ville-Hardouin, c. 33.
[7] *Paschal Chron.*, p. 618.
[8] Theophanes Cont., p. 340 ; Synaxaria, July 29.
[9] *Paschal Chron.*, p. 720.   [10] Attaliotes, p. 251.
[11] Cantacuzene, i. pp. 290, 305 ; iii. p. 501.

charcoal to the city ; as the Bridge of Blachernæ,[1] from the
district in which it stood.   Whether it was the bridge of twelve
arches near St. Mamas mentioned by the Anonymus and
Codinus [2] is uncertain, for we cannot be sure that all references
to the Church of St. Mamas allude to the church of that dedication which stood outside the walls of the city, and overlooked
the head of the Golden Horn.

The bridge crossed the Barbyses [3] (Kiat-haneh Sou, one of
the streams commonly styled "The Sweet Waters of Europe"),
where that stream enters the Golden Horn,[4] in the district of the
Cosmidion [5] (Eyoub).   When Gyllius visited the city the stone
piers of an ancient bridge could be seen, in summer, when the
water was low, standing opposite a point between the northern
extremity of the land walls and Aivan Serai : " Liquet pontem
illum fuisse ubi pilæ cernuntur lapideæ antiqui pontis, sed non
extra aquam eminentes nisi aliquando æstate, sitæ inter angulum
urbis Blacherneum et suburbium, quod Turci appellant Aiba-
sarium." [6]

In the siege of 627 the flotilla of log-boats, which the
Slavonian allies of the Avars brought to take part in the operations, was moored behind this bridge, watching for an opportunity
to descend into the Golden Horn, and harass the northern side
of the city.[7]   Over it Heraclius came to make his triumphal
entrance into the city, after his return from the Persian War.   It
was a circuitous road for him to take from the Palace of the

[1] John Tzetzes, as quoted by Gyllius and Du Cange, *ut infra.*

[2] III. p. 58.   Page 30.

[3] Nicephorus Patriarcha CP., p. 30 ; where it is named τοῦ Βαρνύσσου :
Theophanes Cont., p. 340, τοῦ Βαθύρσου.

[4] Leo Diaconus, p. 129; Cinnamus, p. 75.

[5] Anna Comn., x. p. 47.   Nicetas Choniates, p. 719, adds that near the bridge
stood a perforated rock, τρυπετὸν λίθον.

[6] De Top. CP., iv. c. 6; see, on the whole subject, Du Cange, *Constantinopolis
Christiana,* iv. p. 179.   [7] *Paschal Chron.,* p. 720.

Hiereia (Fener Bagtchèssi, on the Bay of Moda, near Kadikeui),
which he occupied upon his arrival within sight of the capital.
His most direct course was to proceed from that palace to the
Golden Gate by boat across the Sea of Marmora.   But the hero
of seven glorious campaigns was possessed by such an insuper-
able dread of the water that, for a long time, nothing, not even
a conspiracy against his throne, could induce him to overcome
his fear and cross to the city.   At length the difficulty was met
in the following manner.   A bridge of boats was placed across
the Bosporus, from the bay of Phedalia (Balta Liman)[1] to the
opposite Asiatic shore, the parapets of the bridge being constructed of great branches and dense foliage, so as to hide from
view the water on either hand ;   and over this roadway the
emperor was persuaded to pass on horseback, as through a
thicket on *terra firma*.   Once on the European side of the straits,
it would have been natural for him to take the road leading
towards the city along the shore.   But rather than keep near the
water, Heraclius struck inland, for the valley at the head of the
Golden Horn, to reach the side of the harbour on which the city
stood, by the bridge over the narrow stream of the Barbyses.[2]

Near the bridge the Crusaders, under Godfrey de Bouillon,
encamped in 1096.[3]   Over it the Crusaders, under the Emperor
Conrad, passed in 1147, to ravage the suburbs on the northern
side of the harbour.[4]   To it, in 1203, the army of the Fourth
Crusade marched, from Galata, in battle array, and, finding it
had been cut down by the Greeks, repaired it, and crossed to
encamp on the hill fronting the Palace of Blachernæ.   "Et là
(*i.e.* au bout du port)," to quote the picturesque language of
Ville-Hardouin,[5] "il y a un fleuve qui se jette dans la mer, qu' on

---

[1] Gyllius, *De Bosporo Thracio*, ii. c. 13.

[2] Nicephorus Patriarcha CP., pp. 28-30.

[3] Anna Comn., x. p. 47.   [4] Cinnamus, p. 75.   [5] Chap. 33.

ne peut pas passer sinon par un pont de pierre. Les Grecs avaient coupé le pont ; et les barons firent travailler l'armée tout le jour et toute la nuit pour arranger le pont. Le pont fut ainsi arrangé, et les corps de bataille armés au matin ; et ils chevauchèrent l'un après l'autre, ainsi qu' ils avaient été ordonnés. Et ils vout devant la ville." Twice in 1328, and once in 1345, Cantacuzene[1] encamped his troops on the meadows beside the bridge, while he endeavoured to gain the city by parleying with its defenders at the Gate of Gyrolimnè.

[1] Lib. i. pp. 290, 305 ; iii. p. 501.

CHAPTER XIII.

THE SEAWARD WALLS.

OWING to the unique maritime position occupied by Constantinople, the defence of the shores of the capital was a matter of secondary importance.   So long as the Empire retained the command of the sea, a city accessible by water only through the narrow defiles of the Hellespont and the Bosporus had little reason to apprehend a naval attack.

This immunity was, it is true, seriously affected when the Saracens and the Republics of Italy became great sea-powers. Still, even then, the situation of the city rendered an assault with ships an extremely difficult operation.   The northern shore of the city could be put beyond the reach of the enemy by a chain extended across the narrow entrance of the Golden Horn ; while the currents that swept the Marmora shore were ready to carry a fleet out to sea, or to hurl it against the rocks.   According to Ville-Hardouin,[1] it was the dread of those currents that, in 1204, deterred the Venetian fleet, under Dandolo, from attacking the walls beside the Sea of Marmora, after the failure of the attempt upon the fortifications along the Golden Horn.

---

[1] *La Conquête de Constantinople,* c. 52 : "Et il y en eut assez qui conseillièrent qu'on allât de l'autre côté de la ville, du côté où elle n'était pas si fortifiée.   Et les Vénitiens, qui connaissaient mieux la mer, dirent que s'ils y allaient, le courant de l'eau les emmènerait en aval du Bras ; et ils ne pourraient arrêter leurs vaisseaux." Compare with this Pachymeres, vol. i. p. 365.

Other natural allies to withstand a naval attack were, moreover, found in the violent storms to which the waters around the city are liable. Such a storm discomfited the great Saracen fleet in the siege of 718.[1] In 825, a tempest compelled Thomas, the rival of Michael II., to withdraw his ships from action;[2] while in 865 a storm destroyed the first Russian flotilla that entered the Bosporus.[3] In the long history of the Byzantine Empire there is only one instance of a successful naval assault upon Constantinople, the gallant capture of the city in 1204 by the Venetians. That victory, however, was due as much to the feeble spirit exhibited by the defenders, notwithstanding the advantages of their position, as to the bravery and skill of the assailants.

But though the seaward walls did not possess the military consequence of the land walls, they are interesting on account of their connection with important political events, and, above all, for their intimate association with the commercial activity of the greatest emporium of trade during the Middle Ages.

The history of the construction of these walls has already been noticed incidentally, when tracing the gradual expansion of the city.[4] In the days of Byzantium they proceeded, we have seen, from the Acropolis (Seraglio Point) to the Neorium, on the Golden Horn; and to the point subsequently called Topi, on the Sea of Marmora. Under Constantine the Great they were carried to the Church of St. Antony Harmatius, on the northern side of the city; and to the Church of St. Æmilianus, on the southern. In 439, Theodosius II. prolonged the lines to meet the extremities of the land wall at Blachernæ, on the one hand, and the Golden Gate, on the other.

The history of the repair of these walls from time to time is

---

[1] Theophanes, pp. 607, 608. [2] Cedrenus, vol. ii. p. 82.

[3] Leo Gram., p. 241. [4] See Map of Byzantine Constantinople.

a long one. For while comparatively secure from injury by the accidents of war, they were liable to be rudely shaken by earthquakes, like other public buildings of the city, while their proximity to the sea exposed them in a special manner to damage by damp and storm.

During the earlier days of the Empire, indeed, when the Imperial navy ruled the sea, and no hostile fleet dared approach the city, the condition of these fortifications was often neglected ; but as the sea-power of the Empire decayed, and that of other nations grew stronger, the defences along the shores of the city assumed greater interest, and their maintenance in proper order became one of the principal cares of the State.

The earthquake of 447, so ruinous to the new land wall of Anthemius, injured also the seaward walls, especially the portion beside the Sea of Marmora. As an inscription over Yeni Kapou [1] —the gate at the eastern end of Vlanga Bostan—proclaimed, the damage was repaired by the Prefect Constantine when he restored the other fortifications of the city which had suffered from that terrible earthquake.[2]

There is no record of repairs for the next two hundred and fifty years. But the state of these walls could not have been altogether unsatisfactory during that period, for they were prepared to withstand two fleets which threatened the southern side of the city in the seventh century : first, when the ships of Heraclius came, in 610, to overthrow the tyranny of the infamous Phocas ; and again, when the Saracens besieged Constantinople from 673-678.

With the accession of Tiberius Apsimarus the shore defences entered upon a new era of their history. Admiral of the Imperial

---

[1] See below, p. 263.

[2] Patriarch Constantius, *Ancient and Modern Constantinople*, p. 21. The inscription was in the same terms as that in honour of Constantine on the Porta Rhousiou. See above, p. 47.

fleet in the Ægean when the Saracens marched victoriously from the banks of the Nile to the Atlantic, and alive to the power of the enemy upon the sea, as well as upon land, he was in a position to appreciate the necessity of being ready to repel attack at every point. Hence, upon his return to Constantinople, he ordered the walls of the capital, which had for some time been grossly neglected, to be put into a state of defence.[1] Some eight years later, however, Anastasius II. found it expedient to attend to the seaward walls again,[2] in view of the formidable preparations made by the Saracens for their second attack upon the capital of Eastern Christendom ; and so effective was the work done, that, in the great crisis of 718, the city defied a fleet of 1200 vessels.

In the spring of 764 an unusual occurrence shook the walls about the point of the Acropolis. The preceding winter had been one of Arctic severity. If the figures of Theophanes may be trusted, the sea along the northern and western shores of the Euxine was frozen to a distance of one hundred miles from land, and to a depth of sixty feet ; and upon this foundation of solid ice a mass of snow forty-five feet high accumulated. As soon as the breath of spring liberated the frost-bound waters, a long procession of ice-floes came filing down the Bosporus, on their way to the southern seas. They came in such numbers that they packed in the narrow channel, and formed an ice-pile at the opening into the Sea of Marmora, extending from the Palace of Hiereia (Fener Bagtchessi) to the city, and from Chrysopolis to Galata, and as far as Mamas at the head of the Golden Horn.[3]

At length the ice divided again, and as its several parts swayed in the swollen currents, one huge iceberg came dashing

---

[1] Anonymus, iii. p. 56.   [2] Theophanes, p. 589.
[3] Theophanes, pp. 670, 671 ; Nicephorus Patriarcha CP., pp. 76, 77.

against the pier at the point of the Acropolis. Another, larger, followed, and hurled itself against the adjacent wall with a violence which shook the whole neighbourhood. The monstrous mass was broken by the concussion in three fragments, still so large that they overtopped the city bulwarks and invested the apex of the promontory from the Mangana to the Port Bosporus, overawing the city, and crushing, it would appear, the fortifications.

Extensive repairs of these walls were commenced in the reign of Michael II., and completed by his son Theophilus on a scale which amounted to a work of reconstruction.[1] Under the former emperor the rebel Thomas had besieged the city and forced the chain across the entrance of the Golden Horn, proving, for the first time, that even the fortifications in that quarter might be attacked by a bold enemy. The Saracens, moreover, displaying new vigour, had taken Sicily and Crete, and in 829 defeated the Imperial fleet in the Ægean. Accordingly, it is not strange that Theophilus ordered the old ramparts along the shores of the city to be replaced by loftier and stronger fortifications, and that in the execution of the undertaking he spared no labour or expense. "The gold coins of the realm," says the chronicler, " were spent as freely as if worthless pebbles." [2]

The satisfaction of Theophilus with the result was displayed in the extraordinary number of the inscriptions which he placed upon the new walls and towers, to commemorate his work. No other emperor has inscribed his name upon the walls so frequently. And the fortifications he erected endured, with but little change, to the last days of the Empire, and bear his stamp even in their ruin.

Of the inscriptions referred to, the following are found on the walls along the Sea of Marmora :

[1] Genesius, p. 75 ; Cedrenus, vol. ii. p. 107.   [2] Manasses, 4824–4829.

On the curtain-wall immediately to the north of Deïrmen Kapoussi, in one long line of sixty feet, is the legend :

"Possessing Thee, O Christ, a Wall that cannot be broken, Theophilus, King and pious Emperor, erected this wall upon new foundations : which (wall), Lord of All, guard with Thy might, and display to the end of time standing unshaken and unmoved."

These words read like a dedication prayer for the preservation of the whole line of the fortifications erected by Theophilus.

On the first tower to the south of Deïrmen Kapoussi are the words:

† ΠΥΡΓΟϹ ΘΕΟΦΙΛΟΥ ΠΙϹΤΟΥ ΕΝ Χω ΜΕΓΑΛΟΥ ΒΑϹΙΛΕωϹ. ΑΥΤΟΚΡΑΤΟΡΟϹ †

"Tower of Theophilus, faithful and great King and Emperor in Christ."

Above the legend is a slab, with the Cross and the battle-cry of the Empire, " Jesus Christ conquers."

IϹ	XP
NI	KA

A similar inscription stands on the second tower south of the gate :

† ΠΥΡΓΟϹ ΘΕΟΦΙΛΟΥ ΕΝ ΧΡΙϹΤω ΑΥΤΟΚΡΑΤΟΡΟϹ †[1]

"Tower of Theophilus, Emperor in Christ."

Fragmentary inscriptions to the same effect are seen on the third, sixth, seventh, and ninth towers south of Deïrmen Kapoussi.

[1] See illustration facing p. 248.

In addition to these inscriptions, copies of others which have disappeared are preserved by Von Hammer, in the appendix to his work, *Constantinopolis und Bosporos*.[1]

The Gate of St. Barbara (Top Kapoussi) bore the inscription :

ΘΕΟΦΙΛΟϹ . . . ΕΚΑΙΝΙϹΑϹ ΠΟΛΙΝ.

"Theophilus . . . having renovated the city."

This inscription was repeated on the wall adjoining the gate. And on the two towers which flanked the gate was the customary legend which marked the work of Theophilus :

ΠΥΡΓΟϹ ΘΕΟΦΙΛΟΥ ΕΝ ΧѠ ΑΥΤΟΚΡΑΤΟΡΟϹ

According to the same author,[2] a similar inscription was found in the vicinity of the Seven Towers, as well as an inscription in honour of Theophilus and his son, Michael III., who, though a mere child, had been appointed his Imperial colleague.

According to Aristarki Bey and Canon Curtis,[3] two other inscriptions in honour of Theophilus and Michael occurred also on two towers in the immediate vicinity of Top Kapoussi. All these inscriptions indicate the great extent of the repairs executed by Theophilus ; the last three give, moreover, the approximate date of one portion of the work, Michael III. being the associate of his father from 839-842.

Upon the fortifications along the Golden Horn some twenty inscriptions in honour of Theophilus have been noted, similar to those found on the fortifications beside the Sea of Marmora, but they have for the most part disappeared in the destruction of the walls, from time to time, in carrying out city improvements. The most important to recall are the legends in which the name

---

[1] Vol. i. numbers 8, 10, 19.

[2] Von Hammer, *Constantinopolis und Bosporos*, vol. i. appendix, numbers 23, 24. These inscriptions are noted also by Tournefort, *Voyage du Levant*, lettre xi. p. 180.

[3] *Proceedings of the Greek Literary Syllogos of Consple.*, vol. xvi., 1885 ; *Archæological Supplement*, p. 31.

INSCRIPTION IN HONOUR OF THE EMPEROR MICHAEL III.

Michael was associated with that of Theophilus. In two instances the former name preceded the latter; while in five instances the latter name preceded the former. The only satisfactory explanation of this variation is that in the first case the Michael intended was Michael II., the father of Theophilus; and that in the second case the allusion was to Michael III., the son of Theophilus. Hence it appears that the restoration of the seaward walls was commenced in the reign of Michael II., soon after the appointment of Theophilus as his colleague, in 825.

Immediately to the north of the ruins of Indjili Kiosk, beside the Sea of Marmora, three inscribed slabs were, until recently, found built into the city wall. As the legend was mutilated, its full meaning cannot be determined, but it seemed to commemorate the restoration of a portion of the wall by Michael III., under the superintendence of his maternal uncle, the famous Bardas, the commander of the body-guard known as the Scholai (αἱ Σχολαί, οἱ Σχολάριοι).

First Slab.

ωΝΚΡΑΤΑΙωϹΔΕϹΠΟϹΑΝΤωΝΤΟΥϹ
ΠΤωϹΜΙΧΑΗλΟΔΕϹΠΟΤΗϹ ΔΙΑΒΑΡ

Second Slab.

ΙΔΕΝΟϹΠΡΟϹΥΨΟϹΗΕΥΚΟϹΙΙΙΑΙΙΤΟ
ωΝϹΧΟ^ωΝΔωΜΕϹΤΙΚΟΥΗξ ξΙΡΕΤΕΡ

Third Slab.

ΗΘΕΝΕΙϹΓΗΝΤΕΙΧΟϹΕΞΕΓΕΡΚΟΤΟ
ΝΟΝωΡΑΕΙϹΜΑΤΗΠΟλΕΙᘓ ᚿ ᖰᘐ [1]

---

[1] Cf. *Proceedings of the Greek Literary Syllogos of Consple.*, vol. xvi., 1885; *Archæological Supplement*, p. 32. The following reading of the inscription has been suggested:

> Πολλῶν κραταιῶς δεσποσάντων τοῦ σάλου
> Ἀλλ' οὐδενὸς πρὸς ὕψος [εἴκοσιν ποδῶν] [2]
> Τὸ βληθὲν εἰς γῆν τεῖχος ἐξηγερκότος

[2] Read instead, *ἢ εὐκοσμίαν.* Cf. Mordtmann, p. 53.

An inscription on a tower at the eastern side of the entrance to the old harbour at Koum Kapoussi (Kontoscalion) commemorated repairs by Leo the Wise and his brother and colleague Alexander :

† ΠΥΡΓΟϹ ΛΕΟΝΤΟϹ Κ ΑΛΕΞΑΝ †

The first tower west of Ahour Kapoussi was rebuilt by Basil II. in 1024, after its overthrow by storms. It bears the inscription :

ΟΝ ΤΗϹ ΘΑΛΛΑϹϹΗϹ ΘΡΑΥϹΜΟϹ ΕΝ ΜΑΚΡꞶ ΧΡΟΝꞶ
ΚΛΥΔꞶΝΙ ΠΟΛΛꞶ ΚΑΙ ΟΦΟΔΡꞶ ΡΗΓΝΥΜΕΝΗϹ ΠΕϹΕΙΝ
ΚΑΤΑΝΑΓΚΑϹΕ ΠΥΡΓΟΝ ΕΚ ΒΑΘΡꞶΝ ΒΑϹΙΛΕΙΟϹ
ΗΓΕΙΡΕΝ ΕΥϹΕΒΗϹ ΑΝΑΞ ΕΤΟΥϹ ϚΘΛΒ

"In the year 1024, Basil, the pious Sovereign, erected from the foundations, this tower, which the dashing of the sea, shattering it for a long time with many and violent waves, compelled to fall."

One of the most interesting incidents of the siege of 1453, reflecting credit both upon the conqueror and the conquered, was associated with "the towers of Basil, Leo, and Alexius" (τῶν πύργων τῶν λεγομένων Βασιλείου, Λέοντος, καὶ Ἀλεξίου). Although the Turkish troops were in command of the city, the defenders of those towers—the crew of a ship from Crete—refused to surrender, preferring to perish rather than to be reduced to slavery. The stand they made was reported to the Sultan, and he was so impressed by the heroism of the men that he offered, if they would submit, to allow them to leave the city with all the honours of war. The generous terms were accepted, though with great reluctance, and the brave men

---

[Τανῦν] ἀκάμπτως Μιχαὴλ ὁ δεσπότης
Διὰ Βάρδα [μαΐστρου][1] σχολῶν δομεστίκου
[Τὸ δ' ἦρε κλεινὸν][2] ὡράεισμα τῇ Πόλει.

[1] Read instead, τῶν.
[2] Read instead, ἤγειρε τερπνὸν. Dr. Mordtmann reads ΕΥΚΟϹΜΙΑΝ instead of ΕΙΚΟϹΙΝ ΠΟΔꞶΝ, ΘΕΟΜΕΙΚΟΤΑ instead of ΕΞΕΓΕΡΚΟΤΟϹ, and adds ϹΟΥ to the last line.

returned home in their own vessel, and with all their posses-sions.[1] Dr. Paspates[2] suggests that the tower connected with this incident was the tower bearing the inscription in honour of Leo and Alexander.

The tower at the foot of the landing below Narli Kapoussi was repaired, according to the inscription upon it, by Manuel Comnenus.

" Restored by Manuel Comnenus, the Christ-loving King, Porphyrogenitus,
and Emperor of the Romans, in the year 1164."

According to Cinnamus,[3] the Emperor Manuel Comnenus repaired the city walls, wherever necessary.[4]

[1] Phrantzes, pp. 287, 288.

[2] Page 101. The supposition is probable ; but one or two points are not clear. Phrantzes describes the post held by the Cretans as consisting of more than one tower (p. 101, τῶν πύργων), and as a single tower (p. 288, τοῦ πύργου). (1) Is the plural number to be understood literally or rhetorically ? (2) Is the Basil associated by Phrantzes with Leo and Alexius (Alexander) their father, Basil I., or does the historian refer to Basil II. and the tower erected by that emperor ? If the former alternative be adopted, only one tower was concerned in the matter, and the name of Basil I. must have dropped out of the inscription of Leo and Alexander when the tower, as the reversed position of part of the inscription proved, was injured and repaired. If, on the other hand, the historian, in referring to the tower of Basil, had the tower of Basil II. in view, then more than one tower was defended by the Cretans. It should be added that Phrantzes (p. 254) speaks of the crew of a Cretan ship as defending the fortifications near the Beautiful Gate, on the Golden Horn (see below, pp. 221, 222), and this may be thought to imply that the tower or towers he had in mind stood beside the harbour. But as three ships (p. 238) from Crete were present at the siege, Cretans could be found taking part in the defence at different points. The tower of Leo and Alexander has disappeared.

[3] Page 274.

[4] Two fragmentary inscriptions of doubtful import, on the walls beside the Sea of Marmora, may be cited here.

The first is found on the seventh tower south of Deïrmen Kapoussi, and reads :

ΟΥ ΤΟΝ ΦΗΛωΧΡΙΟΤΟΝ ΔΕΟΠΟΤΟΝ
ΕΤΟΟ ΚΟΟΜΟΥ ΤΕΟΟΑΡΗΟ ΚΑΙ ΔΕΚΑΤΟΥ

The second is on the second tower west of Ahour Kapoussi :

ΜΒΑΙωΝΝΘΟΜ ΤΕΙΧ ΗΝΕΟΥΡΓΕΙ ΚΑΙ ΦΥΛΑΤΕΙ

Upon the restoration of the Greek Empire in 1261 the condition of the seaward walls became a matter of graver importance than it had been at any previous period in the history of the city. For, until the rise of the Ottoman power, the enemies whom Constantinople had then most reason to fear were the maritime States of Western Europe, with their formidable fleets.

The loss of the city by the Latins put a new strain upon the relations between the East and the West. It provoked more intense political antagonism, keener commercial rivalries, and a fanatical religious hatred, which all the attempts to unite the Churches of divided Christendom only fanned into fiercer flames. Nor was the situation improved when Michael Palæologus established the Genoese at Galata. A hostile power was then planted at the very gates of the capital; a foreign fleet commanded the Golden Horn; occasions for misunderstandings were multiplied; and selfish intriguers were at hand to foment the domestic quarrels of the Empire, and involve it in disputes with the rivals of Genoa. " The Roman Empire," as Gibbon observes, "might soon have sunk into a province of Genoa, if the Republic had not been checked by the ruin of her freedom and naval power."

The earliest concern of Michael Palæologus, therefore, after the recovery of the city, was to put the fortifications in a condition to repel the expected attempt of the Latins to regain the place.[1] Having no time to lose, and as lime and stone were difficult to procure, the emperor was satisfied, at first, with heightening the walls, especially those near the sea, by the erection upon the summit, of great wooden screens, covered with hide to render them fire-proof. In this way he raised the walls some seven feet.[2]

But later in his reign he conceived the ambitious idea of

[1] Pachymeres, vol. i. pp. 186, 187.   [2] Three pikes.

making the walls along the shores of the city, like the land walls, a double line of bulwarks.[1] The new fortifications, however, cannot have been a piece of solid work, for no traces of them have survived.[2]

Repairs were again executed upon the seaward walls when Andronicus II. undertook the general restoration of the for-

COAT-OF-ARMS OF ANDRONICUS II. PALÆOLOGUS.[3]

tifications of the city.[4] Until recently a slab bearing the monogram and coat-of-arms of that emperor, a lion rampant,

---

[1] Pachymeres, vol. i. p. 364; Nicephoras Greg., v. p. 124; *Metrical Chronicle*, pp. 657–661.

[2] Dr. Paspates (pp. 208, 209) considered the land wall of the Seraglio enclosure to be the work of Michael Palæologus. His argument for the opinion that the Seraglio grounds were enclosed by walls before the Turkish Conquest, and formed, after 1261, part of the domain attached to the palace of the Byzantine emperors, is the statement of Cantacuzene (iii. pp. 47, 66) that the Church of St. Demetrius stood within the palace (τῶν βασιλείων ἐντὸς). That church Dr. Paspates identified with the Church of St. Demetrius, near the Seraglio Point; hence his conclusion that the territory about that point was included in the grounds of the Byzantine palace. But Dr. Paspates must have forgotten, for a moment, that the Church of St. Demetrius, which formed the chapel of the emperors, was not near the Seraglio Point, but near the Pharos and the Chrysotriclinium of the Great Palace, buildings placed by Dr. Paspates himself at Domus-Dama, a short distance to the east of the Hippodrome, and to the west of the Seraglio enclosure. See his work on the Great Palace, Βυζαντινὰ Ἀνάκτορα, p. 183. There is an English translation of this work by Mr. Metcalfe.

[3] From *Broken Bits of Byzantium*. (By kind permission of Mrs. Walker.)

[4] Nicephorus Greg., vii. p. 275; Nicephorus Callistus, in the Dedication of his *History* to Andronicus II.

crowned and holding an upright sword, was to be seen on a tower
of the wall surrounding the ancient harbour at Koum Kapoussi.

So far, at least, as the wall beside the Sea of Marmora was
concerned, the work of Andronicus II. was soon injured. For
on the very eve of his death, on the 12th of February, 1332, a
furious storm from the south burst upon the fortifications beside
that sea. The waves leaped over the battlements, opened
breaches in the wall, forced the gates, and rushed in like a
hostile army to devastate every quarter they could overwhelm.[1]

Although the fact is not recorded, the damage done on that
occasion must have been repaired by Andronicus III.

Occasion for attending to the state of the seaward fortifications, especially along the Golden Horn, was again given, in the
course of the conflicts between Cantacuzene and the Genoese of
Galata.

In 1348 the latter made a violent assault upon the northern
side of the city, and, although failing to carry the walls, did much
harm to the shipping, timber-stores, and houses near the water.[2]

Matters assumed a more serious aspect in 1351. A powerful
fleet then sailed from Genoa, under the command of Doria, to
attack Constantinople in support of certain claims put forth by
the colony at Galata, and on its way up the Sea of Marmora,
captured the fortified town of Heraclea. The event caused the
greatest consternation in the capital, and, in view of the enemy's
approach, Cantacuzene promptly set the seaward walls in order,
repairing them where ruined, raising their height, and ordering
all houses before them to be removed.[3] He also carried the
towers higher, by erecting, in the manner usual on such occasions, constructions of timber on their summits. And not

---

[1] Nicephorus Greg., ix. p. 460.
[2] Cantacuzene, iv. p. 70; Nicephorus Greg., xvii. chaps. i.–vii.
[3] Cantacuzene, iv. pp. 212, 213 ; Nicephorus Greg., xxvi. pp. 83, 84.

satisfied with these precautions, he even excavated a deep
moat in front of the Harbour Walls, all the way from the Gate
Xylinè, at Aivan Serai, to the Gate of Eugenius (Yali Kiosk
Kapoussi), near the Seraglio Point.

A trace of these repairs is found in a slab on the tower

Remains of inscription above the heads

OΙΑιｉひ   CΠΑ‖

BAS-RELIEF, ON THE TOWER EAST OF DJUBALI KAPOUSSI, RE-
PRESENTING THE THREE HEBREW YOUTHS CAST INTO THE FIERY
FURNACE OF BABYLON, AS DESCRIBED IN THE BOOK OF DANIEL.[1]

immediately to the east of the gate Djubali Kapoussi,[2] bearing a
lion rampant, and the name of Manuel Phakrasè Catacuzene
(MANOYHΛ ΦAKPACH TOY KATAKOYCHNOY), who was
Proto-strator under Cantacuzene, and distinguished himself by

---

[1] From *Broken Bits of Byzantium.* (By kind permission of Mrs. Walker.) The
bas-relief has been removed to the Imperial Museum.

[2] See below, p. 209.

his conduct in the defence of Selivria, in 1341, and in the siege of Galata, ten years later.[1]

In 1434 the Harbour Walls called for some slight repair, in consequence of another Genoese attack upon them.   An expedition which had been sent from Genoa to take the town of Kaffa, having failed in that object, returned to the Bosporus, and sought to compensate for defeat in the Crimea by nothing less than the capture of Constantinople itself.   The bold attempt made with ships carrying 8000 troops, was repulsed, and the baffled fleet returned to Italy.   But the Genoese of Galata determined to continue the struggle ; and in the bombardment of the walls with cannon, destroyed several warehouses in the city, and a tower beside the Gate Basilikè.   This attack, likewise, ended in failure, and the colony was compelled to pay an indemnity of a thousand pieces of gold, to make good the damage caused by the bombardment.[2]

Two inscriptions, preserved by Dr. A. D. Mordtmann[3] in his work on the last siege of the city,[4] are noteworthy as records of repairs made on the fortifications beside the Sea of Marmora, when Constantinople trembled before the Ottoman power. They are also interesting on account of the personages whom they commemorate as restorers of the walls.

One stood, somewhere, on the wall between Ahour Kapoussi and Tchatlady Kapou, and read :

ΛΟΥΚ
ΝΟΤΑΡΑς
ΔΙΕΡΜΗΝΕΥΤΟΥ

"Of Luke Notaras, the Interpreter."

---

[1] Cantacuzene, iii. p. 585 ; iv. p. 196.   See *Proceedings of Greek Literary Syllogos of Consple.*, 1885 ; *Archæological Supplement*, pp. 37, 38.

[2] Chalcocondylas, pp. 285, 286.

[3] The father of Dr. Mordtmann, whose work on the topography of the city has been so often cited.

[4] *Belagerung und Eroberung Constantinopels durch die Türken in Jahre* 1453, note 27, p. 132 ; Stuttgart, J. G., *Cottascher Verlag.*

This was Lucas Notaras, who subsequently became Grand Duke, and was the most prominent citizen of Constantinople in the catastrophe of 1453. When he executed these repairs he held the office of interpreter, or dragoman, under the Emperor John VII. Palæologus, in carrying on negotiations with Sultan Murad.[1] The office had, naturally, come into existence owing to the frequent diplomatic intercourse between the Byzantine Government and foreigners, and was of great importance and distinction. In the reign of Manuel Palæologus it had been held by Nicholas Notaras, the father of Lucas Notaras.[2]

The second inscription stood on a tower between Koum Kapoussi and Yeni Kapou. It commemorated repairs executed in 1448 at the expense of the celebrated George Brankovitch, Despot of Servia.

> † ANEKENIO
> ΘΗΝ ΟΥΤΟϹ
> Ο ΠΥΡΓΟϹ ΚΑΙ
> ΚΟΡΤΙΝΑ Υ
> ΠΟ ΓΕωΡΓΙ
> ΟΥ ΔΕϹΠΟΤΟΥ
> ϹΕΡΒΙΑϹ · ⁖ · +
> ΕΝ ΕΤΕΙ ϛϡΥϛ

"This tower and curtain-wall were restored by George, Despot of Servia; in the year 6956 (1448)."

It will be remembered that some of the funds furnished by the Servian king were employed in repairs on the land walls.[3]

---

[1] Ducas, pp. 196, 275; cf. Phrantzes, p. 118.

[2] Ducas, pp. 93, 94. See Schlumberger, *Un Empereur Byzantin au Dixième Siècle*, pp. 48, 49, for an account of the interpreters attached to the Varangian Guard. Ville-Hardouin (c. 39) speaks of the dragoman who assisted Isaac Angelus in the negotiations with the envoys of the Crusaders in 1203 : " Et il (the emperor) se leva, et entra en une chambre ; et n'emmena avec lui que l'impératrice, et son chancelier, et son drogman, et les quatre messagers " (of the Crusaders).

[3] See above, p. 107.

O

CHAPTER XIV.

THE WALLS ALONG THE GOLDEN HORN.

THE Harbour Fortifications guarded the northern side of the city, from the Acropolis (Seraglio Point) to the terminus of the land walls at Blachernæ, and, excepting a small portion, consisted of a single wall, flanked, according to Bondelmontius, by a hundred and ten towers.[1]

To accommodate the commerce and traffic of the city, the wall was built, for the most part, at a short distance from the water ; but the strip of ground thus left without the fortifications was even narrower in ancient times than it is at present, much of the land outside the wall having been made by recent deposits of earth and rubbish. This explains how the Venetian fleet, in 1203 and 1204, was able to approach so near the ramparts that troops standing on the flying bridges attached to the ships' yards came to close quarters with the defenders on the walls. Indeed, in one case, at least, such a bridge spanned the distance between ship and tower, and permitted the assailants to cross over and seize the latter.[2] At the actual distance, however, of the wall from the water, such a feat would be impossible, except in the vicinity of the Seraglio Point, which was not the quarter attacked by the Venetians.

---

[1] *Librum Insularum Archipelagi.*   [2] Ville-Hardouin, c. xxxvi., lii., liii.

GATES.

At a short distance to the east of the Xylo Porta a breach in the wall marks the site of a gateway named by the Turks Kutchuk Aivan Serai Kapoussi—"the Small Gate of Aivan Serai."[1]   It stands at the head of a short street leading southwards to the site of the famous Church of the Theotokos of Blachernæ, while to the north is the landing of Aivan Serai Iskelessi, which accommodates this quarter of the city.   Here, probably, was the Porta Kiliomenè (Κοιλιωμένη Πόρτα),[2] at which the emperors—as late, at least, as the beginning of the thirteenth century—landed and were received by the Senate, when proceeding by water to visit the Church or the Palace of Blachernæ. Nowhere else could one disembark so near that sanctuary and that palace.

The landing-stage before the gate must, therefore, have been the Imperial Pier ('Αποβάθρα τοῦ βασιλέως) mentioned by Nicetas Choniates.   Some authorities, it is true, place that landing at Balat Kapoussi.   But it could not have been there when Nicetas Choniates wrote ; for that historian [3] refers to the Apobathra of the Emperor to indicate the position of the Wall of Leo, which was attacked by the Latins in 1203.   Now, points which could thus serve to identify each other must have been in close proximity.   But Balat Kapoussi and the Wall of Leo are too far apart for the former to indicate the site of the latter.   On the other hand, the Wall of Leo and Aivan Serai Iskelessi are very near each other.

---

[1] Evlia Tchelebi.   Aivan Serai means the Palace of the Porch, or Verandah. The name refers, probably, to the Palace of Blachernæ.

[2] Constant. Porphyr., *De Cer.*, p. 542, cf. p. 551.   In the Bonn Edition the term is translated, "Depressa et in humilius deducta."

[3] Page 721, τὸ τεῖχος ὅ παρατείναι πρὸς θάλασσαν περὶ τόπον ὅς ἀποβάθρα τοῦ βασιλέως ὠνόμασται.   Cf. Ville-Hardouin, c. 35 : "un avant-mur . . . près de la mer."

Over the northern entrance to the lower chamber in the tower west of the gateway were found, until recently, two blocks of stone, upon which the name of St. Pantoleon was rudely carved between the figures of two peacocks, or phœnixes, symbols of the immortality that rose from the fires of martyrdom. Possibly, the chamber was a chapel in which persons entering or leaving the city could perform their devotions. According to Stephen of Novgorod, the relics of St. Panteleon reposed in the adjoining Church of the Theotokos of Blachernæ.[1]

In the street to the rear of the tower is the small Mosque Toklou Dedè Mesdjidi, formerly, it is supposed, the Church of St. Thekla,[2] in the quarter of Blachernæ.

On the east side of the street leading from the Porta Kiliomenè to the Church of Blachernæ remains are found of a large two-storied Byzantine edifice, with three aisles. Its original destination cannot be determined with any degree of certainty. By some authorities[3] the building is supposed to have been the Porticus Cariana (Καριανὸν Ἐμβολον), which the Emperor Maurice erected, and upon the walls of which scenes in his life, from his childhood until his accession to the throne, were pourtrayed.[4]

The Bay of Aivan Serai was called the Bay of Blachernæ (ὁ πρὸς Βλαχέρνας κόλπος), and had a dockyard known as the Neorion at Blachernæ (τὸ ἐν Βλαχέρναις νεώριον).[5]

Proceeding eastwards, a few paces bring us to a breach in the wall leading to the Mosque Atik Mustapha Pasha Djamissi,

[1] *Itinéraires Russes en Orient*, p. 124.

[2] Paspates, pp. 357–360. Cf. Theophanes Cont., pp. 147, 148 ; Anna Comn., iii. p. 166.

[3] Mordtmann, p. 39.

[4] Theophanes, p. 402. The building is ninety-eight feet long by sixty feet wide. The central aisle is twenty feet wide ; the side aisles fifteen feet. The dividing walls, pierced by seven arches, are five feet thick.

[5] Pachymeres, vol. i. p. 365.

supposed to be the Byzantine Church of SS. Peter and Mark, which was erected in 458 by two patricians, Galbius and Candidus, upon the shore of the Golden Horn, in the quarter of Blachernæ. The sanctuary claimed the honour of having enshrined "the Girdle of the Blessed Virgin," before that relic was placed in the church specially dedicated to the Theotokos in this part of the city.[1] In the street to the west of the mosque lies the marble baptismal font of the church, cruciform, and having three steps within it leading to the bottom.

In a chrysoboullon of John Palæologus dated 1342, mention is made of the Gate of St. Anastasia (Πύλη τῆς ἁγίας ᾽Αναστασίας) in this part of the city.[2] The Russian pilgrim, who visited Constantinople in the fifteenth century (1424-1453), speaks of a chapel containing the relics of St. Anastasia near the Church of Blachernæ.[3]

Considerable interest is attached to the Church of St. Demetrius, situated within the walls a few paces to the east of Atik Mustapha Pasha Djamissi; for although the present edifice dates only from the beginning of the eighteenth century, the original building was a Byzantine foundation, adorned with mosaics and surmounted by a dome. Its full style was the Church of St. Demetrius of Kanabus (τοῦ Καναβοῦ), and may, as the Patriarch Constantius suggests,[4] have been erected by a member of the family of the Nicholas Kanabus who became emperor for a few days, in the interval between the overthrow of the Angeli and the usurpation of Murtzuphlus, during the troublous times of the Fourth Crusade.[5] In 1334, the church

---

[1] Paspates, p. 317 ; Du Cange, _Constantinopolis Christiana_, iv. p. 116.

[2] Νεολόγου ᾽Εβδομαδιαία ᾽Επιθεώρησις, January 3, 1893, p. 203.

[3] _Itinéraires Russes en Orient_, p. 233.

[4] Συγγραφαὶ αἱ ᾽Ελάσσονες, p. 441.   [5] Nicetas Chon., pp. 744-746.

was the property of George Pepagomenos, a relative of Andronicus III.[1]   After the Turkish Conquest the church became, from 1597 to 1601, the cathedral of the Greek Patriarch, when he was deprived of the use of the Church of the Pammakaristos (Fethiyeh Djamissi).[2]

Soon after leaving the Church of St. Demetrius, and before reaching the gate now styled Balat Kapoussi, the city wall was pierced by three large archways, 45 to 55 paces apart, and alternating with three towers.   Balat Kapoussi being only 55 paces beyond the easternmost archway, here stood four entrances into the city, in most unusual proximity to one another.   The first, or westernmost archway was, at one time, adorned with a bas-relief on either side.   Tafferner, chaplain to Count Walter of Leslie, ambassador from the German Emperor Leopold I. to the Ottoman Court in the seventeenth century, describes the archway as follows: "In decensu clivi defluentis in Euxini brachium, porta perampla et obstructa muro conspicitur.   Fama fert limitum hunc fuisse aulæ magni Constantini.   Ad dextrum portæ latus adstat Angelus a candido et eleganti marmore effigiatus, statura celsior, ac virilem præ se ferens, et inserto muro.   Ad lævam, Deipara visitur, proportione priore consimilis, atque ab Angelo consulatuta." [3]

Only the bas-relief which stood on the eastern side of the archway has survived to our time.[4]   It represents a winged female figure, attired in a flowing robe, and holding in her left hand a palm leaf—beyond all controversy a Nikè, not, as Tafferner imagined, the Angel of the Annunciation, nor, as the Patriarch Constantius supposed, the Archangel Michael.[5]

[1] *Acta Patriarchatus CP.*, vol. i. p. 568.
[2] Gedeon, Χρονικὰ τοῦ Πατριαρχικοῦ Οἴκου καὶ τοῦ Ναοῦ, pp. 72–75.
[3] *Cæsarea Legatio*, pars. iii. p. 94 (Vienna, 1668).
[4] It is now in the Imperial Museum.
[5] *Ancient and Modern Constantinople*, p. 15.

NIKÉ (FORMERLY ADORNING ARCHWAY NEAR BALAT KAPOUSSI).

Regarding the precise object of these four entrances, and the names to be attached to them, a serious difference of opinion prevails. Most authorities maintain that the archway adorned with the bas-relief was the Gate of the Kynegos, of the Hunter (τοῦ Κυνηγοῦ, τῶν Κυνηγῶν), so frequently mentioned in the later days of the Empire; and that Balat Kapoussi was the Pylè Basilikè (Πύλη Βασιλικὴ) referred to by writers of the same period. On the other hand, Gyllius identified Balat Kapoussi with the Gate of the Kynegos, and regarded the three archways above mentioned as entrances to a small artificial port within the line of the fortifications. His reason for the latter opinion was the existence of a great depression in the ground to the rear of the archways, which was occupied, in his day, by market-gardens, but which seemed to him the basin of an old harbour: "Ultra Portam Palatinam"—to give his own words—" progressus circiter centum viginti passus, animadverti tres magnus arcus, astructos urbis muro, et substructos, per quos olim Imperatores subducebant triremes in portum opere factum, nunc exiccatus et conversus in hortos concavos, præ se gerentes speciem portus obruti."[1]

As appears from the passage just quoted, Gyllius styled Balat Kapoussi not only the Gate of the Hunter, but also the Porta Palatina. Whether in doing so he meant to identify the Gate of the Kynegos with the Basilikè Pylè, or simply gave the Latin rendering of the name by which Balat Kapoussi was popularly known when he visited the city, is not perfectly clear. The latter supposition is, however, more in harmony with that author's usage in the case of other gates.

Stephen Gerlach and Leunclavius agree with Gyllius in regarding Balat Kapoussi as the Gate of the Kynegos, but place the

---

[1] *De Top. CP.*, iv. c. 4 ; *De Bosporo Thracio*, ii. c. 2. This depression was visible as late as 1852, according to Scarlatus Byzantius, vol. i. p. 582. It was then known as a Tchoukour Bostan, the usual Turkish designation for a garden in a hollow.

Basilikè Pylè near the eastern extremity of the Harbour Walls,
Gerlach[1] identifying it with Yali Kiosk Kapoussi, Leunclavius[2]
with Bagtchè Kapoussi.   Neither Gerlach nor Leunclavius
refers to the three arches on the west of Balat Kapoussi. The
latter, however, speaks of the hollow ground to their rear,
describing it in the following terms: "Locus depressus et con-
cavus, ubi Patriarchion erat meæ peregrinationis tempore,"
and supposed it to have been the arena of a theatre for the
exhibition of wild animals.   From that theatre, he thought, the
Gate of the Kynegos obtained its name.

The question to which gates the names Gate of the Kynegos
and Basilikè Pylè respectively belonged is the most difficult
problem connected with the history of the harbour fortifications.
To discuss it satisfactorily at this stage of our inquiries is, however, impossible; for the opinion that the Basilikè Pylè was not at
Balat Kapoussi, but near the eastern extremity of the Harbour
Walls, is a point which can be determined only after all the facts
relative to the gates near that end of the fortifications are
before us.   The full discussion of the subject must therefore be
deferred,[3] and, meantime, little more can be done than to state
the conclusions which appear to have most evidence in their
favour.

There can be no doubt, in the first place, that the Gate of the
Kynegos was in this vicinity, and was either Balat Kapoussi or
the archway adorned with the bas-relief.   This is established
by all the indications in regard to the situation of the entrance.
The Gate of the Kynegos stood, according to Phrantzes,[4] between the Xylo Porta and the Petrion; according to Pusculus,[5]

---

[1] *Tagebuch der Gesandschaft an die Ottomanische Pforte durch David Ungnad,*
p. 454. All subsequent references to Gerlach are to this Diary of his visit to Constantinople, 1573–1578.

[2] *Pand. Hist. Turc.*, s. 200.   [3] See below, pp. 230–240.

[4] Page 254.   [5] IV. p. 181.

between the Xylo Porta and the Porta Phani (Fener Kapoussi), and not far from the former. It was in the neighbourhood of the emperor's palace,[1] and the point at which persons approaching that palace from the Golden Horn disembarked and took horses to reach the Imperial residence.[2] Both Balat Kapoussi and the adjoining archways answer to this description, and they are the only entrances which can pretend to be city gates in the portion of the walls between the Xylo Porta and the Gate of the Phanar. Therefore, one or other of them was the Gate of the Kynegos.

It is a corroboration of this conclusion to find that the district named after the Gate of the Kynegos occupied the level tract beside the Golden Horn within and without the line of the walls in the vicinity of these entrances. The Church of St. Demetrius, for instance, which stood a short distance to the west of Balat Kapoussi and the adjoining archways, is described as near a gate in the quarter of the Kynegon.[3] The bridge which the Turks threw out into the harbour from Haskeui, to carry a battery with which to bombard this part of the fortifications, was in front of the Kynegon.[4] Nicholas Barbaro[5] applies the name even to the territory near the Xylo Porta ; for, according to him, the land walls extended from the Golden Gate to the Kynegon : " Le mure de tera, che jera mia sie, che sun de la Cresca per fina al Chinigo." With this agrees also the

---

[1] N. Barbaro, p. 789.

[2] Clavijo, p. 14, " Il fut décidé que les ambassadeurs retourneraient (from Pera) à Constantinople mercredi, par la porte nomée ' Quinigo,' où ils devaient trouver le sieur Hilaire . . . ainsi que des chevaux de monture, et qu'ils visiteraient alors la plus grande partie de la ville." Cf. p. 15, " Les dits ambassadeurs passèrent à Constantinople et trouvèrent bientôt le dit sieur Hilaire et d'autres personnes de la cour, près de la porte de ' Quinigo,' où ils les attendaient ; ils montèrent à cheval et partirent pour visiter une église nommée Sancta Maria de la Cherne (St. Mary of Blachernæ)."

[3] *Acta Patriarchatus CP.*, i. p. 568, year 1334.

[4] Ducas, p. 279 ; cf. Barbaro, p. 789.   [5] Page 728.

statement of the same author that the Kynegon was the point
where Diedo and Gabriel of Treviso landed the crews of their
galleys, to excavate the moat which the emperor asked to be
constructed before the land walls protecting his palace.[1] The
quarter of the Kynegon thus comprised the modern quarters
of Balata and Aivan Serai.

In the second place, it is exceedingly doubtful whether the
archway with the Nikè, to which the name Gate of the Kynegos
is commonly ascribed, was, after all, a city gate in the ordinary
sense of the term. It does not stand alone, but is one
of three archways which pierce, respectively, the curtain-walls
between three towers. And these three openings were in
close proximity to a gate (Balat Kapoussi), amply sufficient for
the requirements of public traffic in this quarter of the capital.
Such facts do not accord with the idea that any one of these
archways was a gateway. Furthermore, when their real destination could be more accurately ascertained than at present,
Gyllius found that they formed the entrances to an artificial harbour within the line of the fortifications. This explanation of
their presence in the wall is perfectly satisfactory, and any other
is superfluous. But if Balat Kapoussi was the only gate in this
vicinity, it must have been the Gate of the Kynegos, which
certainly stood in this part of the city.

There is nothing strange in the existence of a harbour within
the line of the fortifications in the quarter of the Kynegon. It is
what might be expected when we remember how closely the
quarter was connected with the Palace of the Porphyrogenitus
and the Palace of Blachernæ, and how necessary such a harbour
was for the accommodation and protection of the boats and galleys
at the service of the Court. That the harbour behind the three
archways near Balat Kapoussi was the Neorion of Blachernæ is

[1] Page 720.

unlikely ; the most probable situation of that Neorion being at Aivan Serai Iskelessi. But it may very well have been the harbour on the shore of the Kynegon at which, during the period of the Palæologi, the emperor and visitors to the palaces in the vicinity embarked or disembarked in moving to and fro by water. The landing at which the Spanish ambassadors to the Byzantine Court were received is described as near the Gate of the Kynegos : "Près de la porte de Quinigo."[1] The galleys sent by the Council of Basle to convey John VII. Palæologus to the West, and which reached Constantinople fifteen days after the arrival of four Papal galleys on a similar errand, were detained for one day at Psamathia, until the rival parties had been prevailed upon to keep the peace, and then came and moored at the Kynegon (εἰς τὸν Κυνηγὸν). There the emperor embarked for Italy, under the escort of the Papal galleys ; there the galley having on board the patriarch, who was to accompany the emperor, joined the Imperial squadron ; and there the emperor disembarked upon his return from the Councils of Ferrara and Florence.[2] During the siege of 1453 a fire-ship, with forty young men on board, proceeded from the Gate of the Kynegos to burn the Turkish vessels which had been conveyed over the hills into the Golden Horn.[3] All this implies the existence of a port somewhere on the shore of the quarter of the Kynegon.

In the third place, all discussion in regard to the proper application of the names Basilikè Pylè, and Gate of the Kynegos must proceed upon the indisputable fact that the epithet "Imperial,"

[1] Clavijo, *Constantinople, Ses Sanctuaires et ses Reliques*, pp. 14, 15.

[2] See *History of the Council of Florence*, by Sgyropoulos, who attended the Council in the suite of the patriarch. The Greek original and a Latin translation are found in *Veræ Historia Unionis non Veræ inter Græcos et Latinos, sive Concilii Florentini.* The translation, published in 1670, is by Robert Creyghton, and was dedicated to Charles II. For the account of the matters referred to above, see that work, pp. 51, 54, 55, 67, 318. Cf. Scarlatus Byzantius, vol. i. p. 582.

[3] *Historia Politica*, p. 19.

belonged to an entrance at the eastern extremity of the Harbour Walls. In proof of this, it is enough to cite, meantime, the statement of Phrantzes[1] that Gabriel of Treviso was entrusted with the defence of a tower which guarded the entrance of the Golden Horn, and which stood opposite the Basilikè Pylè. Unless, therefore, it can be shown that there was more than one Basilikè Pylè in the fortifications beside the Golden Horn, the claim of Balat Kapoussi to the Imperial epithet falls to the ground. If the existence of two Imperial gates in the Harbour Walls can be established, then Balat Kapoussi has the best right to be regarded as the second entrance bearing that designation. In that case, however, the conclusion most in harmony with the facts involved in the matter is that the second Basilikè Pylè was only the Gate of the Kynegos under another name.[2]

Why, precisely, the entrance was styled the Gate of the Hunter is a matter of conjecture. Some explain the name as derived from a Kynegion, or theatre for the exhibition of wild animals,[3] such as existed on the side of the city facing Scutari; and in favour of this opinion is the term "Kynegesion" (τοῦ Κυνηγεσίου), employed by Phrantzes[4] to designate the quarter adjoining the entrance. But the ordinary style of the name lends more countenance to the view that the gate was in some way connected with the huntsmen attached to the Byzantine Court, hunting being always a favourite pastime of the emperors of Constantinople. Their head huntsman (ὁ πρωτοκυνηγὸς) was an official of some importance. Besides directing his subordinates,

---

[1] Pages 254, 255.

[2] On the supposition that there was no Imperial Gate near the eastern extremity of the Harbour Walls, it is impossible to identify the Basilikè Pylè and the Gate of the Kynegos, for these names are sometimes employed in a way which renders it perfectly evident that they referred to different gates. See Phrantzes, *ut supra;* Pusculus, iv. 179-221; Dolfin, s. 55; Ducas, p. 275.

[3] Leunclavius, *Pand. Hist. Turc.*, s. 200.

[4] Page 254.

it was his prerogative to hold the stirrup when the emperor mounted horse, and the Imperial hunting-suit was his perquisite, if stained with blood in the course of the chase.[1]

A gate, known as the Gate of St. John the Forerunner and Baptist (Πόρτα τοῦ ἁγίου Προδρόμου καὶ Βαπτιστοῦ), was also situated in the quarter of the Kynegon, and near the Church of St. Demetrius.[2] That name might readily be given to a gate in this vicinity, either in honour of the great Church and Monastery of St. John the Baptist in Petra, on the heights above Balat Kapoussi, or in honour of the church of the same dedication, which, there is reason to think, stood on the site of the Church of St. John the Baptist, found, at present, on the shore to the north-east of that entrance. Whether the Gate of St. John has disappeared, or was the Gate of the Kynegos under another name, is a point upon which there may be a difference of opinion. Dr. Mordtmann[3] identifies it with the Gate of the Kynegos, which, according to him, was the archway adorned with the Nikè. It may be identified with the Gate of the Kynegos, even on the view that the latter was Balat Kapoussi. That a Church of St. John stood in the neighbourhood of the Gate of the Kynegos is also intimated by Pachymeres, who records a fire which, in 1308, burnt down the quarter extending from that gate to the Monastery of the Forerunner.[4]

---

[1] Codinus, *De Officiis CP.*, p. 39.

[2] *Acta Patriarchatus CP.*, vol. i. p. 568, year 1334 : Ὁ πλησίον τῶν οἰκημάτων αὐτοῦ, τῶν περὶ τὴν πόρταν τοῦ ἁγίου καὶ ἐνδόξου Προδρόμου καὶ Βαπτιστοῦ κατὰ τῶν Κυνηγῶν, διακείμενος πάνσεπτος ναὸς τοῦ ἐν μάρτυσι περιβοήτου, μυροβλύτου καὶ θαυματουργοῦ ἁγίου Δημητρίου.

Beyond all reasonable doubt, this was the same gate as the Gate of St. John mentioned in the *Chrysobullon of John Palæologus*, p. 203, cited above on p. 197. The latter, also, was a gate near the water, with a considerable territory outside the entrance, occupied by numerous buildings. See p. 203 of the Νεολόγου Ἑβδομα-διαία Ἐπιθεώρησις, of January 3, 1893. The identity of the two gates is confirmed by the reference in the *Chrysobullon* to Kanabus (τοῦ Κανάβη), the eponym of the Church of St. Demetrius.

[3] Page 40.

[4] Vol. ii. p. 582.

The gate next in order, as its Turkish name, Fener Kapoussi, proves, is the entrance which the foreign historians of the last siege style Porta Phani, Porta del Pharo.[1] This designation was, doubtless, the rendering of the Byzantine name of the gate, for the adjoining quarter, as appears first in a document dated 1351, went by its present name, Phanari (τοποθεσία τοῦ φανάρι),[2] also before the Turkish Conquest. A beacon light must have stood at this point of the harbour.

From the Porta Phani eastwards to Petri Kapoussi, the next gate, the fortifications consisted of two lines of wall which enclosed a considerable territory, the inner wall describing a great curve on the steep northern front of the Fifth Hill. The enclosure was called the Castron of the Petrion[3] (τὸ κάστρον τῶν Πετρίων), after Petrus, Master of the Offices in the reign of Justinian the Great;[4] and the surrounding district was named the Petrion (Πετρίον, τὰ Πετρία,[5] "Regio Petri Patricii").[6] It must be carefully distinguished from the district of Petra (Πέτρα), at Kesmè Kaya, above Balat Kapoussi.

In the angle formed by the junction of the two walls, a little to the west of the Porta Phani, was a small gate, Diplophanarion,[7] which led from the Castron into the city.

Petri Kapoussi, at the eastern extremity of the Castron, and in the outer wall, communicated with the street skirting the Golden Horn, and retains the ancient name of the district.[8] Dr. Mordtmann[9] identifies it with the Porta Sidhera (Σιδηρᾶ Πύλη), near the Convent of the Petrion.[10] That the Petrion was not confined to the Castron, but included territory on either

---

[1] Pusculus, iv. 189 ; Zorzo Dolfin, s. 55.
[2] *Acta Patriarchatus CP.*, vol. i. p. 321.
[3] *Ibid.*, p. 721.   [4] Anonymus, ii. p. 35 ; cf. i. p. 20.
[5] Nicetas Chon., p. 753.
[6] Antony of Novgorod, in *Itinéraires Russes en Orient*, p. 99.
[7] Leunclavius, *Pand. Hist. Turc.*, s. 200.   [8] *Metrical Chronicle*, line 259.
[9] Page 41.   [10] Anna Comn., iii. p. 103 ; Bryennius, iii. p. 126.

side of the enclosure, is manifest from the fact that whereas the wall between the Porta Phani and the Porta Petri is without a single tower, mention is yet made of towers in the Petrion.[1]

Of the churches in this quarter, St. Stephen of the Romans, St. Julianè, St. Elias, and St. Euphemia, the two last were the most important.   The Church of St. Euphemia claimed to be an older foundation than Constantinople itself, being attributed to Castinus, Bishop of Byzantium, 230-237. It was restored by Basil I., and his daughters entered the convent attached to the church.[2] The Convent of Petrion, as it was called, must have been of considerable importance, for it was on several occasions selected as the place in which ladies of high rank, who had become politically inconvenient, were interned ; as, for instance, Zoe, the dowager-empress of Leo the Wise, for conspiracy against Romanus Lecapenus ;[3] Theodora, by her sister the Empress Zoe ;[4] and Delassaina, the mother of the Comneni, with her daughters and daughters - in - law, by Nicephorus Botoniates.[5]

In the assaults made by foreign fleets upon the Harbour Walls, the Petrion, or Phanar, occupied a conspicuous place.

It was before the Petrion[6] that the Venetian galleys under Dandolo stood, July 17, 1203, and established the free end of their flying bridges upon the summit of the walls, whereby twenty-five towers were captured, and the city was recovered for Isaac Angelus.   The Petrion was again prominent in the assault which the Crusaders delivered on April 12, 1204, when Constantinople passed into their hands and became the seat of a Latin Empire.   Here the flying bridge of the ship *Pelerine* lodged itself on a tower, and allowed a bold Venetian and a

---

[1] Ville-Hardouin, c. 36 ; Nicetas Chon., p. 722.
[2] Anonymus, ii. p. 39.   [3] Cedrenus, vol. ii. p. 296.   [4] *Ibid.*, p. 537.
[5] Anna Comn., ii. p. 103.   [6] Nicetas Chon. ; Ville-Hardouin, *ut supra.*

French knight, André d'Urboise, to rush across, seize the tower, and clear a way for their comrades to follow. Here ladders were then landed, the walls scaled, three gates forced, and the city thrown open to the whole host of the invaders.[1]

In the siege of 1453, early on the morning of the 29th of May, the Phanar was fiercely attacked by the Turkish ships in the Golden Horn.[2] The attack was repulsed, and the Greeks remained masters of the situation, until the occupation of the city by the enemy's land forces made further resistance impossible. The memory of the struggle is said to be preserved in the quarter by the name of the street Sandjakdar Youcousou (the Ascent of the Standard-bearer) and by the Turkish name for the Church of St. Mary Mougouliotissa, Kan Klissè (the Church of Blood).[3]

The succeeding gate, Yeni Aya Kapou, was opened, it would seem, in Turkish times, being first mentioned by Evlia Tchelebi. There is, however, one circumstance in favour of regarding it as a small Byzantine entrance, enlarged after the Conquest. On the right of the gate, within the line of the walls, are the remains of a large Byzantine edifice, which could hardly have dispensed with a postern.

Aya Kapou, the next entrance, as its Turkish name intimates, and the order of Pusculus requires, is the Porta Divæ Theodosiæ (Πύλη τῆς Ἁγίας Θεοδοσίας),[4] so named in honour of the adjoining Church of St. Theodosia (now Gul Djamissi), the first martyr

---

[1] Nicetas Chon., pp. 753, 754; Ville-Hardouin, c. 52, 53.

[2] N. Barbaro, p. 818.

[3] Patriarch Constantius, *Ancient and Modern Consple.*, pp. 85, 86. The church was erected or restored by Maria, the natural daughter of Michael Palæologus, upon her return to Constantinople, after the death of her husband, the Khan of the Mongols. It has remained in the possession of the Greek community, in virtue of a firman of Mehemet the Conqueror, who presented the church to Christodoulos, the architect of the mosque erected by the Sultan on the Fifth Hill (*Acta Patriarchatus CP.*, vol. i. p. 321, year 1351).

[4] Phrantzes, p. 254; Pusculus, iv. 190.

in the cause of Icons, under Leo the Isaurian.   The gate was
also known by the name Porta Dexiocrates, after the district of
Dexiocrates in which it stood.[1]   This identification rests upon
the fact that while Pachymeres[2] affirms that the body of St.
Theodosia lay in the church dedicated to her memory, the
Synaxaristes declares that she was buried in the Monastery of
Dexiocrates.[3]   Only by the supposition that the Church of St.
Theodosia stood in the district of Dexiocrates can these statements be reconciled.   The church is first mentioned by Antony
of Novgorod.[4]   The festival of the saint, falling on May 29th,
coincided with the day on which, in 1453, the city was captured
by the Turks.   As usual, a large crowd of worshippers, many
of them ladies, filled the sacred edifice, little thinking of the
tragedy which would interrupt their devotions, when suddenly
Turkish troops burst into the church and carried the congre-
gation off into slavery.[5]

The next gate, Djubali Kapoussi, must be the entrance
styled Porta Puteæ by Pusculus,[6] and Porta del Pozzo by Zorzo
Dolfin ;[7] for it is the only entrance between the Gate of St.
Theodosia (Aya Kapou) and the Porta Platea (Oun Kapan
Kapoussi), the gates between which the writers above mentioned
place the Porta Puteæ.   Although no Byzantine author has
mentioned the Porta Puteæ by its Greek name, there can be no
doubt that the name in vogue among foreigners was the translation, more or less exact, of the native style of the entrance,
and that consequently the gate marks the point designated
Ispigas (εἰς Πηγὰς) by the Chronista Novgorodensis, in his account
of the operations of the Venetian fleet against the harbour fortifications on the 12th of April, 1204.   The ships of the Crusaders,

---

[1] Codinus, *De S. Sophia*, p. 147 ; Anonymus, ii. p. 34.
[2] Vol. ii. pp. 452–455.   [3] *Synaxaria*, May 29.
[4] *Itinéraires Russes en Orient*, p. 104.   [5] Ducas, p. 293.
[6] IV. 191.   [7] S. 55.

says that authority, were then drawn up before the walls, in a line extending from the Monastery of Christ the Benefactor and Ispigas, on the east, to Blachernæ, on the west : " Cum solis ortu steterunt, in conspectu ecclesiæ Sancti Redemptoris, quæ dicitur τοῦ Εὐεργέτου, et Ispigarum, Blachernis tenus." [1]

The name of the gate alluded to the suburb of Pegæ (Πηγαί), situated directly opposite, on the northern shore of the harbour, and noted for its numerous springs of water. Dionysius Byzantius, in his *Anaplus of the Golden Horn and the Bosporus*,[2] describes the locality at length, naming it Krenides (Κρηνίδες). on account of its flowing springs (πηγαίων), which gave the district the character of marshy ground. The suburb appears under the name Pegæ in the history of the siege of the city by the Avars, when the Imperial fleet formed a cordon across the harbour, from the Church of St. Nicholas at Blachernæ to the Church of St. Conon and the suburb of Pegæ, to prevent the enemy's flotilla of boats in the streams at the head of the Golden Horn from descending into the harbour.[3]

According to Antony of Novgorod, the suburb was situated to the west of St. Irene of Galata ; it contained several churches, and was largely inhabited by Jews.[4] It appears again in the old Records of the Genoese colony of Galata in the fourteenth

---

[1] *Chroniques Græco-Romaines*, pp. 96, 97. Dr. Mordtmann thinks that this point is referred to also in the Treaty of Michael Palæologus with the Venetians in 1265, when that emperor allowed the Venetians to occupy any point from the old Arsenal to Pegæ (ἀπὸ τῆς παλαιᾶς ἐξαρτύσις μέχρι καὶ τῶν Πηγῶν). The passage is ambiguous, for there was an old arsenal and a suburb Pegæ on the northern side of the Golden Horn, and the concession was outside the city.

[2] Edition of C. Weseler, Paris, 1874. Cf. Gyllius, *De Bosporo Thracio*, ii. c. iv.

[3] *Paschal Chron.*, p. 720, 721.

[4] *Itinéraires Russes en Orient*, pp. 88, 107, 108. Among its churches was the Church of St. Conon (*Paschal Chron.*, p. 721), memorable in the Sedition of the Nika, as the church of the monks who rescued two of the seven rioters condemned to death from the hands of the clumsy executioner, and carried them across the Golden Horn in a boat to the Church of St. Laurentius for sanctuary (Malalas, p. 473).

century, under the name Spiga, or De Spiga, to the west of that town.[1] Critobulus calls it the Cold Waters (Ψυχρὰ Ὕδατα), placing it on the bay into which Sultan Mehemet brought his ships over the hills from the Bosporus.[2]

As appears from the passage of the Chronista Novgorodensis, cited above, near the Porta Puteæ stood the Monastery of Christ the Benefactor, interesting as a conspicuous landmark in the scenes associated with the Latin Conquest of the city.

The fire which the Venetians set near the portion of the Harbour Walls captured in 1203, reduced to ashes the quarters extending from Blachernæ as far east as that monastery.[3] The monastery marked also the eastern extremity of the line of battle in which the ships of the Crusaders delivered the final attack upon the walls on April 12, 1204 ;[4] while the fire which illuminated the victory of that day started in the neighbourhood of that religious house, and raged eastwards to the quarter of Drungarius.[5] During the Latin occupation the Venetians established a dockyard on the shore in the vicinity of the monastery ;[6] the adjoining district, including the Church of Pantocrator [7] (now Zeirek Klissè Djamissi) and the Church of Pantopoptes [8] (now Eski Imaret Mesdjidi), on the Fourth Hill, being their head-quarters.

[1] Desimoni, *Giornale Ligustico*, anno iii., Genoa, 1876.

[2] Lib. i. c. 42 ; cf. Mordtmann, p. 43.

[3] Nicetas Chon., iii. p. 722 ; Ville-Hardouin, c. 36.

[4] *Ibid.*, p. 754; *Chroniques Græco-Romaines*, p. 96.

[5] *Ibid.*, *ut supra ;* Ville-Hardouin, c. 54.

[6] Pachymeres, vol. i. p. 365 ; *Tafel und Thomas*, ii. p. 284.

[7] *Tafel und Thomas*, ii. pp. 46, 348.

[8] *Ibid.*, p. 423. Dr. Mordtmann (pp. 73, 74) identifies the Monastery of Christ the Benefactor with the ruined Byzantine church known as Sinan Pasha Mesdjidi, to the south of St. Theodosia (see Dr. Paspates, pp. 384, 385). But the prominence of the monastery suggests a position nearer the shore. For incidents connected with it, see Pachymeres, vol. ii. p. 579 ; Cantacuzene, iii. p. 493. A tower near the monastery ("ab ultima turri de Virgioti versus Wlachernam") marked the eastern limit of certain fishery rights in the Golden Horn granted to the Monastery of St. Giorgio Majore, at Venice (*Tafel und Thomas*, ii. pp. 47–49).

CHAPTER XV.

THE WALLS ALONG THE GOLDEN HORN—*continued.*

THE next gate on the list of Pusculus and Dolfin is the Porta
Platea, or Porta ala Piazza,[1] evidently the Porta of the Platea
(Πόρτα τῆς Πλατέας) mentioned by Ducas.[2]   The entrance, judging
by its name, was situated beside a wide tract of level ground,
and is, consequently, represented by Oun Kapan Kapoussi, which
stands on the plain near the Inner Bridge, at the head of the
important street running across the city from sea to sea, through
the valley between the Fourth and Fifth Hills.   The district
beside the gate was known as the Plateia (Πλατεῖα),[3] and contained
the churches dedicated respectively to St. Laurentius and the
Prophet Isaiah.[4]   The blockade of the Harbour Walls in 1453 by
the Turkish ships in the Golden Horn extended from the Xylo
Porta to the Gate of the Platea.[5]   If the legend on Bondelmontius' map may be trusted, this gate bore also the name
Mesè, the Central Gate, a suitable designation for an entrance
at the middle point in the line of the harbour fortifications.

The succeeding gate, Ayasma Kapoussi, was opened, it would

[1] Pusculus, iv. 192; Dolfin, s. 55.   [2] Ducas, p. 282.
[3] Anonymus, ii. p. 39; *Acta Patriarchatus CP.*, ii. p. 461; *Itinéraires Russes
en Orient*, pp. 104, 105.
[4] According to Dr. Paspates (pp. 381–383), respectively, Pour Kouyou Mesdjidi,
and Sheik Mourad Mesdjidi.
[5] Ducas, *ut supra.*

seem, after the Turkish Conquest. It is not mentioned by
Gyllius, or Leunclavius, or Gerlach. The conjecture that it
represents a gate in the Wall of Constantine, styled Porta
Basilikè, situated near the Church of St. Acacius ad Caream (τὸν
ἅγιον Ἀκάκιον, τὴν Καρυὰν, ἐν τῇ Βασιλικῇ Πόρτα)[1] does not appear
very probable. The Church of St. Acacius, situated in the
Tenth Region,[2] was the sanctuary to which Macedonius, the bishop
of the city, removed the sarcophagus of Constantine the Great,
from the Church of the Holy Apostles on the summit of the
Fourth Hill, when the latter edifice threatened to fall and crush
the Imperial tomb.[3] The bishop's action encountered the
violent opposition of a large class of the citizens, and led to a
riot in which much blood was shed. Under these circumstances,
it is difficult to believe that the sarcophagus of Constantine was
transported from its original resting-place to a point so distant
as the neighbourhood of Ayasma Kapoussi, especially when the
removal was a temporary arrangement, made until the repairs on
the Church of the Holy Apostles should be completed. It is
more probable that St. Acacius was near the Church of the Holy
Apostles. Furthermore, we cannot be sure that the Porta Basilikè
was a gate in the Wall of Constantine. The Church of St. Acacius
stood near a palace erected by that emperor (πλησίον τῶν
οἰκημάτων τοῦ μεγάλου Κωνσταντίνου) :[4] or, as described elsewhere,
was a small chapel (οἰκίσκον εὐκτήριον) near a palace named
Karya, because close to a walnut-tree on which the saint
was supposed to have suffered martyrdom by hanging.[5] The
Porta Basilikè may have been a gate leading into the court of
that palace.

The three succeeding gates, Odoun Kapan Kapoussi, Zindan

[1] Mordtmann, pp. 7, 8, 45 ; Du Cange, iv. ad St. Acacium. See above, p. 32.
[2] *Notitia, ad Reg. X.*   [3] Socrates, ii. c. xx. ; Theophanes, p. 70.
[4] Du Cange, *ut supra.*   [5] *Ibid.,* vi. c. xxi.

Kapoussi, Balouk Bazaar Kapoussi, bore respectively the names Gate of the Drungarii (τῶν Δρουγγαρίων) ; Gate of the Forerunner (Porta juxta parvum templum Precursoris, known also as St. Johannes de Cornibus); Gate of the Perama or Ferry (τοῦ Περάματος). They can be identified, perhaps, most readily and clearly by the following line of argument :—

The three Byzantine gates just named were situated in the quarter assigned to the Venetians in Constantinople by successive Imperial grants from the time of Alexius Comnenus to the close of the Empire. The Gate of the Drungarii marked the western extremity of the quarter ;[1] the Gate of the Perama, its eastern extremity ;[2] while the gate beside the Church of the Forerunner was between the two points. Where the Gate of the Perama stood admits of no doubt. All students of the topography of the city are agreed in the opinion that the entrance so named was at Balouk Bazaar Kapoussi. Consequently, the two other gates in the Venetian quarter lay to the west of Balouk Bazaar Kapoussi, in the portion of the fortifications between that entrance and the Gate of the Platea, all gates further west being out of the question. But as the only two gates in that portion of the walls are Zindan Kapoussi and Oun Kapan Kapoussi, they must represent, respectively, the Gate of the Forerunner and the Gate of the Drungarii.

The Gate of the Drungarii (τῶν Δρουγγαρίων) derived its name from the term " Drungarius," a title given to various officials in the Byzantine service ;[3] as, for example, to the admiral of the fleet (μέγας δρουγγάριος τοῦ θεοσώστου στόλου), and to the head of the city police, the Drungarius Vigiliæ (ὁ τῆς Βίγλας δρουγγάριος).

---

[1] *Miklosich et Müller*, iii. p. 88.   [2] *Ibid., ut supra.*

[3] According to Du Cange, Glossarium Mediæ et Infimæ Latinitatis, *ad vocem*, from Drungus, "company of soldiers." The word is connected with the German "Gedrung" and the English "throng."

In this particular case the reference was to the latter officer, for in the neighbourhood of the gate stood an important Vigla, or police-station, which is sometimes mentioned instead of the Gate of the Drungarii, as the western limit of the Venetian quarter.[1]

The street running eastwards, outside the city wall, was known as the Via Drungariou (De Longario),[2] and the pier in front of the next gate bore the name Scala de Drongario.[3]

The practice of storing timber on the shore without the gate has come down from an early period in the history of the city. One of the questions put to Justinian the Great by the Greens, during the altercation between him and the Factions in the Hippodrome, on the eve of the Nika riot was, "Who murdered the timber-merchant at the Zeugma?"[4]—another name for this part of the shore. An inscription on the gate reminded the passing crowd that to remember death is profitable to life (Μνήμη θανάτου χρησιμεύει τῷ βίῳ).[5]

It is in favour of the identification of Zindan Kapoussi with the Gate near the Church of St. John (Porta juxta parvum templum Precursoris) to find only a few yards within the entrance a Holy Well, venerated alike by Christian and Moslem, beside which stood, until recently, the ruins of a Byzantine chapel answering to the small Church of the Forerunner mentioned in the Venetian charters.[6]

Leunclavius found the gate called in his day Porta Caravion, because of the large number of ships which were moored in front of it.[7] The landing before the gate, the old Scala de

[1] Anna Comn., vi. p. 286 ; cf. Luitprandus, as quoted by Du Cange, in *Anna Comn.*, vol. ii. p. 544.

[2] *Tafel und Thomas*, ii. pp. 27, 28 : "Via quæ dicitur De Longaria, extra murum civitatis CP."

[3] *Ibid.*, pp. 11, 60 : " Scala de Drongario."   [4] Theophanes, p. 281.

[5] Gerlach, p. 454 ; Smith, *Epistolæ Quatuor*, p. 88.

[6] Mordtmann, p. 46.   [7] *Pand. Hist. Turc.*, s. 200.

Drongario, now Yemish Iskelessi, in front of the Dried Fruit-Market, is one of the most important piers on the Golden Horn.

Dr. Paspates[1] and M. Heyd[2] identify this entrance with the Gate of the Drungarii. But this opinion is inconsistent with the fact that whereas the gate near St. John's stood between the Gate of the Drungarii and the Gate of the Perama, no entrance which can be identified with the gate near St. John's intervenes between Zindan Kapoussi and Balouk Bazaar Kapoussi (Gate of the Perama).

M. Heyd, moreover, identifies Zindan Kapoussi with the Porta Hebraica,[3] mentioned in the charters granted to the Venetians in the thirteenth century. But, as will appear in the sequel, the Porta Hebraica of that period was either the Gate of the Perama itself, or an entrance a little to the east of it.

The Gate of the Perama (τοῦ Περάματος), as its name implies, stood where Balouk Bazaar Kapoussi is found to-day, close to the principal ferry between the city and the suburb of Galata ; communication between the opposite shores being maintained in ancient times by boats, for the only bridge across the harbour was that near the head of the Golden Horn. The Perama is first mentioned by Theophanes,[4] in recording the dedication of the Church of St. Irene at Sycæ (Galata), after the reconstruction of that sanctuary by Justinian the Great. Special importance attached to the event, as the emperor attributed his recovery from an attack of the terrible plague that raged in Constantinople, in 542, to the touch of the relics of the Forty Martyrs which had been discovered in pulling down the old church, and which were to be enshrined in the new building. Menas, Patriarch of Constantinople, and Apollinarius, Patriarch

[1] Paspates, p. 166.
[2] Heyd, *Histoire du Commerce du Levant*, vol. i. p. 251.   [3] *Ibid.*, p. 251.
[4] Theophanes, p. 353 ; cf. Procopius, *De Æd.*, i. c. vii.

of Alexandria—who was then in the capital—were appointed
to celebrate the service of the day ; and the two prelates, seated
in the Imperial chariot, and bearing upon their knees the sacred
relics, drove through the city from St. Sophia to the Perama,
to take boat for Sycæ, where Justinian awaited them.   The
ferry was also styled Trajectus Sycenus ;[1] Transitus Sycarum,
after the oldest name for Galata.   It was, moreover, known as
Transitus Justinianarum,[2] from the name Justinianopolis, given
to the suburb in honour of Justinian, who rebuilt its walls and
theatre, and conferred upon it the privileges of a city.[3]   The pier
at the city end of the ferry was known as the Scala Sycena.[4]

It would seem that there was a spice-market [5] in the vicinity
of the Gate of the Perama, like the one which exists to-day to
the rear of Balouk Bazaar Kapoussi, the latter being only the
continuation of the former.   According to Bondelmontius, the
fish-market of Byzantine Constantinople was held before this
gate, as the practice is at present ; for upon his map he names
the entrance Porta Piscaria.   So fixed are the habits of a city.

Besides bearing the name Gate of the Perama, the entrance
was also styled the Porta Hebraica.   This appears from the
employment of the two names as equivalent terms in descriptions of the territory occupied by the Venetians in Constantinople.   For example, according to Anna Comnena,[6] the quarter
which her father, the Emperor Alexis Comnenus, conceded to the
Venetians, extended from the old Hebrew pier to the Vigla.   In
the charter by which the Doge Faletri granted that district to the
Church of San Georgio Majore of Venice, the quarter is described
in one passage, as extending from the Vigla to the Porta Perame,
as far as the Judeca ("ad Portam Perame, usque ad Judecam ") ;[7]

[1] *Notitia, ad Reg. VI.*
[2] *Novella LIX.*, c. v.
[3] *Paschal Chron.*, p. 618.
[4] *Notitia, ut supra.*
[5] *Ptochoprodromus*, line 113 ; cf. Paspates, pp. 164, 165.
[6] VII. p. 286.
[7] *Tafel und Thomas*, i. p. 50.

and in a subsequent passage, as proceeding from the Vigla to the
Judeca (" a comprehenso dicto sacro Viglæ usque ad Judecam ").[1]
In the grants made to the Venetians after the Restoration of the
Greek Empire in 1261, the extreme points of the Venetian
quarter are named, respectively, the Gate of the Drungarii and
the Gate of the Perama.[2]

To this identification of the Porta Hebraica with the Gate
of the Perama it may be objected that on the map of Bondelmontius these names are applied to different gates, and this, it
may further be urged, accords with the fact that after the Turkish
Conquest, also, a distinction was maintained between the Gate of
the Perama and the gate styled Tchifout Kapoussi, the Hebrew
Gate. But in reply to this objection it must be noted that the
Tchifout Kapoussi of Turkish days was the gate now known as
Bagtchè Kapoussi,[3] beside the Stamboul Custom House, while
the "Porta Judece" on the map of Bondelmontius stands close
to the Seraglio Point. Nothing, however, is more certain than
that the Venetian quarter [4] did not extend so far east as Bagtchè
Kapoussi, much less so far in that direction as the neighbourhood of the head of the promontory. Bagtchè Kapoussi corresponds to the Byzantine Porta Neoriou (the Gate of the Dockyard), which had no connection whatever with the quarter
assigned to the Venetian merchants in the city, but was
separated from that quarter, on the west, by the quarters which
the traders from Amalfi and Pisa occupied, while to the east

---

[1] *Tafel und Thomas,* i. pp. 55-63.

[2] *Ibid.,* ii. p. 4 ; iii. pp. 133-149.

[3] Gyllius, *De Top. CP.,* iii. c. i. ; Leunclavius, *Pand. Hist. Turc.,* s. 200.

[4] On the subject of the Italian and other foreign colonies settled in Byzantine
Constantinople, the reader may consult Paspates, pp. 127-276 ; Mordtmann, pp.
46-50 ; Desmoni, *Giornale Ligustico,* vol. i. ; *Sui Quartieri dei Genovesi a Constantinopoli nel Secolo XII.;* Heyd, *Histoire du Commerce du Levant;* Sauli, *Della Colonia
dei Genovesi in Galata ;* Pears, *Fall of Constantinople,* c. 6 ; Miklosich et Müller,
Acta et Diplomata Græca ; Tafel und Thomas, *Urkunden zur Alteren Handels-und
Staatsgeschichte der Republik Venedig.*

of the gate was the settlement of the Genoese. Consequently, the fact that in the age of Bondelmontius and after the Turkish Conquest the Porta Hebraica was a different entrance from the Gate of the Perama affords no ground for rejecting the evidence that in the twelfth and thirteenth centuries the two names designated the same gate. It only proves that the epithet "Hebrew" had meantime been transferred from one gate to another.[1]

At the distance of seventy-seven feet to the east of the Porta Hebraica, or Gate of the Perama, there stood, according to a Venetian document of 1229, an entrance known as the Gate of St. Mark (Porta San Marci).[2] It probably obtained its name during the Latin occupation, after the patron saint of Venice, but whether it was a gate then opened for the first time, or an old gate under a new name, cannot be determined.

Yet further east, at a point 115 pikes before reaching Bagtchè Kapoussi, stood an entrance styled the Gate of the Hicanatissa (Πόρτα τῆς Ἱκανατίσσης).[3] The adjoining quarter went by the same name, and there probably stood the "Residence of the Kanatissa" (τὸν οἶκον τῆς Κανατίσης) mentioned by Codinus.[4]

---

[1] The Russian pilgrim, Stephen of Novgorod (*Itinéraires Russes en Orient*, p. 121), who visited Constantinople about 1350, found a gate near the sea, and beside a Church of St. Demetrius, named "Portes Juives," on account of the many Jews settled in the vicinity. From the connection in which the fact is mentioned, it appears that the gate stood on the Marmora side of the city, somewhere in the neighbourhood of Vlanga; thus showing how the same name might belong to different gates at different periods in the history of the city. Nicolo Barbaro (p. 817) confirms the existence of a Jewish quarter on the Marmora shore of the city, when he says that the Turkish fleet, finding itself unable to force the chain across the harbour, abandoned the attempt, and proceeded to the side towards the Dardanelles ("de la band del Dardanelo"), and there landed to plunder the Jewish quarter ("muntò in tera de la banda de la Zudeca"). It is possible, indeed, to contend that the Russian pilgrim referred to a gate near the Church of St. Demetrius beside the Seraglio Point. This view does not affect the argument presented in the text.

[2] *Tafel und Thomas*, ii. pp. 270–272; cf. *Ibid.*, pp. 4–11.

[3] *Miklosich et Müller*, iii. pp. 12, 16, 19; cf. *Ibid.*, p. 6.

[4] Codinus, p. 22; cf. Paspates, p. 158.

The designation is best explained as derived from the body of palace troops known as the Hicanati.[1]

Between the Gate of the Perama and that of the Hicanatissa was situated the quarter of the merchants from Amalfi; at the latter gate the quarter of the Pisans commenced.[2]

The Gate of the Neorion (Πόρτα τοῦ Νεωρίου),[3] the Gate of the Dockyard, stood, as its name implies, beside the Dockyard on the shore of the bay at Bagtchè Kapoussi, close to the site now occupied by the Stamboul Custom House. It is first mentioned in a chrysoboullon of Isaac Angelus, confirming the right granted to the Pisan merchants by his predecessors, Alexius Comnenus and Manuel Comnenus, to reside in the neighbourhood of the gate.[4] While the western limit of the quarter thus conceded to Pisans was marked, as already intimated, by the Gate Hicanatissa,[5] the eastern limit of the settlement extended to a short distance beyond the Gate of the Neorion.

The Neorion dated from the time of Byzantium, when it stood at the western extremity of the Harbour Walls of the city.[6] It was, therefore, distinguished from all other dockyards in Constantinople as the Ancient Neorion (τὸ Παλαιὸν Νεώριον), or the Ancient Exartesis (Ἐξάρτησις). Nicolo Barbaro calls it "l'arsenada de l'imperador."

Here the Imperial fleet assembled to refit or to guard the entrance of the harbour;[8] here, until the reign of Justin II., was the Marine Exchange;[9] and here was a factory of oars

---

[1] Constant. Porphyr., *De Cer.*, p. 737.
[2] *Miklosich et Müller*, iii. pp. 19-21.
[3] Pachymeres, vol. i. p. 365; Gyllius, *De Top. CP.*, iii. c. i.
[4] *Miklosich et Müller*, iii. pp. 19, 21.   [5] *Ibid.*, p. 19.
[6] See above, p. 10.   [7] Pachymeres, *ut supra; Miklosich et Müller*, p. 72.
[8] Nicephorus Patriarcha, *CP.*, p. 57; Theophanes, p. 591; Theophanes Cont., p. 391.
[9] Anonymus, ii. p. 30; Codinus, p. 52.

(coparia),[1] in addition to the one mentioned in the Justinian Code, which stood elsewhere. As might be expected, several destructive fires originated in the Neorion.[2]

According to Gyllius,[3] Gerlach,[4] and Leunclavius,[5] this entrance was in their day named by the Turks, Tchifout Kapoussi, and was regarded by the Greeks as the Πύλη Ὡραία (the Beautiful Gate), mentioned by Phrantzes[6] and Ducas[7] in the history of the last siege. The epithet Horaia is supposed to be a corruption of the original name for the entrance (τοῦ Νεωρίου); the Turkish designation of the gate being explained by the fact that a Jewish community was settled in the neighbourhood of the gate.[8]

As to the transformation of Neorion into Horaia, it seems somewhat far-fetched; still, Greeks think it conceivable.[9] If both names, indeed, belonged to the gate, a simpler and more probable explanation of the fact would be that the two names had no connection with each other, and that the epithet "Beautiful" was bestowed upon the entrance, towards the close of the Empire, in view of embellishments made in the course of repairs.

The identification of the Gate of the Neorion with the Horaia

---

[1] *Miklosich et Müller*, iii. p. 6. Such a factory can be seen to-day at Keurekdjilar, in Galata.

[2] *Paschal Chron.*, p. 582; Cedrenus, vol. i. pp. 609, 610; ii. p. 529.

[3] *De Top. CP.*, iii. c. i.; *De Bosporo Thracio*, ii. c. ii.

[4] Page 454.   [5] *Pand. Hist Turc.*, s. 200.

[6] Phrantzes, p. 254.

[7] Ducas, p. 282. Phrantzes and Ducas are the only Byzantine writers who mention the Beautiful Gate.

[8] Gyllius, *De Top. CP.*, iii. c. i.; cf. Paspates, pp. 166, 167. The ground on which Yeni Validè Djamissi stands, near the Stamboul end of the Outer Bridge, belonged, as late as the seventeenth century, to Karaïte Jews, who claimed that the territory had been granted to their ancestors under the Byzantine Empire. In return for the seizure of the ground to build the mosque (1615-1655), the community received houses at Haskeui, and forty members of the community were exempted from taxation for life. As the site of the synagogue could not be sold, the mosque has had to pay the community an annual rent of thirty-two piastres.

[9] Patriarch Constantius, *Ancient and Modern Consple.*, p. 12.

Pylè involves, however, a difficulty. It makes Ducas contradict other historians, as regards the point to which the southern end of the chain across the Golden Horn was attached during the siege of 1453.

According to Ducas,[1] that extremity of the chain was fastened to the Beautiful Gate. Critobulus,[2] on the other hand, affirms that it was attached to the Gate of Eugenius (Yali Kiosk Kapoussi), the gate nearest the head of the promontory, and his statement is supported by Phrantzes [3] and Chalcocondylas,[4] when they, respectively, say that the chain was at the harbour's mouth, and fixed to the wall of the Acropolis. Now, the correctness of the position assigned to the chain by the three latter historians cannot be called in question. It was the position prescribed for the chain by all the rules of strategy. To have placed the chain at the Gate of the Neorion would have left a large portion of the northern side of the city exposed to the enemy, and permitted the Turkish fleet to command the Neorion and the ships stationed before it. Hence the accuracy of Ducas can be maintained only by the identification of the Beautiful Gate with the Gate of Eugenius instead of with the Gate of the Neorion.

We are, therefore, confronted with the question whether the historian is mistaken as regards the gate to which the city end of the chain was attached, or whether the view prevalent in Constantinople in the sixteenth century respecting the position of the Horaia Pylè should be rejected as unfounded.

In favour of the accuracy of Ducas, it must be admitted that his statements concerning the Horaia Pylè, in other passages of his work, convey the impression that under that name he refers to the entrance nearest the head of the promontory, the Gate of Eugenius (Yali Kiosk Kapoussi). Speaking of the arrangements made for the defence of the sea-board of the city, he

[1] Page 268.   [2] I. c. 18.   [3] Page 238.   [4] Page 384.

describes them as extending, in the first place, from the Xylinè
Porta, at the western extremity of the Harbour Walls, to the
Horaia Pylè; and then from the Horaia Pylè to the Golden
Gate, near the western extremity of the walls along the Sea of
Marmora.[1]   Again, when he describes the blockade of the shore
of the city outside the chain by the Sultan's fleet, he represents
the blockade as commencing at the Horaia Pylè and proceeding
thence past the point of the Acropolis, the Church of St. Demetrius, the Gate of the Hodegetria, the Great Palace, and the
harbour (Kontoscalion), as far as Vlanga.[2]

Now, the gate which would naturally form the pivot, so to
speak, of these operations was the Gate of Eugenius.   There the
two shores of the city divide; and that was the farthest point
to which the Turkish fleet outside the chain could advance into
the Golden Horn.   It would be strange if Ducas ascribed the
strategical importance of the Gate of Eugenius to another gate.
And yet, it must be also admitted that Ducas can be inaccurate.
He is inaccurate, for example, in the matter of the gate before
which the Sultan's tent was pitched during the siege,[3] and at
which the Emperor Constantine fell,[4] for he associates these
incidents with the Gate of Charisius, instead of with the Gate
of St. Romanus; he is inaccurate, as we have seen, in his
account of the entry of the Turks through the Kerko Porta;[5]
and he is inaccurate, again, in saying that the ships which the
Sultan carried across the hills from the Bosporus to the Golden
Horn were launched into the harbour at a point opposite the
Cosmidion (Eyoub),[6] instead of at Cassim Pasha.   Under these
circumstances it is impossible to maintain his accuracy as to the
connection of the chain with Horaia Pylè at all hazards, and in
the face of all difficulties.   His credit will depend upon the value

[1] Pages 283, 284.   [2] Pages 282, 283.   [3] Page 263.
[4] Page 300.   [5] See above, p. 93.   [6] Pages 270, 271.

attached to the evidence we have, that the Horaia Pylè was
another name for the Gate of the Neorion during the last days
of Byzantine Constantinople.

The application of both names to the same gate rests upon
the authority of tradition, upon the use and wont followed in
the matter by the Greek population of the city in the sixteenth
century. If this is really the case, no evidence can be more
decisive on the question at issue. Use and wont in respect to
the name of a conspicuous public gate, in a much-frequented
part of the city, constitutes an irrefutable argument, provided
that use and wont goes far enough back in the history of the
entrance. In that case, Ducas would be convicted of having
mistaken the gate to which the chain was attached, and all
the importance which he ascribes to the Horaia Pylè, in his
account of the actions of friends and foes along the shores of
the city, is only the consistent following up of that error. For
any gate to which the chain was supposed, however erroneously,
to have been affixed would be represented in the narrative of
subsequent events as the point about which the assault and the
defence of the sea-board turned, although the gate was not
situated where it could, naturally, have sustained that character.

Now, according to Gyllius,[1] the gate anciently styled the Gate
of the Neorion was called in his day Tchifout Kapoussi ("Hebrew
Gate") by the Turks, and Horaia Pylè by the Greeks, as a
matter of common practice. The brief statement of Gerlach [2]
that the second gate west of the Seraglio Point was named
at once the Beautiful Gate and the Jewish Gate implies that

---

[1] Gyllius' statement (*De Top. CP.*, III. c. i.) on the subject is: " Portum, quem
vocunt Neorion, quod prope portam, quam Græci appellant Oraiam, corruptè quasi
Neorii portam, aut non longe ab ea, fuisse existimo. Hodie inter mare et Portam
Oraiam, quam Turci appellant Siphont (Tsifout), id est, Judæorum eam accolentium,
spatium latum . . . videre licet." Cf. *De Bosporo Thracio,* II. c. i. " Pro porta
quam vulgo vocant Oriam corruptè, quasi olim Neorii portam."

[2] Page 454: " Die Prächtige, itzund die Juden-Pfort."

these were the names of the gate in current use.   Leunclavius[1] puts the facts in a somewhat different light.   According to him, the common designation of the entrance was "Huræa" (*Ebraia,* "Hebrew Gate"), and it was only when the Greeks of the city wished to show themselves better acquainted with the truth on the subject that they claimed for the gate the epithet "Horaia."

This may, perhaps, excite the suspicion that the application of the epithet "Horaia" to the Gate of the Neorion, in the sixteenth century, was due to the fact that it was then known also as the Hebrew Gate (Ebraia).   But, on the whole, the more probable view is that the epithet was correctly applied, and, consequently, that Ducas, who was not present at the siege, is mistaken in associating the chain with the Beautiful Gate.

In the charters defining the privileges granted to the Genoese colony in Constantinople during the twelfth century, mention is made of a "Porta Bonu" and a "Porta Veteris Rectoris."[2] As both were associated with the Scala, or Pier, at the service of that colony, they were doubtless the same gate under different names ; the former appellation designating it by the proper name of the officer connected in some way with the entrance, the latter by his official title.   Nothing is known concerning the Rector Bonus ; the name and title are at once Byzantine and Italian. Now, the Genoese quarter in the twelfth century lay to the east of the Gate of the Neorion, and consequently the Porta Bonu, or Porta Veteris Rectoris, must be sought in that direction.   It stood, probably, where Sirkedji Iskelessi is now situated.

Near this gate must have been the Scala Chalcedonensis and the Portus Prosphorianus, which the *Notitia* places in the Fifth

---

[1] *Pand. Hist. Turc.,* s. 200. "Porta quæ Græci quotquot vederi peritores volunt Porta Horæa ('Ωραία), vulgo Huræa (Ebraia) dicitur."

[2] *Miklosich et Müller,* iii. pp. ix., 53 ; Desimoni, *Giornale Ligustico,* vol. i. p. 37 ; *Sui Quartieri dei Genovesi a Constantinopoli, nel secolo XII.,* p. 46.

Region.[1] The former, as its name implies, was the pier frequented by boats plying between the city and Chalcedon; it is mentioned twice, as the point at which relics were landed in solemn state to be carried thence to St. Sophia.[2]

The Portus Prosphorianus[3] was in the bay which once indented the shore immediately to the east of the Gate of Bonus, where the line of the city walls described a deep curve. The name is probably derived from the word Πρόσφορον, and denoted that the harbour was the resort of the craft which brought products from the country to the markets of the city.[4] The harbour was also called the Phosphorion, as though associated with the sudden illumination of the heavens which saved the city from capture by Philip of Macedon. But its most common designation was τὸ Βοσπόριον, ὁ Βοόσπορος, ὁ Βόσπορος, probably because the point to which cattle were ferried across from Asia. The cattle-market was held here until the reign of Constantine Copronymus, who transferred it to the Forum of Taurus;[5] here also stood warehouses for the storage of oil, and granaries, such as the Horrea Olearia, Horrea Troadensia, Horrea Valentiaca and Horrea Constantiaca.[6] The granaries were inspected annually by the emperor.[7] According to Demosthenes, the three statues erected by Byzantium and Perinthus in honour of Athens for the aid rendered against Philip of Macedon were set up at the Bosporus.[8] But it is not certain whether the great orator used the name in a general sense, or with special reference to this port. The great fire in the fifth year of Leo I. started in the

---

[1] *Notitia, ad Reg. V.*   [2] *Paschal Chron.*, ad ann. 406, 415.

[3] *Cod. Theod. De Calcis Coctor.*, Lex V.; Stephanus Byzantius, *De Urbibus et Populis*, ad vocem; Evagrius, ii. c. xiii.

[4] Mordtmann, p. 49.

[5] Anonymus, ii. p. 29. The point at Scutari where cattle are embarked to be ferried to the city is called by the Turks "Ukooz-Limani," the Ox-Port.

[6] *Notitia, ad Reg. V.*   [7] Constant. Porphyr., *De Cer.*, p. 699.

[8] *De Corona*, p. 134, Edition Didot.

market near this harbour, through the carelessness of a woman who left a lighted candle on a stall at which she had bought some salt fish.[1]

We reach, next, the last gate in the line of the Harbour Walls, the Gate of Eugenius (Πόρτα τοῦ Εὐγενίου), represented now by Yali Kiosk Kapoussi. Its identity is established by the following indications. It marked the eastern extremity of the fortifications along the Golden Horn,[2] as the Xylo Porta marked their western terminus. Hence, the ditch constructed by Cantacuzene in front of those fortifications is described as extending from the Gate of Eugenius to the Gate Xylinè.[3] In the next place, the gate was close to the head of the promontory, or Acropolis, for ships outward bound rounded the promontory soon after passing the gate, while incoming ships passed the gate soon after rounding the promontory.[4] Again, the Church of St. Paul which stood near the gate is described, as situated in the quarter of the Acropolis, at the opening of the harbour.[5] This is consistent with the fact that the gate was at a point from which St. Sophia could be easily reached.[6]

Eugenius, after whom the gate, the adjacent tower, and the neighbouring district were named,[7] was probably a distinguished proprietor in this part of the city. The gate bore an inscription commemorating repairs executed by a certain Julian;[8] possibly, Julian who was Prefect of the City in the reign of Zeno, when Constantinople was shaken by a severe earthquake.

There is reason to believe that besides its ordinary designation

[1] Evagrius, ii. c. xiii.   [2] Anonymus, i. p. 2.
[3] Cantacuzene, iv. pp. 213, 214.   [4] *Ibid.*, iv. pp. 76, 232.
[5] Anna Comn., xv. p. 345.
[6] Pachymeres, vol. ii. p. 175; Nicephorus Greg., vi. p. 167.
[7] Anonymus, i. p. 2; *Acta Patriarchatus C.P.*, p. 563.
[8] Banduri, *Imp. Orient.*, vii. p. 149.

this gate bore also, at one time, the name Marmora Porta ; for certain ecclesiastical documents of the year 1399 and the year 1441 speak of an entrance in the quarter of Eugenius, under the name Marmora Porta, Μαρμαροπόρτα ἐν τῇ ἐνορίᾳ τοῦ Εὐγενίου.[1]

The Scala Timasii, so named after Timasius, a celebrated general in the reign of Arcadius, was in the Fourth Region,[2] and must therefore have been a pier near the Gate of Eugenius.

At this entrance it was customary for the bride-elect of an emperor to land, upon reaching the capital by sea ; here she was received in state by her future consort, and having been invested with the Imperial buskins and other insignia of her rank, was conducted on horseback to the palace.[3] But what lends most interest to the gate is the fact that beside it rose the tower which held the southern end of the chain drawn across the harbour in time of war.[4] Originally, the building, styled Kentenarion (Κεντενάριον), was a stately structure, but after its overthrow by an earthquake, Theophilus restored it as an ordinary tower.[5] The chain was supported in the water by wooden floats,[6] and its northern end was made fast to a tower in the fortifications of Galata, known as the Tower of Galata, "Le Tour de Galatas."[7] According to Gyllius, the gate near that tower was called Porta Catena,[8] but, unfortunately, he does not indicate

[1] *Miklosich et Müller*, ii. pp. 467, 564.   [2] *Notitia, ad Reg. IV.*

[3] Codinus, *De Officiis*, pp. 107, 108 ; cf. Cantacuzene, iv. p. 11.

[4] Critobulus, i. c. 18.

[5] Leo Diaconus, pp. 78, 79 ; Anonymus, iii. p. 56.   This was probably the tower to which N. Barbaro (p. 733) refers when, speaking of the two towers, on the opposite sides of the entrance to the Golden Horn, which supported the chain, he says, "Etiam una tore per ladi de la zilade, zoè una de la banda de Constantinopoli, l'altra de la banda de Pera, le qual tore vignia a far defexa assai."

[6] N. Barbaro, pp. 722, 723.   [7] Ville-Hardouin, c. 32.

[8] Gyllius, *De Top. CP.*, iv. c. x.   "Adhuc Galatæ porta est, quæ appellatur Catena, ex eo, quod ab Acropoli usque ad eam portam catena extenderetur." Cf. Theophanes, p. 609.

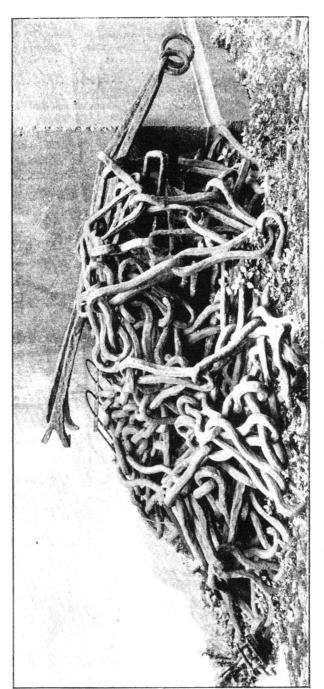

PORTION OF THE CHAIN STRETCHED ACROSS THE ENTRANCE OF THE GOLDEN HORN IN 1453.

its precise position. From the nature of the case, however, it must have been near Kiretch Kapoussi, directly opposite the Gate of Eugenius.[1]

The employment of a chain to bar the entrance of the Golden Horn is mentioned for the first time in the famous siege of the city by the Saracens in 717–718, when the Emperor Leo lowered the chain with the hope of tempting the enemy's ships into the narrow waters of the harbour.[2] It appears next in the reign of Michael II., who thereby endeavoured, but in vain, to keep out the fleet with which his rival Thomas attacked the city.[3] It was again employed by Nicephorus Phocas, in expectation of a Russian descent into the Bosporus.[4] The Venetians found it obstructing their path when they stood before Constantinople in 1203, but removed it after capturing the Tower of Galata, to which it was secured.[5] Finally, in 1453, it proved too strong for Sultan Mehemet to force, and drove him to devise the expedient of carrying his ships into the Golden Horn across the hills to Cassim Pasha.[6] A portion of the chain used on the last occasion is preserved in the Church of St. Irene, within the Seraglio grounds.

In the district of Eugenius were some of the most noted charitable institutions of the city, among which the great Orphanage[7] and the Hospitia,[8] built on the site of the old Stadium of Byzantium by Justinian the Great and Theodora,

[1] Dr. Paspates (Πολιορκία καὶ Ἅλωσις τῆς ΚΠ., p. 63) thinks the tower stood beside the Offices of the Board of Health, between the Galata Bridge and the Galata Custom House. He grounds this opinion on the existence of old ruins at that point. But the chain would never be placed aslant the harbour, as this view implies.

[2] Theophanes, p. 609.   [3] Cedrenus, vol. ii. p. 80.   [4] Leo Diaconus, p. 79.

[5] Nicetas Chon., p. 718 ; cf. Ville-Hardouin, c. xxxii.

[6] Phrantzes, p. 251. See below, pp. 241–247, for the discussion regarding the precise route taken by the ships.

[7] *Acta Patriarchatus CP.*, ii. p. 467 ; Anna Comn., xv. p. 345.

[8] Procopius, *De Æd.*, i. c. xi.

for the free accommodation of poor strangers, were conspicuous. There, also, stood the Church of St. Michael and the Church of St. Paul.[1]

THE BASILIKÈ PYLÈ.

Before concluding the study of the Harbour Walls we must recur to the question which presented itself at an earlier stage of our inquiries, but was reserved for consideration at the close of this chapter, as more favourable to an intelligent and thorough discussion of the subject.

Where was the Basilikè Pylè which Byzantine historians, after the Restoration of the Empire, associate with this line of the city's bulwarks? Was it, as some authorities maintain, at Balat Kapoussi,[2] or, as others hold, in the neighbourhood of the Seraglio Point?[3] Or is it possible that a gate bearing that epithet was found at both points?

In favour of the opinion that the Imperial Gate was near the Seraglio Point there is, first, the statement of Phrantzes, already cited, to that effect. "To Gabriel of Treviso," says the historian,[4] "captain of the Venetian triremes, with fifty men under him, was entrusted the defence of the tower, in the middle of the current, guarding the entrance of the harbour; and he was opposite the Imperial Gate."

What Phrantzes means by the "entrance of the harbour" (τὴν εἴσοδον τοῦ λιμένος) admits of no dispute, for the phrase has only one signification. But, as though to render mistake impossible,

---

[1] Nicephorus Greg., vii. p. 275.

[2] Patriarch Constantius, *Ancient and Modern Consple.*, p. 15. With him agree Von Hammer, Paspates, Mordtmann, etc.

[3] Gerlach, p. 454; Leunclavius, Pand. Hist. Turc. s. 200.

[4] Pages 254, 255, Ἐδόθη φυλάττειν τὸν πύργον τὸν ἐν μέσῳ τοῦ ῥεύματος, τὸν φυλάσσοντα τὴν εἴσοδον τοῦ λιμένος, καὶ ἦν ἀντικρὺς τῆς πύλης τῆς βασιλικῆς.

he repeats the expression, in that sense, several times.   The
Greek ships, which were moored beside the chain across the
mouth of the harbour, and which the Sultan endeavoured to sink
or drive away by the fire of a battery planted on the hill of St.
Theodore, to the north-east of Galata, Phrantzes [1] observes, were
stationed "at the entrance of the harbour" (ἐν τῇ εἰσόδῳ τοῦ
λιμένος). The object of this bombardment, adds the historian [2] in
the next sentence, was not simply to force "the entrance to the
harbour" (διὰ τὴν εἴσοδον τοῦ λιμένος), but also to injure the
Genoese shipping at that point, and thus show that the Sultan
dared to act in any way he pleased, even towards the Italians
of Galata.   Again, Phrantzes [3] remarks that the ships moored
along the chain at the mouth of the harbour (ἐν τῷ στόματι
τοῦ λιμένος) were placed here to render entrance into the
harbour more difficult to the enemy (ὅπως ἰσχυροτέρως κωλύσωσι
τὴν εἴσοδον).

Equally decisive is the indication given regarding the tower
which stood opposite the Imperial Gate.   It was "in the middle
of the current."   This statement carries the mind, at first, to the
tower which stood on the rock off Scutari (Damalis, Arcla), where
the lighthouse Kiz Kalehssi has been erected.   But the idea that
Phrantzes had that tower in view cannot be entertained for more
than a moment ; for to have stationed Gabriel there, with the
Turkish fleet in complete command of the Bosporus and the Sea

---

[1] Page 259.   Dr. Paspates, in his work on the siege of the city (Πολιορκία
καὶ Ἅλωσις τῆς Κωνσταντινουπόλεως, p. 141), represents the Hill of St. Theodore
and the battery upon it as commanding the Bay of Cassim Pasha.   This, however, is
in harmony neither with the statements of Phrantzes, nor with local configuration. The
requirements of the case are met by the supposition that the Hill of St. Theodore was
the ridge to the north-east of Top Haneh, and that the Sultan's battery stood nearer
the Bosporus than the present Italian Hospital. Cf. Zorzo Dolfin, s. 44 : "Acceso
el Turcho da disdegno, da i montè orientali de Pera penso a profondar con machine
e morteri, o trar quelle de la cathena.   Mezzo adonque le bombarde 'a segno dal
occidente " (*i.e.* aiming towards west), " se sforza con bombardieri profundar le naue."

[2] Page 259.   [3] Page 238.

of Marmora, was not simply useless, but impossible. The current intended can be none other than the strong current at the head of the Seraglio Point, where it divides in two swift streams, which Nicephorus Gregoras [1] compares to Scylla and Charybdis, one running up the Golden Horn, the other out into the Sea of Marmora. A tower near a point with rushing waters on either hand might aptly be described as "in the middle of the current." [2] Furthermore, Phrantzes [3] mentions the tower referred to, in close connection with what stood, unquestionably, near the head of the promontory. He speaks of it immediately after the Horaia Pylè, and immediately before the ships which defended the chain across the harbour's mouth, as though in the same vicinity.

In the second place, the view that the Imperial Gate was near the Seraglio Point is supported by the testimony of Leonard of Scio, when he makes the statement that Gabriel of Treviso fought bravely, with his men, on the portion of the walls extending from the Beacon-tower as far as the Imperial Gate, at the entrance of the bay (of the Golden Horn): "Gabriel Trevsianus cordatissime a Turri Phani usque ad Imperialem Portam, antes inum, decertabat." [4] The archbishop's phrase "ante sinum" corresponds to Phrantzes' ἐν τῇ εἰσόδῳ τοῦ λιμένος.

Thirdly, it remains to add, on this side of the question, that the order in which Pusculus mentions the gates in the Harbour Walls favours the view that the Basilikè Pylè was not at Balat

---

[1] XVII., p. 860; cf. Cantacuzene, iv. p. 232.

[2] Dr. Paspates (see p. 111 of his work on the siege of the city, cited above) understands Phrantzes in the same way. He identifies the tower with one which stood, until 1817, between the Gate of St. Barbara (Top Kapoussi) and the Gate of Eugenius (Yali Kiosk Kapoussi). It was probably the tower to which Nicolo Barbaro refers (see above, p. 228).

[3] Pages 254, 255.

[4] See his Epistle to the Pope on the Capture of Constantinople.

Kapoussi. Proceeding from west to east in his account of the defence of the fortifications along the Golden Horn, that author refers to seven gates in the following order: Xylina, Cynegon, Phani, Theodosia, Puteæ, Platea, Basilea,[1] thus putting the Imperial Gate somewhere to the east of Oun Kapan Kapoussi. Had the Basilea stood at Balat Kapoussi it should have been mentioned immediately after Cynegon.

This is the main evidence in support of the opinion that the Basilikè Pylè was near the Seraglio Point, and it is difficult to conceive of evidence more clear and conclusive.

The argument countenancing the view which identifies the Imperial Gate with Balat Kapoussi may be stated, briefly, thus: In the first place, when Leonard of Scio declares that Gabriel of Treviso defended the walls "a Turri Phani ad Imperialem Portam" he associates the Imperial Gate with the quarter of the Phanar. Again, when Ducas affirms that the Venetians assisted the Greeks in the defence of the walls from the Imperial Gate to the Kynegon,[2] that entrance is associated with the district so named. The Imperial Gate, therefore, must have stood at a point between the Phanar and the Kynegon. But that is exactly the situation of Balat Kapoussi, with the quarter of the Phanar on its east, and the Kynegon on its west; hence the two gates were one and the same.

In the next place, the epithet "Imperial" was eminently suitable for an entrance which stood at the foot of a hill surmounted by the Palace of the Porphyrogenitus, and from which the Palace of Blachernæ could be readily reached. How appropriate the epithet was is proved by the actual name of the gate, Balat Kapoussi (the Gate of the Palace), so similar in meaning to Basilikè Pylè.

In the third place, on the shore outside the Basilikè Pylè

---

[1] Pusculus, iv. pp. 179–221.   [2] Ducas, p. 275.

stood a Church of St. John the Baptist.[1] And in keeping with this fact, there is a Church of St. John the Baptist (the metochion of the Monastery of St. Catherine on Mount Sinai) outside Balat Kapoussi.

These arguments are, however, open to criticism. So far as the statement of Leonard of Scio is concerned, it should be noted that he does not speak of the Turris Phani absolutely. Had he done so, the presumption would certainly be in favour of the view which understands him to refer to the district of the Phanar, half-way up the Golden Horn.[2] But his complete statement on the subject is that the Turris Phani of which he was speaking stood, with the Imperial Gate beside it, "ante sinum," at the entrance of the bay of the Golden Horn, thus making it manifest that he had in mind another beacon-tower than the one in the district commonly known as the Phanar. That the shore of the Golden Horn was lighted at more than one point during the night, and especially at the entrance of the harbour, is only what might be expected. Nor is there in the assertion of Ducas, that the Venetians and Greeks united their forces to defend the fortifications from the Imperial Gate to the Kynegon, anything to determine the distance between the two points. They might be very near, or they might be as far apart as the extremities of the Harbour Walls; for there is no reason to think that the Venetians defended only the small portion of the walls between Balat Kapoussi and the three archways to the west of that gate.

[1] *Acta Patriarchatus C.P.*, vol. ii. p. 391, year 1400; cf. pp. 297, 487.

[2] Speaking of the bridge which the Sultan built out into the Golden Horn, and on which he placed cannon to batter the walls in the Kynegon, Leonard of Scio (p. 931) says the bridge was built that the army might advance near the wall, beside the "fanum" of the city: "Decurreret ad murum prope, juxta fanum urbis." The term is ambiguous. Zorzo Dolfin translates it, "Appresso la giesia" (the church). But more probably the reference is to the Phanar quarter, although the bridge was not exactly opposite to it.

The remaining arguments under consideration have more force, but are by no means decisive. The appropriateness of the epithet "Imperial" to an entrance in the situation of Balat Kapoussi affords, certainly, a presumption in favour of the view that the entrance was so named, although it cannot, alone, prove that such was the fact. The name Balat Kapoussi appears only after the Turkish Conquest, and may or may not be borrowed from the Byzantine designation of the gate. The strongest argument on this side of the question is, undoubtedly, that drawn from the presence of the Church of St. John the Baptist on the shore to the north-east of Balat Kapoussi,[1] the possible representative of the ancient church of that dedication "on the shore outside the Basilikè Pylè."[2]

But, in any case, these arguments do not refute the proof adduced for the existence of a Basilikè Pylè near the Seraglio Point. They leave that fact undisturbed; and can only claim to give countenance to the idea that another Basilikè Pylè stood at Balat Kapoussi.

Two questions, accordingly, are involved in the problem before us. Which of the gates near the Seraglio Point was styled the Basilikè Pylè? Was that gate the only Imperial Gate in the line of the Harbour Walls, or do some statements of Byzantine historians on the subject imply the existence of a second Basilikè Pylè?

In the opinion of Leunclavius, the Imperial Gate is to be identified with the Horaia Pylè (the Gate of the Neorion) at

---

[1] How old this church is cannot be precisely determined. It is known to have been in existence, as a small chapel, before 1640, when it was burned down. It was then reconstructed, but was again destroyed by fire, after which it was rebuilt at the expense of the monastery on Mount Sinai. For some time it was the fashionable church of the Phanariotes. See Patriarch Constantius, *Ancient and Modern Consple.*, pp. 104, 105. Mr. Gedeon ascribes it to the 14th century (*Proceedings of the Greek Syllogos of Consple.*, vol. xxvi. p. 148. 1896).

[2] *Acta Patriarchatus CP.*, ii. p. 391.

Bagtchè Kapoussi.[1] But if the Horaia Pylè was at Bagtchè Kapoussi, the Basilikè Pylè could not be there also. The two entrances are unmistakably distinguished by Phrantzes, who mentions both in the same connection, the one immediately after the other, and states that, in the defence of the fortifications along the harbour, the Beautiful Gate was in charge of the crew of a vessel from Crete, while the Imperial Gate was under the care of Gabriel of Treviso.

But this is an objection which has force only against those who adopt the view that the Horaia Pylè stood at Bagtchè Kapoussi.

A more general objection to the view of Leunclavius is that Bagtchè Kapoussi does not occupy the situation attributed to the Imperial Gate by Phrantzes and Leonard of Scio. It is not opposite a tower guarding the entrance of the harbour; it is too far up the Golden Horn to be described as " ante sinum."

This being so there are only two gates with one or other of which the Imperial Gate can be identified, if the indications furnished on the subject by Phrantzes and Leonard of Scio are strictly followed. It was either the Gate of Eugenius (Yali Kiosk Kapoussi), as Gerlach maintains,[2] or the Gate of St. Barbara (Top Kapoussi), which stands immediately to the south of Seraglio Point, and was, therefore, so near the Harbour Walls that it might be included in an account of their defence.

The description of the Imperial Gate given by the historians above mentioned, applies equally well to both these entrances. Both stand near the mouth of the harbour, and opposite a tower " in the middle of the current ; " both occupy a point of great strategical importance, such as the Basilikè Pylè must have

---

[1] *Pand. Hist. Turc.*, s. 200.

[2] Page 454, where he styles the first gate west of the Seraglio Point " Die König-liche Pforte."

occupied, if we may judge from the fact that it was entrusted to commanders like Gabriel of Treviso and the Duke Notaras ; both entrances were, in the course of history, associated with the Court[1] in a way which might have earned for them the distinction of the epithet, "Imperial."

It is not easy to decide, directly, between conflicting claims so nicely balanced. Judgment on the point at issue will doubtless be determined, largely, by the views adopted on questions indirectly connected with the matter in dispute, especially by what view is taken as regards the situation of the Horaia Pylè. Any one who upholds the accuracy of Ducas regarding the point to which the southern end of the chain was attached, and identifies the Beautiful Gate with Yali Kiosk Kapoussi (the Gate of Eugenius) will, necessarily, identify the Imperial Gate with Top Kapoussi. On the other hand, those who accept the opinion that the Beautiful Gate stood, as the Greeks in the sixteenth century maintained, at Bagtchè Kapoussi, may, though still free to place the Imperial Gate at Top Kapoussi, nevertheless prefer to place it at Yali Kiosk Kapoussi, as, on the whole, more in accordance with the indications of its position. If at the latter point, one can understand more readily why the Imperial Gate should have been associated with the Harbour Walls, and why Phrantzes mentions it immediately after the Horaia Pylè, and before the chain and the ships at the harbour's mouth.

Having thus indicated which of the gates near the Seraglio Point have the strongest claim to be regarded as the Basilikè Pylè, it remains to consider the question whether either of those gates was the only entrance bearing that epithet, in the Harbour Walls.

Are there, in other words, any statements made by Byzantine

---

[1] See above, p. 228 ; see below, p. 250.

writers in reference to the Basilikè Pylè which cannot be applied to the Gate of Eugenius or to the Gate of St. Barbara, and which, therefore, imply the existence of another gate of that name ? So far as the Gate of St. Barbara is concerned, there are several such statements. The narrow quay outside Top Kapoussi could not afford room for the Church of St. John, the hospitium, and the other buildings, which are described as situated on the shore outside the Basilikè Pylè.[1] Nor could a ship be moored in front of that gate, as the ship of the Catalan chief Berenger was moored in front of the Imperial Gate.[2] Nor was it necessary, before that gate could be attacked by the Turkish fleet, that the chain across the entrance of the Golden Horn should be forced, as we are told was necessary in the case of the Basilikè Pylè to which Critobulus alludes.[3] Hence the opinion that the Basilikè Pylè was another name for the Gate of St. Barbara involves the view that there were two Imperial Gates.

The claim of the Gate of Eugenius to be the sole Basilikè Pylè encounters but one serious objection. Critobulus, it would appear, distinguishes the two entrances. He refers to the former to indicate where the southern end of the chain across the harbour was attached ;[4] he speaks of the latter to mark the point which the Turkish fleet attacked on the last day of the siege, after breaking the chain, and becoming master of the Golden Horn.[5] For as soon as the Turkish admiral perceived that the Sultan's troops had entered the city, and were busily engaged in the work of plunder, he made a desperate attempt upon the chain, cut it asunder, and forced his way into the harbour. Then, having captured or sunk the Greek galleys found

---

[1] *Acta Patriarchatus CP.*, ii. pp. 297, 391, 487.
[2] Pachymeres, vol. ii. p. 503.
[3] Lib. i. c. 65.
[4] Lib. i. c. 18.
[5] Lib. i. c. 65.

in the port, he led his ships to the Imperial Gate (ταῖς βασιλικαῖς
πύλαις) and landed his sailors in quest of booty.   The gate was,
however, still held by the Greeks, as the Turkish troops had not
yet reached it from within the city.   A fierce struggle therefore
ensued.   But at last the gate was burst open, its brave defenders
were slain to a man, their blood pouring through it like a
stream, and the assailants rushed in to share the spoils of
victory.

What is here related might hold true of the Gate of
Eugenius.   Such facts as that the Imperial Gate stood within
the chain, that before attacking it the Greek vessels in the
harbour had to be disposed of, that it was held for a considerable
time after the Turkish army had entered the city, are all consistent with the idea that the Basilikè Pylè, to which Critobulus
refers, was the Gate of Eugenius.   But, on the other hand, if
the Gate of Eugenius was both the entrance to which the chain
was attached and the entrance captured by the Turkish
admiral after the chain had been broken, it comes very near
defying all the laws of the association of ideas for the historian to speak of the entrance by different names, when the
matters he records were so closely connected.   This is a very
serious objection to the identification of the Imperial Gate
which Critobulus had in mind with the Gate of Eugenius.   Hence,
if this objection cannot be removed by saying that he could
speak of the same gate by different names in different passages
of his work, it follows that the epithet "Basilikè" did not belong
exclusively to the Gate of Eugenius (any more than to the Gate
of St. Barbara), but was bestowed also upon a gate higher up
the Golden Horn.

This being the case, there can be no hesitation where the
latter was situated.   Balat Kapoussi, by the significance of its
name, by its proximity to Imperial palaces, and by the presence

of a Church of St. John, with room for other buildings, on the
territory outside the gate, establishes the best claim to be considered the second Basilikè Pylè in the line of the harbour
fortifications.[1]

Why the Turkish admiral selected it as the point at which
to land his sailors is explained by the wealthy character of the
adjoining quarter of the city.[2]

[1] If the Basilikè Pylè could be identified with the gate which went by the names
Porta Boni, Porta Veteris Rectoris, at Sirkedji Iskelessi, all statements concerning
the Imperial Gate might be applied to that single entrance. But this would be to
interpret the language of Phrantzes and Leonard of Scio on the subject too loosely.
Nor is there any reason apparent for bestowing such an epithet upon that gate, or for
regarding that gate important during the last siege.

[2] The Basilikè Pylè is mentioned in Byzantine history by the following writers :—
Pachymeres, vol. ii. pp. 178–180.—As the starting-point of a great conflagration,
in 1291, which extended far into the interior of the city, and caused immense loss of
houses and merchandise.

Ibid., p. 503.—As the gate to which Berenger, in 1306, took his ship from the
harbour at Blachernæ, in order to leave Constantinople more readily, as soon as a
favourable wind sprang up.

Acta Patriarchatus CP., vol. ii. p. 297. Year 1399.—As the gate beside the
shore on which a certain priest had his residence.

Ibid., p. 391. Year 1400.—As the gate before which a Church of St. John the
Baptist stood upon the seashore.

Ibid., p. 487. Year uncertain.—As the gate before which there was a hospitium
on the sea-shore, near the Church of St. John the Baptist.

Ducas, pp. 184–186.—As the gate guarded by soldiers from Crete during the
siege of 1422. At the demand of those loyal troops the Emperor Manuel Palæologus,
who had taken up his quarters in the monastery of the Peribleptos (Soulou Monastir),
allowed his minister Theologus to be tried on the charge of accepting bribes from
the Turks to betray the city. Having been found guilty, Theologus was forthwith
dragged by the Cretans along the street to the Basilikè Pylè, and there had his eyes
put out, in a manner that resulted in his death three days after the horrible operation.

Chalcocondylas, pp. 285, 286.—As the gate beside which stood the tower injured
by the cannon of the Genoese in 1434.

Ducas, pp. 275, 283, 295, 300.—As the gate defended by the Venetians, and by
the Grand Duke Notaras, in the siege of 1453.

Phrantzes, p. 255 ; Leonard of Scio, in his Letter to Pope Nicholas.—As the
gate defended, in 1453, by Gabriel of Treviso.

Pusculus, iv. p. 193.—As the gate defended, in 1453, by the Grand Duke
Notaras.

Critobulus, i. c. 65.—As the gate attacked by the Turkish fleet which entered
the Golden Horn, after forcing the chain across the mouth of the harbour.

THE ROUTE TAKEN IN CARRYING THE TURKISH SHIPS ACROSS
THE HILLS FROM THE BOSPORUS TO THE GOLDEN HORN.

Owing to the conflicting statements of contemporary historians
on the subject, the precise route followed in carrying the Sultan's
ships, across the hills, from the Bosporus to the Golden Horn,
is not fully settled.   So far, indeed, as the point at which
the ships reached the Golden Horn is concerned, there can be
little, if any, room for doubt, though the historians differ even
on that matter.   The most reliable testimony, however, and
the configuration of the territory on the northern side of the
harbour, are in favour of the view that the Bay of Cassim Pasha
was the point in question.   Critobulus[1] names the point the
Cold Waters,[2] and describes it as situated at a short distance
from Galata (Ψυχρὰ Ὕδατα, μικρὸν ἀπωτέρω τοῦ Γαλατᾶ).   Nicolò
Barbaro[3] designates it as the Harbour of Pera, or Galata—
"Abiando tragetà dentro dal porto de Constantinopoli ben fuste
setantado, e redusele in porto dentro del navarchio de Pera"—
and explains the possibility of the occupation of a point so near
Galata by the excellent relations existing between the Turks
and the Genoese : "E questo perchè lor Turchi avea bona paxe
con Zenovexi."   At variance with these statements, Ducas[4]
says the ships were launched into the harbour opposite Eyoub
(Cosmidion), but that is contrary to all the probabilities of the
case.   Phrantzes[5] sheds no light upon the question.

In regard to the starting-point from the Bosporus, there is
general agreement that it was somewhere on the shore between
Beshiktash and Top Haneh ; Andreossy[6] being singular in
supposing that the vessels left the Bosporus at Balta Liman.

[1] Lib. i. c. 42.   [2] See above, p. 211.   [3] Page 753.
[4] Page 271.   [5] Page 251.   [6] *Constantinople et le Bosphore*, p. 364.

R

Now, there are four ravines or valleys that run inland from the shore between Beshiktash and Top Haneh towards the ridge dividing the Bosporus and the Golden Horn : the valleys of Beshiktash, Dolma Bagtchè, Sali Bazaar, and Top Haneh, which reach the top of the ridge, respectively at Ferikeui, the Municipal Gardens, Taxim, and Asmali-Medjid Sokaki. And the decision of the question which of these valleys was the one actually selected by the Sultan will depend partly upon our estimate of the respective merits of the historians whose testimony has to be considered, and partly upon the comparative suitableness of the various routes to serve the object in view.

Of the four routes indicated above, the two which proceed, respectively, by the valley of Top Haneh and the valley of Dolma Bagtchè present, both on the ground of history and natural fitness, the strongest claims for consideration.

In favour of the Top Haneh route, there is, first, the fact that it was the shortest route ; and secondly, that its length corresponds to that which Critobulus[1] assigns to the road taken by the ships across the hills, viz. eight stadia, or one mile. Accordingly, Dr. Dethier[2] and Dr. Paspates[3] maintain that the Sultan's ships were transported from the Bosporus to the Golden Horn by way of Top Haneh, Koumbaradji Sokaki, Asmali-Medjid Sokaki, and the Petits Champs.

On the other hand, the Dolma Bagtchè route has in its favour, first, the statement made by several historians, including Critobulus himself, that the point on the Bosporus from which the ships started to cross the hills was near the Diplokionion, the name for Beshiktash in Byzantine times. Ducas[4] describes

---

[1] Lib. i. c. 42.

[2] *Siège de Constantinople ;* Nicolò Barbaro, *Giornale,* p. 752.

[3] See his work on the Siege of the City in 1453, p. 139.

[4] Page 270 : Προστάττει τοῦ εὐθυδρομηθῆναι τὰς νάπας τὰς ὄπισθεν κειμένας τοῦ Γαλατᾶ, ἀπὸ τὸ μέρος τὸ πρὸς ἀνατολὴν, κάτωθεν τοῦ διπλοῦ κίονος.

that point as situated to the east of Galata, below the Diplokionion.   Pusculus[1] speaks of it as not far from the twin
columns : "Columnis haud longè a geminis, surgunt quæ ad sidera
rectæ."   Nicolò Barbaro[2] is, if possible, even more explicit.
According to him, the levelling of the road across the hill above
Pera commenced from the shore where the columns, and the
station of the Turkish fleet, were found : "*Siando tuta la sua
armada sorta a le colone*, che sun mia de luntan de la tera, fexe
che tute le zurme muntasse in tera, e fexe spianar tuto el monte
che son de sopra a zitade de Pera, *comenzando da la marina, zae
da li da le colone dove che era armada*."   Critobulus,[3] as already
intimated, styles the starting-point of the expedition the Diplokionion.   Now, the Diplokionion was not at Top Haneh, but at
Beshiktash, and the harbour of the Diplokionion must have been
the bay which formerly occupied the site of Dolma Bagtchè.[4]

In the second place, in the Dolma Bagtchè route we have
the distance which Nicolò Barbaro[5] declares was traversed by
the Turkish ships in their overland passage, *i.e.* three miles :
"Comenzando de la marina, zae da li da le colone dove che era
armada, per infino dentro dal porte de Constantinopoli, *che son
mia tre.*"

Great weight attaches to the testimony of Barbaro upon this
point ; for Critobulus was not present at the siege, while
Nicolò Barbaro was surgeon of one of the Venetian galleys

---

[1] IV. 550–551.   [2] Page 753.

[3] Lib. i. c. 42.   Charles Müller thinks the correct reading in the text of Critobulus
was not "eight stadia," but "eighteen stadia."

[4] For the site of the Diplokionion, see Gyllius, *De Bosporo Thracio*, ii. c. 7.   See
also, Bondelmontius' Map (the columns are more distinctly shown in the copy of that
map found in Du Cange and Banduri, than in the copy which accompanies this work).
The idea of Dr. Dethier, expressed in a note on Pusculus (*Siège de Constantinople*, p.
237), that the Diplokionion stood, in Byzantine days, at Cabatash, and was removed—
columns and inhabitants together—to Beshiktash, after the Turkish Conquest, has
no foundation whatever.

[5] Page 753.

which took part in the defence of the chain across the entrance
to the Golden Horn, kept a diary of the incidents of the siege,
must have taken particular interest in the movements of the
Turkish fleet, and was in the way of obtaining the best available
information on the subject.   Certainly, if the transport of the
Turkish ships started from a point so near the chain and the
Greek and foreign ships guarding it as the site of Top Haneh,
Barbaro had every opportunity to know the fact, and it is
inexplicable how he could have made the mistake of representing
another locality as the scene of the achievement.

With Barbaro agrees another competent witness, Jacques
Tedaldi, a Florentine merchant, who took part in the defence
of the city, and who gives the distance over which the ships
were carried as from two to three miles : "Fit porter de la mer
par terre deux ou trois milles, de soixant dix a quatre-vingts
gallées que aultres fustes armées, dedans le gouffle de Mandra-
quins qui est entre les deux citez, auxquieuls est le port de
Constantinople." [1]

If, in the next place, we judge between the two routes by
their comparative fitness to facilitate the accomplishment of the
Sultan's design, the Dolma Bagtchè route can claim the superiority
in that respect.   Had the matter of distance been all the Sultan
required to consider in choosing the road for his ships, the decision
would necessarily have been in favour of the Top Haneh route.
But, surely, other matters also had to be taken into account.   It
was desirable, for example, that the route should be situated where
all the preparations necessary to effect the passage could be readily
made, where they would be beyond the reach of interference on
the part of the Greeks, where they would, as the conveyance of
the ships by night proves was the Sultan's wish, be screened
from hostile observation, and result in taking the enemy by

---

[1] Dethier, *Siège de Constantinople*, No. xviii. p. 893.

surprise. All this was impossible at the site now occupied by Top Haneh, which stood but a short distance outside the chain and its guard-ships. There the Sultan's preparations—the levelling of the ground, the laying down of sleepers and planks along which the cradles carrying the ships were to be drawn, the gathering of seventy to eighty vessels, the army of men collected to draw the ships out of the water and overland,—would be too much in the public eye to satisfy the requirements of the case.

On the other hand, although the Dolma Bagtchè route laboured under the disadvantage of being longer than the road from Top Haneh, the distance it presented was not excessive, while it offered ample compensation for the additional efforts which its greater length occasioned. It started from the usual station of the Turkish fleet in the Bosporus, where all requisite means for executing the Sultan's purpose could be obtained with the least difficulty, where no attack was to be apprehended, where the presence of a large number of ships would excite no suspicions, and where, it was reasonable to expect, the great secret could be kept as long as necessary. From the point of fitness to serve the scheme contemplated, the route from Dolma Bagtchè had most to recommend it, taking all things into consideration.

Turkish historians do not afford any assistance to solve the problem under discussion. Evlia Tchelebi pretends that the ships were not brought from the Bosporus, but that some of them were constructed at Kiathaneh, the Sweet Waters, at the head of the harbour, and others at Levend Tchiflik (probably the Kutchuk Levend Tchiflik situated, in old Turkish times, high up the longer arm of the Dolma Bagtchè valley, not the Levend Tchiflik above the head of the valley of Balta Liman) ; and that the latter portion of the flotilla was carried to the Golden Horn by way of the Ok Meidan behind Haskeui, and the gardens of the Arsenal (Tersaneh Bagtchessi). Another Turkish authority says the ships were transported from Dolma Bagtchè to Cassim Pasha.

NOTE.

According to Leonard of Scio (p. 920), the distance over which the Turkish ships were conveyed was seventy stadia, "ad stadia septuaginta trahi biremes." This statement involves so many questions which are difficult, if not impossible, to decide, that it affords no assistance in determining where the ships crossed the hills. The archbishop's account of the Sultan's action is given in the following words: "Quare ut coangustaret circumvalleratque magis urbem, jussit invia æquare; exque colle, suppositis lenitis vasis lacertorum sex, ad stadia septuaginta trahi biremes, quæ ascensu gravius sublatæ, posthac ex apice in declivum, in ripam sinus levissime introrsum vehebantur."

Now, if the "seventy stadia" in this passage are to be understood in the ordinary sense of the words, the route taken by the ships was over eight English miles in length. But from no point between Top Haneh and Beshiktash is the distance to the Golden Horn, across the hills, so great. Hence the language of Leonard has been variously interpreted, in the hope of bringing it into accord with what his commentators deemed the real facts in the case. Dethier, in his annotations to Zorzo Dolfin (*Siège de Constantinople*, No. xxii. p. 998), maintains that the numeral seventy gives the number of the ships transported over the hills, and not the length of the road tranversed: "Non sono 70 stadia, ma 70 galere o fuste." Charles Müller, the editor of Critobulus, referring to the statement of Leonard, expresses the same opinion as Dethier, and thinks that the number for the stadia has dropped out of the text of Leonard: "Stadiorum numerus excedisse videtur, nam septuaginta vox ad navium numerum, quem eundem etiam Chalcocondylas, p. 387, 8 præbet, referenda est" (*Fragm. Hist. Græc.*, v. p. 87). Another possible view is that the number seventy is due to an error in the text. Or, finally, it may be supposed that Leonard employed the term "stadium" in a peculiar sense. One presumption in favour of this supposition is the fact that elsewhere in his epistle, the measurements of Leonard by stadia seem too gross mistakes to be made by such a man as the archbishop, with the ordinary idea of a stadium in his mind. The bridge, for example, which the Sultan built at Haskeui, to bring his cannon closer to the Harbour Walls, and which Phrantzes (p. 252) says was one hundred ortygia long, or one stadium, Leonard (p. 931) represents as about thirty stadia in length, *i.e.*, according to the ordinary computation, between three and four miles in length, where the harbour is not half a mile wide. Again, Leonard (p. 970) speaks of the Turkish fleet as anchoring at a point less than one hundred stadia from the shore of the Propontis: "Minus ad stadia centum Propontidis ripa anchoras figunt"—a statement which, if it refers to the distance of Beshiktash from the Seraglio Point, would make that part of the Bosporus about ten miles broad! It should also be added that Charles Müller thinks that the stadium of the later Byzantine writers was one-third less than the Olympic stadium: "Adeo ut stadium tertia parte minus quam vetus stadium Olympicum subesse videri possit" (*Fragm. Hist. Græc.*, v. p. 76). Du Cange (*Glossarium Med. et Infim.*

Latinitatis) says, respecting the use of the term " stadium " by mediæval writers, " Mensuræ species, sed ignota prorsus."

Zorzo Dolfin translates the account which Leonard gives of the ships' passage across the hills, as follows: " Et per coangustar, et circumuallar piu la terra, commando, fusse spianato le uie, et sopra i colli messi in terra i uasi a forza de brazze . . . per 70 stadia che sono circa miglia . . . introdusse le fuste nel mandrachio, le qual per . . . miglia con fatica se tiranno in suxo " (Dethier, *Siège de Constantinople*, No. xxii. p. 997). If the number of miles had been given, or had not disappeared, how much discussion would have been spared !

CHAPTER XVI.

THE WALLS ALONG THE SEA OF MARMORA.

THE fortifications extending along the Sea of Marmora[1] from the Acropolis (Seraglio Point) to the southern extremity of the land walls consisted of a single wall flanked, according to Bondelmontius, by 188 towers—a line of defence some five miles in length. Almost everywhere along their course these fortifications stood close to the water's edge, making it almost impossible to land troops at their foot, and giving them only the comparatively easy task of repelling an attack upon them with ships.

What they had most reason to dread was the open sea upon whose margin they stood, its ceaseless, unwearied sap and mine of their foundations, and the furious assaults of its angry waves. This explains some peculiarities noticeable in their construction. The line of their course, for instance, was extremely irregular, turning in and out with every bend of the shore, to present always as short and sharp a front as possible to the waves that dashed against them. They were protected, moreover, by a breakwater of loose boulders,[2] scattered in the sea along their base. And the extent to which marble shafts were built, as bonds, into the lower courses of the walls and towers was, doubtless, another

---

[1] See Map of Byzantine Constantinople.
[2] Mentioned by the Anonymus, iii. p. 61; Nicetas Chon., p. 169; Cantacuzene, iv. p. 221.

INSCRIPTION IN HONOUR OF THEODOSIUS II. AND THE PREFECT CONSTANTINE.
(*See page* 46.)

INSCRIPTION IN HONOUR OF THE EMPEROR THEOPHILUS.
(*See page* 183.)

INSCRIPTION IN HONOUR OF THE EMPEROR ISAAC ANGELUS.
(*See page* 132.)

precaution adopted to maintain the stability of these fortifications. A large portion of these walls is built in arches closed on their outer face, and seems to be the work of a late age.

The walls had at least thirteen entrances.

The first gate, Top Kapoussi, a short distance to the south of the apex of the promontory, was known as the Gate of St. Barbara (ἡ τῆς μάρτυρος Βαρβάρας καλουμένη Πύλη),[1] after a church of that dedication in the vicinity ; the presence of a sanctuary consecrated to the patroness of fire-arms at this point being explained by the fact that the Mangana, or great military arsenal of the city, stood a little to the south of the gate.

The gate was guarded also on the north-west, by the Church of St. Demetrius, another military saint, and was therefore sometimes styled by the Greeks, after the Turkish Conquest, the Gate of St. Demetrius.[2] It was likewise known as the Eastern Gate,[3] owing to its position on the eastern shore of the city.

Here, probably, stood one of the gates of old Byzantium ; for when the city was occupied by the Greeks under Xenophon, the Spartan admiral, Anaxibius, escaped to the Acropolis by taking boat in the Golden Horn, and rounding the promontory to the side facing Chalcedon.[4] The pier in front of the gate was called the Pier of the Acropolis (ἡ τῆς ἀκροπόλεως σκάλα) ;[5] and for the convenience of the boatmen and sailors frequenting it, a chapel of St. Nicholas, their patron saint, was attached to the Church of St. Barbara.[6]

According to the inscriptions[7] found upon the gate, it was included in the repairs of the seaward walls in the reign of

[1] Anonymus, iii. p. 61 ; Cantacuzene, iv. p. 232 ; Pachymeres, vol. i. p. 270.

[2] Gyllius, *De Top. CP.*, i. c. xxi.

[3] Nicetas Chon., p. 205, ἀπὸ τῆς ἑώας πύλης, ἥτις ἀνέῳγε κατὰ τὴν ἀκρόπολιν. Cf. *Ibid.*, p. 26 ; Pachymeres, vol. i. p. 270.

[4] Anabasis, vii. c. i. See above, p. 5.

[5] Theophanes, p. 671 ; Cedrenus, vol. ii. p. 12.

[6] Pachymeres, *ut supra.*   [7] See above, p. 184.

Theophilus. As became its important position, it was a handsome portal, flanked, like the Golden Gate, by two large towers of white marble,[1] and beside it, if not in it, Nicephorus Phocas placed the beautiful gates which he carried away from Tarsus as trophies of his Cilician campaigns.[2] On two occasions it served as a triumphal entrance into the city, John Comnenus using it for that purpose in 1126, to celebrate the capture of Castamon;[3] and Manuel Comnenus in 1168, on his return from the Hungarian War.[4] In 1816 the towers of the gate furnished material for the Marble Kiosk which Sultan Mahmoud IV. erected in the neighbourhood;[5] and in 1871 the gate disappeared during the construction of the Roumelian railway.

Proceeding southwards from the Gate of St. Barbara, we reach the entrance known as Deïrmen Kapoussi. It is clearly Byzantine, but its Greek name is lost.

Between it and the Gate of St. Barbara must have stood the Mangana (τὰ Μάγγανα),[6] or Arsenal, with its workshops, materials of war, and library of books on military art. Its site is identified by the statement of Nicetas Choniates,[7] that it faced the rocky islet off the shore of Chrysopolis, on which the beacon tower Kiz Kalehssi, or Leander's Tower, is now built. For, according to that historian, Manuel Comnenus, with the view of closing the Bosporus against naval attack from the south, erected two towers between which he might suspend a chain across the entrance of the straits; one of them, named Damalis and Arcla (Δάμαλις, Ἄρκλα), being on the rock off Chrysopolis,[8]

---

[1] Nicephorus Greg., xvii. p. 860.   [2] Cedrenus, vol. ii. p. 363.

[3] Nicetas Chon., p. 26.   [4] *Ibid.*, p. 205.

[5] Patriarch Constantius, *Ancient and Modern Consple.*, p. 23.

[6] Anonymus, ii. p. 26 ; Glycas, p. 468.

[7] Page 268, Ὁ ἀντίπορθμος οὗτος πύργος τῆς τῶν Μαγγάνων ἄγχιστα δεδομημένος μονῆς.

[8] The rock is associated with the history of Byzantium. Upon it Chares, admiral of the Athenian fleet, sent to aid Byzantium against Philip of Macedon, erected a

the other, opposite to it, very close to the Monastery of Mangana.

The Tower of the Mangana was exceedingly strong, capable of withstanding a siege by the whole city.[1] Hence, in the struggle between Apocaucus and Cantacuzene, the former held it with great determination.

To the rear of Deïrmen Kapoussi a hollow, now occupied by market-gardens, indicates the site of the Kynegion, the amphitheatre erected by Severus when he restored Byzantium.[2] A combat of wild animals was held here as late as the reign of Justinian the Great, in honour of his consulship.[3] Subsequently, the Kynegion became a place of execution for important political offenders. There, Justinian II., on his restoration to the throne, put his rivals, Leontius and Apsimarus, to death, after subjecting them to public humiliation in the Hippodrome, by resting his feet upon their necks, while he viewed the games.[4]

A little to the south of the Kynegion stood the Church and Monastery of St. George at the Mangana (Μοναστήριον κατὰ τὰ λεγόμενα Μάγγανα, ἐπ' ὀνόματι τοῦ ἁγίου μεγάλου μάρτυρος Γεωργίου). It was an erection of Constantine Monomachus,[5] and one of the most splendid and important monasteries in the city. Its site is determined by the following indications; the church was opposite Chrysopolis,[6] and near the Mangana and the Kynegion;[7] it stood in the midst of meadows, and to it were

pillar surmounted by the figure of a heifer as a monument to the memory of his wife, Damalis, who had accompanied him on the expedition, and died at Chrysopolis. Hence that suburb and the rock were sometimes called Damalis. A palace of the Byzantine emperors at Damalis was named Scutarion (Nicetas Chon., p. 280 ; Ville-Hardouin, c. lxix.). It was noted for its pleasant air and quiet. Cf. Gyllius, *De Bosporo Thracio*, iii. c. ix.

[1] Cantacuzene, iii. pp. 438, 495, 541.

[2] *Paschal Chron.*, p. 495 ; *Notitia, ad Reg. II.* See above, p. 13.

[3] Marcellinus Comes.

[4] Theophanes, p. 574. For other executions under Constantine Copronymus, see Theophanes, pp. 647, 677, 683.

[5] Zonaras, xvii. p. 55.   [6] Nicetas Chon., p. 268.   [7] Zonaras, *ut supra.*

attached gardens and a hospital.[1] "There was," says Clavijo, the Spanish envoy, "before the entrance (of the church), a wide court containing many gardens and houses ; the church itself stood in the middle of these gardens."[2]   Now, room for a church with such surroundings existed only to the south of the Kynegion, where a comparatively extensive plain is found ; while the territory to the north was contracted, and was, moreover, otherwise occupied.   This·conclusion is corroborated by the statement of the Russian pilgrims that the Monastery of the Mangana lay to the *west* of the Church of St. Saviour.[3] That church, we shall find, stood at Indjili Kiosk.[4]   Hence, a building to the west of that point would be on the plain above indicated.

From the Church of St. George mediæval writers derived the name of Braz Saint George for the Sea of Marmora and the Hellespont.[5]   The Emperor John Cantacuzene, upon his abdication, was for some time a monk in the Monastery of Mangana, under the name Joasaph ('Ιωάσαφ), until he withdrew to the deeper seclusion of the Monastery of Batopedi, on Mount Athos.[6]

The next gate, Demir Kapoussi, is a Turkish erection that may have replaced an older entrance.[7]

A little further south, arched buttresses, forming the substructures on which the villa known as Indjili Kiosk, in the Seraglio grounds, once stood, are seen built against the walls. Through these buttresses the water of a Holy Spring within

[1] M. Attaliota, p. 48.

[2] *Constantinople, ses Sanctuaires et ses reliques, au commencement du XV. Siècle.* Traduit par Bruun, Odessa, 1883.

[3] *Itinéraires Russes en Orient*, pp. 162.

[4] See below, pp. 253, 254.

[5] Ville-Hardouin, cs. xxv.–xxvii. ; *William of Tyre*, lib. xx. c. xxiv.

[6] Cantacuzene, iv. pp. 307, 308.

[7] Large chambers and galleries are found in the body of the portion of the wall between this gate and a short distance beyond Indjili Kiosk.   One gallery measures 123½ feet long by 21 feet wide ; one of the chambers is 52½ feet by 51 feet.

the city was, until recently, conducted to the outer side of the
walls, and thus rendered accessible to the Christians of the Greek
Orthodox Church, who sought the benefit of its healing virtues.
This was the Holy Spring of the Church of St. Saviour, cele-
brated as a fountain of health long before the Turkish Conquest.
"Tout cet endroit ressemble la piscine de Salomon qui est à
Jérusalem!" exclaims one of the Russian pilgrims, who visited
the shrine during the period of the Palæologi.[1]

Its identity cannot be disputed. For the memory of the fact
that the Church of St. Saviour stood at this point has been
preserved by the annual pilgrimages made to the spot, on the
Festival of the Transfiguration, from the time of the Turkish
Conquest until the year 1821, when the privilege of frequenting
the spring was withdrawn, on account of the political events of
the day. Such popular customs afford strong evidence.

The first writer who refers to the church and spring after
1453 is Gyllius,[2] who, speaking of the water-gates in the walls
around the Seraglio, describes the position of Demir Kapoussi
thus: "The fourth gate (counting from Yali Kiosk Kapoussi)
faces south-east (solis exortum spectat hibernum), and is not far
from the ruins of the church dedicated to Christ, for the remains
of which, found built in the wall, the Greeks show much rever-
ence, by visiting them in great crowds." Thevenot[3] and Grelot[4]
give a long account of the animated scene witnessed here on the
Festival of the Transfiguration, in their day. The Sultan himself
would sometimes come to Indjili Kiosk to be entertained by
the spectacle presented on that occasion, particularly by seeing
sick persons buried up to the neck in the sand on the sea-
shore, as a method of cure. Hammer writes to the same effect,

---

[1] *Itinéraires Russes en Orient*, p. 119.

[2] Gyllius, *De Top. CP.*, i. c. vii.

[3] *Relation d'un Voyage fait au Levant*, c. xviii. (1665).

[4] *Relation d'un Voyage de Constantinople*, p. 83 (1670).

but supposed the spring to be the Hagiasma of the Virgin, and thought it marked the site of the Church of the Theotokos Hodegetria, which was in this vicinity, and to which also a Holy Spring was attached.[1] But this opinion, adopted also by Labarte,[2] is opposed to all the evidence upon the subject.

Finally, there is the testimony of the Patriarch Constantius, already alluded to, that from 1453 to 1821 the Hagiasma at Indjili Kiosk was annually frequented on the 6th of August, as the Holy Well associated with the Church of St. Saviour : "The Greeks still revered, until a few years ago, as a matter of tradition, the Hagiasma of the Saviour, which was under Indjili Kiosk."[3]

In striking agreement with this evidence since the Turkish Conquest, are the accounts given regarding the Church of St. Saviour by writers previous to that event. According to them, the church was in the neighbourhood of the Church of St. George Mangana, and to the east of that sanctuary ; it stood close to the sea, immediately behind the city walls ; its Holy Spring was enclosed within the walls, and yet could be reached from without ; in front of the walls through which the sacred stream flowed, was a beach of sand endowed with healing properties.[4] Nothing can be more conclusive.

This identification is of the greatest importance for the topographical reconstruction of the quarters of Byzantine Constantinople along the eastern shore of the promontory, for, with that church as a fixed point, it becomes comparatively easy to determine the positions of other noted buildings in the neighbourhood.

By means of that landmark, for example, the situation of

[1] *Constantinopolis und der Bosporos*, vol. i. p. 238.
[2] *Le Palais Impérial de Constantinople et ses Abords*, p. 99.
[3] *Ancient and Modern Consple.*, p. 26 ; cf. Scarlatus Byzantius, vol. i. p. 181.
[4] *Itinéraires Russes en Orient*, pp. 119, 202, 231.

the Church of St. George Mangana can, we have seen, be fixed.[1]
It enables us also to settle, without prolonged discussion, the
question raised by the extensive ruins discovered behind Indjili
Kiosk, when the ground was cleared, in 1871, for the construction
of the Roumelian railroad.   The walls of an edifice 322 feet long
by 53 feet wide, were then brought to view, and among the *débris*
marble pillars and capitals were found in such numbers, as to
prove that the building to which they belonged had been one of
considerable importance.[2]   Because some of the capitals seemed
ornamented with the heads of bulls and lions, Dr. Paspates
came to the conclusion that the ruins were the remains of the
celebrated Palace of the Bucoleon.[3]   On the other hand,
Dr. Mordtmann thinks that here was the site of the Imperial
residence, known as the Palace of Mangana,[4] an erection of
Basil I.[5]

That the latter opinion is the correct one may be proved by
means of the fact that the Church of St. Saviour stood at Indjili
Kiosk.   In the first place, the Palace of Mangana was near the
Church of St. George Mangana—so near that the destruction
of that palace by Isaac Angelus, to obtain material for edifices
of his own construction, was viewed as an act of sacrilege committed against the property of the great saint.[6]   But the Church
of St. George Mangana, we have found, lay a short distance to
the west of the Church of St. Saviour,[7] near the site of Indjili
Kiosk.   Consequently the remains of a palace near that kiosk
must be those of the Palace of Mangana.   This conclusion

---

[1] See above, p. 252.

[2] For a description of the ruins, see Dr. Paspates, pp. 106–109.

[3] *Ibid.*, p. 107.

[4] Page 52.   As to the opinion of Paspates that the heads on the capitals found
among the ruins represented lions and bulls, Dr. Mordtmann remarks, " explication
qui n'a point été admise par ses contradicteurs."

[5] Theophanes Cont., p. 337.

[6] Nicetas Chon., p. 581.   [7] See above, p. 252.

agrees, furthermore, with the fact that the Mangana, which gave name to the palace, was in this vicinity.[1] It is also consistent with the circumstance that the Palace of Mangana was noted for its coolness,[2] as would be characteristic of a residence in the position of Indjili Kiosk, which is exposed to the north wind that sweeps down the Bosporus from the Black Sea.

Thus, also, the site of the Church of St. Lazarus can be approximately determined. From the order in which the churches visited by the Deacon Zosimus [3] between St. Sophia and St. George Mangana are mentioned, it is clear that the Church of St. Lazarus lay to the south of the Church of St. Saviour, and consequently somewhere between Indjili Kiosk and the Seraglio Lighthouse. The identification is important ; for near the Church of St. Lazarus was found the tier of seats, known as the Topi, which marked the southern extremity of the walls of old Byzantium on the side of the Sea of Marmora.[4]

Thus, also, the eastern limit of the grounds of the palace erected by Constantine the Great is determined. " The Triclinia erected by Constantine the Great," says Codinus,[5] " reached to that point," *i.e.* the Topi. Furthermore, the Tzycanisterion, or polo-ground, attached to the Great Palace, extended, we are told, as far as the neighbourhood of the Church of St. Lazarus and the Topi.[6] Dr. Paspates is therefore mistaken in making the palace grounds reach to within a short distance of the Seraglio Point.

---

[1] See above, p. 250. [2] Anna Comn., xv. pp. 372, 377.

[3] *Itinéraires Russes en Orient*, pp. 201, 202 : "Non loin de ce couvent (Hodegetria, proceeding towards the Seraglio Point) sont deux autres, celui de Lazare le Ressuscité, où ses reliques et (celles de) sa sœur Marie sont incrustées dans une colonne ; et secondement celui de Lazare, évêque de Galassie."

[4] Codinus, pp. 25, 79. Can the Topi have been remains of one of the theatres erected by Severus in Byzantium ?

[5] Page 79.

[6] Leo Gram., p. 273, Εἰς τὸν ἅγιον Λάζαρον, εἰς τὸ καταβάσιον τοῦ Τζυκανιστηρίου : p. 274, εἰς τοὺς λεγομένους Τόπους. Cf. Theophanes Cont., pp. 859, 860.

Near the Topi likewise stood the Thermæ Arcadianæ,[1] constructed by the Emperor Arcadius, and one of the finest ornaments of the capital.   There, also, was a church dedicated to the Archangel Michael, ἐν Ἀρκαδιαναῖς.[2]

In this neighbourhood, moreover, must have stood the Atrium of Justinian the Great,[3] a favourite public resort towards sunset, when the eastern side of the city was in shade, to admire the magnificent display of colour then reflected on the Sea of Marmora and the Asiatic coast and mountains.   It was built of white marble and adorned with statuary, among which the statue of the Empress Theodora, upon a pillar of porphyry, was specially remarkable.[4]

Still further south of the Church of St. Saviour rose one of the most venerated shrines in Constantinople, the Church of the Theotokos Hodegetria (τῶν Ὀδηγῶν) founded by the Empress Pulcheria, and reconstructed by Michael III.[5]   It boasted of a Holy Well famed for marvellous cures,[6] and of an Icon of the Virgin, attributed to St. Luke, which was regarded as the palladium of the city and the leader (Ὀδηγητρία) of the hosts of the Empire to victory.   Generals on leaving the city to engage in war paid their devotions at this shrine, and the sacred picture had the first place of honour in a triumphal procession, taking precedence of the emperor himself.[7]   In view of the siege of the city by Branas, in the reign of Isaac Angelus, the Icon was carried round the fortifications ;[8] while in 1453 it was placed in the Church of the Chora, not far from the Gate of Charisius,

---

[1] Procopius, *De Æd.*, i. c. xi.

[2] Codinus, p. 33 ; Suidas, *ad vocem* στήλη.

[3] Procopius, *De Æd.*, i. c. xi.   [4] *Ibid., ut supra.*

[5] Pachymeres, vol. i. p. 160 ; Codinus, p. 80.

[6] *Itinéraires Russes en Orient*, p. 229.

[7] Genesius, iv. p. 103 ; Cantacuzene, iii. p. 607 ; Nicetas Chon., p. 26 ; Pachymeres, *ut supra.*

[8] Nicetas Chon., pp. 496, 497.

to support the defence. There, upon the capture of the city, it was found by the Turks, and cut to pieces.[1]

According to the Russian pilgrims, the Church of the Hodegetria was situated to the south of St. George Mangana, and to the east of St. Sophia, on the right of the street conducting from the cathedral to the sea.[2] These indications support the opinion of Dr. Mordtmann[3] that the position of the church is marked by a neglected Hagiasma in the large vegetable garden at the south-eastern corner of the Seraglio grounds.

Two small gates in the city walls were respectively named after the two churches just mentioned, one being styled the Postern of St. Lazarus (τοῦ ἁγίου Λαζάρου πυλίς),[4] the other the Small Gate of the Hodegetria (ἡ μίκρα πύλη τῆς Ὁδηγητρίας).[5] They must have stood to the south of Indjili Kiosk; and, in fact, at the distance of some 145 paces from that point the marble frames of two small gateways are seen built in the wall. On the lintel of the one more to the south is a cross, and on two slabs built into the inner side of the gateway are the words, "Open to me the gates of righteousness, that entering into them I may worship the Lord."[6] Two similar gates are seen still further south, one on either side of the second tower beyond Indjili Kiosk. These four entrances must have belonged to some of the numerous churches which were situated, according to the Russian pilgrims, in this part of the city. One

---

[1] Ducas, p. 288.

[2] *Itinéraires Russes en Orient*, p. 230, "Au nord du couvent d'Odigitria, dans la direction de Mangana ;" p. 229, "à l'est de Sainte Sophie, dans la direction de la mer, à droite, s'élève un couvent appelé Odigitria."

[3] Page 52.   [4] Pachymeres, vol. ii. p. 238.

[5] Ducas, pp. 41, 42, 283.

[6] Psalm cxviii. 19.   † ΑΝΥΞΑΤΑΙ ΜΟΙ ΠΥΛΑϹ ΔΙΚΑΙΩϹΥΝΗϹ ΙΝΑ ΕΙϹΕΛΘΩΝ ΕΝ ΑΥΤΑΙϹ ΕΞΟΜΟΛΟΓΗϹΩΜΑΙ Τῳ ΚΥΡΙῳ †. Cf. *Proceedings of Greek Literary Syllogos of Consple.*, vol. xvi., 1885; *Archæological Supplement*, pp. 23, 24; cf. Mordtmann, p. 53.

of them, doubtless, represents the Postern of St. Lazarus, while another may claim to be the Small Gate of the Hodegetria.

The Postern of St. Lazarus is mentioned in history on the occasion of the sudden appearance, in 1269, of seventy-five Venetian galleys in the offing.[1] As soon as the fleet was sighted, all the gates of the city were closed, with the exception of this postern ; and from it envoys were despatched in a boat to ascertain the object of the expedition.   The public anxiety was relieved, when it was found that the Venetians had come to settle disputes with the Genoese at Galata and not to molest the capital.

According to Ducas [2] it was through the Gate of the Hodegetria that John VI. Palæologus penetrated, in 1355, into the city to overthrow John Cantacuzene.   The voyage of the conspirators from Tenedos had been accomplished in rough weather ; and it was dark and stormy when they arrived before Constantinople. As their force consisted of but two galleys, with 2000 men, the assailants could hope to enter the city only by stratagem. Approaching, therefore, the Gate of the Hodegetria, they proceeded to hurl empty oil-jars against the walls, and to rend the air with loud cries of distress.   The startled sentinels, imagining it was a case of shipwreck, and touched by appeals to their humanity and by promises of a share in the rich cargo of oil reported to be on board the galleys, opened the gate and rushed to the rescue.   When they discovered their mistake, it was too late.   They were promptly overpowered and killed, and the Italian adventurers seized the gate, mounted the adjoining towers, and raised the cry in favour of Palæologus.

It was at the Gate of the Hodegetria, probably, that Bardas,

[1] Pachymeres, vol. ii. p. 238.

[2] Ducas, pp. 41, 42 ; Cantacuzene (iv. p. 284) says that John Palæologus took the city by surprise, entering the Harbour of the Heptascalon during the night.

in 866, embarked to conduct an expedition against the Saracens in Crete, after invoking the aid of the Virgin Hodegetria.[1] Here, the troops sent by Alexius III. to suppress the insurrection under John the Fat landed to gain the Great Palace, which the rebel leader was occupying.[2] The gate appears in the last siege, as a point blockaded by the Turkish fleet which invested the walls along the Sea of Marmora.[3]

In the recess of the shore immediately beyond the Seraglio Lighthouse, where the coast bends westwards, are two gates, known, respectively, as Balouk Haneh Kapoussi and Ahour Kapoussi. The former, the Gate of the Fish House, obtained its name from the circumstance that it led to the quarters of the fishermen in the service of the Turkish Court ; the latter was styled the Stable Gate, because it conducted to the Sultan's Mews.

The Patriarch Constantius[4] identified Balouk Haneh Kapoussi with the Postern of Michael the Protovestarius, mentioned once in Byzantine history. That was the gate by which Constantine Ducas, in 913, entered the city to join the conspirators who sought to place him upon the throne instead of Constantine Porphyrogenitus, then a minor under the tutelage of his uncle and colleague, Alexander.[5] The fact that Constantine Ducas reached the gate by sea without being immediately discovered, and that he was then able to reach the Hippodrome quickly, is in favour of the view that the entrance stood upon the Sea of Marmora. But if, as seems probable, the entrance at Balouk Haneh Kapoussi was within the limits of the Great Palace, it cannot be the Parapylis of Michael Protovestarius ; for that postern did not conduct Ducas into the grounds of the Imperial residence, but

---

[1] Genesius, iv. p. 103 ; Cedrenus, vol. ii. p. 179.
[2] Nicetas Chon., p. 698.
[3] Ducas, p. 283.
[4] *Ancient and Modern Consple.*, p. 23.
[5] Leo Gramm., p. 289.

to the private house of his father-in-law Gregoras, without the palace precincts.   Possibly one of the small gates between the Lighthouse and Indjili Kiosk represents the postern.

The ancient name of Ahour Kapoussi is not known.   The Patriarch Constantius,[1] it is true, identifies it with the Gate of the Hodegetria.   But the Gate of the Hodegetria was remarkable for its small size, and stood outside the enclosure of the Great Palace ; whereas Ahour Kapoussi was within the palace grounds, and is of ordinary dimensions.

Equally erroneous is the view of Labarte[2] that the recess in the shore at this point marks the site of the Port of the Bucoleon, the harbour attached to the Imperial palace.   Doubtless, the small bay before Ahour Kapoussi, as its position implies, served the convenience of the Byzantine Court, but it was not the Port of Bucoleon strictly so called.   That harbour, we shall find, lay further west at Tchatlady Kapou, the gate next in order.

The splendid marble stables erected by Michael III. at the Tzycanisterion[3] were in this vicinity.   May this gate not have been at their service ?   It would not be strange if the Sultan's Mews were built upon the site of the Mews of his Byzantine predecessors.

Passing next to Tchatlady Kapou (the Broken or Cracked Gate), we reach the entrance attached, as already intimated, to the Imperial Port of the Bucoleon.   Its Byzantine name has not been preserved, but in the time of Gyllius[4] it was called the Gate of the Lion (Porta Leonis), after the marble figure of a lion near the entrance.   Upon the maps of Constantinople, made in the sixteenth century, it is styled " Porta liona della riva."   Leunclavius names it the Gate of the Bears (Πόρτα

---

[1] *Ancient and Modern Consple.*, p. 23.
[2] *Le Palais Impérial de Consple.*, p. 207.
[3] Anonymus, ii. p. 23.   [4] *De Top. CP.*, ii. c. xv.

ταῖς Ἀρκούδαις), a designation derived, doubtless, from the figures of bears which once adorned the adjoining quay.[1]

Some authorities[2] have identified the entrance with the Sidhera Porta (the Iron Gate), which stood on this side of the city. But this is a mistake. The Iron Gate opened on the Harbour of Sophia,[3] and was near the Church of St. Thomas Amantiou;[4] and both these points were to the west of Tchatlady Kapou. Therefore Tchatlady Kapou itself cannot have been the Iron Gate.

That the Harbour of Sophia lay in that direction is unquestionable, for it stood at Kadriga Limani,[5] which is to the west of Tchatlady Kapou. And that the same was true of the Church of St. Thomas is clear from the fact that this sanctuary and the Church of SS. Sergius and Bacchus marked, respectively, the western and eastern limits of the ravages made beside the Sea of Marmora, by the great fire in the reign of Leo I.[6] The Church of St. Thomas lay, therefore, to the west of SS. Sergius and Bacchus, and, consequently, as the latter stands to the west of Tchatlady Kapou, the former, also, must have occupied a similar position.

In the city walls, a little to the west of Tchatlady Kapou, opposite the beautiful Church of SS. Sergius and Bacchus, is a small postern, opened, doubtless, for the use of the monastery attached to that church. Its side-posts are shafts of marble,

---

[1] *Pand. Hist. Turc.*, s. 200, Πόρτα ταῖς Ἀρκούδες ; *Itinéraires Russes en Orient*, p. 235 : "Sous la muraille au pied de la mer, se trouvent des ours et des aurochs en pierre."

[2] Patriarch Constantius, *Ancient and Modern Consple.*, p. 22.

[3] Anonymus, iii. p. 46.

[4] Cedrenus, vol. ii. p. 250. Symeon Magister (*De Leone Basilii Filio*, c. i.) records a fire near the Harbour of Sophia and the Iron Gate, which burned the Church of St. Thomas—a proof that these points stood near one another.

[5] See below, p. 290.

[6] Cedrenus, vol. i. pp. 609–611 ; Zonaras, xiv. p. 1205.

Postern with inscribed posts.   SS. Sergius and Bacchus.   Mosque of Sultan Achmet.

PORTION OF WALLS BESIDE THE SEA OF MARMORA.

covered with a remarkable inscription, and were evidently
brought from some other building, when the postern was constructed or repaired.

The inscription is a cento of verses, taken, with slight
modifications, from the Prophet Habakkuk and the Psalter, to
form a pæan in honour of the triumph of some emperor over
his foes.

ΕΠΙΒΗΟΙ ΕΠΙ ΤΟΥΟ ΙΠΠΟΥΟ ΟΟΥ Κ. Η ΙΠΠΑΟΙΑ
ΟΟΥ Οω [ΤΗΡ] ΙΑ :[1] ΟΤΙ Ο ΒΑΟΙΛΕΥΟ ΗΜωΝ ΕΛΠΙΖΙ
ΕΠΙ ΚΝ. ΕΝ Τω ΕΛΕΙ ΤΟ [Υ ΥΨΙΟΤΟΥ ΟΥ ΜΗ]
ΟΑΛΕΥΘΗ :[2] ΟΥΚ ΟΦΕΛΗΟΙ ΕΚΘΡΟΟ ΕΝ ΑΥΤω Κ. ΥΙΟΟ
ΑΝΟΜΙΑΟ ΟΥ ΠΡΟΟΘΗΟΗ ΤΟΥ ΚΑΚωΟΙ ΕΑΥΤΟΝ :[3]
ΑΙΝωΝ ΕΠΙΚΑΛΙΟΕΤΟ [ΚΝ.] : ΕΚ ΤωΝ ΕΚΘΡωΝ ΑΥΤΟΥ
ΟωΘΗΟΕΤΕ :[4] ΕΞΟΥΔΕΝωΤΕ ΕΝωΠΙΟΝ ΑΥΤΟΥ ΠΟΝΗ-
ΡΕΥΟΜΕΝΟΟ, ΤΟΥΟ ΔΕ ΦΟΒΟΥ [ΜΕΝΟΥΟ ΚΝ.] ΔΟΞΑΟΙ.[5]

The next entrance, the Gate of Sophia (Πόρτα τῶν Σοφιῶν),[6]
as its name implies, was attached to the Harbour of Sophia. It
was known also as the Porta Sidhera (Πόρτα Σιδηρᾶ),[7] from the
material of its construction, and after the Turkish Conquest was
designated Porta Katerga Limani,[8] the Gate of the Harbour of
the Galleys, from κάτεργον, the Greek word for a galley.

The Porta Kontoscalion (τὸ δὲ λεγόμενον Κοντοσκάλιον ἡ
Πόρτα)[9] communicated with the Harbour of the Kontoscalion,[10]
and stood at Koum Kapoussi.

Next follows the gate Yeni Kapou, in the quarter of Vlanga.
The Latin inscription which was found over the gate[11] proves it to
have been a Byzantine entrance, but its ancient name has not been

[1] Habakkuk iii. 8.　　　　　　　[2] Psalm xxi. 7.
[3] Psalm lxxxix. 22.　　　　　　[4] Psalm xviii. 3.
[5] Psalm xv. 4. Possibly the inscription commemorated the triumph of Justinian
over the Factions in 532.
[6] Codinus, p. 101 ; Anonymus, iii. p. 45.　　[7] *Ibid. ut supra ; ibid.*, p. 46.
[8] Leunclavius, *Pand. Hist. Turc.*, s. 200.
[9] Codinus, p. 109.　　　[10] See below, p. 295.　　　[11] See above, p. 180.

preserved. The gate was beside the Harbour of Theodosius, or Eleutherius[1] (Vlanga Bostan). Its Turkish name must allude to repairs made after 1453.

The next gate, Daoud Pasha Kapoussi, immediately to the west of Vlanga Bostan, is the Gate of St. Æmilianus (ἡ Πόρτα τοῦ ἁγίου Αἰμιλιανοῦ),[2] named so after a church of that dedication in the vicinity. It is identified by its situation. On the one hand, the Gate of St. Æmilianus was the westernmost entrance in the line of the Constantinian Walls beside the Sea of Marmora.[3] It must, therefore, have been a gate to the west of the old harbour at Vlanga Bostan, which, under the name of the Harbour of Eleutherius, stood within the city of Constantine.[4] On the other hand, it cannot have been a gate further west than Daoud Pasha Kapoussi, for the two gates which pierce the city wall in that direction can be identified with other gates, and were, moreover, beyond the original bounds of Constantinople. Near the Gate of St. Æmilianus stood the Church of St. Mary Rhabdou, venerated as the shrine in which the rod of Moses was kept.[5]

The next gate retains its old name, Gate of Psamathia (Πόρτα τοῦ Ψαμαθᾶ),[6] derived from the ancient quarter Psamathia (τοῦ Ψαμαθᾶ). The name alludes to the sand thrown up on the beach here, as at Koum Kapoussi (the Sand Gate).

Narli Kapoussi (the Pomegranate Gate), the succeeding entrance, accommodated the quarter around the celebrated Church

---

[1] See below, p. 296. [2] *Paschal Chron.*, p. 494; Codinus, pp. 102, 103.
[3] Anonymus, i. p. 2; Codinus, p. 25. See above, p. 31.
[4] *Ibid.*, iii. p. 46; *ibid.*, p. 49. [5] *Ibid.*, iii. p. 49; *ibid.*, pp. 102, 103.
[6] Anonymus, iii. p. 48. The name appears also under the forms Ψαμάθεα (Codinus, p. 109); τῶν Ὑψωμαθίων (Phrantzes, p. 253); τοῦ Ψωμαθέως (Constant. Porphyr., *De Administratione Imperii*, c. 43). The quarter boasted of a palace and gerocomion, ascribed to St. Helena (Anonymus, *ut supra*), a monastery (Constant. Porphyr., *ut supra*), and the Church of the Theotokos Peribleptos (Soulou Monastir).

and Monastery of St. John the Baptist, known as the Studion,
because founded, in 463, by Studius, a patrician from Rome.
The gate is never mentioned by name, but is clearly referred
to by Constantine Porphyrogenitus[1] in his account of the
Imperial visit paid, annually, to the Studion on the 29th of
August, in commemoration of the martyrdom of the Baptist.
On that occasion it was usual for the emperor to come from the
Great Palace by water, in his state barge, and to land at this
gate, where he was received by the abbot and monks of the
monastery, and conducted to the services of the day.

On the cliff outside the gate is an Armenian Chapel of St.
John the Baptist, which Dr. Paspates[2] thinks belonged originally
to the Studion.

The excavations made in laying out the public garden beside
the city walls west of the Gas Works at Yedi Koulè, brought to
light substructures of an ancient edifice, in the construction of
which bricks stamped with the monogram of Basil I. and with a
portion of the name Diomed were employed.   The ruins marked,
undoubtedly, the site of the Church and Monastery of St. Diomed,
upon whose steps Basil flung himself to sleep the evening he
entered the city, a poor homeless adventurer from Macedonia,
in search of fortune.   The kindness shown to the stranger by
the abbot of the House was never forgotten ; and when Basil
reached the throne he rebuilt the church and the monastery on a
more extensive scale, and enriched them with ample endow-
ments.[3]   The large number of pillars strewn upon the adjoining
beach belonged, probably, to the church.

Somewhere in the neighbourhood was the prison, known as
the Prison of St. Diomed.   In it, Pope Martin I. was detained
by the Emperor Constans in 654 ;[4] and there Maria, the wife of

---

[1] *De Cer.*, pp. 562, 563.   [2] Page 349.   [3] Theophanes Cont., p. 223.
[4] See account of his treatment at Constantinople in his fifteenth Epistle.

Manuel Comnenus and mother of Alexius II., was confined by the infamous Andronicus Comnenus.[1]

The last tower in this line of fortifications, situated on a small promontory commanding a wide view of the Sea of Marmora, is a very striking and picturesque object. It has four stories, and is constructed mostly of large blocks of marble. To it was attached a two-storied building, forming, with the tower, a small château or castle at this point. Only the foundations of the western and northern walls of the building are left, but the eastern wall, pierced by two tiers of small windows, and ornamented with string-courses, stands almost intact. The castle must have been the residence of some superior military officer. Here, some think, was the Prison of St. Diomed. In the recess of the shore immediately beyond the tower was a small postern for the use of the garrison at this point.

One cannot bring this account of the Walls of Constantinople to a close without calling to mind, again, the splendid part they played in the history of the world. To them the Queen of Cities, as her sons loved to call her, owed her long life, and her noble opportunity to advance the higher welfare of mankind. How great her services in that respect have been, we are coming to recognize more clearly, through a better acquaintance with her achievements, and a fairer judgment upon her faults. The city which preserved Greek learning, maintained Roman justice, sounded the depths of religious thought, and gave to Art new forms of beauty, was no mean city, and had reason to be proud of her record.

But never was she so grand as in her attitude towards the barbarous tribes and Oriental peoples which threatened her existence, and sought to render European civilization impossible.

[1] Nicetas Chon., p. 347.

CHATEAU AND MARBLE TOWER NEAR THE WESTERN EXTREMITY OF THE WALLS BESIDE THE
SEA OF MARMORA.

Some of her foes—the Goths and the great Slavic race—she not only fought, but also gathered within the pale of civilized Christendom. With others, like the Huns, Persians, Saracens, Turks, she waged a relentless warfare, often achieving signal triumphs, sometimes worsted in the struggle, always contesting every inch of her ground, retarding for a thousand years the day of her fall, perishing sword in hand, and giving Western Europe, meantime, scope to become worthy to take from her dying hands the banner of the world's hope. This is service similar to that which has earned for Ancient Greece men's eternal gratitude, and has made Marathon, Thermopylæ, Salamis, Platæa, names which will never die.

Among the monuments brought by Constantine from various parts of the Empire to adorn his city was the serpent column which had stood for eight centuries before the shrine of Delphi, inscribed with the names of the Greek States whose valour on the field of Platæa hurled the Persian out of Greece. In placing that column in the Hippodrome of New Rome, did he divine the mission of the new capital? It was Greece transferring to the city founded on the banks of the Bosporus the championship of the world's best life. And as we look backwards upon the tremendous conflict between barbarism and civilization, which forms the very core of Byzantine history, we see that nowhere could that venerable monument have been placed more appropriately, and that if the name of the City of Constantine were inscribed upon it no dishonour would be cast upon the names already there, and only justice would be done to the Empire which assumed their task and emulated their renown.

But the shield of the city in that long heroic contest were the Walls whose history we have reviewed.

CHAPTER XVII.

THE HARBOURS ON THE SEA OF MARMORA.

THE number of harbours found, at one time or other, on the southern shore of the city formed one of the most striking features in the aspect of Byzantine Constantinople. This was not due to any natural facilities offered by that shore for the purpose. On the contrary, although the outline of the coast is very irregular, it presents no bay where ships may be moored for the convenience of commerce, or into which they can find refuge from storms. The waves, moreover, cast up great quantities of sand upon the beach. Hence, all the harbours on this side of the city were, to a great measure, artificial extensions of some indentation of the coast, and their construction and maintenance involved great labour and expense. They ranked, in fact, among the principal public works of the capital. But the interests of commerce with the regions around the Sea of Marmora and with the Mediterranean were so great, and the difficulty which vessels coming from those regions often found to make the Golden Horn, owing to the prevalence of north winds, was so serious as to outweigh all drawbacks or impediments, and secured for the accommodation of the shipping frequenting this side of the city no less than five harbours. These harbours were probably constructed in the following chronological order: the Harbour of Eleutherius, known also as the

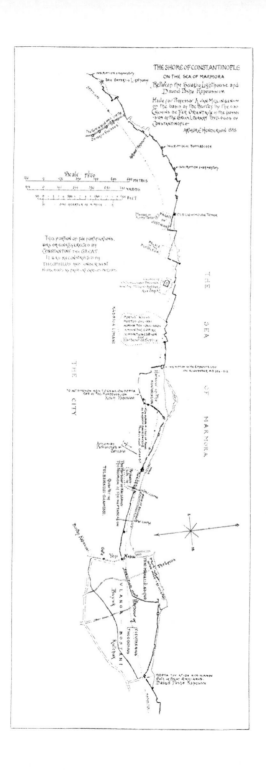

Harbour of Theodosius; the Harbour of the Emperor Julian, known also as the New Harbour, and as the Harbour of Sophia; the Harbour of Kaisarius, the same probably as the Neorion at the Heptascalon; the Harbour of the Bucoleon; and the Kontoscalion. We shall consider them in the order of their position on the shore, proceeding from east to west.

HARBOUR OF THE BUCOLEON.

The Harbour of the Bucoleon was attached to the Great Palace [1] (τὸ τοῦ παλατίου νεώριον ἐν τῷ Βουκολέοντι) for the convenience of the emperor, who in a city like Constantinople would have frequent occasion to move to and fro by water. Its name was derived from a marble group of a Lion and a Bull upon the harbour's quay, the lion being represented with his left foot upon a horn of the bull, in the act of twisting his victim's head round to get at the throat.[2] The harbour, partly artificial, was protected by two jetties from the violence of the winds and waves; [3] and, in keeping with its destination, displayed considerable architectural splendour. Its quay was paved with marble,[4] and adorned with figures of lions, bulls, bears, and ostriches; [5] a handsome flight of marble steps led to the water; [6] and upon the adjoining city walls rose two Imperial villas, known as the Palace of the Bucoleon (τὰ παλάτια τοῦ Βουκολέοντος).[7]

Strangely enough, the site of a harbour so prominent, and so fully described, has been a point concerning which students of the topography of the city have widely differed. Dr. Paspates [8]

---

[1] Cedrenus, vol. ii. p. 292.

[2] Anna Comn., iii. p. 137; Zonaras, xvi. c. xxviii. p. 131.

[3] Bondelmontius' Map.   [4] William of Tyre, xx. c. xxiii. p. 983.

[5] Theophanes Cont., p. 447; Anna Comn., vii. pp. 334, 335; *Itinéraires Russes en Orient*, p. 235.

[6] William of Tyre, *ut supra.*

[7] Anna Comn., iii. p. 137; Anonymus, i. p. 9.   [8] Page 118.

placed the harbour at a distance of 104 feet to the south of Indjili Kiosk, consistently with his opinion that the ruins discovered behind that Kiosk marked the site of the Palace of the Bucoleon.[1] With much learning and ingenuity, Labarte argues that the Harbour of the Bucoleon was in the recess of the shore at Ahour Kapoussi.[2] Von Hammer wavered in his opinion, placing the harbour at one time at Tchatlady Kapou, and at another at Kadriga Limani.[3] And yet to Von Hammer is due the discovery of the evidence that puts an end to all uncertainty on the subject, by showing us that the marble group of the Lion and the Bull, which gave the harbour its name, stood at Tchatlady Kapou.

The evidence on the subject is found in a report which Pietro Zen, Venetian envoy to the Turkish Court, sent to his Government in 1532, where he describes the monument at great length, as he saw it after it had been shaken by an earthquake. In quoting this description,[4] Von Hammer, however, not only fails to use it for the settlement of the question at issue, but also omits portions of the report which are of the utmost importance for determining the exact site of the famous group. Dr. Mordtmann, citing Von Hammer, has appreciated the significance of the passage referred to, and employs it more successfully, but with the same omissions.[5]

The original manuscript of the report is preserved in the Marciana Library, among the unpublished Archives of the Venetian Republic,[6] and the passage with which we are concerned reads to the following effect :

---

[1] See above, p. 255.   [2] *Le Palais Impérial de Consple.*, pp. 201–210.
[3] *Constantinopolis und der Bosporos*, vol. i. pp. 119, 121, 124.
[4] *Histoire de l'Empire Ottoman*, vol. v., note xxxv.   [5] Pages 53, 54.
[6] Marin Sanuto, *Diarii Autographi*, vol. lvii., Carta 158, recto, 14 Decembrio, 1532. The document was addressed to the Doge Gritti, who had been in Constantinople, and knew the localities to which allusion was made.

"At the gate at which animals are slaughtered (near the columns of the Hippodrome, on the road below), which in Turkish is named Chiachadi Capisso, which in the Frank language means 'Gate of the Crack,' outside the said water-gate, and beneath the three ancient windows which have a lion at either end (of the row) ; there, down beside the shore, on two columns, is a marble block upon which is a very large bull, much larger than life, attacked at the throat by a lion, which has mounted upon the back of the (bull's) neck, and thrown him down, and strikes at a horn of the bull with great force. This lion is considerably larger than life, all cut out of one piece of stone of very fine quality.   These animals used to stand with their heads turned towards Asia, but it seems that on that night (the night of the catastrophe) they turned themselves with their heads towards the city. When this was observed next morning, the whole population of the place ran together to the spot, full of amazement and stupefaction.   And every one went about discoursing upon the significance of the event according to his own turn of mind ; a comet also appearing for many nights."

The original is as follows, the words in .italics being omitted by Von Hammer: "Alla porta dove si amaza animali, acosto dile colone dilprodramo, da basso via, *c in Turcho si chiama chiachadi capisso, c in francho vol dir para di crepido,* fuora dila dita porta de marina, *sotto quelle tre fenestre antiquissime che hanno uno lione per banda,* li abasso alla marina, sopra due colone, e una lastra di marmoro sopra la qual e uno granmo tauro, maior bonamente che il vivo, acanatto de uno lione, el qual li e montato sopra la schena, et lo ho atterato, et da una brancha ad un corno dil tauro in un grandissimo atto ; e questo leone assai maior del vivo e tutto di una piera de una bona vena ouer miner.   Questi animali soleano esser con le teste voltate

verso Anatolia, et par che quella medema notte i se voltasseno
con le teste verso Conple., il che la matina veduto tutta questa
terra li e concorsa et ha fatto stupir e stornir tutta quest terra ;
et ogni uno va discorendo secondo le passione dil animo suo,
stante una cometa apparsa per molte notte, questa cosa per il
preditto rispetto ho voluto significar." [1]

Nothing can be more explicit or more decisive.

There is no room to doubt that the monument described by
Zen was the group of the Lion and the Bull, described, before
him, by Anna Comnena and Zonaras.[2] His description might
be a translation of the account given of the group by those
writers. Nor is there any uncertainty as to the locality where
Zen saw the monument. He indicates the site with a re-
dundancy which makes misunderstanding simply impossible,
and for which he may be pardoned, since minute particularity
seldom distinguishes the statements of authorities on the topography of the city. According to the Venetian envoy, the
monument stood on the quay outside the water-gate named
Tchatlady Kapou, which was a gate below the Hippodrome, and

---

[1] Von Hammer (*Histoire de L'Empire Ottoman*, vol. v. note xxxv.) quotes also
from Cornelius, the ambassador of Charles V. to Sultan Suleiman, who alludes to
the subject in the following words : "Est mamor quoddam hic propere ad mare, in
quo sculptus est leo ingens tenens taurum cornibus, tam vasta moles ut a mille
hominibus moveri non possit."

The Venetian historian Sagrado, in his *Memorie Istoriche de Monarchi Ottomani*,
adds that the monument fell to the ground. "In Constantinopoli un Leone di
pietra, il quale stava fuori della porta a Marina, che con una zanna afferava on toro,
guardava prima verso Levante, si ritrovo che stava rivolto a Ponente. E perche,
era situato sopra due colonne, precipito unitamente col toro, che si ruppe una coscia
e cade con la testa nel fiume, in cui parea in certo modo che bevese" (*Libro*, iv.
p. 319. Venezia, 1677).

With the above compare the statement found in the *Spectator* of April 20, 1895,
p. 519, when describing the effects of recent earthquakes in Southern Austria,
Northern Italy, and Hungary : "At Fiume and Trieste there was also a good deal
of disturbance, and at Trieste the statue of the Emperor Charles is reported to have
twisted round on its pedestal and now faces opposite to where it faced before. What
an omen that would have been considered three hundred years ago !"

[2] See above, p. 269, ref. 2.

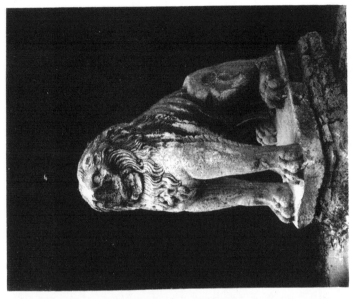

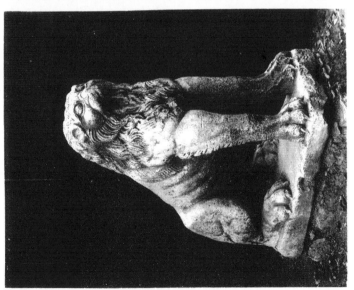

MARBLE FIGURES OF LIONS ATTACHED TO THE BALCONY IN THE PALACE OF THE BUCOLEON.

near a slaughter-house.   The group stood, he adds, beneath a row
of three windows, adorned with a lion at either end, belonging
to a very ancient building.

Now, the gate to which the name Tchatlady pertains is a
matter of public notoriety, and every particular by which Zen
marks the entrance he had in mind holds good of that gate.
It is near the Hippodrome, and on the level ground below
the race-course.   On the western headland of the little bay
in front of it, is an old slaughter-house, by which Leunclavius,
likewise, identifies the gate Tchatlady Kapou, and from which
he derived the name of the entrance;[1] while to the east of
the gate stood, until recent times, a Byzantine palace, in the
façade of which was a row of three windows, supported at either
end by the figure of a lion.   The palace is thus described by
Leunclavius: "This gate (Tchatlady Kapou) has on one side
of it the marble-framed windows of an ancient building or
palace, which rests upon the city walls themselves."[2]   Gyllius
refers to it in the following terms: "Below the Hippodrome
towards the south is the Gate of the Marble Lion, which stands
without the city among the ruins of the Palace of Leo Marcellus.
The windows of the palace are of ancient workmanship, and
are in the city wall."[3]   Choiseul-Gouffier[4] gives a view of the
palace as seen in his day, and so does Canon Curtis, in his
Broken Bits of Byzantium.   The façade was torn down in 1871,
and the lions have been placed at the foot of the steps

[1] *Pand. Hist. Turc.*, s. 200 : " Tchatladi capsi, a mactatione pecudum. . . .
Ædificium rotundum extra muros, ipso mari vicinum, ac vetus habet undique cir-
cumfluum nisi qua terræ jungitur, in quo mactantur, excoriantur et exenterantur
pecudes."

[2] *Ibid., ut supra:* " Fenestres habet hæc porta (Tchatlady Kapou) marmoreas
a latere, cujusdam ædificii vel palatii veteris, quod ipsis, muris urbanis incumbit."

[3] *De Top. CP.*, lib. i. c. vii. ; lib. ii. c. xv. : "Sub Hippodromo versus meridiem
est Porta Leonis Marmorei, extra urbem siti, in ruderibus Palatii Leonis Marcelli ;
cujus fenestræ antiquo opere laboratæ extant in muro inclusæ."

[4] *Voyage Pittoresque dans l'Empire Ottoman, etc.*, vol. iv.

leading to the Imperial School of Art, within the Seraglio enclosure.[1]

With this evidence as regards the site of the group of the Lion and the Bull, it is impossible to doubt that the Harbour of the Bucoleon was in the little bay before Tchatlady Kapou. And with this conclusion every statement made by Byzantine writers regarding the harbour will be found to agree.

That the shore of this bay was, like the Harbour of the

RUINS OF THE PALACE OF THE BUCOLEON.[2]

Bucoleon, once richly adorned with monumental buildings, is manifest from the beautiful pieces of sculptured marble found upon its beach and in the water. Furthermore, the bay stands, as the Harbour of the Bucoleon stood, within easy reach of the site of the Great Palace. Here also are found the ruins of two Imperial villas, situated in the very position ascribed to the

[1] The palace stood on a terraced platform, the area of which was some 200 by 175 feet. See Map facing p. 269.
[2] From *Broken Bits of Byzantium.* (By kind permission of Mrs. Walker.)

Palaces of the Bucoleon ; namely, upon the city walls, at the water's edge, and one of them on a lower level than the other.[1] Such correspondence goes to make the site of the Harbour of the Bucoleon one of the best authenticated localities in the topography of Byzantine Constantinople.

Here, however, a question arises. How far is this conclusion, regarding the site of the Harbour of the Bucoleon, compatible with the received opinion that the palace on the bay before Tchatlady Kapou was the Palace of Hormisdas, the residence of Justinian the Great while heir-apparent ;[2] and that the bay itself was the Harbour of Hormisdas (ὁ λιμὴν τὰ 'Ορμίσδου) ?[3]

In the face of all the evidence we have that the Harbour and the Palace of the Bucoleon were in the bay to the east of Tchatlady Kapou, there is but one answer to the question. We must either abandon the view that the Harbour and the Palace of Hormisdas had anything to do with that bay, and maintain that they stood elsewhere, or we must conclude that they were the Harbour and the Palace of the Bucoleon, under an earlier designation.

Two considerations may be urged in favour of the former alternative. First, the Anonymus distinguishes between the two palaces in a way which seems to imply that they were different buildings. " The Palace of the Bucoleon," he says, " which stands upon the fortifications, was erected by Theodosius the Younger ; "[4] while of the Palace of Hormisdas he remarks : " The very large buildings near St. Sergius were the residence of Justinian when a patrician." [5]

In the second place, the Anonymus[6] identifies the Harbour

---

[1] See above, p. 269. Anna Comnena (iii. p. 137) speaks of a lower and a higher palace, Ἐν τῷ κάτω παλατίῳ : εἰς τὸ ὑπερκείμενον παλάτιον.

[2] Procopius, *De Æd.*, i. c. iv. ; Bondelmontius, *Librum Insularum*, p. 121.

[3] Labarte, *Le Palais Imperial de Consple.*, pp. 208-210.   [4] Lib. i. p. 9.

[5] Lib. iii. p. 42 ; cf. Codinus, p. 125.   [6] Lib. iii. p. 45.

of Hormisdas with that of Julian. "What is called τὰ τοῦ ʽΟρμίσδου," observes the former writer, "was a small harbour where Justinian the Great built a monastery and called it Sergius and Bacchus, and another church, that of the Holy Apostles (SS. Peter and Paul), after receiving unction at the foot of the seats (of the Hippodrome), because of the massacre in the Hippodrome. It was named the Harbour of Julian, from its constructor." Codinus[1] also identifies the two harbours, and adds, that the Harbour of Julian had served for the accommodation of ships before the Harbour of the Sophiôn was constructed; that it had long been filled up; and that Justinian the Great had lived there before his accession to the throne. But if on the ground of these statements we identify the Harbour of Hormisdas with that of Julian, as Banduri[2] and Labarte[3] maintain, then the Harbour of Hormisdas was not situated in the bay to the east of Tchatlady Kapou, but at Kadriga Limani, the undoubted site of the Harbour of Julian, to the west of the gate.[4] The Palace of Hormisdas, also, must then have been in that direction.

In the light, however, of all our knowledge on the subject, the identity of the two harbours just named cannot be maintained. John of Antioch,[5] a far more reliable authority than the Anonymus or Codinus, makes it perfectly clear that the Harbour of Julian (which he calls by its later name, the Harbour of Sophia) was different from any harbour in the quarter of Hormisdas. According to him, the troops collected by Phocas for the defence of the city against Heraclius occupied three positions—the Harbour of Kaisarius, the Harbour of Sophia, and the quarter of Hormisdas. At the first two points were placed the Greens, while the third position was held by the Blues. From this

[1] Codinus, p. 87.   [2] *Imperium Orientale*, vol. ii. pp. 678, 679.
[3] *Le Palais Imperial de Consple.*, pp. 208, 209.   [4] See below, p. 290.
[5] *Fragm. Hist. Græc.*, vol. iv. p. 107.

account of the matter it is evident that the Harbour of Julian was not the harbour in the quarter of Hormisdas. It is a corroboration of this conclusion to find that in the narrative of the same events, given in the *Paschal Chronicle*,[1] while no mention is made of the Harbour of Hormisdas, the Harbour of Julian is described as situated in another quarter, the quarter of Maurus (κατὰ τὰ λεγόμενα Μαύρου).

In favour of the alternative that the Palace and Harbour of Hormisdas were the Palace and Harbour of the Bucoleon under

PORTION OF THE PALACE OF HORMISDAS.[2]

another name, may be urged all that goes to show that the former stood where the evidence furnished by Pietro Zen has obliged us to place the latter. The bay and palace on the east of Tchatlady Kapou stand close to what was unquestionably the district of Hormisdas; for the Church of SS. Sergius and Bacchus (Kutchuk Aya Sophia), a short distance to the west of the gate, was in that district.[3] It would be strange if a palace and harbour so near that district were not those known by its name.

[1] Page 700.
[2] From *Broken Bits of Byzantium.* (By kind permission of Mrs. Walker.)
[3] Procopius, *De Æd.,* i. c. iv.

The palace at Tchatlady Kapou answers, moreover, to the description which Procopius gives of the Palace of Hormisdas, the residence of Justinian, as near SS. Sergius and the Great Palace.[1] Its position agrees also with the statement of John of Ephesus that the Palace of Hormisdas was below the great Imperial residence.[2] Again, the style of the capitals and other pieces of marble, which have fallen from the palace at Tchatlady Kapou into the water, resemble the sculptured work in the Church of SS. Sergius and Bacchus, erected by Justinian. And lastly, the palace at this point was regarded as the Palace of Justinian when Bondelmontius visited the city in 1422. "Beyond Condoscali (Koum Kapoussi)," says that traveller, as he proceeds eastward, along the Marmora shore of the city, "was the very large Palace of Justinian upon the city walls" ("Ultra fuit supra mœnia amplissimum Justiniani Palatium").

All this being the case, it seems unavoidable to conclude that the Palace and Harbour of Hormisdas were the Palace and Harbour of the Bucoleon, under an earlier name. The circumstance that the palaces are distinguished by the Anonymus presents, after all, no serious difficulty, but the reverse ; for, as a matter of fact, there are two palatial buildings on the bay east of Tchatlady Kapou, at a distance of some 110 yards from each other, and on different levels. One of the buildings, probably the lower, might be the Palace of Hormisdas; the other, on higher ground, and nearer the gate—may be the palace to which the Anonymus referred as the Bucoleon.

It is in keeping with this view of the subject to find that the terms "Palace of Hormisdas," "Port of Hormisdas," are not employed by Byzantine authors to designate an Imperial residence or harbour, after the name Bucoleon came into vogue.

The earliest writer who refers to the Harbour of the Bucoleon

---

[1] Procopius, *De Æd.*, i. c. iv.   [2] Translation by R. Payne Smith, p. 179.

is the Emperor Constantine Porphyrogenitus,[1] in the tenth
century.   Later writers,[2] it is true, employ the name when
speaking of events which occurred in the reign of Michael I.,
and in that of Theophilus, in the course of the ninth century.
But whether these writers do so because the name was
contemporary with the events narrated, or because, when the
historians wrote, it was the more familiar appellation for the
scene of those events, is uncertain.   Should the former supposition be preferred, it was early in the ninth century that the
term "Bucoleon" first appeared.

On the other hand, the last author who alludes to the Palace
of Hormisdas is the historian Theophanes, who died in 818.
The passage in which the allusion is found refers, indeed, to
matters which transpired in the seventh century, viz. to the
execution of a certain David, Chartophylax of (the Palace of)
Hormisdas, in the reign of Phocas.   But the historian could
hardly have described an official position in terms not still
familiar to his readers.[3]

Accordingly, the designation "Palace of Hormisdas" dis-
appears about the time when the term "Bucoleon" appears,
and this is consistent with the supposition that the two names
denoted the same building at different periods of its history.[4]

The Palace of Hormisdas was so named in honour of the
Persian Prince Hormisdas, who had been deprived of the
succession to the throne of his country by a conspiracy of
nobles, and confined in a tower; but who escaped from his prison

---

[1] *De Cer.*, p. 601.   [2] Theophanes Cont., p. 22 ; Cedrenus, vol. ii. p. 49.

[3] Theophanes, p. 456.   May David, however, in opposition to the view of Du
Cange, adopted in the text, not have been Keeper of the Archives of SS. Sergius and
Bacchus?

[4] Against this view it may be objected that the Anonymus ascribes the Palace of
the Bucoleon to Theodosius II.   But the authority of the Anonymus on points of
history is not very great.   Or, it may be held, that the palace was founded by
Theodosius II., and that the name Bucoleon was given to it later.

through the ingenuity of his wife, and fled to New Rome for protection at the hands of Constantine the Great. The royal fugitive was received with the honour due to his rank, and this residence was assigned to him because near the emperor's own palace.[1]   Later, the residence was occupied, as already intimated, by Justinian while Crown Prince, with his consort Theodora ; and after his accession to the throne, was by his orders, improved and annexed to the Great Palace.[2]   It appears in the reign of Justin II. as the abode of Tiberius, upon his being appointed Cæsar.[3]   Under ordinary circumstances, Tiberius should have occupied apartments in the Great Palace. But the Empress Sophia was bitterly jealous of his wife Ino, and forbade her to show herself at Court, on any pretext whatever.   Obliged, consequently, to find a home elsewhere, the Cæsar selected the Palace of Hormisdas, because its proximity to the Grèat Palace would allow him to enjoy the society of his family, and attend to his official duties.   But the jealousy of the empress was not to be allayed so readily.   It followed Ino to the Palace of Hormisdas with such intensity that the ladies of the Court dared not visit her even there ; and it compelled her at last to leave the capital and retire to Daphnusium.

As already stated, when Heraclius appeared with a fleet, in 610, before the city to put an end to the tyranny of Phocas, he found the quarter of Hormisdas defended by the Faction of the Blues.[4]

During the tenth century, the port and palace, then called Bucoleon, received special marks of Imperial favour.   Constantine Porphyrogenitus, noted for his devotion to the Fine Arts, adorned the quay of the harbour with figures of animals, brought from various parts of the Empire.[5]   Possibly, the group of the

---

[1] Zosimus, ii. pp. 92, 93 ; iii. pp. 140, 158.   [2] Procopius, *De Æd.*, i. c. iv.
[3] *John of Ephesus*, translation by R. Payne Smith, pp. 179, 180.
[4] John of Antioch, *Fragm. Hist. Græc.*, vol. iv. p. 107.
[5] Theophanes Cont., p. 447.

Lion and the Bull was placed there by him. He also attached a fishpond to the palace.

Later, Nicephorus Phocas added a villa, which he made his usual place of residence.[1] It was probably the building with the row of three windows, supported by a lion at either end. A still more important change was introduced by the same emperor. His austere character, and the heavy taxes he imposed for the maintenance of the army, made him exceedingly unpopular, notwithstanding his eminent services as the conqueror of the Saracens. So strong did the hostile feeling against him become, that, returning once from a visit to the Holy Spring of the Pegè, he was mobbed at the Forum of Constantine, and narrowly escaped being stoned to death before he could reach the palace.[2] Rumours of a plot to dethrone and kill him were also in circulation. He therefore decided to convert the Great Palace into a fortress, and to provision it with everything requisite to withstand a siege.[3]

Accordingly, he surrounded the grounds of the Imperial residence with a strong and lofty wall, which described a great arc from the neighbourhood of Ahour Kapoussi on the east to Tchatlady Kapou on the west, and thus cut off the palace from the rest of the city.[4] Luitprand,[5] who saw the wall soon after its erection, says of it: "The palace at Constantinople surpasses

---

[1] Nicetas Chon., iii. p. 149.   [2] Leo Diac., iv. p. 63-65.

[3] *Ibid.*, iv. p. 64; Cedrenus, vol. ii. 369, 370; Zonaras, xvi. c. xxvi. p. 123. The last author describes the work thus : Τῷ νῦν ὁρωμένῳ τείχει τὰ βασίλεια ἐστεφάνωσεν. Ἀκρόπολιν δ' οἱ πολῖται τοῦτο καὶ τυραννεῖον καθ' ἑαυτῶν γινόμενον ἔκρινον.

[4] *Ibid.*, iv. p. 64, Περίβολον ἐκ τοῦ θατέρου μέρους τοῦ πρὸς θάλατταν ἐπικλινοὺς τῶν ἀνακτόρων τειχίζειν ἀρξάμενος, κατὰ θάτερον πρὸς θάλατταν συνεπέρανε, καὶ τεῖχος, τὸ νῦν ὁρώμενον ὑψηλόν τε καὶ ὀχυρὸν ἐδομήσατο, καὶ τὴν βασίλειον ἑστίαν ὡς ὑπετόπαζεν, ἠσφαλίσατο. Not, as Schlumberger supposes, from the Golden Horn to the Sea of Marmora, across the promontory (*Un Empereur Byzantin au Dixième Siècle*, p. 544).

[5] Lib. v. c. ix. ; Migne, *Patrologia Latina*, vol. cxxxvi.

in beauty and strength any fortifications that I have ever seen." Within this wall the Palace of Bucoleon was, of course, included.

Labarte [1] and Schlumberger [2] maintain, indeed, that Nicephorus surrounded the Palace of Bucoleon with special works of defence, and constituted it a citadel within the fortifications of the Great Palace. But Leo Diaconus, Cedrenus and Zonaras, our authorities on the subject, make no such statement.[3]

As might be expected, historical events of considerable importance transpired at the Port and the Palace of the Bucoleon.

Here, in 919, Romanus Lecapenus, admiral of the fleet, made the naval demonstration which compelled Constantine VII. Porphyrogenitus to accept him as a colleague, and to surrender the administration of affairs into his hands.[4]

---

[1] *Le Palais Impérial de Consple.*, p. 210.   [2] *Op. cit.*, p. 545.

[3] Still, the Palaces of the Bucoleon may have been protected by a special enclosure, although the historians do not refer to it particularly.

In the garden of a Turkish house to the north of the lower palace, a portion of a Byzantine wall, about 130 feet in length and 40 feet high, is found standing. It was discovered, when walls and houses in the neighbourhood were demolished for the construction of the Roumelian Railway, and was then pierced by a very large vaulted gateway, over 18 feet high, supported by four great marble columns. Gate and columns have disappeared. If produced southwards, the wall would join the tower at the eastern end of the lower palace ; while if produced northwards, the wall would abut against the retaining wall of the terrace on which the Mosque of Sultan Achmet and its courtyards are built. The wall is pierced with loopholes, facing *east,* and behind them a passage runs along the rear of the wall, through arches occurring at intervals.

Dr. Paspates (p. 120) regarded the wall as part of the Peridromi of Marcian (see Labarte, *Le Palais Impérial de Consple.*, p. 214), attached to the Great Palace. But this view of its character is not consistent with the fact that the loopholes look eastwards. That fact indicates that the wall belonged to the Palaces of the Bucoleon which stood to the rear. The gate in the wall, likewise, shows that these palaces were separated from the area of the Great Palace. May the wall not have turned westwards, at its present northern extremity, to protect the Palaces of the Bucoleon along the north, and then southwards, to connect with the city wall at Tchatlady Kapou, and protect the palaces on the west ? This, with the city wall along the southern front of the palaces, would put them within a fortified enclosure of their own.

[4] Theophanes Cont., p. 393.

RUINS OF THE PALACE OF HORMISDAS.

It was here that the memorable conspiracy against Nicephorus Phocas was carried out, in 969, by John Zimisces, with
the connivance of the Empress Theophano.[1]   Under cover of the
night, the conspirators embarked at Chalcedon, the residence of
Zimisces at the time, and in the teeth of a strong north wind, and
with snow falling heavily, crossed to the Bucoleon.   A low whistle
announced their arrival to their accomplices, who were watching
on the terrace of the palace ; and in response, a basket held
fast by ropes was stealthily lowered and raised, again and again,
until one by one all in the boat were lifted to the summit.   The
last to ascend was Zimisces himself.   Then the traitors made
for the apartment in which they expected to find the emperor.
Nicephorus, who had received some intimation of the plot, was
not in his usual chamber, and the conspirators, fearing they had
been betrayed, were about to leap into the sea and make their
escape, when a eunuch appeared and guided them to the room
in which the doomed sovereign lay fast asleep on the floor, on a
leopard's skin, and covered with a scarlet woollen blanket.   Not
to spare their victim a single pang, they first awakened the
slumberer, and then assailed him with their swords as he
prayed, "Lord, have mercy upon me."   As if to add irony to the
event, Nicephorus met his fate, it is said, on the very day on
which the fortifications around the palace were completed.
After this, guards were stationed, at night, on the quay of the
Harbour of the Bucoleon, to warn off boats that approached
the shore.[2]

From this point, Alexius Comnenus entered the Great
Palace, after the deposition of Nicephorus Botoniates ; leaving
his young wife and her immediate relatives in the residence
by the shore, while he himself, with the members of his own

[1] Leo Diaconus, v. p. 87 ; Cedrenus, vol. ii. p. 375.
[2] Nicetas Chon., pp. 169, 170.

family, proceeded to the higher palace (τὸ ὑπερκείμενον παλά-τιον).[1]   Here, also, in 1170, Amaury, King of Jerusalem, landed on the occasion of his visit to Manuel Comnenus, to seek the emperor's aid against Saladin.   Access to the palace by this landing, says William of Tyre,[2] in his account of that visit, was reserved, as a rule, for the emperor exclusively.   But it was granted to Amaury as a special honour, and here he was welcomed by the great officers of the palace, and then conducted through galleries and halls of wonderful variety of style, to the palace on an eminence, where Manuel and the great dignitaries of State awaited the arrival of the king.

In the course of time, as the prominent position of the Palace and the Harbour of Bucoleon rendered natural, the name Bucoleon, it would appear, was extended to the whole collection of buildings which formed the Great Palace, facing the Sea of Marmora.   That is certainly the sense in which Ville-Hardouin employs the term in his work on the Conquest of Constantinople by the Crusaders.   He associates "le palais de Bouchelyon" with the Palace of Blachernæ, as one of the principal residences of the Greek emperors.   In the division of the spoils of the city, the Palace of "Bouchelyon," like the Palace of Blachernæ, was to belong to the prince whom the Crusaders would elect Emperor of Constantinople ;[3] upon the capture of the city, the Marquis of Montferrat hastened to seize the Palace of Bucoleon, while Henry, the brother of Baldwin, secured the surrender of the Palace of Blachernæ ;[4] the treasure found in the former is described as equal to that in the latter: "Il n'en faut pas parler ; car il y en avait tant que c'était sans fin ni mesure."   Indeed, the statements of Ville-Hardouin concerning the Palace of Buco-leon make the impression that of the two Imperial residences

---

[1] Anna Comn., iii. p. 137.   [2] Lib. xx. c. 23.
[3] *Conquête de Consple.*, c. li.   [4] *Ibid.*, c. lv.

which he names, it was, if anything, the more important.[1]
Thither Murtzuphlus fled when his troops were discomfited.[2]
There, the Marquis of Montferrat found congregated for safety
most of the great ladies of the Court, including Agnes of France,
wife of Alexius II., and Margaret of Hungary, wife of Isaac
Angelus.[3]   And to the Palace of Bucoleon, the richest in the
world ("el riche palais de Bochelyon, qui onques plus riches ne fu
veuz"), the Latin Emperor Baldwin proceeded in great state,
after his coronation in St. Sophia, to celebrate the festivities
attending his accession to the throne.[4]   There, also, were held
the festivities in honour of the marriage of the Emperor Henry
with Agnes, the daughter of the Marquis of Montferrat.[5]   It
is not possible that the two comparatively small buildings at
Tchatlady Kapou could be the palace which Ville-Hardouin
had in mind in connection with these events.   The terms he
employs, in speaking on the subject, were appropriate only to
the Great Palace as a whole.

The designation of the Palace of Bucoleon as " Chastel de
Bouchelyon "[6] is no evidence that Ville-Hardouin used the
name in its restricted sense, as Labarte contends.   For the
Great Palace was within a fortified enclosure, and could therefore be styled a castle with perfect propriety, just as the same
historian, for a similar reason, speaks of the Palace of Blachernæ
as a "chastel."   Nor does the fact that the Marquis of Montferrat reached the Palace of Bucoleon by riding along the shore
("chevaucha tout le long du rivage, droit vers Bouchelion")[7]
prove that the residence beside Tchatlady Kapou was the one
he wished specially to secure.   For the grounds of the Great

---

[1] *Conquête de Consple.*, c. li.   [2] *Ibid.*, c. liii.   [3] *Ibid.*, c. lv.
[4] Ville-Hardouin, c. lviii.   [5] *Ibid.*, c. cvi.   [6] *Ibid.*, c. liii., lv.
[7] *Ibid.*, c. lv.   The position assigned by Labarte to the Palace of
Bucoleon, at Ahour Kapoussi, explains his interpretation of the statements of Ville-
Hardouin.

Palace were thus accessible by a gate which stood at the eastern extremity of the Tzycanisterion, on the plain beside the Sea of Marmora, and which communicated with the quarter of the city near the head of the promontory.

Two incidents in Byzantine history, cited by Labarte [1] himself, establish the existence of such a gate, beyond contradiction. When Stephen and Constantine, the sons of the Emperor Romanus Lecapenus, deposed their father, in 944, and sent him to a monastery on the island of Proti,[2] great fears were entertained in the city, that a similar, if not a worse, fate had befallen his associate upon the throne, the popular Constantine VII., Porphyrogenitus. The people, therefore, crowded about the palace to ascertain the truth, and were reassured that their favourite was safe by his appearance, with dishevelled hair, at the iron bars of the gate which stood at the end of the Tzycanisterion ("Ex ea parte qua Zucanistrii magnitudo portenditur, Constantinus crines solutus per cancellos caput exposuit.") The existence of a gate at this point is, if possible, still clearer from the statement of Constantine Porphyrogenitus,[3] that the Saracen ambassadors, after their audience of the emperor, left the palace grounds by descending to the Tzycanisterion, and mounting horse there. To approach the palace by that entrance evinced, therefore, no particular intention on the part of the Marquis of Montferrat to reach the buildings to which the name of Bucoleon strictly belonged. On the contrary, by that entrance one would reach the principal apartments of the Great Palace, sooner than the palaces beside the group of the Lion and the Bull, at Tchatlady Kapou.

The Bucoleon is mentioned for the last time in Byzantine

---

[1] *Le Palais Impérial de Consple.*, p. 201. Labarte quotes Luitprandi Antapodosis, lib. v. s. 21, ap. Pertz, *Mon. Germ. Hist.*, t. v. p. 333.

[2] Theophanes Cont., p. 393.   [3] *De Cer.*, p. 586.

history, in connection with the events of the final fall of the city. "To Peter Guliano, consul of the Catalans, was entrusted," says Phrantzes,[1] "the defence of the quarter of the Bucoleon, and the districts as far as the neighbourhood of the Kontoscalion."

[1] Page 253.

CHAPTER XVIII.

THE HARBOURS ON THE SEA OF MARMORA—*continued*.

The NEW HARBOUR[1] (Portus Novus), known also as the HARBOUR OF
    JULIAN[2] (Portus Divi Juliani : Λιμὴν τοῦ Ἰουλιανοῦ), and the HARBOUR
    OF SOPHIA,[3] or the SOPHIAS[4] (Λιμὴν τῆς Σοφίας, τῶν Σοφιῶν).

ABOUT 327 yards to the west of SS. Sergius and Bacchus
traces are found of an ancient harbour extending inland to the
foot of the steep slope above which the Hippodrome is situated.
The Turkish name for the locality, Kadriga Limani, "the
Harbour of the Galleys," is in itself an indication of the
presence of an old harbour at that point.   When Gyllius visited
Constantinople, the port was enclosed by walls and almost filled
in, but still contained a pool of water, in which the women of
the district washed their clothes, and at the bottom of which,
it was reported, submerged triremes could sometimes be seen.[5]

Here, as we shall immediately find, was the site of the
harbour known by the three names Portus Novus, the Harbour
of Julian, the Harbour of Sophia.

The harbour obtained its first name, when newly opened in
the fourth century, to distinguish it from the earlier harbours of
the city ; while its other names were, respectively, bestowed in

---

[1] *Notitia, ad Reg. III.*   [2] Theod. Cod., *De Calcis Coctor.*
[3] Theophanes, p. 284.   [4] Nicetas Chon., p. 585.
[5] *De Top. CP.*, ii. c. xv.

honour of the Emperor Julian, the constructor of the harbour, and of the Empress Sophia, who restored it when fallen into decay.

That these three names designated the same harbour can be proved, most briefly and directly, by showing first the identity of the Portus Novus with the Harbour of Sophia, and then the identity of the latter with the Harbour of Julian.

The former point is established by the fact that the Portus Novus and the Harbour of Sophia occupied the same position ; both were situated on the southern side of the city, and at the foot of the steep slope descending from the Hipprodrome towards the Sea of Marmora.[1]

The evidence for the identity of the Harbour of Sophia with that of Julian rests upon express declarations to that effect. There is, first, the statement of Leo the Grammarian[2] that the Emperor Justin II. built the Palace of Sophia at the Harbour of Julian, and having cleaned the latter, changed its name to the Harbour of Sophia. Then, we have two passages in which Theophanes[3] takes particular care to explain that the Harbour of Julian went also by the name of Sophia. Furthermore, both names are used to designate the scene of the same events, and the position of the same buildings. For instance ; whereas the *Paschal Chronicle*[4] states that the final action in the struggle between Phocas and Heraclius took place in the Harbour of Julian, John of Antioch[5] and Cedrenus[6] say it occurred at the Harbour of Sophia. Again, while some authors[7] put the Residence of Probus, the district of Maurus, and the Palace of

---

[1] *Notitia, ad Reg. III.;* Nicetas Chon., p. 585 ; Leo Diaconus, v. pp. 83, 84.

[2] Page 135. Cf. Cedrenus, vol. i. p. 685.

[3] Pages 284, 564, Εἰς τὸν Ἰουλιανοῦ τῆς Σοφίας λεγόμενον λιμένα: ἐν τῷ Ἰουλιανισίῳ λιμένι τῆς Σοφίας.

[4] Page 700.   [5] *Fragm. Hist. Græc.*, v. p. 38.   [6] Cedrenus, vol. i. p. 712.

[7] *Paschal Chron.*, pp. 622, 700 ; Theophanes, pp. 284, 364, 564.

Sophia, beside the Harbour of Julian, others[1] place them beside the Harbour of Sophia.

That the harbour known under these different names was at Kadriga Limani admits of no doubt, seeing the Portus Novus and the Harbour of Sophia were, as already intimated, at the foot of the steep ascent below the Hippodrome,[2] where Kadriga Limani is found.   Or the same conclusion may be reached by another line of argument.   The Portus Juliani (identical with the Portus Novus and the Harbour of Sophia) was a large harbour on the southern side of the city,[3] and close to the Church of SS. Sergius and Bacchus.[4]   It could not, however, have stood to the east of that church, for not only are all traces of such a harbour wanting in that direction, but no large harbour could possibly have been constructed there, on account of the character of the coast.   The Portus Juliani, therefore, lay to the west of SS. Sergius and Bacchus.   But it could have been very near that church (the other indication of its site), only if at Kadriga Limani.

The construction of the harbour was ordered by Julian during his stay of ten months in Constantinople, on his way to the scene of war in Persia.[5]   He likewise erected beside it, for the convenience of merchants and traders frequenting the harbour, a fine crescent-shaped portico styled, from its form, the Sigma (Σίγμα);[6] and there, also, his statue stood until 535, when it fell in an earthquake, and was replaced by a cross.[7]   In promoting such public works, Julian was actuated not only by the dictates of enlightened policy, but also by the affection he cherished for the city of his birth.[8]

[1] Leo Gramm., p. 135; Theophanes, p. 564.
[2] *Notitia ad Reg. III.*; Leo Diaconus, v. pp. 83, 84.
[3] Zosimus, p. 139; Evagrius, ii. c. xiii.; Cedrenus, vol. i. p. 611.
[4] Zonaras, xiv. c. i. p. 1205.   [5] Zosimus, pp. 139, 140.
[6] Zosimus, *ut supra.*   [7] Malalas, p. 479.   [8] See Epistle 58.

After one hundred and fifty years, the harbour was so injured by the accumulation of the sand thrown up on this coast as to call for extensive repairs ; and accordingly, at the order of Anastasius I., it was, in 509, dredged, and protected by a mole.[1]

Nevertheless, further restoration was required sixty years later, in the reign of Justin II. The work was then executed under the superintendence of Narses and the Protovestarius Troilus, at the urgent solicitation of the Empress Sophia, whose sympathies had been greatly stirred by seeing, from her palace windows, ships in distress during a violent storm on the Sea of Marmora. It was in recognition of the empress's interest in the matter that the harbour received her name,[2] and was adorned with her statue, as well as with the statues of Justin II., her daughter Arabia, and Narses.[3] Owing to the improvements made on the harbour at this time, the Marine Exchange of the city was transferred to it from the Neorion on the Golden Horn.[4] The port continued in use to the end of the Empire, and also for some sixty years after the Turkish Conquest. The entrance (now closed) was between the two large towers immediately to the west of SS. Sergius and Bacchus.

With the harbour the following historical events are associated : Here the body of St. Chrysostom was landed, and placed for a time in the neighbouring Church of St. Thomas Amantiou, when brought from the land of his exile to be entombed in the Church of the Holy Apostles.[5] In the riot of the Nika, the

---

[1] Marcellinus Comes, "Portus Juliani, undis suis rotalibus exhaustus cœno effoso purgatus est ;" Suidas, ad Anastasium.

[2] The plural form of the name (τῶν Σοφιῶν) may allude to the two divisions of the harbour. See Mordtmann, p. 55 : "La configuration actuelle permet encore de distinguer un port intérieur et un port extérieur, séparés par une étroite digne."

[3] Leo Gramm., p. 135 ; Anonymus, iii. p. 45.   [4] Anonymus, ii. p. 30.

[5] *Menæa*, January 27. This point was known also as ἐν τῷ μούλῳ τοῦ ἁγίου Θωμᾶ (Theophanes, p. 673).

Residence of Probus, which stood beside the harbour, was first searched for arms, and then set on fire by the Factions.[1] Here Phocas placed a division of the Green Faction, to prevent the landing of troops from the fleet of Heraclius ;[2] and hither the tyrant himself was dragged from his palace, thrown into a boat, and taken to Heraclius, in whose presence he was put to death.[3] Here Leontius, upon his appointment as Governor of the Theme of Hellas, embarked to proceed to his post ; but, at the instance of his friends, landed to head the revolution which overthrew Justinian II.[4]

Several of the great fires to which Constantinople was so liable reached this harbour. Among them was the terrible conflagration in the reign of Leo the Great, which devastated the principal quarters of the city, from the Golden Horn to the Sea of Marmora.[5] The equally destructive fire of 1203, which started with the burning, by the Crusaders, of the Saracen Mosque beside the Golden Horn, near Sirkedji Iskelessi, likewise swept across the city to this point.[6] Other fires of minor importance occurred here in 561, 863, 887, and 956.

To the list of the noted buildings and districts near the Harbour of Julian, already mentioned, may be added the Residence of Bardas, father of Nicephorus Phocas ;[8] the Residence of Isaac Sevastocrator, which was converted by Isaac Angelus into a khan or hostelry (Pandocheion), with accommodation for one hundred men and as many horses ;[9] the Churches of St. Thekla ;[10] St. Thomas, Amantiou ;[11] the Archangel Michael, of Adda (τοῦ

---

[1] *Paschal Chron.*, p. 622.   [2] *Ibid.*, p. 700.
[3] *Ibid.*, *ut supra*.   [4] Theophanes, p. 564.
[5] Evagrius, ii. c. xiii.   [6] Nicetas Chon., p. 733.
[7] Theophanes, p. 364 ; Nicet. Paphl. (Unger, *Quellen der Byzantinischen Kunstgeschicte*, p. 89) ; Cedrenus, vol. ii. 250 ; Theophanes Cont., p. 462.
[8] Leo Diaconus, v. pp. 83, 84.   [9] Nicetas Chon., p. 585.
[10] Procopius, *De Æd.*, i. c. iv.   [11] Theophanes, p. 385.

'Αδδᾶ) ;[1] St. Julian Perdix ; and St. John the Forerunner, near the Residence of Probus.[2]

Close to the Harbour of Sophia stood a tower known as the Bukanon, or the Trumpet (τὸ Βύκανον).[3] It was so named, according to the Anonymus,[4] both because trumpets were kept there, and because the tower itself, being hollow, resounded like a trumpet when struck by the waves. Whenever the Imperial fleet, the same writer adds, sailed from the city, it was customary for the ships to assemble before this tower and exchange musical salutes with it ; a legend, which is probably a fanciful travesty of the simple fact that the tower was a station from which the movements of vessels were directed by trumpet signals.

If the order in which the Anonymus mentions the tower, between the SS. Sergius and Bacchus and the Harbour of Sophia, indicates its actual position, the Bukanon stood on the eastern side of the harbour.

HARBOUR OF THE KONTOSCALION (τὸ Κοντοσκάλιον).

Another harbour on the Marmora side of the city was the Harbour of Kontoscalion.

The first reference to the Kontoscalion occurs in the Anonymus,[5] in the eleventh century, but the harbour acquired its greatest importance after 1261, when it was selected by Michael Palæologus to be the dockyard and principal station of the Imperial navy. Here the emperor thought his fleet could lie more secure from attack, and in a better position to assail an

---

[1] Anonymus, iii. p. 46. [2] Codinus, p. 105.

[3] Nicetas Chon., p. 733 ; Michael Psellus (Sathas, *Bibl. Græc. Med. Ævi.,* vol. v. p. 214).

[4] Lib. iii. p. 45. [5] Lib. ii. p. 34.

enemy, than in any other haven of the city.   For the force of
the current along this shore would soon oblige hostile ships
approaching the port to beat a hasty retreat, lest they should be
driven upon the coast, and consequently expose them, as they
withdrew, to be taken in the rear by the Imperial vessels that
would then sally forth in pursuit.   Great labour was therefore
expended upon the old harbour.   It was dredged and deepened
to render it more commodious ; and to make it more secure, it
was surrounded with immense blocks, closed with iron gates, and
protected by a mole.[1]   Subsequently, as his coat-of-arms on
the western tower of the harbour indicated, the Kontoscalion
was repaired by Andronicus II.[2]

A Russian pilgrim who visited the city about 1350 has drawn
a vivid picture of the harbour when crowded with triremes on
account of contrary weather :—

"De l'Hippodrome on passe devant Cantoscopie ; là est la
superbe et très grande porte en fer à grillage de la ville.   C'est
par cette porte que la mer pénétre dans la ville.   Si la mer est
agitée, jusqu'a trois cents galères y trouvent place ; ces galères
ont les unes deux cents et les autres trois cents rames.   Ces
vaisseaux sont employés au transport des troupes.   Si le vent est
contraire, ils ne peuvent avancer, et doivent attendre le beau
temps." [3]

The Kontoscalion is generally held to have stood in front
of Koum Kapoussi, where the traces of an old harbour, about
270 yards wide and some 217 yards long, are still discernible in
an extensive mole off the shore, and in the great bend described
by the city walls at that point to enclose an area which, at one
time, was evidently a basin of water.

There is scarcely any room for doubt that this view is correct.

---

[1] Pachymeres, vol. i. pp. 365, 366.   [2] See below, p. 295, note 5.
[3] *Itinéraires Russes en Orient*, pp. 120, 121.

The adherence of the name Kontoscalion to this quarter, apparently, ever since the Turkish Conquest,[1] is in favour of the opinion. So, likewise, is the fact that thus it becomes intelligible how Pachymeres[2] and Bondelmontius[3] associate the harbour with Vlanga, on the one hand, while Nicephorus Gregoras[4] associates it with the Hippodrome on the other. It is also a corroboration of this view to find on the walls of the harbour the coat-of-arms of Andronicus II., who is declared, by one authority, to have restored the Kontoscalion.[5] The only objection to this identification is found in the difference between the character of the actual enclosure around the harbour at Koum Kapoussi and the character of the enclosure which Michael Palæologus placed around the Kontoscalion. The former consists of the ordinary walls of the city; the latter consisted, according to Pachymeres,[6] of very large blocks of stone: ὥστε γυρῶσαι μὲν μεγίσταις πέτραις τὸν κύκλῳ τόπον. But in reply to this objection it may be said, either (though not without some violence to the words of the historian) that the great blocks of stone referred to were the boulders which form the mole of the harbour; or

---

[1] Leunclavius, *Pand. Hist. Turc.*, s. 200, is the first writer after the Conquest who refers to it: "Ipsa porta (*i.e.* Contoscalion) velut intra sinum quemdam abscedit versus unbem, et ab altera parte proximum sibi portum habet, pro triremibus, in mare se porrigentem et muris circumdatum." The silence of Gyllius regarding the Kontoscalion is strange, unless he has confounded it with Kadriga Limani.

[2] Vol. i. p. 365.

[3] *Liber Insularum Archipelagi*, p. 121. "Propinqua huic (Vlanga) Condoscali vel Arsena restat."

[4] Lib. xvii. p. 854. Cf. Cantacuzene, iv. pp. 72, 74.

[5] In a copy of the Anonymus, Codex Colbertinus, made in the thirteenth century, the copyist, under the heading Περὶ τὸν Σοφιανῶν λιμένα, adds the note that the harbour εἰς τὸ Κοντοσκάλον was constructed by Justin, and had been deepened and surrounded by a remarkable enclosure in his own day by Andronicus Comnenus Palæologus. See Banduri, *Imperium Orientale*, vol. ii. pp. 678–680. The copyist is at fault in identifying the Harbour of Sophia with the Kontoscalion, which was a historical question, but he may be trusted in regard to the restoration of the Kontoscalion, which was a contemporary event.

[6] Vol. i. p. 365.

that the work done under Michael Palæologus was temporary, and was superseded by the improvements executed in the reign of his son and successor Andronicus II. The objection must not be ignored.[1]

HARBOUR OF ELEUTHERIUS AND THEODOSIUS.

According to the *Notitia*,[2] Constantinople possessed a harbour called Portus Theodosianus, in the Twelfth Region of the city. As that Region comprised within its limits the shore of the Sea of Marmora at the southern base of the Seventh Hill, the Harbour of Theodosius must have been found at Vlanga Bostan, where the basin of a very ancient harbour, now filled in and converted into market-gardens, is distinctly visible.

There can be little doubt that this harbour was also the one which went by the name Harbour of Eleutherius[3] (ὁ λιμὴν τοῦ Ἐλευθερίου) : for the district of Eleutherius, and the palace of that name,[4] were situated in the valley leading from Vlanga Bostan to Ak Serai, and the Et Meidan. The harbour at Vlanga Bostan, moreover, corresponds to the description given of the Harbour of Eleutherius by the Anonymus,[5] who speaks of it as a very ancient harbour, situated to the west of that of Sophia, and abandoned long before his time.

If this be so, then the name Harbour of Eleutherius was its earlier designation, and the port itself was the oldest on the side of the city towards the Sea of Marmora, its construction being ascribed to a certain Eleutherius, who was present at the foundation of Constantinople.[6] Its antiquity is supported

---

[1] See below, pp. 312, 313.

[2] *Ad Reg. XII.*

[3] Anonymus, iii. p. 46.

[4] *Ibid.*, p. 47.

[5] Lib. iii. p. 46 ; cf. *ibid.*, p. 45.

[6] Anonymus, iii. p. 46.

by the aspect of its remains, for the walls enclosing it on the
north are the oldest portion of the fortifications of the city,
and possibly belong to the time of Constantine the Great.
Here the statue of Eleutherius was erected, in the appropriate
equipment of an excavator, with a spade in his hand and a
basket on his back.[1]

TOWER GUARDING THE HARBOUR OF ELEUTHERIUS AND THEODOSIUS.[2]

From the fact that the harbour was called Portus Theodosianus, it is evident that it was improved by Theodosius I.,
to whom the city owed so many public works.

[1] Anonymus, iii. p. 46.
[2] From *Broken Bits of Byzantium.* (By kind permission of Mrs. Walker.)

When precisely the harbour was filled in is a question not easily settled. The Anonymus declares, indeed, that this was done in the reign of Theodosius I., with the earth excavated in laying the foundations of the column of that emperor in the Forum of Taurus.[1] But, had that been the case, the *Notitia* would scarcely have mentioned an abandoned harbour among the objects for which the Twelfth Region of the city was remarkable. What is certain is that the harbour was destroyed some time before the eleventh century; probably because the earth brought by the stream of the Lycus, which flows into the harbour, and the sand cast up by the sea, proved too troublesome for the maintenance of a sufficient depth of water.

The harbour measured 786 yards from east to west and 218 yards from south to north. Along its southern side, as well as along a portion of its side towards the east, it was protected by a mole twelve feet thick, carefully constructed of masonry, and extending from the Gate of St. Æmilianus (Daoud Pasha Kapoussi) eastwards for about 436 yards, and then northwards for 327 yards more.[2] Upon the greater portion of the mole, walls were constructed for the military defence of the harbour.

The entrance was at the north-eastern end, between the head of the mole and the site of the Gate Yeni Kapou, the opening through which the Roumelian Railway now runs, and was guarded by a tower built at a short distance out in the sea.[3]

[1] Lib. iii. p. 46.

[2] Gyllius, *De Top. CP.*, iii. c. viii.; iv. c. viii. According to this authority the circuit of the harbour was over a mile; the mole being 600 paces long and 12 feet broad.

[3] Gyllius, *ut supra.* "Cujus ostium vergebat ad solis ortum æstivum, a quo moles extendebatur ad occasum æstivum, supra quam nunc muri adstricti existunt."

As stated already, the adjacent quarter was called the quarter of Eleutherius (τὰ τοῦ Ἐλευθερίου). It is mentioned under that name in 1203, as the farthest point reached by the great fire which then devastated the city through the folly of the Crusaders.[1] The present name of the quarter, Vlanga, appears

PORTION OF THE WALL AROUND THE HARBOUR OF ELEUTHERIUS AND THEODOSIUS.[2]

first in the eleventh century, as the designation of the residence of Andronicus Comnenus in this part of the city (οἶκος ὅς τοῦ Βλάγγα ἐπικέκληται),[3] and it is the name by which writers

"In faucibus portus, adhuc navium capacibus, extra murum urbis, etiamnum videtur turris undique mari circumdata, et saxa, reliquæ ruinarum."

Grelot, in his *Relation Nouvelle d'un Voyage de Constantinople*, pp. 79, 80, refers to the tower thus (to quote the quaint English translation of his work by J. Philips, London, 1683, p. 68): "Going by sea from the Seven Towers to the Seraglio, you meet with a square tower upon the left hand, that stands in the sea, distant from the city wall about twenty paces. The inhabitants of the country call it Belisarius Tower, affirming that it was in this tower where that great and famous commander, for the recompense of all those signal services which he had done the Emperor Justinian, in subduing his enemies, as well in Asia and Africa as in Europe, being despoyled of all his estate and honour, and reduced to the extremity of necessity, after he had endured putting out both his eyes, was at length shut up and forced for his subsistence to hang out a bag from the grate of his chamber, and cry to the passengers, 'Give poor Belisarius a farthing, whom envy and no crime has deprived of his eyes.' Near to the place where stands this tower was formerly the harbour where Theodosius, Arcadius, and their successors kept their galleys."

[1] Nicetas Chon., p. 733.
[2] From *Broken Bits of Byzantium*. (By kind permission of Mrs. Walker.)
[3] Nicetas Chon., p. 170.

subsequent to the Restoration of the Greek Empire refer to the district.[1]

In the vicinity stood the Palace of the Empress Irene,[2] the unnatural mother of Constantine VI., in which Basil II. entertained the Legates of Pope Hadrian II.[3]

The Church of St. Panteleemon, erected by Theodora the wife of Justinian the Great, on the site of her humble dwelling when a poor woman earning her bread by spinning wool,[4] and the district of Narses (τὰ Ναρσοῦ)[5] were in this neighbourhood ; so also was the district of Canicleius (τὰ Κανικλείου), where the emperor landed when proceeding to pay his annual visit to that church.[6] The modern Greek church of St. Theodore, to the south of Boudroum Djamissi (Myrelaion), marks, Dr. Mordtmann[7] suggests, the district of Claudius (τὰ Κλανδίου).

THE HARBOUR OF THE GOLDEN GATE.

Another harbour on this side of the city was the Harbour of the Golden Gate (ὁ λιμὴν τῆς Χρυσῆς),[8] in the bay to the west of the entrance of that name. This is implied in the statement of Ducas, that during the siege of 1453 the right wing of the Turkish army extended southwards from the Gate of St. Romanus to the Harbour of the Golden Gate.[9]

On the occasion of a triumph celebrating a victorious campaign in Asia Minor, the harbour presented an animated

---

[1] Pachymeres, vol. i. p. 365 ; *Actus Patriarchatus Constantinopolitani*, year 1400, p. 394, where a vivid description of the site of the old harbour is given : Κῆπος περὶ τὸν Βλάγκαν, ἔξω που καὶ σύνεγγυς τοῦ τείχους τῆς πόλεως.

[2] Anonymus, iii. p. 47 ; Theophanes, p. 723.

[3] Guillelmus Bibliothecarius.   [4] Anonymus, iii. p. 47.

[5] *Ibid.*, p. 48.   [6] Constant. Porphyr., *De Cer.*, p. 560.

[7] Page 59.   [8] Ducas, p. 283.   [9] *Ibid.*, *ut supra*.

scene; for the spoils and prisoners which were to figure in the procession, were ferried across from Chrysopolis, and landed at this point, to be marshalled on the plain before the Golden Gate.[1]

It was off this point that the Turkish fleet, in 1453, waited to intercept the five gallant ships, which brought provisions to the city from the island of Scio, and which forced their way to the Golden Horn, notwithstanding all the efforts of 305 vessels of the Sultan to capture them.[2]

THE HARBOUR OF KAISARIUS AND THE NEORION AT THE HEPTASCALON.

Before concluding this account of the city harbours on the Sea of Marmora, a point of some importance remains to be settled.

Byzantine historians speak of the Harbour of Kaisarius, and of the Neorion at the Heptascalon, on the southern shore of the city. Now, as traces of an additional harbour to those already mentioned, on this side of the city, may be disputed, the question presents itself: Have the Harbour of Kaisarius and the Neorion at the Heptascalon disappeared, or were they one or other of the harbours already identified?

The Harbour of Kaisarius (Λιμὴν τοῦ Καισαρείου) is mentioned for the first time in the Acts of the Fifth General Council of Constantinople,[3] held in 553, under Justinian the Great. Near it, we are there informed, stood the Residence of Germanus:

---

[1] Constant. Porphyr., *De Cer.*, pp. 438, 499, 504.

[2] Ducas, pp. 268, 269. The principal part of the engagement took place off the entrance to the Bosporus; for Leonard of Scio (p. 931) says that the Sultan viewed the contest from the hill of Pera; "ex Colle Perensi, fortunæ expectans eventum."

[3] Act II.

"In domo Germani, prope portum Cæsarii." The harbour is mentioned for the last time by Cedrenus,[1] in what is manifestly a quotation from Theophanes.[2] Beside it stood a district,[3] and a palace,[4] known respectively as the District and the Palace of Kaisarius (ἐν τοῖς Καισαρείου : κυράτωρ τῶν Καισαρείου) ; the latter being probably the residence of Germanus above mentioned.

After whom the harbour was named is uncertain. Du Cange[5] suggests three persons from whom the designation may have been derived : Kaisarius, Prefect of the City under Valentinian ; Kaisarius, Prætorian Prefect under Theodosius I.; and Kaisarius, a personage of some note in the reign of Leo I. If the choice lies between these persons, the preference must be given to the last ; for the *Notitia*, which describes the city in the reign of Theodosius II., makes no mention of this harbour. In all probability, therefore, the Harbour of Kaisarius was constructed towards the close of the fifth century.

That it stood on the Sea of Marmora is evident ; first, from its association with the Harbours of Julian and of Hormisdas, as one of the points at which the tyrant Phocas placed troops to prevent the landing of Heraclius on the southern side of the city ;[6] and secondly, from the fact that it was there that Constantine Pogonatus, in 673, placed his ships, armed with the newly invented tubes for squirting Greek fire, to await the Saracen fleet coming up against the city from the Ægean.[7]

Passing next to the Neorion at the Heptascalon, we find that

---

[1] Vol. i. p. 679.   [2] Page 364.   [3] *Ibid., ut supra.*

[4] *Ibid., ut supra.*   [5] Du Cange, *Constantinopolis Christiana,* ii. p. 169.

[6] John of Antioch, *Fragm. Hist. Græc.*, vol. v. p. 38. Ἐπιτρέπει φυλάττεσθαι ἐκ τῶν Πρασίνων τὸν λιμένα τοῦ Καισαρείου καὶ τὸν Σοφίας, τοὺς δὲ Βενετοὺς τὰ ἐπὶ Ὁρμίσδου. Cf. *Paschal Chron.*, p. 700.

[7] Theophanes, p. 541, who uses the expression, Ἐν τῷ Προκλιανισίῳ τῷ Καισαρίου λιμένι. What does Προκλιανισίῳ mean ?

the term "Heptascalon" is employed by Byzantine writers only in two connections : first, and then generally in the corrupt form Πασχάλῳ or Πασκάλῳ, it serves to mark the site of a church dedicated to St. Acacius ; the earliest writer who uses it for that purpose being Constantine Porphyrogenitus,[1] in his biography of Basil I., by whom the church was restored: secondly, Cantacuzene[2] employs the phrase to indicate the situation of the harbour now under discussion.

In 1351 Cantacuzene[3] found the harbour in a very unsatisfactory condition. Owing to the sand which had accumulated in it for many years, it could hardly float a ship laden with cargo ; and accordingly, in pursuance of his policy to develop the naval resources of the Empire, he caused the harbour to be dredged at much labour and expense, to the great convenience of public business. So extensive was the work of restoration that in one passage the harbour is styled the New Neorion.[4]

Du Cange,[5] misled by the fact that a Church of St. Acacius was found in the Tenth Region—one of the Regions on the northern side of the city—has classed the Neorion at the Heptascalon among the harbours on the Golden Horn. But to identify a site in Byzantine Constantinople by means of a church alone is a precarious proceeding, for churches of the same dedication were to be found in different quarters of the city. This, Du Cange[6] himself admits, was possible in the case before us ; since, besides the Church of St. Acacius at the Heptascalon, writers speak of a Church of St. Acacius ad Caream (ἐν τῇ Καρύᾳ), and the identity of the two sanctuaries cannot be assumed. But the existence of a second church dedicated to St. Acacius is not a mere possibility.

[1] Theophanes Cont., p. 324 ; *Synaxaria*, May 7, July 21.
[2] Lib. iv. pp. 165, 212, 220, 284.
[3] *Ibid.*, p. 165.
[4] *Ibid.*, p. 290.
[5] Constantinopolis Christiana, i. p. 56.
[6] *Ibid.*, iv. p. 118.

According to Antony of Novgorod,[1] there was a church of that dedication also on the southern side of the city, not far from the Church of SS. Sergius and Bacchus. The Neorion at the Heptascalon may, therefore, have been on the Sea of Marmora.

And that it was there, as a matter of fact, is evident from the statements made regarding that harbour by Cantacuzene and Nicephorus Gregoras, in their account of the naval engagement fought in the Bosporus in 1351, between a Genoese fleet on the one hand, and the Greeks, supported by Venetian and Spanish ships, on the other.

Upon coming up from the Ægean to take part in the war, the Venetians and the Spaniards, says the former historian,[2] anchored off the Prince's Island, to rest their crews after the hardships of the winter. There they remained three days. Then, quitting their moorings, the two allies made for the Neorion at the Heptascalon, or, as it is also styled, the Neorion of the Byzantines (τὸ Βυζαντίων νεώριον),[3] to join the Imperial fleet which was stationed there, all ready for action, and awaiting their arrival. Meanwhile, the Genoese admiral, with seventy ships, had taken up his position at Chalcedon (Kadikeui), to watch and oppose the movements of the allied squadrons. The wind was blowing a gale from the south, and though the Venetians and Spaniards had started for the Heptascalon very early in the morning, it was with the utmost difficulty, and late in the afternoon, that they succeeded in crossing from the island to the city. Even at the last moment they narrowly escaped destruction, by

---

[1] *Itinéraires Russes en Orient*, p. 106. Immediately after speaking of the Church of St. Acacius, he proceeds to say, "Au pied de la montagne, se trouve l'eglise des saints Serge et Bacchus." In the Latin version given in Riant's *Exuviæ CP.*, ii. pp. 228, 229, the passage is rendered, "Ex altera parte monticuli posita est Ecclesia SS. Sergii et Bacchi."

[2] Cantacuzene, iv. pp. 218–234.   [3] *Ibid.*, p. 220.

being dashed to pieces against the boulders scattered along the foot of the walls as a breakwater.

The Byzantine admiral, encouraged by the arrival of his allies, then sallied forth from the Heptascalon, and led the way towards the Genoese ships at Chalcedon. The latter, finding it impossible to make head against the wind, retired towards Galata, and skilfully entrenched themselves among the shoals and rocks off Beshiktash, preferring to be attacked in that advantageous situation.[1] The allies came on, and a desperate conflict, partly on the water, partly on the rocks, ensued, until night parted the combatants without a decisive victory on either side.

With this narrative of Cantacuzene in view, no one familiar with the vicinity of Constantinople can doubt for a moment that the Neorion at the Heptascalon was upon the Sea of Marmora. The single circumstance that the walls in the neighbourhood of the harbour were protected by boulders placed in the sea as a breakwater is alone sufficient to prove the fact; for only the walls bordering the Sea of Marmora were defended in that manner. Equally conclusive is the circumstance that the Venetian and Spanish ships found it difficult to make the harbour from the Prince's Island with a strong south wind on their left. Such a wind would drive them towards the Bosporus with a violence that would render it almost impossible for them to put into any port on the Marmora shore of the city. Nor is it less decisive to find, as the historian's account makes perfectly clear, that the

---

[1] But for the statement of Nicephorus Gregoras (xxvi. p. 87), one would suppose that the scene of this amphibious struggle was among the reefs and shoals off the shore between Kadikeui and Scutari. But Nicephorus says explicitly that the conflict took place off the Diplokionion (Beshiktash), ὅπη κίονες διπλοῖ σχῆμα τάφου τινὸς ἀνέχοντες ἵστανται. According to Gyllius, the sea off the shore between Beshiktash and Galata was in his day shallow and full of rocks. *De Bosporo Thracio*, ii. c. 8, "Alluitur mari vadoso, crebris petris supra aquam eminentibus inculcato." The Turkish names of two points on this shore, Beshiktash, Cabatash, refer to these rocks.

X

harbour was so situated ; that the approach to it, and possible shipwrecks at its entrance, could be observed by the Genoese admiral stationed off Chalcedon ; that an enemy at Chalcedon found it hard to advance towards the Heptascalon in a strong south wind ; and that vessels proceeding from the harbour to Galata could, on the way, touch at Chalcedon. These facts hold true only of a harbour on the Sea of Marmora.

This conclusion, based on the narrative of Cantacuzene, is corroborated by the indications which Nicephorus Gregoras[1] furnishes regarding the site of the Neorion. The events which transpired, according to the former historian, at the Neorion at the Heptascalon, or the Neorion of the Byzantines, took place, according to the latter, in the Harbour of the Byzantines, or, more definitely, "the Harbour of the Byzantines facing the east" (τοῦ τῶν Βυζαντίων λιμένος, τοῦ πρὸς ἔω βλέποντος).[2] That the expression "facing the east" denoted the shore of the city facing the Sea of Marmora and the Asiatic coast is manifest, from the use which Nicephorus Gregoras makes of that expression in other passages of his work. The Golden Gate, which stands near the Sea of Marmora, on what would generally be described as the southern shore of the city, stood, according to him, near the city's *eastern* shore.[3] Again, the gale from the south, which damaged the city fortifications along the Sea of Marmora in the year 1341, assailed, he says, the *eastern* walls of the capital.[4] This way of speaking, if not strictly accurate, is justified by the fact that extensive portions of the city beside the Sea of Marmora face east or south-east.

Nor is this all. The harbour in question, adds Nicephorus Gregoras,[5] stood where the walls of the city were protected by

---

[1] Lib. xxvi. pp. 85–92.   [2] *Ibid.*, pp. 86, 90 ; cf. Cantacuzene, iv. p. 220.
[3] Lib. xiv. p. 711 ; cf. Theophanes Cont., p. 614.
[4] Lib. ix. p. 460.   [5] Lib. xxvi. p. 87.

boulders; ships issuing from it, in a south wind, could readily make the Bosporus;[1] while ships proceeding from the Bosporus to the harbour passed Chalcedon on the left, and could be watched from Chalcedon, upon their arrival at their destination.[2]

Such facts, we repeat, hold good only of a harbour situated on the shore of the city beside the Sea of Marmora.

It being thus proved that the Harbour of Kaisarius and the Neorion at the Heptascalon were situated on the Marmora side of the city, we return to the question, whether they have disappeared, or were different names for one or other of the harbours already identified.

So far as room for harbours additional to those already identified is concerned, such room could be found only in the level ground at the foot of the Third Hill, extending from the Kontoscalion at Koum Kapoussi to the Harbour of Theodosius at Vlanga, points some 910 yards apart. An additional harbour elsewhere was impossible, owing to the character of the coast. Accordingly, if the Harbour of Kaisarius and the Neorion at the Heptascalon cannot be identified with one or other of the well-known harbours on the Sea of Marmora, they must have been situated between Koum Kapoussi and Vlanga.

So far as the Harbour of Kaisarius is concerned, it could not have been another name for the Harbour of the Bucoleon, or the Harbour of Julian and Sophia, or the Harbour of the Golden Gate. For, as John of Antioch[3] makes perfectly clear in his account of the defence of the city by Phocas against Heraclius, the Harbour of Kaisarius was situated in the same general district as the two former harbours, and to the west of them. Nor can the Harbour of Kaisarius be identified with the Harbour of Theodosius, inasmuch as the latter had

---

[1] Lib. xxvi. p. 87.   [2] *Ibid.*, p. 90.
[3] *Fragm. Hist. Græc.*, iv. p. 38.

been filled in and abandoned [1] before the reigns of Phocas and
Constantine IV., in the seventh century, when the Harbour of
Kaisarius was still one of the principal ports on the southern
coast of the city.[2]

The Harbour of Kaisarius must, therefore, have been either
the Kontoscalion, at Koum Kapoussi, or another harbour between
that gate and Vlanga.   To suppose that it was the Kontoscalion,
under an earlier name, is possible, since the name Kontoscalion,
we have seen,[3] appears for the first time in the eleventh century.
Still the circumstance that a fire which started beside the
Harbour of Kaisarius extended to the Forum of the Ox (ἕως τοῦ
Βοός),[4] situated at Ak Serai far up the valley that runs northwards from Yeni Kapou, suggests a situation nearer Vlanga.

Turning, next, to the Neorion at the Heptascalon, it could,
obviously, not be the Harbour of the Bucoleon, attached to the
Imperial Palace ; nor the Harbour of the Golden Gate, which
was beyond the city limits ; nor the Harbour of Theodosius,
which had been filled in long before the reign of Cantacuzene,
and which in 1400 and 1422, dates respectively not fifty and
seventy years after that emperor's reign, is described as a garden.[5]
The Neorion at the Heptascalon, therefore, must have been
either the Harbour of Julian and Sophia, or the Kontoscalion,
or an additional harbour between Koum Kapoussi and Vlanga.
One objection to the first supposition is that the Harbour of
Julian and Sophia was so notoriously known under its own
special name, that reference to it by another designation is extremely improbable.   Another objection is that the indications
respecting the site of St. Acacius at the Heptascalon, however

---

[1] Anonymus, iii. p. 46.
[2] *Fragm. Hist. Græc.*, iv. p. 38 ; Theophanes, p. 541.
[3] See above, p. 293.   [4] Theophanes, p. 364.
[5] *Actus Patriarchatus Constantinopolitani*, year 1400, p. 394 ; Bondelmontius,
" In quibus mœnibus est campus ab extra, et olim portus Vlanga." See above,
p. 300, ref. 1.

vague their character, furnish no ground for believing that the church stood in the vicinity of the Harbour of Julian and Sophia, but support, rather, the opinion that it stood in the neighbourhood of Boudroum Djamissi, in the quarter of Laleli Hamam, situated to the north-west of Koum Kapoussi.[1]

The supposition that the Neorion at the Heptascalon was the same as the Kontoscalion is open to objections equally, if not more, serious.   The identity of the two harbours is inconsistent with the fact that the two names occur in the writings of the same author, Cantacuzene,[2] in the same section of his work, in passages not widely separated and treating of kindred matters, without the slightest hint that under the different names he refers to the same thing.   The natural impression made by the use of the two names in such a way is that they denote different things.   Then, there is an opposition between the respective meanings of the two names, which makes their application to the same object incompatible; a harbour distinguished by a short pier cannot also be a harbour distinguished by seven piers.   In the next place, the different accounts which Cantacuzene gives of the condition of the two harbours in his reign imply that he is not speaking of the same port.   He refers

[1] The indications for the site of the Church of St. Acacius are: (1) It was ἐν Ἑπτασκάλῳ (Anonymus, ii. p. 33); (2) near the Church of St. Metrophanes (*Synaxaria*, June 4; *Itinéraires Russes en Orient*, p. 106); (3) near the Residence of Moselè (Μωσηλὲ), and the monument named the Christocamaron (Χριστοκάμαρον), after a gilt Icon of Christ upon it (Anonymus, ii. p. 38).   (4) The Christocamaron, it is supposed, was the same as the Chrysocamaron (Χρυσοκάμαρον: Anonymus, iii. p. 48).   Supporters of that identity are Banduri (*Imp. Orient.*, ii. p. 688) and Dr. Mordtmann (p. 59).   (5) The Chrysocamaron stood to the rear of the Myrelaion (Anonymus, iii. p. 48).   (6) The Myrelaion was the church, now the Mosque Boudroum Djamissi (Gyllius, *De Top. CP.*, iii. c. 8; Patriarch Constantius, *Ancient and Modern Consple.*, p. 75).   (7) Therefore, the Church of St. Acacius was situated to the rear, or to the east of Boudroum Djamissi.   There are two weak points in this chain of arguments; Codinus (pp. 107, 108) distinguishes the two monuments which are identified above, and speaks of two places in Constantinople that were named Myrelaion.

[2] He refers to the Kontoscalion in the Fourth Book of his work, pp. 72, 74; and to the Neorion at the Heptascalon in the same Book, pp. 165, 212, 220, 284.

to the Kontoscalion,[1] in 1348, without a note of disparagement,
as a harbour in which he constructed several large triremes for
the increase of his fleet ; while he describes the Neorion at the
Heptascalon,[2] only three years later, as a harbour which had
long been neglected, which was full of silt, and which he restored
at great expense, for the public advantage, on a scale which
entitled it to be styled the New Neorion.[3]

And just as all that Cantacuzene states regarding the two
harbours implies that they were different, so does the language
of Nicephorus Gregoras. When the latter writer alludes to the
Kontoscalion, he describes it as the harbour near the Hippodrome ;[4] when he alludes to the Neorion at the Heptascalon, he
describes it as the harbour facing the east.[5]   Different marks are
generally employed to distinguish different objects.[6]   This being
so, the unavoidable conclusion is that the Neorion at the Heptascalon was a harbour situated between Koum Kapoussi and Yeni
Kapou, the only possible situation for an additional harbour.

We should feel obliged to insist upon this conclusion, even
in the absence of any remains of a harbour in the situation
indicated. Our task, however, is not so arduous ; for manifest
traces of such a harbour have been identified. In the first
place, traces of a harbour in the district above mentioned came

---

[1] Codinus, p. 72.   [2] Cantacuzene, iv. p. 165.

[3] *Ibid.*, p. 290.   Taken in conjunction with the other arguments on the subject,
the epithet New, bestowed upon the Neorion at the Heptascalon, implied not only
that the harbour was no longer its old self, but, also, that it was to be distinguished
from another and earlier Neorion. But the only other conspicuous Neorion during
the reign of Cantacuzene was the Kontoscalion.

[4] Lib. xvii. p. 854: Ἐς τὸ περὶ τὸν τοῦ Βυζαντίου ἱππόδρομον νεώριον.
Cf. Cantacuzene, iv. p. 72.

[5] Lib. xxvi. p. 90.

[6] Unger (*Quellen der Byzantinischen Kunstgeschichte*, p. 264), without discussing
the question at length, holds, as the result of his study of the texts, that the Kontoscalion cannot be identified with either the Harbour of Sophia or the Heptascalon.
Scarlatus Byzantius (Ἡ Κωνσταντινούπολις, vol. i. pp. 268, 277) also maintains
that the three names designated different harbours.

to view in 1819, and were then officially noted by so competent an authority as the Patriarch Constantius.[1] In that year a great fire burned down a large part of the Turkish quarter near Yeni Kapou—Tulbenkdji Djamissi—and brought to light a portion of an ancient circular enclosure around that quarter. The discovery excited considerable attention, and the patriarch was specially instructed by the Turkish Government of the day to examine the wall and report the result of his investigations Accompanied by two distinguished members of the Greek community, the prelate proceeded to the scene of the conflagration, and found a wall built of huge blocks of stone, about seven feet long, four and a half feet wide, and over a foot thick. The stones were carefully hewn and placed in three tiers ; the blocks in the two lower tiers being the ordinary limestone found on the banks of the Bosporus, while the blocks in the highest row were of marble from the Island of Marmora. The territory enclosed by the wall presented the appearance of a great hollow which had been filled in, since the Turkish Conquest, and raised to afford ground for building. All that the patriarch saw convinced him that he stood upon the site of one of the ancient harbours of the city. The wall has disappeared, as the excellent building material it provided rendered natural. But other remains of a harbour at this point, the complement of those discovered by the patriarch, have been recognized, and can, to some extent, be still distinguished.

Off the shore in front of the territory enclosed by the wall described above is a mole formed with boulders (marked " Molotrümmer" on Stolpe's map of the city), similar to the mole before the old harbour at Koum Kapoussi. At a point about half-way between Koum Kapoussi and Yeni Kapou, there is a wide gap in this mole, dividing it in two unequal

---

[1] Συγγραφαὶ Ἐλάσσονες, pp. 443, 444. He was not patriarch at the time.

parts, and forming a passage through it.   The shore[1] opposite
the gap was, until the construction of a quay in 1870 for the
Roumelian railroad, a sandy beach extending back to the foot
of the city walls.   The portion of the walls at the rear of the
beach was, however, not Byzantine ; but a piece of Turkish
work[2] inserted between the Byzantine walls on either hand to
close an opening which gave admittance to the area occupied by
the quarter of Tulbenkdji Djamissi.

Here, accordingly, we have traces of all that constitutes a
harbour: its mole, its entrance, its basin and enclosure, indicating where the Neorion at the Heptascalon, which the language of Cantacuzene and Nicephorus Gregoras obliges us to
distinguish from the Kontoscalion, was probably situated.   At
this point, it seems reasonable to think, stood also the Harbour
of Kaisarius, if we may judge from the circumstance that a fire
which originated at that harbour extended up the valley from
Vlanga to Ak Serai.[3]

In the opinion of the Patriarch Constantius,[4] indeed, the
harbour discovered in 1819 was the Kontoscalion.   The statement of Pachymeres[5] and Bondelmontius,[6] that the Kontoscalion was near Vlanga, cannot, perhaps, be held to lend much
countenance to this supposition, for in view of the short distance
between Vlanga and Koum Kapoussi, the Kontoscalion might
be thus described, although situated in front of the latter.   But
what presents a most serious consideration in favour of the
patriarch's opinion is the fact that the wall which he examined
answered exactly to the description of the wall with which
Michael Palæologus enclosed the Kontoscalion.

---

[1] For the following information I am indebted to the Rev. H. O. Dwight, LL.D.,
who knew the quarter of Yeni Kapou in 1854, and was for many years a resident there.
[2] It is still standing.   [3] See above, p. 308.   [4] *Ut supra.*
[5] Pachymeres, vol. i. p. 365, Τὸ πρὸς τὸν Βλάγκα Κοντοσκέλιον.
[6] *Librum Insularum Archipelago,* p. 121.

That emperor, according to Pachymeres,[1] surrounded the Kontoscalion with very large stones; and closed the entrance in the stones with iron gates ("Ωστε γυρῶσαι μὲν μεγίσταις πέτραις τὸν κύκλῳ τόπον, . . . πύλας δ᾽ ἐπιθεῖναι ἀραρυίας ἐκ σιδήρου τῇ ἐν ταῖς πέτραις εἰσίθμῃ ἔξωθεν).

No language could describe better the enclosure of large blocks discovered in 1819; while the expression "the entrance in the stones" applies admirably to the gap in the mole which protected the harbour. Nothing of the kind is found at the harbour before Koum Kapoussi, which lay within a mole and a great curve of the ordinary city walls. This, it must be admitted, is an exceedingly strong argument in support of the patriarch's contention. On the other hand, we have seen how strong also are the arguments in favour of the view that the Kontoscalion stood at Koum Kapoussi.[2] Perhaps the solution of the difficulty is found in the supposition that while the name Kontoscalion strictly belonged to the harbour at Koum Kapoussi, it was sometimes applied also to other harbours in the vicinity, because the name of the most important member of the group.

NOTE ON THE LOCALITY WHERE THE ANCIENT HARBOUR WALL, DISCOVERED IN 1819, WAS FOUND.

The Patriarch Constantius, our sole informant on the subject, refers to this discovery twice; first, in his work on *Ancient and Modern Constantinople* (Κωνσταντινιὰς Παλαιὰ τε καὶ Νεωτέρα), published in 1844; secondly, in a letter, dated April 12, 1852, which is found in the collection of his minor works (Συγγραφαὶ αἱ Ἐλάσσωνες), and which was addressed to Mr. Scarlatus Byzantius, upon the publication of that gentleman's work on the history and antiquities of the city. In that letter the patriarch corrects several mistakes made in his own work on the same subject, and gives additional information on other points.

The earlier reference to the discovery is brief, and when viewed in the light of the later statements, altogether misleading. It occurs in the paragraph upon Koum Kapoussi, the ancient Gate of Kontoscalion (English translation, p. 21; Greek original, p. 30). After expressing the opinion that the Neorion of the Kontoscalion

---

[1] Vol. i. p. 365. [2] See above, p. 295.

stood at that gate, and quoting the description which Pachymeres gives of the wall around the harbour, the reverend author adds : "A portion of this circular enclosure appeared in 1819, consisting of three layers of very large stones placed one upon the other " (Ἕν μέρος δὲ τούτου τοῦ κυκλικοῦ περιφράγματος τοῦ λιμένος ἀνεφάνη τῷ 1819 ἔτει, συνιστάμενον ἐκ τριῶν θέσεων παμμεγίστων ἀλλεπαλλήλων πετρῶν).

There can be but one meaning to this language, namely, that the enclosure referred to stood beside the harbour at Koum Kapoussi. But the difficulty with this language has always been how to make it coincide with the facts in the case. For, as already intimated, the enclosure around the harbour at Koum Kapoussi is almost intact, and consists of the ordinary walls of the city at their usual elevation. There has never been room at that point for another enclosure such as the patriarch describes. But his later, and, fortunately, fuller statements (Συγγραφαὶ αἱ Ἐλάσσωνες, pp. 443, 444) make the matter clear, although, at the same time, they convict the patriarch of inaccuracy in his first statement, so far as the locality of the discovery is concerned. According to the patriarch's letter, the locality in question was not at Koum Kapoussi, but between that gate and the gate Yeni Kapou of Vlanga, and nearer to the latter entrance than to the former. This fact is confirmed by the additional indication that the discovery was made in a Turkish quarter; for the only Turkish quarter near the shore between Kadriga Limani, on the east of Koum Kapoussi, and Daoud Pasha Kapoussi, on the west of Vlanga, is the quarter of Tulbenkdji Djamissi near Yeni Kapou. But to render all doubt as to the situation of the locality impossible, the route taken to reach it is minutely described; the patriarch and his friends passed first through Kadriga Limani and the parishes of St. Kyriakè and St. Elpis; then they went beyond Koum Kapoussi itself, and, keeping within the line of the walls, proceeded to the neighbourhood of the gate of Yeni Kapou at Vlanga, where the wall had come to light. These particulars are, indeed, at variance with the statement found in *Ancient and Modern Constantinople,* but as they constitute the patriarch's clearest and fullest declarations on the point at issue, and are made in a letter correcting mistakes in his former work, they have been adopted as his most authoritative statements. The subject being important and the patriarch's letter but little known, the passages bearing most directly upon the question are here appended : Περὶ τοῦ κατὰ τὴν Προποντίδα λιμένος, περὶ οὖ σημειοῦμεν ἐν τῷ ἡμετέρῳ Συγγράμματι, τοῦ παρὰ Μιχαὴλ τοῦ Παλαιολόγου κατασκευασθέντος, αὐτὸς κεῖται ἐν τῷ μέσῳ τῆς Πύλης Κοντοσκαλίου (Κούμ-καπουσοῦ) καὶ τῆς τοῦ Γενὶ-καπουσοῦ τῆς Βλάγκας, καὶ ὑπῆρχε, διὰ τὸ ἀσφαλέστερον, ἔνδον τῶν παραλίων τειχῶν κατεσκευασμένος. . . . Ἀλλ' ὅλου τοῦ μέρους, ἐν ᾧ ὁ τοῦ Παλαιολόγου ἔκειτο, κατοικουμένου ὑπὸ Ὀθωμανῶν, κατὰ τὸ 1819 ἔτος πυρπολυθέντος, ἀνεφάνη τὸ τοῦ λιμένος τούτου κυκλικὸν περίφραγμα, κατὰ τὸν Παχυμέρην, γεγυρωμένον ἐκ τριῶν ἀλλεπαλλήλως τεθειμένων μεγάλων πετρῶν, εἰργασμένων ὡς πλακῶν, ἐχουσῶν μῆκος μὲν τριῶν πήχεων, εὖρος δὲ δύο, καὶ βάθος ἡμίσειαν, τῶν μὲν δύο κάτωθεν ἀλλεπαλλήλων πλακῶν ἐκ πετρῶν τοῦ Βοσπόρου, λευκομελανοχρόων, τῆς δ' ἐπ' αὐτῶν τρίτης σειρᾶς καὶ ἀνωτέρας, ἐκ μαρμάρων ἰσομέτρων Προκονησίων. He then refers to the order received from the Government to investigate the discovery, and mentions the persons who accompanied him on that errand ; after which he continues thus: Διήλθομεν δὲ τὸ Κάτεργα-λιμὰν, τὰς ἐνορίας Ἁγίας Κυριακῆς καὶ Ἐλπίδος, παρήλθομεν τὸ Κοὺμ-καπουσοῦ, καὶ προεχωρήσαμεν ἔχοντες ἀριστερόθεν τὰ παράλια τείχη ἔνδοθεν, ἐγγὺς τῆς Πύλης Γενὶ-καπουσοῦ τῆς Βλάγκας, ὅπου εἴδομεν τὸ ἐκ πετρῶν καὶ μαρμάρων κυκλοτερὲς περίφραγμα, ἐκτεινόμενον ὑποκάτω ἑνὸς τεφρωθέντος Τζαμίου, ἑνὸς μεγάλου Ὀθωμανικοῦ οἴκου καὶ περαιτέρω. Καὶ παραυτίκα ἐγνώκαμεν ὅτι τοῦτο αὐτὸ ἐστι, κατὰ τὸν Παχυμέρην, τὸ πρὸς τὴν Βλάγκαν νεῦον τοῦ Κοντοσκαλίου Νεώριον. Ὅλος ὁ τόπος ὁ περιέχων ποτὲ τὸ Νεώριον αὐτὸ, μετὰ τὴν ἅλωσιν ἐπληρώθη, ἐχερσώθη καὶ ὑψώθη τὸ ἔδαφος, κατοικούμενος ὑπὸ Ὀθωμανῶν· αἱ δὲ ἀραρυῖαι ἐκ σιδήρου πύλαι, δι' ὧν εἰσέπλεεν ὁ στόλος ἐλλιμενιζόμενος, ἀπῳκοδομήθησαν.

CHAPTER XIX.

THE HEBDOMON.

THE Hebdomon (τὸ ῞Εβδομον, " Septimum ") was a suburb of
Constantinople, situated on the Egnatian Road, at the distance of
seven miles from the centre of the city.   It obtained its name, as
so many villages and towns on the great Roman highways did,[1]
from the number of the milestone beside which it stood (ἐν τῷ
῞Εβδόμῳ Μιλίῳ), and holds a noteworthy place in history on
account of its military associations and its connection with the
Court of Constantinople.   Considerable interest attaches to it
also on account of the discussions which the question of its site
has occasioned.

There can be no doubt that the Hebdomon is represented
by the modern village of Makrikeui, situated on the shore of the
Sea of Marmora, three miles to the west of the Golden Gate.
But the opinion which has been generally accepted, and has had
the greatest names in its favour, is that the suburb stood at the
northern extremity of the Theodosian Walls, where the Palace
of the Porphyrogenitus and the quarter of Blachernæ were
found.

Now, of all the mistakes committed by students of the
topography of Byzantine Constantinople, none is so preposterous

[1] A station, eleven miles from Turin, on the line of railway between that city and
Milan, *via* Vercelli, retains in its name, Settimo, the reminiscence of its ancient
designation, ad Septimum.

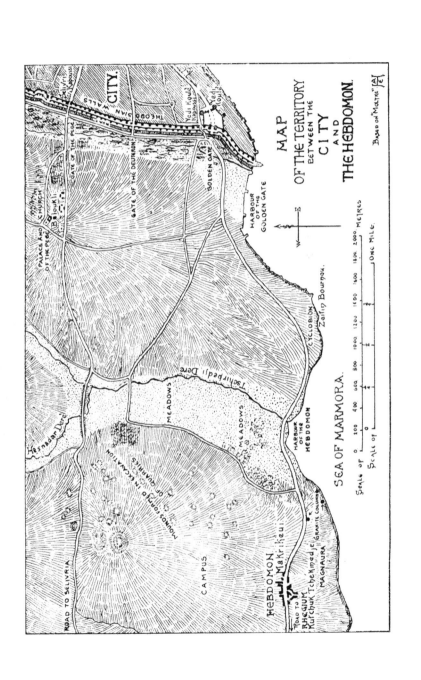

MAP
OF THE TERRITORY
BETWEEN THE
CITY
AND
THE HEBDOMON.

Based on Maltré "AY"

Scale of 0 200 400 600 800 1000 1200 1400 1600 1800 2000 METRES
Scale of 0 ONE MILE.

or inexcusable as this identification. It is a mistake made when to err seems impossible, for it is in direct opposition to the plainest and most convincing evidence that the famous suburb was situated elsewhere. A blind man, Valesius exclaims in his indignation at such a baseless opinion, might see the truth in the matter.

The blunder started with Gyllius, and was afterwards supported with all the immense learning of Du Cange. It was soon denounced by Valesius,[1] and shown to be utterly inconsistent with the most obvious facts in the case ; but the reputation of the great authorities upon its side gave it a vitality which made it the commonly received opinion until the most recent times. Unger, however, contested the error, once more, in his important work entitled *Quellen der Byzantinischen Kunstgeschichte*,[2] published in 1878, and maintained the correct view, but without discussing the question at length. Schlumberger, also, in his monograph on the Emperor Nicephorus Phocas, has seen the facts in their true light.[3]

Under these circumstances one is strongly tempted to let the fallacies with which Gyllius and Du Cange maintained their views pass into oblivion, and to be satisfied with proving the truth on the subject. But the great authority and eminent services of these students of the topography of the city, and the tenacity with which the error they countenanced has held the field demand some account of the arguments which have been employed in support of an untenable position.

Gyllius[4] entered upon the discussion of the subject with the

---

[1] In his annotations to Ammianus Marcellinus. The arguments of Valesius were unknown to me when I adopted the correct view on the subject. It was startling to find, afterwards, that the truth had been established so long ago by substantially the same evidence as convinced my own mind, and that truth so well established had been ignored. My reasons for dissenting from the views of Gyllius and Du Cange were first published in the *Levant Herald*, April 12, 1891.

[2] Pages 113, 114.　　　[3] *Un Empereur Byzantin au Dixième Siècle*, p. 299.

[4] See *De Top. CP.*, iv. c. i. iv.

fixed idea that no locality entitled to be regarded as a suburb could be seven miles distant from the city to which it belonged. With this conviction rooted in his mind, he found himself called to interpret the passage in which Sozomon relates how Theodosius the Great, upon leaving Constantinople for Italy to suppress the rebel Eugenius, stopped at the seventh mile from the city to invoke the Divine blessing upon the expedition, in the Church of St. John the Baptist which the emperor had erected at that point of the road.[1] Gyllius knew his Greek too well not to recognize the obvious meaning of this statement. He acknowledges that the passage may be understood to intimate that the church above mentioned stood at the seventh milestone from Constantinople. But while allowing that this is a possible meaning of the historian's words, he contends that it cannot be his actual meaning, because the Hebdomon, being a suburb, could not be so distant from the city as seven miles. Hence Gyllius separates the numeral adjective "seventh" from the noun "mile," and treating the former as a proper name, construes the passage to signify that the Church of St. John the Baptist, in the suburb of the Hebdomon, was one mile from the capital. The proposed construction is so original that it must be given in its author's own words: "Theodosius egressus unum milliare extra Constantinopolim, in æde Divi Joannis Baptistæ, quam ipse construxerat in Hebdomo suburbio, a Deo precatus est."

Under the guidance of this strange interpretation of Sozomon's statement, the indefatigable explorer of the ancient sites of Constantinople set himself to discover the precise locality which the Hebdomon had occupied. As the suburb

---

[1] Sozomon, vii. c. xxiv., Λέγεται δὲ τότε τῆς Κωνσταντινουπόλεως ἐκδημῶν, πρὸς τῷ Ἑβδόμῳ μιλίῳ γενόμενος, προσεύξασθαι τῷ θεῷ ἐν τῇ ἐνθάδε ἐκκλησίᾳ, ἥν ἐπὶ τιμῇ Ἰωάννου τοῦ Βαπτιστοῦ ἐδείματο·

was in existence before the erection of the Theodosian Walls, the specified distance of one mile had to be measured from the original limits of the city, viz. from the Wall of Constantine. This, Gyllius thought, would put the suburb somewhere in the neighbourhood of the Walls of Theodosius. Searching next for more definite indications, he found the ruins of a splendid church dedicated to St. John the Baptist on the Sixth Hill, at Bogdan Serai near Kesmè Kaya. But a church of St. John the Baptist, as already intimated, adorned the Hebdomon, and so Gyllius leaped to the conclusion that the Hebdomon was the district on the Sixth Hill : "Suburbium Hebdomon appellatum in sexto colle fuisse, qui nunc est intra urbem, ostendit ædes Divi Joannis Baptistæ, quam etiam nunc Græci vulgo vocant Prodromi."

Having adopted this conclusion, it only remained for Gyllius to explain how a suburb only one mile from the city could have been styled the Hebdomon. His explanation is that the extra-mural territory along the Wall of Constantine had been occupied, before its enclosure within the Theodosian lines, by a series of suburbs distinguished from one another by numerals, and that the Hebdomon was so named because it was the seventh suburb in the series. This explanation he supports by pointing to the undoubted fact that one portion of that territory is frequently named the Deuteron [1] by Byzantine writers. And he might have added that other portions of the territory were, respectively, styled the Triton [2] and the Pempton.[3]

Du Cange [4] was unable to accept Gyllius's interpretation of the phrase, Ἑβδόμῳ Μιλίῳ. He insists upon its correct and only signification ; and admits that the suburb derived its name from

---

[1] See above, p. 74.   [2] See above, pp. 77, 78.   [3] See above, pp. 81, 82.
[4] *Constantinopolis Christiana*, ii. pp. 172–174; and the "Excursus on the Hebdomon," appended to the edition of his great work published at Venice.

its situation near the seventh milestone from the capital. Nevertheless he is, impossible though it may seem, in substantial agreement with Gyllius.

The fundamental thesis of Du Cange on the subject is that the term "Hebdomon" had two meanings. Strictly speaking, he grants, it meant the seventh mile; but it was also employed, he maintains, as the designation of the whole district extending between the Wall of Constantine and the seventh milestone. Hence, after the erection of the Theodosian Walls, a considerable portion of the suburb was included within the new city limits, so that the Hebdomon could very well be where Gyllius supposed it stood.

Only, while supporting Gyllius on this point, Du Cange considers that the identification of the Church of St. John at Kesmè Kaya with the Church of St. John the Baptist at the Hebdomon is a mistake. For the latter is described by Constantine Porphyrogenitus[1] as without the city walls in the tenth century, and therefore never stood, like the Church of St. John at Kesmè Kaya, within the Theodosian lines. At the same time, Du Cange does not concede that the church of that dedication in the Hebdomon was near the seventh milestone. In harmony with his view regarding the extent of the area to which the term "Hebdomon" was applied, he holds that the church, though outside the Walls of Theodosius, was close to them. Du Cange differs from Gyllius also in laying great stress upon Tekfour Serai as an indication of the site of the Hebdomon, identifying that palace with the Palace of the Magnaura, one of the noted buildings of the suburb.[2]

---

[1] Theophanes Cont., p. 340.

[2] Gyllius refers to Tekfour Serai under the name of the Palace of Constantine, and recognizes the existence of a Palace of the Magnaura at the Hebdomon; but he neither identifies the two palaces, nor points to Tekfour Serai as an indication of the site of the Hebdomon.

What induced Du Cange to maintain the application of
the term " Hebdomon " to the whole territory extending from
the seventh mile eastwards to the walls of the city was the
opinion, that only thus could certain statements regarding the
suburb become intelligible or credible.   The statement, for
instance, that the plain at the Hebdomon was "adjacent"
($\dot{a}\nu a\kappa\epsilon i\mu\epsilon\nu o\nu$)[1] to the city implies, he thinks, that the plain of
the Hebdomon was contiguous to the city; "quæ (vox) campus
urbi adjacuisse situ prodit."   So does, he contends, the statement
that the Avars, upon approaching to lay siege to the city,
encamped "at what of the city is named the Hebdomon."[2]
For how could an enemy besiege a city without coming close up
to its walls?   The consideration, however, which above everything else led Du Cange to attach a wider meaning to the term
"Hebdomon" than the seventh mile, was the difficulty of believing
that the great religious processions which, on the occasion of a
severe earthquake, went on foot from the city to the Campus
of the Hebdomon to implore Divine Mercy, walked the whole
distance of seven miles on that pious errand.[3]

Such a performance seemed to Du Cange, especially when the
emperor and the patriarch took part in the procession, incredible;
and since he could not imagine the people going to the Hebdomon, in the strict sense of the word, he made the Hebdomon
come to the people, by extending the signification of the term.

But Du Cange forgets that the processions to which he refers
were recognized to be extraordinary performances, even in the
age in which they were undertaken; that they were acts of

---

[1] Theophylactus Simocat., p. 339.   What the historian says is, Τὸ πεδίον τὸ
ἀνακείμενον ἐν τῷ λεγομένῳ Ἑβδόμῳ, ὃν Κάμπον Ῥωμαῖοι κατονομάζουσι.

[2] Nicephorus, *Patriarcha CP.*, pp. 15, 16, Καὶ πρὸς τὸ τῆς πόλεως ὅ
Ἕβδομον καλοῦσι καταλαβόντες ἱδρύσαντο.   What the enemy did was to halt
at the Hebdomon before advancing against the city.

[3] See below, p. 329.

Y

profoundest humiliation in view of a most awful danger; that
they were deeds of penance, whereby men hoped to move the
Almighty to spare His people.   The distance of seven miles
is not too great for men to walk in order to escape a terrible
death.

At the same time, it is quite possible that the Campus of the
Hebdomon extended some distance towards the city.   The
plain was not a mathematical point, and a portion of it may
have been nearer the city than the seventh milestone itself was.
That must be decided by the nature of the ground, not by
subjective considerations.   But to make the plain reach to the
city walls for the reason assigned is preposterous.

This brief account of the arguments with which Gyllius
and Du Cange upheld their views must suffice.   For all the
evidence at our command goes to prove that the suburb
occupied the site of the modern village of Makrikeui.

In support of this proposition there are, first, express
statements to the effect that the Hebdomon, taken as a whole,
was seven miles distant from the city.   That is how Theophylactus Simocatta,[1] for instance, indicates the situation of the
suburb : "It was a place seven miles from the city"—ἐν τῷ
λεγομένῳ Ἑβδόμῳ (τόπος δὲ οὗτος τοῦ ἄστεος ἀπὸ σημείων ἑπτὰ).
That is how Idatius, also, describes the suburb's position,
when speaking of the inauguration of Valens and of Arcadius
there : "Levatus est Constantinopoli in Milliario VII."[2]   And
it is in the same terms that Marcellinus Comes refers to the
suburb, when he records the fact that Honorius was created
Cæsar in it : "Id est, septimo ab urbe regia milliario."   To

---

[1] Page 333; cf. *Ibid.*, p. 236, where the distance of the Hebdomon from the city
is said to be one parasang and a half.   Zosimus (p. 271) gives the distance as forty
stadia.

[2] Cf. *Paschal Chron.*, pp. 556, 562.

understand such expressions as denoting the whole territory
between the walls of the city and the seventh milestone is out
of the question. As employed by these writers, the term
"Hebdomon" or "Septimum" means a definite place, reached
only when a person stood seven miles from the point whence
distances from Constantinople were measured.

In the second place, not only is the Hebdomon, as a whole,
described as being seven miles from the city, but the particular
objects found there are similarly identified. The Church of
St. John the Baptist in that suburb, Sozomon,[1] Socrates,[2] and
John of Antioch[3] state in express words, was seven miles from
the city. The Church of St. John the Evangelist, which
stood in the suburb, is declared by Socrates[4] to have been
at the same distance. Thus, also, the Campus of the Hebdomon is described by Cedrenus as "the plain in front of
the city, seven miles distant."[5] The Imperial Tribune in that
Campus was, according to Idatius and Marcellinus Comes,
at the seventh mile: "In milliario septimo, in Tribunali;"
"Septimo ab urbe regia milliario." So, likewise, the palace
which Justinian the Great built at the Hebdomon[6] is described,
in the subscription to several of his laws, as at the seventh
mile: "Recitata septimo milliario hujus inclytæ civitatis, in
Novo Consistorio Palatii Justiniani."[7] In all these passages the
Hebdomon is defined with a precision that renders any vague
and loose application of the term impossible, if language has
any meaning. So much for the distance of the Hebdomon from
the city.

---

[1] Lib. vii. c. xxiv. See quotation of the passage on p. 318, ref. 1.
[2] Lib. vi. c. vi., Ἀπέχει καὶ τοῦτο ἑπτὰ σημείοις τῆς πόλεως.
[3] *Fragm. Hist. Græc.*, iv. p. 611, Ὃς ζ' σημείοις τῆς πόλεως ἀφειστήκει.
[4] Lib. vi. c. xii., Ἀπέχει καὶ τοῦτο ἑπτὰ σημείοις τῆς πόλεως.
[5] Vol. i. p. 641, Εἰς τὸ πρὸ τῆς πόλεως πεδίον ἑπτὰ σημείοις ἀπέχον.
[6] Procopius, *De Æd.*, i. c. xi.   [7] Lib. xxii., *De Sacros Eccl.*

That the Hebdomon was situated on the shore of the Sea of Marmora is placed beyond dispute by the fact that ships approaching Constantinople from the south reached the Hebdomon before arriving at the city.   When, for example, Epiphanius came by ship from Cyprus to Constantinople, in 402, to attend a synod called to condemn the heresies of Origen, he landed at the Hebdomon, and celebrated divine service there in the Church of St. John the Baptist, before entering the capital.[1] This order in the stages of the bishop's journey implies that the suburb stood on the shore of the Sea of Marmora.   Again, when the fleet of Heraclius came up from Carthage to overthrow Phocas, in 610, the latter proceeded to the Hebdomon to view the ships of the hostile expedition as they stood off the suburb, and there he remained until they advanced towards the city, when he mounted horse and hurried back to fight for his throne.[2]   Such proceedings were possible only if the suburb stood beside the Sea of Marmora.   Yet again ; the Saracen fleets which came against Constantinople, in 673 and 717, put into the harbour of the Hebdomon on their way to the city.   On the first occasion the enemy's vessels anchored, says Theophanes,[3] " off Thrace, from the promontory of the Hebdomon, otherwise named Magnaura, to the promontory of the Cyclobion."   The ships of the second Saracen expedition, likewise, " anchored between the Magnaura and the Cyclobion."   There they waited for two days, and then, taking advantage of a south wind, " they sailed alongside the city," some of them making the ports of Anthemius and Eutropius (at Kadikeui), others of them reaching the Bosporus, and

---

[1] Socrates, vi. c. xii. ; Sozomon, vii. c. xiv.

[2] John of Antioch, *Fragm. Hist. Græc.*, v. p. 38 ; cf. *Paschal Chron.*, pp. 699, 700.

[3] Page 541. Speaking of the same event, the Patriarch Nicephorus (p. 36) describes the Hebdomon as παραθαλάσσιον τόπον. In regard to the situation of the Hebdomon upon the sea, compare Synaxaria, September 2, the Festival of St. John the Faster, Patriarch of Constantinople.

dropping anchor between Galata and Klidion (Ortakeui).[1] Manifestly, the Hebdomon lay to the west of the city, upon the Sea of Marmora.

Let one more proof of this fact suffice. When Pope Constantine visited Constantinople in 708, for the settlement of certain disputes between Eastern and Western Christendom, he came all the way by sea until he reached the Hebdomon. There the Pontiff and his retinue disembarked, and having been welcomed with distinguished honour, mounted horses which had been sent from the Imperial stables, and rode into the city in great state: "A quo loco (the island Cæa) navigantes venerunt a Septimo Milliario Constantinopolim, ubi egressus Tiberius Imperator, filius Justiniani Augusti (Justinian II.) cum Patriciis, cum clero, et populi multitudine, omnes lætantes, et diem festum agentes. Pontifex autem et ejus primates, cum sellaribus imperialibus, sellis et frenis inauratis, simul et mappulis, ingressi sunt civitatem."[2] On the view that the Hebdomon was situated beside the Sea of Marmora, all this is clear.

The data for determining the situation of the Hebdomon therefore are: that the suburb was seven miles from the city; that it stood beside the Sea of Marmora; that it had a harbour, on the one hand, and a plain of considerable extent, on the other.

There is little room for difference of opinion in regard to the point from which the seven miles are to be measured. That point could not have been in the Theodosian Walls, as the Hebdomon is mentioned before they were in existence. For a similar reason, it could not have been in the Wall of Constantine, seeing the Egnatian Road which led from Byzantium to Rome was marked with the seventh milestone before the foundation of

---

[1] Theophanes, p. 608, Ἀπάραντες ἐκεῖθεν παρέπλευσαν τὴν πόλιν.

[2] Anastasius Bibliothecarius, *De Vitis Pontificum Roman*, p. 56. Paris, 1649.

Constantinople. It must, therefore, have been the point whence distances from old Byzantium were measured under the Roman domination. This being so, the choice lies between the Milion near St. Sophia, and the gate of Byzantium near the Column of Constantine. In favour of the former is the fact that it was the point from which distances from Constantinople were afterwards measured; for in all probability that usage was the continuation of the practice of the older city, any change in that respect being not only unnecessary, but exceedingly inconvenient. Still, the result will be substantially the same if the gate of Byzantium is preferred, since the Milion and that gate were at a short distance from each other. Seven miles from either point, westwards, to the Sea of Marmora will bring us to the modern suburb of Makrikeui.

Between the promontory on which that village stands and the promontory of Zeitin Bournou, to the east, is a bay which could serve as a harbour; while to the north and north-east spreads a magnificent plain. Makrikeui, therefore, satisfies all the indications regarding the site of the Hebdomon.

As a corollary from this determination of the real site of the Hebdomon there follows the determination of the real site of the Cyclobion; and thus the correction of another of the mistakes into which students of the topography of Byzantine Constantinople have fallen. The prevalent opinion on the subject, since Du Cange[1] propounded the opinion, has been that the Cyclobion was a fortress attached to the Golden Gate. But this could not have been the case, for the Cyclobion was at the Hebdomon. It was a fortification on the eastern headland of the bay which formed the Harbour of the Hebdomon,[2] and, therefore, stood some two miles and a half from the Golden Gate. This explains how

---

[1] *Constantinopolis Christiana*, i. p. 45. See above, p. 70, ref. 1.
[2] Theophanes, p. 541.

Theophanes [1] describes the engagements between the Greeks and the Saracens, who landed at the Hebdomon in 673, as taking place between the Golden Gate and the Cyclobion. The fortress was so closely connected with the suburb that the latter is sometimes referred to under the name of the former. The Church of St. John the Evangelist at the Hebdomon, for example, is declared by one authority [2] to have stood in the Cyclobion: "Ad Castrum autem Rotundum, in quo est Ecclesia, miræ magnitudinis, Sancti Evangelistæ Johannis nomini dicata." Again, whereas John of Antioch [3] represents the fleet of Heraclius as standing off the Hebdomon, the *Paschal Chronicle*,[4] on the other hand, says the fleet was seen off the Round Tower. In all probability, the Cyclobion stood at Zeitin Bournou, on the tongue of land to the east of Makrikeui. It derived its name, Κυκλόβιον, Στρογγύλον Καστέλλιον (Castrum Rotundum), from its circular form,[5] and was a link in the chain of coast fortifications defending the approach to the city. It was repaired by Justinian the Great, who connected it by a good road with Rhegium [6] (Kutchuk Tchekmedjè), another military post, and drew upon its garrison for troops to suppress the riot of the Nika.[7] There Constantine Copronymus died on board the ship on which he had hoped to reach the capital from Selivria, when forced by his mortal illness to return from an expedition against the Bulgarians.[8]

Whether the Cyclobion was the same as the "Castle of the Theodosiani at the Hebdomon," mentioned by Theophanes,[9] is not certain. On the whole, the fact that the two names are employed by the same historian favours the view that they designated

---

[1] Page 541.
[2] Guillelmus Biblioth. in *Hadriano II.*
[3] *Fragm. Hist. Græc.*, v. p. 38.
[4] Page 699.
[5] Procopius, *De Æd.*, iv. c. viii.
[6] *Ibid., ut supra.*
[7] *Paschal Chron.*, p. 622.
[8] Theophanes, p. 693.
[9] Page 458, Τὸ καστέλλιν τῶν Θεοδοσιανῶν ἐν τῷ Ἑβδόμῳ.

different fortifications. The Theodosiani were a body of troops named in honour of Theodosius the Great.[1]

What gave the Hebdomon its importance and explains its history was, primarily, its favourable situation for the establishment of a large military camp in the neighbourhood of the capital. An extensive plain, with abundance of water, and at a convenient distance from the city, furnished a magnificent camping-ground for the legions of New Rome. This, in view of the military associations of the throne, especially during the earlier period of the Empire, brought the emperors frequently to the suburb to attend great functions of State, and thus converted it also into an Imperial quarter, embellished with the palaces, churches, and monuments which spring up around a Court. To these political reasons for the prosperity of the suburb were added the natural attractions of the place—its pleasant climate, its wide prospect over the Sea of Marmora, and the excellent sport obtained in the surrounding country.

It was on the plain of the Hebdomon that Theodosius the Great joined the army which he led against the usurper Eugenius in Italy.[2] There, the Gothic troops which Arcadius recalled from the war with Alaric took up their quarters under the command of Gainas, and there that emperor, accompanied by his minister Rufinus, held the memorable review of those troops, in the course of which Rufinus was assassinated in the Imperial tribune.[3] It was at the Hebdomon that Gainas gathered the soldiers with which he planned to seize the capital.[4] There Vitalianus encamped with more than sixty thousand men

---

[1] *Notitia Dignitatum*, pp. 12, 14, 16, etc. Edition of Otto Seeck. Du Cange thinks the Castle of the Theodosiani was the Castellion built by Tiberius to protect his fleet against the Bulgarians (see Anonymus, iii. p. 57 ; Codinus, p. 115).

[2] Sozomon, vii. c. xxiv. There, probably, Julian encamped the army with which he advanced from Gaul to Constantinople (Zosimus, p. 139).

[3] Zosimus, pp. 255, 256.   [4] *Ibid.*, pp. 272, 273.

to besiege Constantinople in the reign of Anastasius I.[1] Thither
Phocas[2] and Leo the Armenian[3] brought the armies that enabled
them to win the crown.   And there Avars, Saracens, Bulgarians,
and, doubtless, other foes halted to gaze upon the walls and
towers they hoped to scale, or from which they retired baffled
and broken.[4]

The plain at the Hebdomon was used, also, for military
exercises and athletic sports, and consequently appears under
the name of the Campus Martius,[5] as though to give it the
prestige of the ground devoted to similar purposes on the banks
of the Tiber.   There recruits were drilled and trained in the use
of arms,[6] and there the popular game of polo was played.[7]

Thither, also, on account of the wide and free space afforded
by the plain the population of the city fled, on the occasion of a
violent earthquake, to find a temporary abode, or to take part in
public supplications for the withdrawal of the calamity.[8] Such
services were attended by the emperor and the patriarch, and it
was on such an occasion that the Emperor Maurice, a particularly
devout man, and the Patriarch Anatolius, proceeded from the
city to the Campus, on foot.[9] It was customary, moreover, to
hold religious services at the Campus on the anniversary of a
great earthquake, to avert the recurrence of the disaster, or to
celebrate the fact that it had not been attended with loss of life.[10]

---

[1] Marcellinus Comes, in 513.

[2] Theophanes, pp. 446, 447 ; Theophylactus Simocat., p. 339.

[3] Theophanes, p. 784.

[4] Nicephorus, *Patriarcha C.P.*, pp. 15, 16 ; Theophanes Cont., p. 385.

[5] Constant. Porphyr., *De Cer.*, pp. 414, 416.

[6] Theophanes, p. 458.   [7] Theophanes Cont., p. 379.

[8] *Paschal Chron.*, p. 586 ; Theophanes, pp. 143, 144 ; Cedrenus, vol. i. p. 641 ;
Paschal Chron., p. 702.

[9] Theophanes, p. 169.

[10] *Paschal Chron.*, p. 589 ; Theophanes, p. 355. The Greek Church still commemorates seven of the earthquakes which shook the city during the Byzantine
period.

There, also, public executions took place,[1] or the heads of persons executed elsewhere were set up for public gaze, as in the case of the Emperor Maurice and his five sons.[2]

But the chief interest of the Hebdomon belongs to it on account of the many associations of the suburb with the life of the Byzantine Court. There, in the early days of the Eastern Empire, while old Roman customs prevailed and the army continued to be a great political factor, an emperor often assumed the purple, in the presence of his legions and a vast concourse of the citizens of the capital. At the suburb, also, triumphal processions sometimes commenced their march to the Golden Gate and the city. And there the emperors had a palace to which they resorted for country air, or to escape the turbulence of the Factions, or to take part in the State ceremonies performed on the adjoining Campus.

The earliest reference to the Hebdomon, though not by name, is in connection with the inauguration of Valens there, in 364, as the colleague of his brother, the Emperor Valentinian : "Valentem, in suburbanum, universorum sententiis concinentibus (nec enim audebat quisquam refragari) Augustum pronuntiavit ; decoreque imperatorii cultus ornatum et tempore diademate redimitum in eodem vehiculo secum reduxit."[3] In commemoration of the event Valens erected a tribune, adorned with many statues, for the accommodation of the emperors when taking part in State functions on the Campus of the suburb.[4] It was known as the Tribune of the Hebdomon (ἐν τῷ Τριβουναλίῳ τοῦ Ἑβδόμου).[5]

Valens also provided the Harbour of the Hebdomon with a

---

[1] Theophanes, p. 458.   [2] Theophylactus Simocat., p. 339.

[3] Ammianus Marcellinus, xxvi. c. iv.; cf. Themistius, as cited below ; *Paschal Chron.*, p. 556.

[4] Themistius, *Oratio VI.*, p. 99. Edit. Dindorf.

[5] *Paschal Chron.*, p. 562. The Campus is sometimes styled the Campus of the Tribunal, as for example by Cedrenus, vol. i. p. 707 : ἐν τῷ Κάμπῳ τοῦ Τριβουναλίου.

TRIUMPHUS THEODOSII.
(From Bandusi's *Imperium Orientale*.)

quay, and showed his partiality for the suburb otherwise to such an extent that Themistius ventured to expostulate with him, and to charge him with forgetting to improve and beautify the capital.[1]

After Valens, the following ten emperors were invested with the purple at the Hebdomon: Arcadius,[2] by his father Theodosius the Great, who also raised Honorius to the rank of Cæsar there;[3] Theodosius II.;[4] Marcian;[5] Leo the Great;[6] Zeno;[7] Basiliscus;[8] Maurice;[9] Phocas;[10] Leo the Armenian;[11] and Nicephorus Phocas.[12] Doubtless the fatigue involved in celebrating the ceremony so far from the heart of the city had much to do with transferring the scene of Imperial inaugurations to the Hippodrome.

The custom of installing an emperor thus into his office was the continuation of an old Roman practice which testified to the power acquired by the army in deciding the succession to the throne. We have two accounts of the ceremonies observed on such an occasion at the Hebdomon, given at great length and with minute details by that devoted student and admirer of Byzantine Court etiquette, Constantine Porphyrogenitus.[13] They are interesting, both as an exhibition of public life during the Later Empire, and as an illustration of the extent to which old Roman forms, and even the old Roman spirit, survived the profound changes which the Empire underwent after the capital was removed to the banks of the Bosporus.

When all interested in the event of the day had assembled, the troops present laid their standards prostrate upon the

---

[1] Themistius, *Oratio VI.*, p. 99.   Edit. Dindorf.
[2] *Paschal Chron.*, p. 562.
[3] Marcellinus Comes.
[4] *Paschal Chron.*, p. 568.
[5] *Ibid.*, p. 590.
[6] *Ibid.*, p. 592.
[7] Victor Tunnensis.
[8] Cedrenus, vol. i. p. 615.
[9] Theophanes, p. 388.
[10] *Ibid.*, p. 447.
[11] *Ibid.*, p. 784.
[12] Constant. Porphyr., *De Cer.*, p. 438.
[13] The Coronation of Leo the Great in 475, and that of Nicephorus Phocas in 963. See Constant. Porphyr., *De Cer.*, pp. 410–417, 433–440.

ground, to express the desolation of the State bereft of a
ruler.   Meanwhile, from every point of the Campus rose the
sound of prayer, as the immense multitudes gathered there
joined in supplications that God would approve the man
who had been chosen as the new chief of the Empire.   " Hear
us, O God ; we beseech Thee to hear us, O God.   Grant Leo
life ; let him reign.   O God, Lover of mankind, the public
weal demands Leo ; the army demands him ; the laws wait for
him ; the palace awaits him.   So prays the army, the Senate,
the people.   The world expects Leo ; the army waits for
him.   Let Leo, our common glory, come ; let Leo, our common
good, reign.   Hear us, O God, we beseech Thee." At length the
emperor-elect appeared, and ascended the Imperial tribune.   A
coronet was placed upon his head by one high military officer,
an armlet upon his right arm by another.   And instantly the
prostrate standards were lifted high, and the air shook with
acclamations: " Leo, Augustus, thou hast conquered ; thou art
Pius, August.   God gave thee, God will guard thee.   Ever
conquer, worshipper of Christ.   Long be thy reign.   God will
defend the Christian Empire."[1]   This was the first act in the
dramatic spectacle.   Next came the solemn investiture of the
emperor with the Imperial insignia.   This took place behind a
shield held before him by soldiers of the household-troops
known as the Candidati, and when he had been duly robed,
crowned, and armed with shield and spear, the screen was
removed, and the new sovereign stood before the gaze of his
subjects in all his majesty.[2]

---

[1] The soldiers spoke in Latin at the Coronation of Anastasius I. in the Hippodrome.   See Constant. Porphyr., *De Cer.*, p. 431.   Probably that was the rule.

[2] In older times the emperor was raised upon a shield at this point of the pro-
ceedings.   *E.g.* Julian (Ammianus Marcell. xx. 4) ; Arcadius, Valens (Idatius
Fasti Consulares) ; Theodosius II. (*Paschal Chron.*, p. 568) ; Marcian (*Paschal
Chron.*, p. 590).

The dignitaries of the State now approached, in the order of their rank, and did homage to the monarch, while the crowds around made the air ring again with every acclamation that loyalty or adulation could invent. As soon as this scene terminated, the emperor addressed a brief allocation to the soldiers, through a herald; claiming to reign by the will of God and their suffrage, promising devotion to the welfare of the Empire, and a generous donative to each of his faithful companion-in-arms, announcements which were greeted with storms of applause. Then the sum of money required for the promised largess was handed over by the emperor to the officers charged with its distribution.

Upon the conclusion of this important part of the day's proceedings, the ceremonies assumed a religious character. The emperor now repaired, on foot, to a camp-chapel, a tent of many colours, at a short distance from the Imperial tribune, and, leaving his crown without, entered to bow before the King of kings. It was a simple service conducted by ordinary priests, as the patriarch and higher clergy had left the Campus for St. Sophia. Upon issuing from the chapel, the emperor resumed his crown, and proceeded on a white charger, followed by a brilliant escort of dignitaries also on horseback, to the Church of St. John the Baptist, the principal sanctuary of the Hebdomon. This second service may be described as the Consecration of the Crown. For in this case, the crown, upon being again removed from the emperor's head, was not left in the vestry, but was carried by a court official up to the altar, and then placed by the emperor himself on the sacred table. There it remained until the service closed, when the emperor handed it to the court official, and, having presented a rich gift to the church, returned to the vestry and assumed his diadem once more. This brought the coronation ceremonies, so far as they concerned the Hebdomon, to an end. The stream of life now poured into the city, the Imperial *cortége* gathering more and more pomp as it passed the Golden Gate, the Helenianæ,[1] the Forum of Constantine, and entered St. Sophia for the supreme coronation of the emperor by the patriarch in the Great Cathedral of the capital.[2]

Only one triumphal procession, that of Basil I.,[3] is expressly described as starting from the Hebdomon, but the suburb was in all probability[4] the starting-point also of the processions which celebrated the victories of Theodosius the Great, Heraclius, Constantine Copronymus, Zimisces, and Basil II., if not of Michael Palæologus.

On the occasion of the triumph accorded to Basil I., the Senate and a vast crowd, representing all classes of the population, and carrying wreaths of roses and other flowers, went forth from the city to the Hebdomon to welcome the conqueror, who had crossed to the suburb from the palace at Hiereia (Fener Bagtchè). After the customary salutations had been exchanged, the emperor proceeded to the Church of St. John the Baptist to pray and light tapers at that venerated shrine. Then having put on his "scaramangion triblation," he and his son Constantine mounted horse and took the road towards the Golden Gate, the Senate and people leading the way, with banners waving in the air. A short halt was made at the monastery of the Abramiti (τῶν Ἀβραμιτῶν), which stood between the suburb

---

[1] Near the Forum of Arcadius, on the Seventh Hill.

[2] In the case of Phocas, for manifest reasons, the coronation by the patriarch took place in the Church of St. John the Baptist at the Hebdomon.

So also in the case of Zeno, according to Victor Tunnensis, as quoted by Du Cange, ii. p. 173. "Zeno a Leone Augusto filio in Septimo contra consuetudinem coronatur."

[3] Constant. Porphyr., *De Cer.*, p. 498.

[4] The case of Basil I. is not given by Constantine Porphyrogenitus as exceptional, and may be considered as exemplifying the rule.

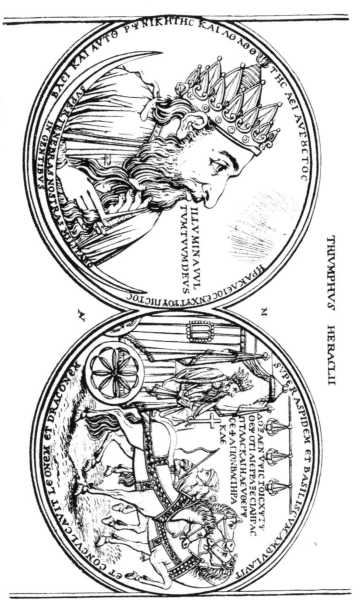

(From Du Cange.)

TRIVMPHVS HERACLII

and the gate, that Basil might offer his devotions in the Church of the Theotokos Acheiropoietos ('Αχειροποίητος), and then the procession resumed its march, and entered through the Golden Gate into the jubilant capital.[1]

The first writer who mentions the Hebdomon by name refers to it as an Imperial country retreat which the emperors gladly frequented. From the connection in which Rufinus[2] makes this statement, it is evident that a palace stood at the Hebdomon before the reign of Theodosius the Great. That residence was either rebuilt or enlarged in the reign of Justinian the Great, when mention is made of "the New Consistorium of the Palace of Justinian, at the seventh mile from this renowned city."[3] How agreeable a retreat the palace was may be inferred from the name bestowed upon it—the Pleasance, Jucundianæ ('Ιουκουν-διαναὶ).[4]

In front of the palace rose the statue of Justinian, on a porphyry column brought for the purpose from the Forum of Constantine, where it had borne the silver statue of Theodosius I.[5] Justinian showed his partiality for the suburb, moreover, by the erection of porticoes, fora, baths, churches, all built in a style worthy of the capital itself, and by having the Harbour of the Hebdomon dredged and provided with jetties for the better accommodation and safety of the shipping frequenting the coast.[6]

---

[1] Constant. Porphyr., *De Cer.*, pp. 498-503.

[2] Rufinus, *De Vitis Patrum*, iii., n. 19. "Fuit quidam nuper monachus in Constantinopoli, temporibus Theodosii imperatoris. Habitabat autem in parva cella foris civitatem prope proastium, qui vocatur in Septimo, ubi solent imperatores, egressi de civitate, libenter degere."

[3] *De Sacro Eccl.*, Lex. 22. "Recitata septimo milliario inclytæ civitatis, in Novo Consistorio Palatii Justiniani;" cf. *Novella*, 118.

[4] Procopius, *De Æd.*, i. c. xi. The name appears, also, under the form Secundianas: "In Septimo, in palatio quod dicitur Secundianas" (Pope Gregory the Great, lib. ii. epist. 1; see Du Cange, lii. p. 141; cf. Malalas, p. 486).

[5] Lydus, p. 229. The column was overthrown by an earthquake in 577, and sank eight feet into the ground (Theophanes, p. 358).

[6] Procopius, *ut supra*; Theophanes, p. 353.

In the seventh and eighth centuries the palace of the Hebdomon appears under the name of Magnaura ; [1] but whether it
was the old residence under a different designation, or a new
building added to the Imperial quarters, in the style of the Hall
of the Magnaura in the Great Palace beside the Hippodrome,[2] it
is impossible to say.

It was to the palace of the Hebdomon, probably, that
Pulcheria retired from the Court of her brother Theodosius II.,
while the influence of the Empress Eudoxia had the ascendency.[3]
Basiliscus withdrew to it from the storm of theological hatred
which his opposition to the creed of Chalcedon had excited
in the capital, and thither the pillar-saint of Anaplus (Arnaout-
keui), Daniel Stylites, went to rebuke him and foretell the loss
of the throne which had been usurped and dishonoured.[4] As
already intimated, it was a favourite resort of Justinian the
Great,[5] and several of his laws were promulgated during his
residence there.   On the occasion of one of his visits, the
Imperial crown mysteriously disappeared and was not heard of
again for eight months, when it as strangely reappeared, without a single gem missing.[6] The palace was occupied also by
Justin II.[7] and Tiberius II., the latter dying in it.[8]

The Hebdomon enjoyed, moreover, a great religious reputation on account of its numerous churches. The oldest sanctuary

---

[1] Theophanes, pp. 541, 608.

[2] See Labarte, *Le Palais Impérial de Consple.*, pp. 185-195. It was a hall in the
form of a basilica, divided in three aisles by two rows of six columns, with an apse at
the eastern end, where the emperor's throne stood on a platform.   In it foreign
princes and ambassadors were received, and there meetings of the great dignitaries of
the State were held.

[3] Theophanes, p. 152.

[4] Symeon Metaphrastes, *Life of Daniel Stylites*, p. 1025.   Patrol. Græca, Migne.

[5] Procopius, *De Æd.*, i. c. xi.   [6] Theophanes, p. 351.

[7] Eustachius, *Vita Eutychii Patriarchæ*, as quoted by Du Cange, *Constantinopolis
Christiana*, iv. p. 177.

[8] *Paschal Chron.*, p. 690.

of the suburb was the Basilica of St. John the Evangelist,[1] which appears first in the reign of Arcadius,[2] but claimed to be a foundation of Constantine the Great. It is described by the Legates of Hadrian II., after its restoration under Basil I.,[3] as remarkable for its size, "miræ magnitudinis,"[4] and continued to be a venerated shrine as late as the Comnenian period,[5] after which it was allowed to fall into decay. Basil II. was interred in it, according to his dying request,[6] and his grave was discovered among the ruins of the church in the thirteenth century, while Michael Palæologus was engaged in the siege of Galata, in 1260. Some members of the Imperial household, in the course of their exploration of the surrounding country, then visited the Hebdomon, and found the church of St. John the Evangelist turned into a fold for sheep and cattle. As the visitors wandered among the ruins, admiring the traces of the building's former beauty, they stumbled upon the dead body of a man. It was naked, but well preserved, and in its mouth a vulgar jester had placed a shepherd's lute by way of derision. As the corpse lay near a sarcophagus upon which was inscribed an epitaph in honour of Basil II., no doubt could be entertained regarding the identity of the body. When the discovery was reported to Michael Palæologus, he commanded the mortal remains of his predecessor to be conveyed in great state to the camp before Galata, to receive once more a tribute of respect, and then sent them with solemn ceremonial to Selivria,[7] for interment in the monastery of St. Saviour.

---

[1] Anonymus, iii. p. 56.
[2] Socrates, vi. c. vi.
[3] Theophanes Cont., p. 340.
[4] Guillelmus Biblioth. in *Hadriano PP.*
[5] Anna Comn., p. 149.
[6] Cinnamus, pp. 176, 177.
[7] Pachymeres, vol. i. pp. 124, 125. The epitaph is given by Banduri, *Imp. Orient.*, vol. ii. vii. p. 179. It mentions the Hebdomon :

IOTIMI TYMBON EN MEϹⲰ ΓHϹ EBΔOMOY

Another of the sanctuaries at the Hebdomon was the church erected, in 407, by the Emperor Arcadius to enshrine the reputed remains of the Prophet Samuel.[1] Such importance was attached to these relics that their conveyance from Palestine to Constantinople, by way of Asia Minor, resembled an Imperial progress through the country. One might have supposed the prophet himself was moving through the land, so great was the interest and devotion displayed by the population along the route.[2] Nor were the relics less honoured upon their arrival at the capital. The emperor and the highest dignitaries of Church and State did homage to them at the Scala Chalcedonensis and carried them in procession to the Church of St. Sophia, where the sacred remains rested until the church built for them at the Hebdomon was completed.[3] The church fell in the earthquake which shook the city in the thirty-first year of the reign of Justinian the Great.[4]

But the most venerated church in the suburb was that dedicated to St. John the Baptist (τὸ μαρτύριον τοῦ Βαπτιστοῦ 'Iωάννου),[5] a domical edifice, built by Theodosius the Great[6] for the reception of the head, it was supposed, of the heroic Forerunner of Christ. The Emperor Valens had already sought to obtain the relic. But its possessors, certain monks of the sect of Macedonius, who had taken it with them from Jerusalem to Cilicia, refused to surrender the treasure, and all that Valens succeeded in doing was to bring it as near to Constantinople as Panticheion (Pendik), on the opposite shore of the Sea of Marmora. There, the mules which drew the car conveying the relic refused to proceed any further, and at that village, accordingly, in obedience to what appeared to be an

[1] *Paschal Chron.*, p. 570.
[2] Jerome, *Adversus Vigilantium*, c. ii. Quoted by Du Cange, iv. p. 105.
[3] *Paschal Chron.*, pp. 569, 570.
[4] Theophanes, p. 357.
[5] Socrates, vi. c. vi.
[6] Anonymus, iii. p. 56.

indication of the Divine will, the sacred head was allowed to remain. When Theodosius the Great endeavoured to acquire the relic, its custodians, a woman Matrona and a priest Vicentius, did everything in their power to prevent the execution of the emperor's design. But the pressure to make them yield was such that at last they gave their reluctant consent. In doing so, however, Matrona cherished the secret belief that Theodosius would be hindered, like Valens, from carrying out his purpose ; while Vicentius laid down a condition which he thought could never be fulfilled, viz. that the emperor in removing the head should walk after the Baptist. Theodosius saw no difficulty in the condition. He reverently wrapped the reliquary in his Imperial mantle and, holding the sacred contents in front of him, took them to the Church of St. John the Evangelist at the Hebdomon, and commenced the erection of a church consecrated to the Forerunner's name as their final shrine. This won Vicentius over to the emperor's side, and he followed the head to the Hebdomon. But Matrona, with a true woman's intensity of feeling, maintained her protest, and would never come near the suburb which had disappointed her faith, and purloined her treasure.[1]

It was the possession of this relic that gave the church its great religious repute. This explains why, as we have seen, Theodosius the Great,[2] Epiphanius of Cyprus,[3] Gainas,[4] at important moments in their lives, performed their devotions there ; and this accounts for the association of the church with the ceremonies attending Imperial inaugurations and triumphs.[5]

In the course of its history the church was twice restored on

---

[1] Sozomon, vii. c. xxi.   [2] *Ibid.*, vii. c. xxiv.
[3] *Ibid.*, viii. c. iv.   [4] Socrates, vi. c. xii.
           [5] Constant. Porphyr., *De Cer.*, pp. 413, 499.

a magnificent scale; first by Justinian the Great,[1] and again by Basil I.[2]

Other churches of less note at the Hebdomon were respectively dedicated to St. Theodotè (τὸ Θεοδότης ἁγίας τέμενος);[3] SS. Menas and Menaius (Μηνᾶς καὶ Μηναίος);[4] SS. Benjamin and Berius (Ἁγίων Βενιαμὶν καὶ Βηρίου);[5] and the Holy Innocents (τῶν Νηπίων).[6] The first two sanctuaries owed their foundation to Justinian the Great, who did so much for the suburb in other ways; at the last church, the Senate welcomed an emperor upon his return to the capital by land, from the West.

Finally, in days when travellers made the first and last stages of a journey short, the Hebdomon enjoyed considerable importance as a halting-place for persons leaving or approaching Constantinople; its proximity to the city rendering it a caravansary, where a traveller could conveniently make his final arrangements to start on his way, or to enter the capital in a suitable manner. The suburb served that purpose, even in the case of the emperors.[7]

Instances of this use of the suburb, by Theodosius the Great, Epiphanius, and Pope Constantine, have already been noticed, when referring to other matters connected with the Hebdomon. There also the Legates of Pope Hormisdas, in 515,[8] and the Legates of Pope Hadrian II., in 869,[9] rested before entering the city. There the Emperor Maurice halted, upon leaving Constantinople, to join the expedition against the Avars;[10] and

---

[1] Procopius, *De Æd.*, i. c. viii.

[2] Theophanes Cont., p. 340. The wealthy monastery at the Hebdomon, mentioned in history, was probably attached to this church (John Scylitzes, in Cedrenus, vol. ii. p. 714).

[3] Procopius, *De Æd.*, i. c. iv.   [4] *Ibid.*, c. ix.

[5] *Menæa*, 29 July, πλησίον τῶν παλατίων τοῦ Ἑβδόμου.

[6] Constant. Porphyr., *De Cer.*, p. 496.   [7] *Ibid.*, *ut supra*.

[8] Anastasius Biblioth. in *Hormisda PP.*

[9] Guillelmus Biblioth. in *Hadriano PP.*

[10] Theophylactus Simocat., pp. 236, 237.

there Peter, King of Bulgaria, stopped on his return home, in
927, with the Princess Maria, the granddaughter of the Emperor
Romanus Lecapenus, as his bride.[1]

On the last occasion, as relatives and friends, doubtless,
often did under similar circumstances, the parents of the princess
accompanied her as far as the suburb to take leave of her there.
The historian has left a vivid picture of the scene. "When
the moment for their daughter's departure approached, father
and mother burst into tears, as is natural for parents about to
part with the dearest pledge of their love. Then having embraced their son-in-law, and entrusted their child to his care,
they returned to the Imperial city. Maria proceeded on her
journey to Bulgaria in the king's charge, with mingled feelings of
grief and joy—sad, because carried away from beloved parents,
Imperial palaces, and the society of her relations and friends ;
happy, because her husband was a king, and she was the Despina
of Bulgaria. She took with her much wealth, and an immense
quantity of baggage."

In keeping with such practices, when the Icon of St. Demetrius was transported from Thessalonica to Constantinople, in the
reign of Manuel Comnenus, to be placed in the Church of the
Pantocrator (now Zeirek Klissè Djamissi, above Oun Kapan
Kapoussi), members of the Senate and a vast multitude of
priests, monks, and laymen, went seven miles from the capital
to receive the sacred picture and escort it with great pomp to its
destination.[2]

---

[1] Theophanes Cont., pp. 906, 907.   [2] *Synaxaria*, 26 October.

CHAPTER XX.

THE ANASTASIAN WALL.

SOME notice, however brief, may here be taken of the wall erected by the Emperor Anastasius I. to increase the security of the capital, and at the same time to protect from hostile incursions the suburbs and a considerable tract of the rich and populous country, outside the Theodosian Walls. This additional line of defence, consisting of a wall twenty feet thick flanked by towers, stood at a distance of forty miles to the west of the city, and was carried from the shore of the Sea of Marmora to the shore of the Black Sea, across a territory fifty-four miles broad, or, as Procopius measures it, what would take two days to traverse.[1] It was known, in view of its length, as the Long Wall (Μακρὸν τεῖχος),[2] the Long Walls (τὰ Μακρὰ τείχη),[3] and, after the emperor by whom it was erected, as the Anastasian Wall (τὸ τεῖχος τὸ Ἀναστασιακὸν).[4] In 559, in the reign of Justinian the Great, it demanded extensive repairs on account of injuries due to earthquakes, and occasion was then taken to introduce a change which, it was hoped, would render the defence of the wall an easier task. All tower-gateways permitting communication between the towers along the summit of the wall were built up,

---

[1] For a description of the wall, see Evagrius, iii. c. 38; Procopius, *De Æd.*, iv. c. ix.

[2] Theophanes, p. 361.   [3] Agathias, p. 305.   [4] Theophanes, p. 360.

so that a tower could be entered only by the gateway at its base; the object of this arrangement being to make every tower an independent fort, which could hold out against an enemy even after he was in possession of the wall itself.[1]   The Anastasian Wall appears in history in connection with the attacks of the Huns and Avars, in the reigns of Justinian the Great,[2] Maurice,[3] and Heraclius.[4]   But it cannot be said to have been of much service.   The attempt to obstruct the march of the enemy, and to join issue with him at a distance from the city, was indeed a wise measure.   It has been imitated by the recent establishment, nearer the city, of a chain of forts across the promontory, from Tchataldja to Derkos; a line of defence occupying a position which makes Constantinople, in the judgment of a competent military authority,[5] the best-fortified capital in the world.   But the weakness of the Anastasian Wall was its great length, which required for its proper defence a larger garrison than the Empire was able to provide for the purpose.[6]   And, of course, it was useless against an enemy advancing upon the capital by sea.[7]   Traces of the wall are, it is said, visible at Koush Kaya and at Karadjakeui.

---

[1] Theophanes, p. 362; Procopius, *De Æd.*, iv. c. ix.

[2] Theophanes, p. 361.   [3] Cedrenus, vol. i. p. 692.   [4] *Paschal Chron.*, p. 712.

[5] Colonel F. V. Greene, United States Army, in his work, *The Russian Army and its Campaigns in Turkey in* 1877-78, p. 362.

[6] Agathias, p. 305; Procopius, *ut supra*.   [7] Theophanes, p. 460.

TABLE OF EMPERORS.

Leontius	695–697
Tiberius III. Apsimarus	697–705
Justinian II. (restored)	705–711
Philippicus	711–713
Anastasius II.	713–715
Theodosius III.	715–717
Leo III., the Isaurian	717–740
Constantine V. Copronymus	740–775
Leo IV.	775–779
Constantine VI.	779–797
Irene	797–802
Nicephorus I.	802–811
Stauricius	811
Michael I. Rhangabe	811–813
Leo V., the Armenian	813–820
Michael II., the Amorian	820–829
Theophilus	829–842
Michael III.	842–867
Basil I., the Macedonian	867–886
Leo VI., the Wise	886–912
Constantine VII. Porphyrogenitus	912–958
Co-Emperors—	
Alexander	912–913
Romanus I. Lecapenus	919–945
Constantine VIII. and Stephanus, sons of	
Romanus I., reigned five weeks ...	944
Romanus II.	958–963
Basil II. Bulgaroktonos	963–1025
Co-Emperors—	
Nicephorus II. Phocas	963–969
John I. Zimisces	969–976
Constantine IX.	976–1025

Constantine IX.	...	...	...	...	1025–1028
Romanus III. Argyrus	...	...	...		1028–1034
Michael IV., the Paphlagonian		...	...		1034–1042
Michael V.	...	...	...	...	...	1042
Zoe and Theodora	...	...	...	...		1042
Constantine X. Monomachus		...	...		1042–1054
Theodora (restored)		...	...	...	1054–1056
Michael VI. Stratioticus	...	...	...		1056–1057
Isaac I. Comnenus	...	...	...	...	1057–1059
Constantine XI. Ducas	...	...	...		1059–1067
Michael VII. Ducas	...	...	...	...	1067–1078

Co-Emperor—

Romanus IV. Diogenes		...	...	1067–1078
Nicephorus III. Botoniates	...	...	...	1078–1081
Alexius I. Comnenus	...	...	...	1081–1118
John II. Comnenus	...	...	...	...	1118–1143
Manuel I. Comnenus	...	...	...	1143–1180
Alexius II. Comnenus	...	...	...	1180–1183
Andronicus I. Comnenus	...	...	...	1183–1185
Isaac II. Angelus	...	...	...	...	1185–1195
Alexius III. Angelus	...	...	...	1195–1203
Isaac II. (restored) ⎱ Alexius IV. Angelus ⎰	...	...	...	1203–1204
Nicolas Canabus	...	...	...	...	1204
Alexius V. Ducas, Murtzuphlus		...	...	1204

LATIN EMPERORS.

Baldwin I.	...	...	...	...	1204–1205
Henry	...	...	...	...	...	1205–1216
Peter	...	...	...	...	...	1217–1219

Robert	...	...	...	...	1219–1228
John of Brienne		...	...	...	1228–1237
Baldwin II.	...	...	...	...	1237–1261

NICÆAN EMPERORS.

Theodore I. Lascaris	...	...	1204–1222
John III. Ducas	...	...	...	1222–1254
Theodore II. Ducas	...	...	1254–1259
John IV. Ducas	...	...	...	1259–1260

EMPIRE RESTORED.

Michael VIII. Palæologus 1260–1282

Andronicus II. Palæologus 1282–1328

Co-Emperor—

    Michael IX. 1295–1320

Andronicus III. Palæologus 1328–1341

John VI. Palæologus 1341–1391

Co-Emperors—

    John V. Cantacuzene 1342–1355

    Andronicus IV. Palæologus (usurped throne) 1376–1379

Manuel II. Palæologus 1391–1425

John VII. Palæologus 1425–1448

Constantine XII. Palæologus 1448–1453

INDEX.

——◇——

THE END.

LONDON: PRINTED BY WILLIAM CLOWES AND SONS, LIMITED, STAMFORD STREET AND CHARING CROSS.

1177805R0

Printed in Great Britain by
Amazon.co.uk, Ltd.,
Marston Gate.